# The British and Irish
# Short Story Handbook

# Blackwell Literature Handbooks

This new series offers the student thorough and lively introductions to literary periods, movements, and, in some instances, authors and genres, from Anglo-Saxon to the Postmodern. Each volume is written by a leading specialist to be invitingly accessible and informative. Chapters are devoted to the coverage of cultural context, the provision of brief but detailed biographical essays on the authors concerned, critical coverage of key works, and surveys of themes and topics, together with bibliographies of selected further reading. Students new to a period of study or to a period genre will discover all they need to know to orientate and ground themselves in their studies, in volumes that are as stimulating to read as they are convenient to use.

## Published

*The Science Fiction Handbook*
M. Keith Booker and Anne-Marie Thomas

*The Seventeenth-Century Literature Handbook*
Marshall Grossman

*The Twentieth-Century American Fiction Handbook*
Christopher MacGowan

*The British and Irish Short Story Handbook*
David Malcolm

# The British and Irish Short Story Handbook

*David Malcolm*

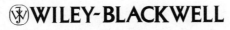
**WILEY-BLACKWELL**

A John Wiley & Sons, Ltd., Publication

This edition first published 2012
© 2012 David Malcolm

Blackwell Publishing was acquired by John Wiley & Sons in February 2007. Blackwell's publishing program
has been merged with Wiley's global Scientific, Technical, and Medical business to form Wiley-Blackwell.

*Registered Office*
John Wiley & Sons Ltd, The Atrium, Southern Gate, Chichester, West Sussex, PO19 8SQ, UK

*Editorial Offices*
350 Main Street, Malden, MA 02148-5020, USA
9600 Garsington Road, Oxford, OX4 2DQ, UK
The Atrium, Southern Gate, Chichester, West Sussex, PO19 8SQ, UK

For details of our global editorial offices, for customer services, and for information about how to
apply for permission to reuse the copyright material in this book please see our website at
www.wiley.com/wiley-blackwell.

The right of David Malcolm to be identified as the author of this work has been asserted in accordance
with the UK Copyright, Designs and Patents Act 1988.

*Library of Congress Cataloging-in-Publication Data*

Malcolm, David, 1952–
  The British and Irish short story handbook / David Malcolm.
    p. cm.
  Includes bibliographical references and index.
  ISBN 978-1-4443-3045-8 (cloth) – ISBN 978-1-4443-3046-5 (pbk.)
  1. Short stories, English–History and criticism–Handbooks, manuals, etc. 2. English fiction–
Irish authors–History and criticism–Handbooks, manuals, etc. 3. Short story–Handbooks,
manuals, etc.  I. Title. II. Title: Short story handbook.
  PR829.M35 2012
  823.009'9417–dc23                                                          2011031900

A catalogue record for this book is available from the British Library.

Set in 10/13pt Sabon Roman by Thomson Digital, Noida, India
Printed in Singapore by Ho Printing Singapore Pte Ltd

1   2012

*for Jennifer*

# Contents

Contents

# Acknowledgments

I thank Zina Rohan, without whose kindness and generosity I could not have written this book.

I thank Cheryl Verdon. Many years ago, she pointed out to me the excellences of short fiction. I have only realized fully over the past few years how right she was. In addition, I have been deeply influenced by our work together on several books.

My thanks also go to William and James Malcolm for their enduring toleration of their father's work.

I also thank Jennifer Carter. Without her unstinting support, this book would never have been written. I am very grateful indeed. This book is dedicated to her.

# Preface

This book is divided into five parts. Part 1 offers a brief history of the short story, first in Britain, and then in Ireland (as far as the developments are distinguishable). Part 2 addresses important issues in short-story studies: the question of the definition of the short story; whether the short story is a genre, or a higher-level category; the importance of the collection for interpretation of short stories; the matter of the short story's predilection for dealing with marginal characters; and the vexed topic of the canonicity or non-canonicity of short fiction. In Part 3, I present the spectrum of genres that has marked British and Irish short fiction from the 1880s through to the present. Part 4 presents brief discussions of almost fifty key authors for the British and Irish short story. I have attempted to strike a balance between well-known and less canonical writers, although I have given substantial space to lesser-known but important writers, such as Richard Aldington, Hubert Crackanthorpe, Julian Maclaren-Ross, Mollie Panter-Downes, and Sylvia Townsend Warner. The final chapter contains extensive discussions of individual key short-story texts, both in the British and Irish traditions.

Writing a book involves discovery and disappointment for the author. While working on this text, I have gained considerable respect for an English tradition (and as a Scot, I use the term "English" advisedly) in short-story writing since 1880. Hubert Crackanthorpe, James Lasdun, W. Somerset Maugham, Michael Moorcock, T. F. Powys, and V. S. Pritchett – these are very fine and very varied English voices. They take their place beside other great English short-story writers, such as H. G Wells, D. H. Lawrence, Virginia Woolf; and alongside their Irish peers, such as James Joyce, Seán O'Faoláin, John McGahern, William Trevor, and Bernard MacLaverty. The motif of immigration that runs throughout so many texts – for example, those by George Moore, Joseph Conrad, William Trevor, and Hanif Kureishi – discussed in this volume has also surprised me (although perhaps it should not have). These are two of the discoveries. On the other hand, one of my disappointments is the exclusion of substantial writers, an exclusion demanded by the scope of the book. I would have liked to have written more (or at all) on short stories by Ella D'Arcy, George Egerton (Mary Chavalita Dunne), Alun Lewis, and Graham Swift, among others. Another disappointment (or perhaps it is, rather, a promising discovery) is an awareness of areas that still need considerable research, for example, the pre-1880s evolution of British short fiction, and the role of institutions (*The New Yorker* and the BBC) in the course followed by twentieth-century British short fiction. I have pointed these out at relevant places in this book.

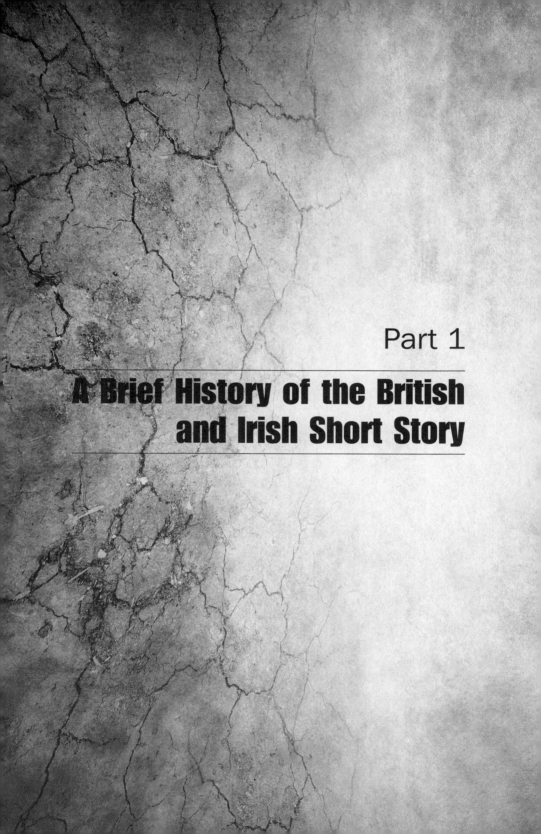

Part 1

# A Brief History of the British and Irish Short Story

It is a widely accepted argument – and one that students of literature should, therefore, beware of – that the modern British short story, and even the British short story *tout court*, dates from around 1880. For example, Clare Hanson writes of her important study of short fiction: "The year 1880 has been chosen as a convenient opening date for this study because it marks a point when the short story began to flower in England" (1985: 8). Valerie Shaw also sees the last two decades of the nineteenth century as being crucial for the development of the short story in Britain. "Only towards the end of the nineteenth century," she writes, "when in fact all branches of literature and the arts were becoming acutely self-conscious, did people begin to acknowledge that short fiction might be shaped according to its own principles" (Shaw 1983: 3). The classic statement of this position is that of Dean Baldwin in his influential essay "The Tardy Evolution of the British Short Story" (1993). He puts it thus:

> One of the more curious anomalies of literary history is why the short story was so late to blossom in Britain. By the 1840s the genre was already established in America, and within two decades it had taken root in Germany, Russia, and France . . . [The] modern short story did not achieve prominence in Britain till the 1880s, even though Britain would appear especially likely to develop the genre, since during the period of the story's "invention" . . . Britain was world leader in the writing and dissemination of fiction.
>
> (Baldwin 1993: 23)

*The British and Irish Short Story Handbook*, First Edition. David Malcolm.
© 2012 David Malcolm. Published 2012 by Blackwell Publishing Ltd.

In his essay, Baldwin argues that a late development of short fiction in Britain can be attributed largely to "literary economics" (23). He points to the mass production of newspapers and magazines in nineteenth-century Britain. By the 1830s, there were titles with large circulations catering for a wide range of readerships. These journals would seem to offer perfect outlets for short fiction. However, Baldwin insists that the short story brought little "financial gain or public fame" to authors in this period (27). The novel's prestige within the literary system of nineteenth-century England meant that it was the form of choice (or of demand) for writers of fiction. The short story had little status (it was a type of fiction associated, if anything, with cheap publications for the semi-educated), and, indeed, made little money for writers. Baldwin contrasts this situation with that of American writers for whom the short story was profitable. There were outlets for short stories in the USA, and such was the standing of the British novel in the US market, that American writers were forced to turn to the shorter form. The 1870s were a watershed in Britain. Influences from the USA, including the personal influence of Henry James and American theorizing about short fiction (Brander Matthews's developments, in the 1880s, of Poe's ideas about the short story), changed the literary interests of a generation of British writers. Baldwin's argument is a powerful one.

Yet there had been short fictional narratives in British literature for centuries before the 1880s. Barbara Korte sets out a full history of early-modern and eighteenth-century short prose narratives. These include jest books, rogue literature, essays and character sketches, oriental tales, senti-mental stories, and moral treatises. Authors of note range from Robert Greene, William Painter, Aphra Behn, and Daniel Defoe, to Richard Steele, Thomas Addison, and Samuel Johnson (Korte 2003: 35–62). In the nine-teenth century, before the 1880s, many important writers tried their hands at short fiction. Ivan Reid describes the short story as *the* Romantic form (Reid 1977: 28), and the Gothic tale is a central Romantic prose genre that lasts throughout the nineteenth century. A role call of nineteenth-century British authors who wrote short stories is impressive: John Galt, Elizabeth Gaskell, Thackeray, Dickens, Wilkie Collins, Trollope, and George Eliot (Fowler 1987: 302–310). But, finally, the short story does not appear to have been very important for them. Harold Orel's study of the Victorian short story is a particularly interesting and nuanced discussion of pre-1880 British short fiction. His argument is set out clearly in the introduction to his book.

The Victorian Age, a richly productive literary period, is notable for (among other things) its nurturing of the short story. The genre had been ill-defined in earlier centuries, and for much of the nineteenth century attracted little critical attention as a new and increasingly popular reading diversion. Many Victorian authors regarded it with suspicion, as a diversion from more profitable novels and plays; even when prospering periodicals paid them decent wages for short stories that pleased readers, authors usually neglected to collect them and reprint them in hard covers.

(Orel 1986: ix)

In detailed discussions of pre-1880 writers of short stories, Orel points to the low place those texts occupied and occupy in their *œuvre*. For example, with regard to Dickens, he writes: "His short stories...were evidently by-products, and on occasions only filler materials" (64). Of Trollope, he notes: "Trollope, like Dickens, earned his bread and butter from his novels, and thought his short stories commercially viable, but on the whole marginal material for the making of a reputation" (79). An essay in *Fraser's Magazine* from 1856 summed up the situation thus: "The English...will have nothing to do with a story unless it is in three volumes" (qtd. in Harris 1979: 91).

All this changed in the last two decades of the nineteenth century. Many factors were involved. There was a relatively large urban literate population eager for inexpensive literate entertainment. Journals and magazines were set up to cater to this market (Newnes's *Tit-Bits* and *The Strand Magazine*, for example). In addition, avant-garde magazines like *The Yellow Book* and *The Savoy* were aimed at a higher-class, bohemian audience. The three-decker novel, for literary and economic reasons, had run out of steam and become *passé*. Writers simply wanted to do something new. The *fin-de-siècle* was a period of expanding intellectual, aesthetic, political and moral horizons. A new form substantially untainted by the past could flourish then, especially among writers who, like Stevenson and Crackanthorpe, had read their short-fiction-writing American or French predecessors and contemporaries. (For fuller discussions of these issues, see: Böker 2005: 32–34; Hunter 2007: 6–7; Orel 1986: 184–192.) At the end of the nineteenth century, H. G. Wells remarked, "short stories broke out everywhere" (qtd. in Hanson 1985: 34), and became, according to Henry James, "an object of almost extravagant dissertation" (qtd. in Shaw 1983: 3). That interest is scarcely surprising, given the number and quality of the writers working in the form: Stevenson, Kipling, Conrad, James, Gissing, Wells, Conan Doyle, M. R. James, Ernest Dowson, Hubert Crackanthorpe, Ella D'Arcy, George Egerton, and Wilde. Writers also reflected on what they were doing with short fiction, in a way that no earlier British writer did. James (an American, but working very substantially within a British literary world) is particularly important in this respect (Hunter 2007: 2, 7).

The rapid development of the short story in Britain in the space of a decade can be illustrated by the sophistication, complexity, and sheer vivid bravura of a text by Rudyard Kipling, "The Mark of the Beast" (published first in Britain in *Life's Handicap: Being Stories of Mine Own People* [1891]). A chilling supernatural story, and a complex story of imperial adventure (both major genres of the period), its action is laid in North India "[s]ome years" prior to the time of narration. On New Year's Eve, British soldiers, planters, and other official and civilian representatives of the Empire, all men, gather at the "club," for a riotous drunken evening of racial and male solidarity. One of their number, a planter called Fleete, on his way home with the narrator, and Strickland, a policeman, desecrates the temple of the Monkey-god Hanuman. The outraged crowd that gathers lets the British go, but only after a leper has touched Fleete on the chest. As the rest of the day progresses, it becomes clear that Fleete has been bewitched by the leper and is turning into a beast. The narrator and Strickland capture the leper and, it is implied, torture him into releasing Fleete from the curse.

The narrator of the text is a figure who recurs in many Kipling stories of this period, a knowledgeable and experienced European, who has excellent connections within the world of British India. The principal character is Strickland, a figure who also recurs in Kipling short stories, a shrewd and also very knowledgeable British colonial police officer. The characters are divided clearly into certain groups. The most obvious division is racial. The men at the club (servants are not mentioned) are all British; they are surrounded by a world of Indians. Indeed, the reader is informed that for many of the British characters, the New Year's Eve festivities are so important because of the racial isolation of the rest of their lives. Characters are also divided into those who know and do not know (a very common division in Kipling's fiction). Strickland "knows as much of natives of India as is good for any man"; the narrator, too, knows a great deal, both about the British in India, and about the wider world, of Hanuman, of lepers, and of horses. Fleete knows nothing of India. He ends up knowing nothing of the plight he has fallen into and from which Strickland and the narrator have saved him. The characters are further divided into the civilized and the not civilized. The leper from the Indian world is scarcely human; he has no face and makes a "noise exactly like the mewing of an otter"; he turns Fleete into an animal that grubs in Strickland's garden and howls like a wolf; he circles the policeman's house, an embodiment of subhuman terror. Against that is set, largely by implication, a British world of doctors, policemen, soldiers, and tea-planters – the inside of Strickland's house. The division is, indeed, clearly marked by spatial contrast: the club and Strickland's house as opposed to the city, the temple, and even Strickland's garden; relative safety as opposed to danger for the unwary or unlucky. But the division of civilized and uncivilized is far from clear by the end of the text. Fleete pollutes Hanuman's temple; one of the priests speaks perfect English; Strickland and the narrator behave with disturbing cruelty to the leper (the narrative's elision here draws attention to their violence).

"The Mark of the Beast" is a skillfully organized tale of supernatural horror. The leper is a truly frightening figure, an emanation from a sinister orientalist nightmare. The text is also a complex story of imperial adventure, both embodying the genre's conventions and querying them. The life of the British in India and the Indian city that surrounds them is captured in economical flashes of detail. Racial lines are clearly drawn, and simultaneously blurred, for the story is, further, a reflection (like other texts in *Life's Handicap*) on the dangers for the British of coming too close to India. The motif of racial and cultural fear, however, is balanced by a complexity, whereby Fleete does behave abominably and his saviors behave worse, and know that they do. It is in part a revisionist recension of the genre to which it partly belongs.

The fin-de-siècle also brought a kind of short story that was to become very important in the twentieth century, the scientific romance that evolved into science fiction by the 1930s. H. G. Wells is most associated with this genre, and "The Star" is a representative example (first published in *Graphic* in 1897, and published in book form in *Tales of Space and Time* [1899]). It is an apocalyptic story. A "vast mass of matter ... bulky, heavy, rushing without warning out of the black mystery of the sky into the radiance of the sun" collides with the planet Neptune. The two "locked in a fiery embrace" draw nearer and nearer the earth, causing cataclysmic earthquakes, floods, tidal waves, the melting of snows and ice, bringing terrible destruction and loss of life. After some days, the new body passes by the earth, and, cautiously, after the catastrophe a new life starts. The story is made credible by traditional verisimilitude devices: the mention of authorities, the figure of the scientist and mathematician, the initially detailed time line.

The story offers different perspectives on the new "star": that of scientists and astronomers, people in the street, women in a dancehall, a schoolboy, tramps, African lovers, a great mathematician, the crowds and masses of the endangered and dying. The story concludes with the point of view of Martian astronomers, for whom the cataclysm is, in fact, minor. It offers its readers the thrill and horror of the apocalypse, stressing the fragility and triviality of human life and civilization in the vast indifference of space and the almost equally vast indifference of another species. Suddenly, our world is seen from a fresh perspective and the old is swept away by a brilliant and deadly new phenomenon. However, the text also draws attention to its own fictive and textual status in a sophisticated manner. The perspective of the Martians is quite unexplained. How does the narrator obtain their point of view? Thus, the story advertises its own imaginative quality. This is augmented by the highly self-advertising syntax of the whole piece. Biblical sentences and lists make it apparent that the story is a rhetorical performance, an elaborate and creative game. For a moment, the reader is to imagine a new world made by art.

The range of fin-de-siècle short fiction was considerable. By the late 1890s, the reader could also encounter a short story like Ella D'Arcy's "The Villa Lucienne" (published in *The Yellow Book* in 1896, and in the collection *Modern Instances* in 1898).

This framed story (written in, by contemporary standards, an informal and accessible English) is mostly an account by Madame Koetlegon of a visit to an abandoned villa on the French Riviera. The frame paragraph, written by an unnamed narrator, recounts the skill with which Madame Koetlegon told her story, so that the audience can share her experience, but, really, the narrator points out, "as you will see, in reality there is no story at all." A group of ladies visits the Villa Lucienne because one of them, presumably the recently widowed Cécile, is considering renting it. They pass from the garden of a nearby villa, the Villa Soleil, through a dark and damp trellised passage to the dilapidated villa in the middle of a garden run wild. A surly caretaker shows them over the house; the ladies become frightened, convinced that something sinister has happened in the past; the child in their company is sure that she saw an old lady watching her. The text achieves its effect through contrasting settings. It is a beautiful day in December; olives are being harvested; the garden of the Villa Soleil is rich and lovely; the view from the villa's balcony is entrancing. These settings are set against the vile passage through which the group passes to the Villa Lucienne, the disorder of its garden, the shabby dilapidation of the once beautiful home, its malevolent guardian and its sinister atmosphere. The story deploys Gothic conventions in a sophisticated way. It is marked as a story from the beginning; it only hints at the horrors of the supernatural. Indeed, it is almost lacking traditional/conventional story materials. But the elisions in the narrative are telling. The reader knows nothing of the past occupants of the Villa Lucienne, but much is hinted at, in, for example, the "long ragged fragment of lace" caught on "the girandole of a pier-glass," torn off from a dress as someone passed by in haste. The elision with regard to the party of ladies is even more marked and more revealing. Cécile's husband Guy has recently died. His absence is made prominent by the presence of his beloved dog, and by Madame Koetlegon's sense that only he could have captured or expressed (how is ambiguous) the experience of the sinister villa. The story finally becomes an evocation of the ladies' sense of loss and their experience of the sadness of things and time.

"The Villa Lucienne" is a subtle, accomplished and powerful story, and a self-conscious one. It, Kipling's "The Mark of the Beast," and Wells's "The

Star" embody the ambition and skill of the British short story by the mid-1880s, and that in the work of both canonical authors, and of a now relatively uncanonical one. Each well represents the two major categories of turn-of-the-century short story noted by Clare Hanson, "stories with a strong plot and 'plotless' short fiction" (Hanson 1985: 6). But the kind of story represented in "The Villa Lucienne," an elliptical, atmospheric, highly organized (and self-advertisingly organized) study of psychology, proved to be extraordinarily fruitful and resilient in the decades following the 1890s. That the movement from the *fin-de-siècle* to literary modernism is very blurred is nowhere more evident than in short fiction (Hanson 1985: 58). The dynamic form of the 1890s is one of the favored genres of the literary avant-garde in the first three decades of the twentieth century. The modernists – if it makes any sense to call them that, for the affiliations and interrelations of the early twentieth-century literary world were very complex and much richer than is usually acknowledged – tackled the short form with gusto. Conrad, James, Joyce, Woolf, Lawrence, and Mansfield all produced major short fiction, and short fiction was a major part of their output. It was most amenable to their desire to capture elusive, shifting psychological movements, and to produce evidently artistic products. It offered yet another way to distance themselves from the Victorian novel and its Edwardian and Georgian imitators (Head 1992: 15–16).

Jean Rhys's "Illusion" was first published in 1927 in her collection *The Left Bank and Other Stories*, with a laudatory preface by the great modernist and modernist patron Ford Madox Ford. It well represents the modernist short story by a writer somewhat outside the central canonical grouping of the avant-garde. The narrator is an unnamed English woman living in Paris. One of her acquaintances is a Miss Bruce, independently wealthy, but living, for seven years now, as an artist in Paris. Sensibly dressed, slightly mannish, Miss Bruce seems to exist at a remove from the hectic, sensual life around her. However, when she falls ill, the narrator, who has been asked to bring her nightdresses to the hospital, on opening a dark solid wardrobe, discovers an array of the most beautiful, colorful dresses, enormously glamorous, extremely expensive. The narrator tries to imagine why she might have bought them. She thinks that after buying one on impulse, Miss Bruce is compelled to seek more such dresses. "Then must have begun the search for *the* dress, the perfect Dress, beautiful, beautifying, possible to be worn. And lastly, the search for illusion – a craving, almost a vice, the stolen waters and the bread eaten in secret of Miss Bruce's life." Once she has recovered, Miss Bruce claims to the narrator that she simply collects "frocks," dresses she will never wear.

Plotless in a traditional sense, "Illusion" aims to capture two psychologies, that of Miss Bruce and that of the narrator. Miss Bruce, with her mannish good sense, nonetheless keeps an armoire full of the riotous color of expensive dresses. The narrator, of whom the reader knows little, imagines her way into Miss Bruce's mind, but simultaneously reveals something about herself as well. The text is notable for implications such as the above. Does the narrator, too, share Miss Bruce's longings? The reader also is prompted to ask about Miss Bruce's interest in pretty women. Her name is male, as is the size of her body parts, while the story's final sentence has her noting the appearance of a girl "in her gentlemanly manner." At the center of the story is the striking motif of the wardrobe full of dresses, the glorious illusion of Miss Bruce's (and the narrator's) life, a metaphor rich in implication. Lawrence, Woolf, Mansfield, and Kipling wrote similar stories. (See, for example, Lawrence's "Odour of Chrysanthemums" [1911/1914], Woolf's "Kew Gardens" [1919/1921], Mansfield's "The Garden Party" [1922], and Kipling's "The Wish House" [1926].)

In 1933, the OED Supplement included for the first time the term "short story" to designate "a particular kind of literary product" (Reid 1977: 1). In 1937, *The Faber Book of Modern Stories* was published, edited and with an introduction by Elizabeth Bowen. Bowen's collection includes work by herself, A. E. Coppard, E. M. Forster, Aldous Huxley, D. H. Lawrence, Walter de la Mare, Somerset Maugham, Frank O'Connor, Seán O'Faoláin, Liam O'Flaherty, and others. She omits Katherine Mansfield because "a story was not available," and Kipling and Wells because their work does not need "further prominence" (17). Bowen's introduction is a celebration of the achievement and possibility of short fiction. "The short story is a young art," she insists, "as we now know it, it is the child of this century" (7). It is modern, like the cinema, unbound by tradition – "both are, accordingly, free" (7). It is a rejection of the length, the dead conventions, the *longueurs* of the novel. It can be fragmentary, inconclusive, allusive. Its weapons are "oblique narration, cutting (as in the cinema), the unlikely placing of emphasis, or symbolism (the telling use of the object both for its own sake and as an image)" (8). It "may thus more nearly than the novel approach aesthetic and moral truth" (15). Bowen herself expresses a fondness for stories with compression, tautness and vital clarity (15). The achievement of short fiction is remarkable. "In this country, within the last fifteen years, the non-commercial or free short story – that is to say, the story unsuitable, not meant to be suitable, for the popular, well-paying magazines, and free, therefore, not to conform with so-called popular taste – has found a wider opening: it has come to have an eclectic vogue" (13). The short story has a future. "The present state of the short story is, on the whole, healthy: its prospects are good" (18).

"The short but extremely fertile period between the two world wars remains the high point of the British short story," notes John H. Rogers

(1996: xv), and certainly the list of its practitioners in this period is impressive. Kipling produced his late and often difficult work in this period. Maugham was prolific, writing *inter alia* the very influential Ashenden espionage stories (1928), and reworking the conventions of stories of colonial adventure (in "Footprints in the Jungle" (1927), for example). It was the golden age of the detective short story (G. K. Chesterton, Agatha Christie, Dorothy L. Sayers, and Margery Allingham). Women writers such as Mansfield, Rhys, Sylvia Townsend Warner, and Frances Bellerby turned to the short story as a form congenial towards the specifically female experience they wished to recount (Coelsch-Foisner 2008 a: 96–113). The Second World War, too, was a good time for the short story. Bowen put it thus in May 1945:

> The short storyist shares – or should share to an extent – the faculties of the poet: he can render the significance of the small event. He can take for the theme of his story a face glimpsed in the street, an unexplained incident, a snatch of talk overheard on bus or train .... Wartime London, blitzed, cosmopolitan, electric with expectation now teems, I feel, with untold but tellable stories, glitters with scenes that cry aloud for the pen.
>
> (qtd. in Beachcroft 1968: 212)

Bernard Bergonzi describes the short story as "the preferred form for new fiction writers" during the 1939–1945 War (Bergonzi 1993: 40). Some might have their work published in *Penguin New Writing* or *Horizon*, but there were other outlets too. Bergonzi points to the irony that in the paper-strapped 1940s, short story writers had more publications in which to place their work than fifty years later (40). Certainly, the conflict inspired some major short fiction: Bowen's own ("Mysterious Kôr" [1944] and "The Demon Lover" [1945], for example), and that of Alun Lewis, Julian Maclaren-Ross, Rose Macaulay, and Mollie Panter-Downes. (The last two writers found an audience and market for their work in the U.S.A.)

Panter-Downes's short stories are some of the most memorable of the 1939–1945 conflict. Her "Good Evening, Mrs. Craven" was first published in 1942. Like all her war-time short fiction, it came out in the United States, in *The New Yorker*. The title is ironic, for the protagonist and central consciousness of the text is Mr. Craven's unnamed mistress, not his wife, her anonymity embodying both her final neglect by her lover and her final irrelevance or non-existence to his family and officialdom. The brief story is divided into four sections, the first setting out the course of the affair before the war, the second sketching the lovers' last meal together before his departure for active service in Libya, the third depicting the mistress's sense of loss as she ceases to receive any letters from Craven and her attempt to have news of him by calling his wife (the real Mrs. Craven), and the fourth presenting the protagonist's utter despair, cut off hopelessly from the man she has loved. The story is elliptical to a high degree. The reader learns the details of the protagonist's and Craven's meeting every Thursday evening in an old-fashioned London restaurant. How she and her lover met is not mentioned; their love-making after their meal is only hinted at by the detail of Mr. Craven's tying his tie as he speaks to her. The protagonist's job before and during the war is never mentioned, nor are details given of her background, education, or even her appearance. Clothes are indicated and one piece of jewelry, but that is all. The focus is firmly on her feelings about her relationship, its stasis (for it scarcely develops) and her vertiginous sadness as she loses touch with Craven. The reader observes her pleasure in meeting her lover every Thursday evening, her joy in being called "Mrs. Craven" by the old waiters, and her consciousness of the compromises she must make to keep this affair (she must not fuss, she must not want too much). The limits of the relationship are, however, clearly signaled in the setting of the restaurant in which the lovers meet. Frozen in time, with ancient waiters, pictures of actors from the past, a bust of Mrs. Siddons above the lovers' favorite table, the "whole place looked as though it had been soaked in Madeira." It is a place of illusion, usually charming, but ultimately fake; on occasions when acquaintances of Mr. Craven are present, they must pretend to be employer and secretary; but here, usually, if only temporarily, she can be Mrs. Craven. The limits of her lover, too, are also evident. He has a most comfortable situation: a successful married life, children he can boast of, and an acquiescent mistress who never cries or demands or causes bother. The war cuts her off and out. There is, as she notes, no War Office procedure for informing mistresses of their lovers' fates. The story's power comes in making the reader know and feel for her; clinging to illusions, her alienated, unacknowledgeable intimacy with Craven's family, and her dizzying lapse into despair at the story's end. It is typical of Panter-Downes's ability to render a wide variety of women's experience of war in complex and moving detail.

Like Bowen in 1937, H. E. Bates in *The Modern Short Story* in 1941 saw the short story as modern, free from the encumbrances of the novel and its conventions. He also, again like Bowen, predicted a great future for short fiction. In 1962, he summed up his view then: "I prophesied . . . that the inevitable distrust and dislocation of war's aftermath would lead new writers to find in the short story the essential medium for what they had to say" (qtd. in Beachcroft 1968: 212). However, in 1972, looking back at his statement in 1941, he noted gloomily that "my prophecy as to the probability of a new golden age of the short story, such as we had on both sides of the Atlantic in the 1920s and 1930s was . . . dismally unfulfilled" (qtd. in Moosmüller 1993: 109). For the British short story, the post-1945 period has been a difficult time. There are two main reasons for this. First, the publishing outlets – journals and magazines – for short fiction disappeared substantially, progressively, and relentlessly after 1945. Second, British publishers became, and still are, very hostile to short stories, arguing that they do not make money (Baldwin 1985: 35; Pickering 1985: 75; Malcolm and Malcolm 2006: xvi). V. S. Pritchett summed up the situation in 1986: "It is very difficult to find anyone to publish a short story" (Pritchett 1986: 36). Anthologies of short fiction were published in post-war Britain; there did exist journals that took short stories. But these were few. The fact that the U.S. magazine *The New Yorker* plays an important role in publishing the work of many important British short story writers in the post-war years is telling. Barry Menikoff mentions, in this respect, Sylvia Townsend Warner, Elizabeth Taylor, Ruth Prawer Jhabvala, Muriel Spark, and V. S. Pritchett (Menikoff 1987: 138). (See also LeStage 1999: 191–203, and Bloom 2006: 65–91.)

British publishers' distaste for short fiction is well documented. Graham Swift records that his collection of short stories *Learning to Swim* was only considered for publication after he had published two successful novels (Moosmüller 1993: 113). There is no evidence that this has changed in the late twentieth and early twenty-first century. Debbie Taylor wrote in the writers' journal *Mislexia* in 2003 of the short story as an "Endangered Species" (Taylor 2003: 9). Announcing a short story competition, Alexander Linklater wrote in 2005 in *Prospect* of an anti-short story "herd mentality among magazines and publishers." "At some point during the last twenty years, the short story came to viewed in Britain as culturally redundant and economically unviable" (Linklater 2005: 24). One would only take issue with Linklater's time limitation. The recent site "The Short Story Website," while admirable, has to some degree the tone of a cause that knows it is fighting a hard battle (www.theshortstory.org.uk).

Disparagement and neglect of the short story is not just commercial, but scholarly as well. Authorities are unanimous that over the last sixty years critics and scholars have not taken the form very seriously. Reid noted in 1977 that "even now it seldom receives serious critical attention commensurate with [its] importance" (Reid 1977: 1). In 1964, Alan Coren exclaimed: "What overtones of dilettantism, of superfluous also-running that title [of short story writer] carries in England" (qtd. in Beachcroft 1968: 213–214). Even Bergonzi turns his nose up at the short story, accusing it of "slightness and slickness" and of being marked by "stereotypes, mannerisms, gimmickry and the like" (qtd. in Reid 1977: 1–2). However, neglect is relative rather than absolute, and the last forty years have brought a substantial body of serious studies of the British short story. The work of T. O. Beachcroft (1968), Walter Allen (1981), Joseph M. Flora (1985), Dennis Vannatta (1985), Valerie Shaw

(1983), and Dominic Head (1992) is important. Nineteenth-century British short fiction has been thoroughly discussed by Harold Orel (1986), while Alastair Fowler dedicates considerable parts of his 1987 *A History of English Literature* to the late nineteenth- and twentieth-century short story and its Romantic and Victorian predecessors (Fowler 1987: 302–310; 335–342). Birgit Moosmüller's *Die experimentelle englische Kurzgeschichte der Gegenwart* (1993) is a major piece of scholarship. Barbara Korte's *The Short Story in Britain* (2003) is an outstanding study of the form, while Arno Löffler's and Eberhard Späth's collection of insightful essays, *Geschichte der englischen Kurzgeschichte* (2005), and Andrew Maunder's comprehensive *The Facts on File Companion to the British Short Story* (2007) also help to shatter the tale of critical neglect. Renate Brosch's *Short Story: Textsorte und Leseerfahrung* (2007) is an extension and expansion of the theoretical approaches to short fiction (including British short fiction) in the work of Charles E. May (1976; 1984; 1994; 1995). Adrian Hunter's excellent *The Cambridge Introduction to the Short Story in English* (2007) is also well worthy of note. In collaboration with Cheryl Alexander Malcolm, my own work has addressed the British short story with an attempt at seriousness (Malcolm and Malcolm 2006; 2008). Günther Jarfe has just published a fine introduction to British short fiction in *Die moderne britische Short Story: Eine Einführung* (2010). *Studies in Short Fiction* and the *Journal of the Short Story in English* contain substantial essays on British short fiction.

Critical study is deserved; for the list of British writers since 1945 who have attempted the shorter form is impressive, and their achievements in short fiction are equally so. Dennis Vannatta's "Selected Bibliography of Short Stories, 1945–1980" includes work by writers of the stature of Stan Barstow, H. E. Bates (ten volumes of short fiction between 1946 and 1968), Christine Brooke-Rose, Elaine Feinstein, Penelope Gilliat, James Hanley, Wilson Harris, L. P. Hartley, Susan Hill, B. S. Johnson, Francis King, Rosamond Lehmann, Wolf Mankowitz, Olivia Manning, Nicholas Mosely, Bill Naughton, William Samson (ten volumes between 1946 and 1963), Paul Scott, Elizabeth Taylor, Henry Treece, Alexander Trocci, Frank Tuohy, John Wain, Sylvia Townsend Warner, and Evelyn Waugh. Major post-war novelists – Graham Greene and Muriel Spark – also have a substantial output of short fiction. A supplementary list of writers of short stories since the early 1980s would include (among others): J. G. Ballard, John Berger, A. S. Byatt, Angela Carter, Patricia Duncker, Michel Faber, Neil Gaiman, Alasdair Gray, Dan Jacobson, Gabriel Josipovici, James Kelman, Doris Lessing, Toby Litt, E. A. Markham, Adam Mars-Jones, Ian McEwan, Julian Maclaren Ross, Michael Moorcock, Ben Okri, Dylis Rose, Salman Rushdie, Iain Crichton Smith, Graham Swift, Fay Weldon, and Arnold Wesker. Not all have written large numbers of short stories, but all have given the form at some point in their careers a serious attention that has produced substantial work.

The writer who devoted himself most closely to the short story in the post-war period was V. S. Pritchett. His *œuvre* is large, complex, and extremely good. Yet little critical attention has been paid to his work. (There are exceptions; see Jeremy Treglown's critical biography [2005], Jonathan Bloom's study [2006], and Andrzej Gąsiorek's essay in Malcolm and Malcolm [2008]: 423–430.) "The Camberwell Beauty," published in the collection of the same name from 1974, shows the strengths of his work.

The story is one of obsession. The narrator, an unnamed failed antique dealer, tells of his fellow dealers and their secret lusts for particular pieces. He also tells of his and other characters' desires for a young woman, Isabel. The narrator first meets her as a child, an orphan, in August's antique shop while he is searching for a rare piece of china. He meets her again briefly, from time to time, over a period of several years. She eventually leaves her adoptive home to marry an elderly antique dealer called Pliny, who keeps her as a semi-willing prisoner in his shop. The narrator comes to desire her and eventually makes contact with her again, even being admitted to Pliny's shop on two occasions. On the second, he appeals to Isabel to leave with him; they are interrupted by Pliny; there is violence; and Isabel dismisses the narrator.

This is the skeleton of the story material, although it only becomes apparent on close reading of the text. The narrative is digressive. The narrator speaks of antique dealers' secrets, the appearance of their shops, their bar-room gossip, what goes on at auctions, various kinds of antique, and his own failed career. The framework only appears through these digressions: August sexually abuses Isabel as a child; she fascinates the elderly Pliny; the narrator becomes increasingly drawn to, and finally obsessed by the girl. The story is, centrally, one of lust. The narrator uses the word frequently for the secret passions of antique dealers, the desire and longing that drive them, the fever of dealing and finding, however dishonestly, a bargain. Each of the central figures in the text is urged on by a lust to possess something or someone: a piece of Meissen china, Isabel. The characters are damaged or disappointed. Antiques offer them dreams and illusions; Isabel is a consolation for an impoverished life. Pliny makes her his prisoner, undresses her although he has no intercourse with her, worships her. Isabel herself, the narrator notes, writes "I S A B" on a dusty shelf in Pliny's antique store – "half a name, written by a living finger in dust." She herself is afraid to leave the back of Pliny's shop.

The story's settings are desolate: lower middle-class shops, South London streets, provincial towns to the north of the capital, and, above all, shabby antique shops, full of unsold items. When the narrator finally persuades Isabel to let him into Pliny's shop, the place is one of "empty hopelessness."

> At night the cold white-washed store-room was silent under the light of its single bulb and the place was mostly in shadow, only the tops of stacked furniture stood out in the yellow light, some of them like buildings.... We walked down alleys between the stacks. It was like walking through a dead, silent city, abandoned by everyone who once lived there. There was a sour smell of upholstery....

"The Camberwell Beauty" depicts a wretched, empty world of shabby unglamorous people and places, but also shows the people in it obeying the promptings of lust and passion. The story's language with its short sentences and neutral lexis and syntax, neither elevated nor picturesque dialect, stands at a similar slant to its subject matter, as do some of the characters' names. Names like August and Pliny hardly belong to this milieu. But all impulses of desire lead to half-pleasures at best: a collector does find the piece of Staffordshire he has been searching for; Pliny possesses Isabel in some measure; Isabel is worshipped and secure, queen of junk. But, like others, the narrator fails. His cocky knowledgeableness at the story's start is shown as hollow. He did not understand his feelings till quite late, and in the end he is rejected by Isabel. "That was the end. I found myself walking in the street. How unreal people looked in the sodium light." "The Camberwell Beauty" is an extraordinary story – of passion among tawdriness, of a seedy lower middle-class inferno of destructive lusts and deviance – a masterpiece of indirect narration.

In the second half of the twentieth century, the dominant conventions in the British short story are those of realism. There is, however, a strong non-realist tendency. This takes two principal forms: metafictional stories and stories that draw on the conventions of non-realist genres, supernatural fiction, gothic fiction, and, above all, science fiction. Metfictional short fiction is represented by work by Christine Brooke-Rose, B. S. Johnson, and Gabriel Josipovici, who write texts that draw attention to themselves as texts, that scrutinize and question the conventions of traditional realist fiction, and focus on problems connected with writing fiction. The influence of the Franco-Irish writer Samuel Beckett is particularly important and evident in Brooke-Rose's, Johnson's, and Josipovici's short fiction. One of Josipovici's most celebrated stories is "Mobius the Stripper" (1974), its pages divided in two, one narrative in the top half, a second in the lower half, the narrator/writer of one half oppressed by the literature of the past and uncertain what to write. (See the Key Works chapter of this book for a full discussion of Josipovici's text.)

More important, however, certainly in terms of numbers of readers, are short stories that operate within the conventions of fantasy and science fiction. In post-war Britain, Sylvia Townsend Warner wrote many short stories, full of changelings, elves, human eunuchs, and cruel supernatural queens, collected in her *Kingdoms of Elfin* (1977). From the 1960s, Michael Moorcock produced a vast number of short stories featuring heroic fantasy figures such as Elric of Melniboné and Earl Aubec. Underrated or ignored by scholarship, these are an important part of the short-story landscape of the late twentieth century. The work of J. G. Ballard has, however, always drawn some serious literary criticism. Like Moorcock's work, it impresses by the sheer dizzying fertility of imagination involved, by its psychological and social suggestiveness, and by its intelligent reworking of literary motifs. One of Ballard's earliest short stories, "Prima Belladonna" (1956) shows his non-realist work in its full colors. The story is set in a non-documented time, "the Recess," a period of inertia and stagnation, before the government "started up all the clocks" again; and in non-documented places, such as Vermilion Sands. The narrator runs a "Choro-Flora" shop that sells musical plants. He offers little explanation of the social, political, and genetic background to his tale. The reader is simply plunged into a different and intriguing universe. The story material is centered on the narrator's relationship with a beautiful, golden-skinned, musical, part-mutant woman who is fascinated by the rarest and most powerful of his stock of plants. In the climax of the text, the woman and the plant appear to have species-transgressing sexual intercourse, after which the gorgeous Jane Ciracylides passes out of the narrator's life. The story mesmerizes the reader with a created world that is close to the empirical one, yet radically different, wildly colorful and absorbing. Its literary credentials are embodied both in its focus on the intoxication of difference and perversion, and in its intelligent reworking of motifs from Hawthorne's "Rappaccini's Daughter" (1844). Ballard's science fiction, like Moorcock's fantasy, is clearly writing with ambitions to be taken seriously. It harks back to Wells's and de la Mare's work, and it is echoed in, for example, Angela Carter's highly regarded collection of revisionings of folk tales and fairy tales, *The Bloody Chamber* (1979), and in the work of a younger generation of short-story writers, such as Michel Faber, China Miéville, and Neil Gaiman.

The strength in depth of the realist British short story can be illustrated by a writer like Hugh Fleetwood. Although he is the author of sixteen novels and four collections of short stories, all critically well received, his work is little known. But a story like "The Last Lesson" from the collection *The Beast* (1978) is, by any standards, an accomplished piece of work.

"The Last Lesson" does what so many short stories do supremely well: it presents a mind; it poses an enigma. Like much of Fleetwood's work, it has a foreign setting. Antonietta Misseri, unattractive, reclusive, spinsterish, on the day of her thirtieth birthday goes to her last English lesson. She lives with her father in Ostia, outside Rome, in a pine forest with a view of the beach and its sybaritic goings-on. It is a view that she never enjoys, for over the years she has ceased to have much contact with the world outside her home. She increasingly feels it to be unreal. The sense of unreality spreads to her home and herself, and only a chance encounter with a foreign language persuades herself that there is something real, somewhere. Consequently she starts to study English, largely at home, although once a week she attends an hour-long tutorial in a suburb of Rome. Three days previously, she has seen what appears to be the first stages of a brutal, sexually perverse murder. An English hitchhiker is picked up by a man in a flame-colored car. Antonietta has, however, told the police nothing. It transpires that she is sure that the car belongs to the gentlemanly English teacher, Mr. Ball, whom she likes best at the language school. She has asked to have her last lesson with him. She reveals that she knows he is the murderer, and then asks for a ride home.

The story is a third-person point-of-view narration that slowly exposes Antonietta's thoughts and feelings in the present and in the past. A world and a mind are vividly presented; Antonietta's psychological disturbance is patiently, carefully, sympathetically unfolded. Her arbitrary leap into a foreign language course is interestingly motivated, and the language school, its overworked and intermittently malign teachers, and its methods reek of authenticity. Antonietta is also not alone. Mr. Ball, too, is perhaps in flight from realities that no longer seem real: England, his everyday life, his work as a tired English teacher. If he is the murderer, he shares Antonietta's madness. The story is deeply enigmatic. Did Antonietta actually see the flame-colored car pick up the murdered tourist? Was it, indeed, Mr. Ball's car? Was he the gallant driver? Why might someone like him savagely sexually assault and murder someone? Why does Antonietta want to be driven and murdered, and in such a fashion? What is to happen next?

In the early twenty-first century, writers continue to address the shorter form. James Lasdun's most recent collection of short stories (his fourth), *It's Beginning to Hurt* was published to acclaim in 2009. The stories range widely in setting and character, although several (with echoes of the work of Henry James) involve English encounters with the U.S.A. One of the most memorable stories in *It's Beginning to Hurt* is "Annals of the Honorary Secretary," a story all the more striking for its allusiveness to a long tradition of British supernatural tales.

The narrator is the anonymous honorary secretary of a spiritualist, mystic group dedicated to discussing and experiencing psychic, supernatural, paranormal phenomena (communication with the dead, hypnotism, thought transference). A new member, Lucille Thomas, an unexceptional young woman, offers after some time to give a "performance." In her case, it is a practical "demonstration" of psychic power. She communicates to her audience unease, despair, "an overwhelming feeling of desolation." In later demonstrations, she makes small objects disappear, once again filling the audience with a deep sense of physical and ethical discomfort. At the group's New Year celebration (held in spring, out of respect for the traditions of older and wiser civilizations), Lucille performs a demonstration that imparts a terrible sense of corruption, decay, and death to all present. The guests flee; Lucille disappears; but her legend endures in the society.

The story is at once humorous and frightening. The narrator's English is formal and mannered. He articulately and carefully presents his and others' experience of Lucille Thomas's gift, meticulously differentiating responses. He wraps the supernatural tale in credibility – his is the voice of authority and good sense – and also adds a strange element of discordant humor to the text. The details he offers of the sites of the society's meetings, the people involved, and the traditions of the society, give an additional layer of credibility (and humor) to the story. The text is a powerful supernatural story, in a long tradition, cast in a contemporary mold. However, it also has grander ambitions, suggested briefly in the text through meanings attached to Lucille, in a manner reminiscent of Hawthorne's short fiction. She is a performer, a kind of artist, with a terrifying gift, a gift that the narrator describes in artistic terms as "lyric rather than epic." He also identifies her as a kind of messiah figure (an inverted one, offering disquiet rather than salvation): her remarks now belong to "apocrypha"; "the critical exegesis" of Lucille's figure, performances, and gifts "has only just begun."

In *The Lonely Voice* (1962), Frank O'Connor wrote that the short story appeared a particularly suitable form for the marginal and excluded voices of the world (O'Connor 1965: 18–19). Angela Carter and Hermione Lee have also argued something similar (Lee 1985: viii; Carter 1986: xii). Although one can have reservations about terms such as "marginal" and "excluded," it is the case that groups and individuals who feel themselves at a slant to mainstream literary and social traditions have found the short story a congenial vehicle for their voices. This is true of women writers such as Doris Lessing and Angela Carter. Lesbian short fiction – Anna Livia's *Saccharin Cyanide* (1989), J. E. Hardy's *Stranger Than Fish* (1989), and Cherry Pott's *Mosaic of Air* (1992) – is published not just in individual author collections, but in a host of anthologies and in many small journals (Grubisic 2008: 368). Following a tradition laid down by Oscar Wilde, E. M. Forster, Angus Wilson, and Noël Coward, gay writers, too, have produced major work in the short story. Anthologies of short stories play an important role in offering an outlet for gay short fiction, although Adam Mars-Jones, Tom Wakefield, Simon Burt, and Joseph Mills have also published individual collections (Grubisic 2008: 369). Salman Rushdie, Hanif Kureishi, Ben Okri, E. A. Markham, and Barbara Burford have also written substantial short fiction that aims to capture the experience of Black and Asian British citizens negotiating the complexities of discordant worlds and cultures. The short fiction of Dan Jacobson, Clive Sinclair, and Ruth Fainlight, among others, has spoken of a specifically Anglo-Jewish experience, while Scottish writers – Iain Crichton Smith, George Mackay Brown, Alan Spence, Alasdair Gray, and James Kelman – have given a Scottish inflection to the short story.

At the beginning of the twenty-first century, the British short story is in an ambiguous situation. Major publishers and literary agents still express distaste for short fiction. Major short-story writers from the past, like Pritchett, are non-canonical. The major literary prizes are still given for novels. But there are other counter-signals – besides the high quality of short stories written and published. In 2005, the National Short Story Prize was announced at the Edinburgh International Book Festival. The first prize is £15,000. Originally sponsored by the National Endowment for Science, Technology and the Arts, it was supported by BBC Radio 4 and *Prospect* magazine. The BBC is now the sponsor and since 2008 the prize has been called the BBC National Short Story Award. The web site www.shortstory. org.uk, supported by the Arts Council England and the Scottish Book Trust, among other organizations, aims to promote the short story in the U.K., and is part of the campaign "Story," the goal of which is to reverse decades of neglect of short fiction. Collections of short stories, partly aimed at younger readers, for example Neil Gaiman's *Smoke and Mirrors* (1999), can have very good sales.

In addition, other recent literary phenomena show an interesting relationship with the short story. There is a tendency for some recent novels to approach the dimensions of long short fiction (Ian McEwan's *On Chesil Beach* [2007], Alan Judd's *Dancing with Eva* [2007]), although this is not a new phenomenon; well-known novelists have produced linked collections of short narratives (Iain Sinclair's *Downriver* [1991], David Mitchell's *Ghostwritten* [1999], Kazuo Ishiguro's *Nocturnes* [2009]). Further, the graphic short story has emerged as a recognizable and recognized form. In *Looking for Jake and Other Stories* (2005), the highly regarded contemporary sciencefiction writer China Miéville incorporates one graphic short story, "On the Way to the Front" (visuals by Liam Sharp). The graphic short texts contained in *It's Dark in London* (1996), edited by Oscar Zarate, are serious and powerful pieces of work. Random House, Jonathan Cape, Comica and the Observer Group has offered a Graphic Short Story Prize since 2007.

The 2009 edition of the competition had a first prize of £1000. The graphic narrative, with the demand that it exist within the relatively short scope of a single issue, bears a similarity to the short story, and individual issues can build up into something reminiscent of a short-story cycle. Gaiman's *Sandman* series (1988–1996) is a good example of such graphic fiction. Perhaps the graphic short story will prove an important variant of short fiction in Britain in the future.

The history and the development of short fiction in Ireland have followed substantially different paths from those of the British short story. First, there is the question of status. In 1979, Declan Kiberd wrote that "For the past eighty years in Ireland, the short story has been the most popular of all literary forms with readers. It has also been the form most widely exploited by writers" (Kiberd 1979: 14). For most of the twentieth century, the short story was the preferred form for many Irish writers, and those writers have usually had little difficulty in publishing their work. Second, the context of the Irish short story has always been different from that of its British equivalent. Ireland's experience has for centuries been closer to that of a colonized country – with all its complexities of affiliation and rejection – than that of any part of mainland Britain. In addition, while Britain in the twentieth century experienced social, economic, military and political disruptions enough, they were certainly different and perhaps less convulsive than those in Ireland – vigorous nationalist agitation, rebellion, military occupation and guerilla warfare, partition, ethnic cleansing, civil war, the attainment of a difficult independence in the south and the creation of a bitterly divided, neo-colonial society in the north.

One of the difficulties of talking about the Irish short story, a difficulty acknowledged by many commentators, is that until the creation of the Irish Free State in 1922, Irish writers were closely involved in the British literary system, publishing in mainland Britain and writing for British audiences. Indeed, even after independence this situation has not completely altered. Many Irish writers have lived extensively out of Ireland, publishing in London rather than in Dublin. Further, the complex affiliations of a colonial society, such as was pre-1922 Ireland, meant that many Irish writers did not identify themselves closely with their fellow Irish for reasons of class or religion. Anthony Trollope, Joseph Sheridan Le Fanu, Edith Somerville and Violet Martin ("Somerville and Ross") are cases in point. (For a fuller discussion of this period and the development of the Irish short story up to 1945, see Lonergan 2008: 51–64).

Attempts are made by commentators to link the nineteenth-century Irish short story with a traditional oral Gaelic narrative tradition (Kiberd 1979: 13–25; Maunder 2007: 207), but these must be speculative. However, it is clear that in nineteenth-century Ireland there was a substantial body of short fiction published in a wide range of journals. Harris writes of a "great flood of fiction portraying Irish life and character," as well as that recounting Irish legends, from the beginning to the end of the nineteenth century (Harris 1979: 39–47). John and Michael Banim's *Tales of the O'Hara Family* (1825), and the work of William Carleton in the 1820s and 1830s are usually mentioned as examples of early nineteenth-century Irish short fiction. Certainly, the contemporary Irish publishing world offered numerous outlets for short fiction. Kilroy lists an impressive range of magazines willing to publish short stories: *Dublin University Magazine* (1833–1877) (edited by Le Fanu from 1861 to 1867), *Comet* (1831–1833), *Dublin Penny Journal* (1832–1836), *Irish Penny Journal* (1840–1841), *Cork Magazine* (1847–1848), *Nation* (1842–1892), *Irish Homestead* (1895–1923) (edited by Æ and the first publisher of Joyce's short stories), and others (Kilroy 1984: 10–12).

A writer whose work illustrates the complexities and strengths of Irish short fiction in the mid-nineteenth century is Joseph Sheridan Le Fanu, who published short stories between the 1830s and 1870s. One of his most interesting is "The Familiar," published in London in 1872 in the collection *In a Glass Darkly*. Like other stories in the collection, "The Familiar" has a complex frame. The unnamed overall editor is a disciple of the German physician-philosopher Dr. Martin Hesselius. "The Familiar" is one of Hesselius's "about two hundred and thirty cases," one selected by the editor. It is in manuscript form with a handwritten note in Hesselius's writing attached to it. Hesselius praises the narrator of the manuscript and places the case it reports, that of Mr. Barton, in a pseudo-scientific context. The editor reveals that the narrator of Mr. Barton's story is "the Reverend Thomas Herbert," a character who does not appear in the subsequent story. In the peculiar manner of all such framing devices (which are part of the tradition of the supernatural story from the time of Defoe's "A Relation of the Apparition of Mrs. Veal" [1705]), this technique in "The Familiar" both makes the account of supernatural events that follows verisimilar (after all, it is textually and scientifically authenticated), and questions its veracity (the reader is distant from the actual events, and why is the account of the Reverend Mr. Herbert to be given any credibility anyway?).

The story told is one of the "strange persecution" and ultimate destruction of Sir James Barton in Dublin and Clontarf by a malevolent supernatural figure. The haunting first takes the form of footsteps that follow Barton in lonely parts of Dublin. Later, letters arrive warning the victim that he is under the eye of "The Watcher." Subsequently, a small, foreign-looking figure, which terrifies the otherwise resolute captain, appears both to Barton and those in his company; however, the figure can never be detained, but always vanishes when pursued. At one point, a shot is fired at the unhappy gentleman by an unknown would-be assassin, as he is walking home alone at night in Dublin. The apparition appears to be recognized by Barton and to recall an episode from his past that he does not wish to divulge to anyone. This small malevolent man (in an account of his sighting by a servant girl, he is described as "a singularly ill-looking little man, whose countenance bore the stamp of menace and malignity") drives Barton to despair; he attempts to flee to the Continent, but in vain; even strict seclusion in a country house outside Dublin does not save him. Barton meets a macabre end, seemingly terrified to death by a supernatural incursion, probably of this familiar figure, into his bedroom. A postscript to the Reverend Herbert's account suggests that the small persecutor may be the ghost of a man that Barton persecuted and indirectly killed, in retaliation for his (the apparition's) brutal treatment of a woman whom Barton had loved.

"The Familiar" has all the powerful machinery of the supernatural story – isolated settings, malevolent persecution, a guilty conscience, inexplicable occurrences that intrude into a recognizable and daylight world, extreme emotions, a macabre and mysterious death. The reader might ask in what sense it can be counted a distinctively Irish story. The settings are certainly largely Irish, and specific and concrete Dublin locales are given. The characters, however, belong almost entirely to the Anglo-Irish ruling class, and, at one level, the story might as well be set in Bath or London. Nonetheless, as in many of Le Fanu's stories, one is tempted to see an Irish resonance in details of the story material. Barton returns to Ireland "[s]omewhere about the year 1794," thus in a period of a major challenge to British rule in Ireland, culminating in the French attempted invasion of Ireland in 1798. In addition, the persecution of Barton takes the form of political violence – scary stalking in dark places, threatening letters, attempted assassination. It is surely important that the small malevolent figure (a sub-human threat from the colonial dark) eventually breaches the defenses of the Irish country house (a symbol of Anglo-Irish power), in which Barton has taken refuge. The tensions of a deeply divided Irish colonial society are present indirectly but intrusively in the supernatural story.

The Irish Literary Revival, which scholars and contemporaries have noted in the years from the mid-1890s through the end of the Irish Civil War in the mid-1920s, produced two main kinds of short fiction: stories based on the subjects and techniques of myth, legend, and folklore, and those (drawing inspiration from the work of Turgenev and Chekhov) focusing on a relatively unvarnished presentation of the *realia* of Irish rural and urban life. The former category contains work by Lady Augusta Gregory, Lady Jane Wilde ("Speranza," Oscar Wilde's mother), James Stephens, and Padraic Colum. It also embraces important parts of Oscar Wilde's output of short stories.

Wilde himself is a peculiarly Irish author, even when he seems least so. His cosmopolitanism, his taking the literary world of London by storm, is typical of the physical displacement of many Irish writers of the late nineteenth and early twentieth century. In addition, his work, while drawing on Irish motifs, transcends national boundaries (Lonergan 2008: 57). Wilde's collection of short stories for children, *The Happy Prince and Other Stories*, was first published in London in 1888. The title story is one of the most memorable. It is a story of love and sacrifice, rich and yet austere at the same time, funny (the Swallow is delightfully self-important on occasion) yet very sad, profoundly satisfying in its morals, yet deeply, and consciously, unsatisfying in its politics. The Happy Prince sacrifices himself to alleviate the sufferings of the poor; the Swallow sacrifices himself too, out of his "good heart" and his love of the Prince. Yet neither changes the world, except temporarily, and individually. It is clear that the whole unjust system grinds on as before, despite their sacrifice. Their only reward is in Heaven. Yet their gestures are grand and moving, and are reflected and invested in a linguistic glamour: in the Prince's "Swallow, Swallow, little Swallow . . . will you not stay with me one night longer?"; and in the Swallow's own evocations of a far land ("I am waited for in Egypt").

Less widely discussed, and yet equally complex and intriguing, and indirectly Irish, is Wilde's "The Portrait of Mr. W.H.," first published in *Blackwood's Magazine* in 1889. The anonymous narrator recounts the story of an obsession, shared at various times by three men, Cyril Graham, Erskine, and himself, that the dedicatee of Shakespeare's *Sonnets* is a handsome young actor, Willie Hughes. Part of the story is a narration within the text. The narrator gives the reader Erskine's account of his beautiful friend Cyril Graham's conviction that he has found the true identity of the young man to whom so many of Shakespeare's sonnets are addressed. His explanation and analysis of the texts convince Erskine too, up to the point when he demands objective evidence of the existence of the boy actor. Graham forges such evidence in the form of a gorgeous miniature of the figure. Erskine, however, discovers that the piece is a forgery, and upbraids his friend, who shoots himself to prove his utter commitment to the truth of his theory. Despite Erskine's warnings, the narrator is seized by Graham's interpretation, and spends three weeks attempting to confirm and develop it. He produces an elaborate and substantial life out of textual analysis and speculation, which he embodies in a passionate letter to Erskine, discovering that once he has written out his fancies, he becomes strangely indifferent to them. Erskine, however, is again inflamed by Graham's theory, and pledges himself to substantiate it. Two years later, the narrator receives a letter from Erskine in France in which he claims that he, too, will commit suicide "for Willie Hughes's sake." The narrator, on traveling to Cannes discovers that Erskine is indeed dead, but of consumption, not by his own hand. He inherits the forged, but beautiful, miniature.

This humorous story has a very serious side to it. It shows three characters who convince themselves of the rightness of a theory, on the basis of a mass of textual evidence. The ultimate lack of key empirical data does not finally shake their commitment to their cause, even in Graham's case to the point of death. The reader shares in their conviction, led on by the plausibility of the three men's arguments. Yet, at the heart of their convictions are lies: the forged portrait, Erskine's faked death. (Or is his death, indeed, by consumption? At that stage of the story, one wonders.) The Willie Hughes theory itself is an important part of the story. It is one of a series of norm-breaking and transgressive motifs. The story starts with a discussion of forgeries; Cyril Graham is so beautiful as to be sexually ambiguous; the Willie Hughes theory is a rejection of conventional wisdom, and also a social offence, for Shakespeare's muse is not an aristocrat, but an inconstant actor; and Wilde's fondness for paradox, an overt transgression of traditional linguistic and cultural expectations, is apparent, especially in Erskine's comments. And, then, there is Ireland. The narrator and Erskine start the story discussing "Macpherson, Ireland and Chatterton." What Ireland is doing between that pair of noted forgers is not immediately clear. Yet the inflammation of young men with an idea, the norm-breaking force of the dedication to the lowly Willie Hughes, and the power of martyrdom ("Cyril Graham sacrificed his life to a great idea," declares the narrator to Erskine, "and if you will not tell of his martyrdom, tell at least of his faith"), all assume a political and national resonance in an Irish context. "The Portrait of Mr. W.H." turns out to be a rather Irish story in the end, a questioning examination of the force of idealistic commitment.

The Irish focus of George Moore's short fiction collected in *The Untilled Field* (1903) cannot be missed. These stories were modeled on Turgenev's *A Sportsman's Sketches/Sketches from a Hunter's Album* (published in Russian in 1852, and published in English as early as 1855), and aimed to redeem the cosmopolitan Moore's status within Irish nationalist circles (Cave 2000: xii–xiii). "The Window" is a representative story from the collection, focused on the details of Irish rural life, and yet also echoing not just Turgenev, but Flaubert's "Un cœur simple" (1877). It tells the story of the elderly, crippled Biddy M'Hale's obsession to sponsor the installation of a window in her local church. Father Maguire, the harassed but authoritarian and interfering parish priest, is constantly annoyed by her stubborn insistence on paying for a window rather than the rebuilding of the church itself. Biddy has once been young and vigorous, but an accident has made her hunchbacked. The story is organized around a tension of the everyday and material (for example,

Biddy's handicap) with the visionary. Maguire is occupied with raising money for the new church (trips to the U.S.A., letters to the bishop, sales of scapulars); Biddy has inherited money and has made money by raising chickens, her Buff Orpingtons, and is cannily aware of her financial status; it is a German traveler for a firm of stained glass manufacturers who allows her to realize her vision. On the other hand, Biddy moves from making a vow after her accident that she will do something for God with her chickens, to visualizing clearly the colors and figures in her window, and then to actual visions of the divine in church during mass and when staring at her window. She eventually steps out of everyday social life, freed from her physical deformity, abandoning her chickens, dressing eccentrically, living only for her translation to another world of spiritual ecstasy and trance, of heavenly visitors, and mystic music. She becomes a burden, a boon (she draws publicity), and a mystery to the worldly Father Maguire. The narration is balanced and objective: the reader understands Biddy and enters her obsessive, practical and mystical world, but also sympathizes with the priest. Biddy's visions are moving, yet also deranged.

Almost contemporary with *The Untilled Field* (in terms of composition, if not of publication), the stories in James Joyce's *Dubliners* (1914), with their sober detailing of the *accidie* of the lives of the denizens of the early twentieth-century provincial imperial capital, are also resolutely Irish in their focus, and, along with Joyce's other longer fiction, have done much to make Dublin one of *the* literary *loci* in Europe. These stories have been so extensively written on that further commentary here is redundant (although Joyce's "An Encounter" is discussed in Part 5 Key Works).

Irish society was transformed and disrupted in the early twentieth century by the Easter Rising (1916), the Anglo-Irish War (1919–1922), the partition of the island (1922), and the Irish Civil War (1922–1923). "All changed, changed utterly," Yeats declares in "Easter 1916." The political and military upheavals of these years find a response in the work of several Irish short-story writers, although there is a not entirely surprising avoidance of the Civil War. One of the most famous of such texts, presenting an incident in the Anglo-Irish War, is Frank O'Connor's "Guests of the Nation" (1931). It is O'Connor's first published work of short fiction, appearing first in the American *Atlantic Monthly*, later in the *Irish Statesman*, and in a collection published in Britain by Macmillan.

Narrated by an anonymous and young Irish guerrilla fighter, in an informal, convincingly authentic oral language (for example, shifting at times from past to present tenses), the story recounts the circumstances surrounding the shooting of hostages in reprisal for the British authorities' execution of prisoners. The hostages are two English soldiers, known only by their surnames, Belcher and Hawkins. One short and talkative, the other tall and laconic, they form a traditional comic duo, a motif that contributes toward the dark absurdity of the story. The two English hostages have no intention of escaping; they feel very much at home with their captors and in the Irish countryside. While held by another I.R.A. battalion, they have danced with local girls, and in their present captivity, they become "chums" with their guards, and with the old lady in whose house they are held. When orders come to shoot the soldiers, both the narrator and his companion, ironically called Noble, are very reluctant to carry them out. However, they assist their superior, Jeremiah Donovan, to carry out the execution. The execution itself, performed in the lonely darkness of a bog, is absurd. Hawkins cannot believe he is to be shot by his new friends; he even offers to join them ("I don't believe in your stuff, but it's no worse than mine"). Belcher achieves a kind of dignity, tying on his own blindfold, caring about Hawkins to the last, refusing to say a prayer, and closing with the austere "I never could make out what duty was myself.... I think you're all good lads, if that's what you mean. I'm not complaining." The story concludes with the consequences of the execution for some of those involved. Noble and the old lady who made such friends with Belcher fall to prayer, but the narrator goes out alone into the empty and desolate night, feeling "very small and very lost and lonely," making it clear that his life has been forever tarnished by the incident. This justly celebrated story shows the war against the British in a profoundly unheroic light, the cause of Irish freedom substantially compromised. A small incident, narrated from one character's point of view, without substantial apportioning of blame, brings the sadness and absurdity of this kind of war powerfully before the reader. Published only nine years after the end of hostilities with the British, it is a brave story.

Equally brave in their exposure of a post-independence *misère*, and one frequently seen from a woman's perspective, are the early short stories of Mary Lavin. *Tales from Bective Bridge*, her first collection, was published in Boston in 1942 and in London in 1943. In 1931, Daniel Corkery had published his influential *Synge and Anglo-Irish Literature*, in which he set out what an authentic Irish literature should concern itself with – land, nationalism and religion – a recipe for an introverted, rural realism endorsing the pieties (literal and metaphorical) of the post-independence Irish Free State, and rejecting cosmopolitanism and a pre-independence literature written, Corkery argued, for foreign consumption. This strident and, in the context of the post-1922 settlement, understandable position neither reflected Corkery's own writing, nor the practice of the writers of the Free State or, indeed, the early years of the Irish Republic after 1947. Corkery's puritanism was contested constantly, in theory and in practice, by O'Connor and by Seán O'Faoláin (the latter especially in the journal *The Bell*, which he edited from 1940 to 1946), and Liam O'Flaherty. These writers published widely in Ireland, but also in the U.S.A. and Britain. *The New Yorker* was an important source of income and status for O'Connor especially, and also offered an outlet free from the censors of the Irish Republic. Along with these writers, Lavin's work, especially *Tales of Bective Bridge*, presents Ireland in a complex fashion. Indeed, the whole collection moves, at times, beyond Ireland ("Miss Holland"), and aims at a universality, grounded, indeed, in Irish *realia*, but achieving a potent timelessness. "At Sallygap" is rightly famous as a treatment of almost Beckettian inertia (for a discussion of this story, see the Key Works chapter of this book), but the volume also contains the bleak and poetic story "The Green Grave and the Black Grave," and in "Brother Boniface" a luminous presentation of an escape from petty worldliness.

Lavin's "Love Is for Lovers" shows a debt to Joyce's *Dubliners*, but also points toward the psychological quirkiness and humor of William Trevor. The central character is Matthew Simmins, a forty-four-year-old manager of a general store. The glamorous widow Mrs. Cooligan sets her sights on him, constantly throwing herself in his way and asking his help, eventually bringing him to her house. Over several weeks, Mrs. Cooligan feeds him fine meals ("delectable dishes"), and he begins to think of marriage with her. One "exceptionally hot" Saturday afternoon in July, as they are taking tea in Mrs. Cooligan's back garden, he becomes aware of her as a disturbing and offensive figure: her dress is fiercely orange, she has unrealistic desires (she wants to go to America with him), she is coarsely suggestive, pushy, and, above all, she has a large and fat dog which she cuddles, pets, talks to, makes much off and which she allows to lick her face. Mr Simmins finds the beast nauseating, and flees the widow's house for the shadowy side of the street outside, for the coolness of a new handkerchief, for the cold air of his own house, for his own dreams of "a fragrant life where love was no warmer than winter sunlight," for his "chill, white bed."

"Love Is for Lovers" is a comic story, its principal (and stock) characters the bosomy widow and the small shop manager. It is, however, a powerful evocation of Simmins's psychology (and much of the story is presented from his point of view and through free indirect speech/thought): the insignificant invisible man who has let middle age creep up on him. He is, however, a man of dreams: he sees himself as really the major "partner" in a shop he does not own; he has entertained desires for the beautiful girls on advertisements. He allows himself, fully conscious of what is happening, to be finagled into a relationship with the lurid and blowsy Mrs. Cooligan, only, in the end, to be repelled by her vivid and forceful personality. The text partly hinges on an opposition between her, her orange furnishings and dress, on one hand, and Mr. Simmins's longing for cool transcendence. The story is both even-handed and quirkily comic: Mrs. Cooligan is a grotesque but rather splendid figure (little Mr. Simmins sees her as a bosomy swan); finally, the reader is meant to see Mr. Simmins's escape as a fortunate one (even dreams of the cool peace of death are preferable to Mrs. Cooligan's dog). It is only Irish by suggestion (the small town, the general store, the characters' names), and aims for and achieves a universality in its depiction of two radically opposed temperaments.

No other Irish writer represents better than Samuel Beckett a profoundly cosmopolitan and experimental tendency within Irish short fiction in the twentieth century. Beckett wrote short fiction throughout his career. After the mid-1940s, however, he did so in French, himself usually, translating his work into English at a later date. Thus, Beckett texts exist from the start in a complex and very cosmopolitan state; they are both French and English texts, neither of which can really take precedence over the other. Beckett himself is a complex figure too: both part of the French and Irish literary worlds. Beckett's early short prose, even the macaronic "Sedendo et Quiescendo" (1932), can be relatively easily assimilated into the conventions of reading European fiction. Even the stories in *Stories and Texts for Nothing* (written in French in 1945, and published in French in 1958; published in English between 1962 and 1967), "The Expelled," "The Calmative," and "The End," have, albeit exiguous and deformed, narrative elements. The "Texts for Nothing" (written between 1950 and 1952, and published at various times in English), however, offer signal challenges to readers.

The thirteen texts are simply given numbers. The overall title is ambiguous. Texts that have no point? Texts offered to nothing? Texts that cost nothing? Texts in praise of nothing? Number 1 is typical of the sequence. Traditional story material is almost entirely absent. The reader encounters a voice that talks about its present situation, elements in its past, and its relationship with some other figures. The situation is one of stasis. "I couldn't any more, I couldn't go on." The voice appears to belong to a character lying face-down on the wet earth in a hole. How long he (or she – even the sex is unclear) has been there, and what brought him there, are unclear. He waits for a change in the weather (which seems poor), and for night to fall. He has lost his hat, perhaps swept away by the wind. He recalls his father's telling him a story when he was a child. At the text's end, it is apparent that the narrator is, in fact, telling himself the story the reader has just overheard. The lack of inciting moment, climax, denouement, and all the other traditional conventions of prose narrative is trumpeted.

Settings are unclear. The landscape in which the narrator/voice finds himself is bleak and isolated. Parts of it are hidden from view. Night is falling. Are there other characters? The narrator hears voices and refers to others standing above him. Yet, these may be parts of his own complex individuality rather than separate entities. Curlews call. The narrator's father told him a story once, about the heroic and active Joe Breem, or Breen. The narrator himself seems to be principally in dialog with himself. He contradicts himself right at the beginning: "Suddenly, no, at last." "I'll describe the place, that's unimportant," he remarks later. The narrator's language is highly self-referential. He speaks to himself in run-on sentences; there are numerous repetitions and examples of syntactic parallelism.

> And how long have I been here, what a question, I've often wondered. And often I could answer, An hour, a month, a year, a century, depending on what I mean by here, and me, and being, and there I never went looking for extravagant meanings, there I never much varied, only the here would sometimes seem to vary.

Other passages are also marked by phonological orchestration. Note the recurrent /t/ and /l/ sounds that mark the story's concluding lines: "Sleep now, as under that ancient lamp, all twined together, tired out with so much talking, so much listening, so much toil and play."

What is the point of all this? Answers are many. Clearly Beckett is pushing at the limits of what readers will find acceptable as story. The text breaks conventions to offer something fresh and demanding, something rather different from the story of the noble Joe Breem. The reader has to work. Further, the story questions the status of the conventions: the lack of traditional setting and character makes us wonder about those often unchallenged devices of narrative. The voice, too, coming from nowhere, restlessly going over certain concerns, questioning itself, is surely not untrue, not unreal (one knows this from nightmare, conversations overheard on trains and planes, the confused jumble of one's own thoughts). Finally, the image of the human being trapped, exhausted, unable to go on or stay, surrounded by voices whose status is unclear, recalling – with night coming on – the consolations of a simpler past, somehow consoling himself with a story of sorts – that image is not unpersuasive. Beckett's short prose may be hard, but it has its rationale and rewards.

It is, also, not without influence in Irish short fiction. The great short-story writer of post-war Ireland, John McGahern, both distances himself from and yet cannily assimilates Beckett's work in his own fiction. In terms of career, McGahern, too, illustrates recurring complexities in Irish fiction. Driven into a brief, but bitter, exile in 1965 by the scandal surrounding his second novel *The Dark*, McGahern never had an Irish publisher, but brought out all his work in London and in the U.S.A. His short fiction illustrates the range, depth and strength of the Irish short story in the last fifty years better than that of any other writer.

"Swallows" from *Getting Through* (1978) is set in a terrain and a time that McGahern and many other twentieth-century Irish short story writers made *the* setting of Irish short fiction: rural Ireland sometime in the mid-century. The drab constraints of time and place are emphasized, in a way that harks back to Joyce's paralyzed Dubliners and Beckett's inert voices, as the rural setting derives ultimately from Moore. The discontents of the muted, occluded lives of the post-independence dispensation are this text's subject, as they are of a multitude of Irish short stories. The protagonists of "Swallows" are unnamed, known only by their jobs, a *Garda* sergeant and a State Surveyor. One is older, the other is younger. The Sergeant was once a talented fiddle-player, vital, attractive to a beautiful girl at local dances. Now he lives in middle age, embittered by the inequities of his society, savage about the tawdry banalities of his world, with a deaf and mentally simple housekeeper, his fiddle case covered with dust, and the instrument itself unplayable. The younger man, too, has opted for the safety of a state job, but he at least keeps his dream of music alive. He owns an old and beautiful instrument; he plays it with the talented proprietor of a Galway hotel. The story is a study in loneliness and failure. The swallows of the title refer to the summer birds in distant, glorious Avignon where the young surveyor buys his lovely violin, a dream and a space of hope and light that is set against the grim weather and the rural inanity and stagnation of the Sergeant's world. They are also a metaphor of passing time and of the summer when the weather will change and the Sergeant can go roach fishing on the lake. As in stories by McGahern's predecessors, Lavin and O'Faoláin, for example, and in many of those by his contemporary William Trevor, there is a desperate sadness about characters' lives, trapped in a limited world that is impoverished materially and mentally. The power of a story like "Swallows" lies in the careful, sympathetic, yet clear-sighted evocation of such a world. In McGahern's case, such power is augmented by a language that drifts towards poetry on several occasions through phonological orchestration and syntactic parallelism, a language that – once noticed – becomes as self-referential as Beckett's prose.

"The Beginning of an Idea" (also from *Getting Through*) moves beyond rural Ireland. The protagonist is Eva Lindberg, a Finnish woman writer – it is never stated explicitly that the opening setting is Finland, but this is indicated by characters' names. Fascinated by an account of one element in Chekhov's death (the fact that his body was transported to Moscow in a wagon that had the word "Oysters" chalked on it) and by Chekhov's story "Oysters," Lindberg decides to leave her director's job in the theatre to travel to Spain and to write about the Russian author. She is also getting away from an unsatisfying love affair with a married man. Her journey to Spain and the initial period there are rewarding. However, she finds it difficult to write and falls into work that takes her away from what she wants to do. Also – for this is Franco's Spain – she is entrapped by corrupt *Guardia Civil* officers, who force her to have sex with them. The story's end is inconclusive. The protagonist is traveling again, but, apart from her immediate destination, it is not clear where she is going.

"The Beginning of an Idea" strikingly presents the experience of a woman and a writer in worlds far from Ireland – a never-explicitly named wintry Helsinki, and a bakingly hot southern Spain. Eva's responses to her Finnish lover and to her abuse at the hands of the *Guardia Civil* officers are rendered powerfully, as is her writer's block. The story demonstrates some of the cosmopolitan ambitions of Irish short fiction, and finds a resonance in the work of a younger generation of Irish short-story writers, such as Mary Dorcey, Neil Jordan, and Hugo Hamilton. McGahern's contemporary, William Trevor, too, casts the net of his fiction beyond Ireland and the Irish, his output including both "The Ballroom of Romance" with its rural Irish setting (from *The Ballroom of Romance and Other Stories* [1972]) and, in the same collection, stories without Irish characters and set far from Ireland, such as "Going Home" or "The Mark-2 Wife." McGahern's choice of a woman's point of view, which he adopts also in his first novel *The Barracks* (1963), reflects that in Edna O'Brien's short fiction, for example the stories in *The Love Object* (1968), and also that in Maeve Binchy's very successful short story collections, such as *The Return Journey and Other Stories* (1998). McGahern's short fiction can be seen as representative, too, of the predominant realist tendency within the Irish short story. Beckett's deviations from the protocols of realism are unusual. The self-referentiality and other metafictional elements that are undeniably present in McGahern's writing are always modestly hidden beneath a traditional surface.

The list of Irish writers, from both the north and south of the island, who have produced substantial work in short fiction over the past fifty years is impressive. It includes (besides those mentioned above): Mary Beckett, Evelyn Conlon, Brian Friel, Jack Harte, Desmond Hogan, Benedict Kiely, Bernard MacLaverty, Bryan MacMahon, and Éilís Ní Dhuibhne. The conventions of realism dominate; the focus is usually on a specifically Irish life and *realia*; however, this is not always the case, and Irish fiction casts its net wide these days, as, indeed, it has always done. One assumes that in the twenty-first century the form will continue to be a favored one for Irish writers.

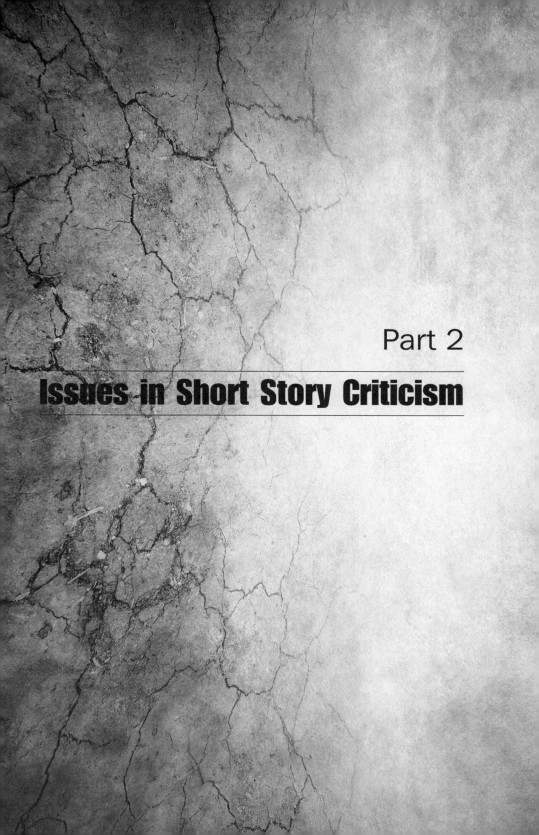

Part 2

# Issues in Short Story Criticism

# Definitions

With justice, it has traditionally been seen as difficult to define the short story. As Renate Brosch remarks: "Die short story ist sympatisch resistant gegnüber Definitionen" (The short story charmingly resists definitions) (2007: 9). There are several reasons for this difficulty.

First, there is a problem of names. The term "short story" is used, according to Reid (1977: 25) and others, only from the 1880s. Neither Poe nor Hawthorne wrote of their narratives, which we would now call short stories, as such, but referred to them as "tales" or "sketches." Such usage endures into the late nineteenth century. Writers like Crackanthorpe and James designated what they wrote as "impressions" or "vignettes" or "nouvelles" (Fowler 1987: 336). Arthur Symons, writing in 1897, praises Maupassant as an unrivalled author of the "nouvelle, or short story" (qtd. in Stanford 1968: 23). Both Orel (1986: 96) and Harris (1979: 10) point to the terminological confusion that bedevils discussions of short fiction in the nineteenth century. Several different terms have traditionally been used to discuss this type of text: tale, sketch, fable, *conte*, novella, and *nouvelle*.

The second reason for difficulty in definition is the lack of distinctive subject matter in the short story. Short fiction, whatever one calls it, deals with the same story materials as novels: supernatural occurrences, love, psychological change, historical conflict, space travel, the adventures of talking animals, and so on. Several short stories do, indeed, present relatively static kinds of action. A great deal happens in Virginia Woolf's "Kew Gardens" or Jean Rhys's "Hunger," but the action is not of the kind that forms the skeleton of so many novels: adultery, invasion, murder, journeys, and social conflict, for example. Head (1992: 16–17) and Hanson (1985: 55–81) write of the importance of the less traditionally plotted story for the development of

*The British and Irish Short Story Handbook*, First Edition. David Malcolm.
© 2012 David Malcolm. Published 2012 by Blackwell Publishing Ltd.

twentieth-century short fiction. However, the relatively inert (only in one respect, of course, for the psychological movements of the stories by Woolf and Rhys mentioned above are very substantial) is only one kind of short story. There are many others, full of the kind of action that equally well appears in longer fictions.

Third, the short story does not seem to deploy specific narrational or narrative strategies/techniques that would distinguish it from the novel. Short stories are texts in the epic mode. The story material is given by a narrator or narrators, first-person or third-person (usually), in logical-chronological sequence or in some other motivated order. Two features, however, of many short stories do point to differences in this respect. Short stories usually eschew substantial amounts of exposition. They also are more frequently open-ended than is the norm in many novels. A classic U.S. short story like Hemingway's "Hills Like White Elephants" illustrates this strategy clearly, but one can observe it in several stories discussed in the introduction to this book: for example, Panter-Downes's "Good Evening, Mrs. Craven," Fleet-wood's "The Last Lesson," Lavin's "Love Is For Lovers," or McGahern's "Swallows." In general, one can suggest that there is a tendency toward narrative ellipsis in short stories. For example, in Pritchett's "The Camberwell Beauty," much of what happens to Isabel is implied rather than given explicitly. What is Jane Ciracylides exactly in Ballard's "Prima Belladona," human or mutant, animal or vegetable, where is she really from, and what is the social-political-economic background of the "Recess," so rudely broken at the text's end? The stories are replete with *Unbestimmtheitsstellen* (spots of indeterminacy) (Ingarden 1973: 246–254).

Nevertheless, there is one clear feature of the short story that, however banal it may seem to note this, does define it, and that is its short length. But brevity is relative. As all commentators who touch on this issue (for example, Pasco 1994: 123–124) rightly ask: short in comparison to what? However, shortness has always been seen as crucial to the short story, whatever it may have been called. Poe's 1842 essay (a review of Hawthorne's *Twice-Told Tales*) insists that a tale should be a narrative that one can read "at one sitting," thus "a half-hour to one or two hours" (Henderson and Hancock 2010: 395–396; Scofield 2006: 31–32). In "The Short Story" (1896), Frederick Wedmore saw the short story as appealing to a reader "who rebels sometimes at the *longueurs* of the conventional novel: the old three volumes or the new fat book" (qtd. in Stanford 1968: 15). In his "Appreciation" in Crackanthorpe's posthumous *Last Studies* (1897), James writes of the author's interest in "the situation that asked for a certain fineness of art and that could best be presented in a kind of foreshortened picture"

(Crackanthorpe 1897: xviii). V. S. Pritchett talks of the short story's "glancing view" (Pritchett 1976: 424).

Throughout the nineteenth and twentieth centuries, this shortness has been seen both negatively and positively. Nineteenth-century British novelists avoided the form, or did not take it seriously, artistically or financially. The long novel carried with it prestige and money. G. K. Chesterton in 1906 remarked that the contemporary interest in short fiction was a "sign of a real sense of fleetingness and fragility; it means that existence is only an impression, and, perhaps, only an illusion.... We have no instinct of anything ultimate and enduring beyond the episode" (qtd. in Shaw 1983: 17). Arnold Bennett was even more obviously scathing in 1914. "A short form," he wrote, "is easier to manipulate than a long form. ... it is lawful and even necessary in it to leave undone many things which are very hard to do" (qtd. in Shaw 1983: 23). In an interview given in 1985, Graham Greene (who wrote several highly regarded short stories) expressed his distaste for the form because it was short, and, thus, its length allowed him no space for surprises and made it impossible to develop characters as he would wish (Greene 1985: 12, 14, 20). Bernard Bergonzi's strictures about the short story are also related to length. For him, short fiction is marked by a reductiveness: it will inevitably "filter down experience to the prime elements of defeat and failure" (qtd. in Reid 1977: 1–2).

But the short story's brevity has also always had advocates. Elizabeth Bowen in 1937 was full of praise for stories with compression, tautness, and clarity, and saw these as vitally inspired. The short story for her was free of the expansive tedium (and conclusiveness) of the novel. By virtue of its shortness, "it may thus more nearly than the novel approach aesthetic and moral truth" (Bowen 1937: 15). Pritchett clearly thought that the "glancing view" could do a great deal (Pritchett 1976: 424). James Lasdun praises the short story for "[o]mission, occlusion, cropping: the ability to cultivate a kind of force-field of negative space within a narrative" (Lasdun 1996: 23). The very shortness of the form, he argues, is the challenge. Clare Hanson argues that the brevity of short fiction allows for the creation of different, non-consensual narratives that can challenge the status quo, and thus allow short fiction to offer a congenial fictional space for women and for other traditionally marginalized groups (Hanson 1989: 6, 25). Hermione Lee even suggests that the short story's terseness makes it a suitable form for women plagued by the interruptions of domestic duties (Lee 1985: viii). In an important recent study of short fiction, Renate Brosch persuasively argues that the constitutive syncope of short fiction encourages and even demands activities of the reader, visualizing and extrapolating from a suggestive paucity of detail, that are intellectually stimulating, timely, and socially and culturally valuable (Brosch 2007: 19–25).

None of this answers the question as to what exactly is meant by shortness. Under 30 000 words? 20 000? Around 10 000? 600 words? A couple of pithy narrative sentences? But should we try to fix an exact upper limit to the short story? Literature is not, usually, a matter of closed categories, but a continuum of texts, a spectrum of possibilities. In prose fiction, one moves from *roman fleuve*-like sequences through heavy and long novels (both in the nineteenth century and the early twenty-first) to much shorter novels and then to short fiction, which itself can now in the twenty-first century come in a wide variety of lengths – long-short, short, short-short, short-short-short. The borders are of necessity obscure, and the undecidability of certain texts – for example, canonical pieces such as "The Turn of the Screw" or "Heart of Darkness" – is an important aspect of their meaning. If a text inhabits an unresolved area and is difficult to assign to one category or another (long short story or short novel), that surely has semantic consequences.

Except for the former's brevity, the short story and the novel are close together. Their subject matters and story materials, and their genres overlap. The argument, as old as Poe, that the short story has an artistic coherence and cohesion beyond that of the novel (Allen 1981: 8; Pasco 1994: 120–121), is questionable. It may have had some validity in Poe's literary environment, but even there it is hard to see how "Young Goodman Brown," for example, is more artistically integrated than *The Scarlet Letter*. Certainly, in the twentieth century it will not hold water. Compare, for example, McGahern's "Swallows" with his novels *The Barracks* or *Amongst Women*. The novels are carefully organized, completely integrated artistic texts. But succinctness is very important. Adrian Hunter writes tellingly of James's insistence that a short story is not a boiled down novel, but a kind of text that, by virtue of its abbreviature, offers exciting technical, emotional, and cognitive possibilities and experiences, for both writers and readers (Hunter 2007: 7–8). Shortness allows and compels elision – curtailment of exposition, ellipses in action, enigmatic endings. What do Strickland and the narrator do to the leper in Kipling's "The Mark of the Beast"? What went on at the Villa Lucienne, and where is Cécile's husband (D'Arcy's "The Villa Lucienne')? What will Eva Lindberg do next (McGahern's "The Beginning of an Idea")? The stories invite speculation, and disturb and fascinate because they omit. Indeed, one could argue that Beckett's mysterious, unplaced and displaced voices are not so distant from a mainstream short-story tradition as it might at first seem.

But brevity comes at a certain cost. It does not permit character development to the degree that the novel can engage in. There is simply not the space. Hence, the short story has the tendency towards what is often called "epiphany," a climactic moment in which a character realizes something about him/herself and about life. The term is particularly associated with Joyce's short fiction, but also with work by Mansfield, Lawrence, and a host of later short-story writers (Hunter 2007: 44–45; Malcolm and Malcolm 2008: 202–205). However, a moment of revelation ("epiphany") or judgment ("epiklesis") is not necessarily part of the short story's action. Among the stories discussed in the Introduction, Le Fanu's "The Familiar" does not have one, nor does Wilde's "The Portrait of Mr. W.H.," nor, indeed, does Lasdun's "Annals of the Honorary Secretary," although they all have enigmas enough. For, if the short story is, in a sense, fragmentary, shunning the *longue durée* for the "glancing view" (Pritchett 1976: 424), that brief episode that constitutes its story material is veined with suggestiveness. It can point to the configuration of a whole life (as in Rhys's "Illusion"), a whole society (as in Le Fanu's "The Familiar"), an entire metaphysics and its reception ("Annals of the Honorary Secretary"), or a disorientingly transgressive universe ("Prima Belladonna"). The shorter form may be shorter, but it can show the world in a grain of sand.

# Genre?

What is one to call the short story? Is it a genre? Does it matter what we call it? Certainly, usage in English varies. Many commentators refer to it as a genre. Reid (1977: 54–65), Harris (1979: 11), Shaw (1983: 21), and Head (1992: 190) do so. Orel's important study of nineteenth-century short stories is subtitled "Development and Triumph of a Literary Genre" (Orel 1986). The other widely used term is "form." Kiberd (1979: 14) and Pritchett (1976: 424) refer to short fiction thus. Hunter (2007) favors "form." Some scholars use both terms: Feddersen (2001: xvii, xxi) and May (1976: 289; 1996: 470–471), for example.

On one level, it does not matter what one calls a group of texts. Readers do and should just read them and enjoy. But, on another level, it does. Literary studies is bedeviled with enough problems without seeking more in terminological confusion, and the term one chooses (genre or form) carries implications for the sense of further discussion.

It is difficult to see how one can call the short story a genre. Genres are groups of texts like sonnets or villanelles, Westerns or gothic fiction. They are defined by a variety of features or genre markers: technical criteria (traditional villanelles have to consist of nineteen lines with a specific stanza arrangement, rhythmic pattern, and rhyme scheme), or the kind of characters, settings and action one can expect to find in them (for example, Westerns are set in specific parts of the U.S.A., usually in the 1860s through the 1890s, and involve gunmen, cowpokes, saloon girls, and schoolmarms, usually caught up in violent action that follows a set pattern leading to a climactic shoot-out). Historical consensus is also important: readers' recognition of a genre is crucial. Genres are, it must be stressed however, not fixed groups of texts. A prose text may show, and almost certainly will show, features of more than

*The British and Irish Short Story Handbook*, First Edition. David Malcolm.
© 2012 David Malcolm. Published 2012 by Blackwell Publishing Ltd.

one genre (1950s Hollywood Westerns sometimes take on complex psychological themes). Specific texts may be very mixed in terms of genre (very few late twentieth-century British novels are not promiscuous in their genre markers). In addition, the markers of a genre may well alter over time. Even rigid genres like the sonnet change historically in, for example, the relation of octave to sestet, or the use of a final couplet. Blasons mutate into anti-blasons. Detective fiction may become more violent, deploy female detectives, and leave crimes unsolved. But the term 'genre' has a great deal of usefulness and reflects a reality, a literary fact, and should be reserved for the level of category represented by *terza rima*, film noir (perhaps), or historical fiction.

The short story is a much larger category, like the novel or film. It includes a wide range of genres (see Chapter 3 of this book). One can identify, and readers and scholars have identified, supernatural short stories, gothic short stories, historical short stories, beast fable short fiction, crime short fiction, short stories of colonial adventure, science-fiction and fantasy short fiction, indeed the whole gamut of narrative prose fiction. If one reserves genre for a group of texts such as science fiction, then one needs another term for the short story. "Kind of text" is clumsy and not helpful. "Form," favored by Hunter (2007), and a term that I have attempted (with mixed success) to stick to in books under my editorship, seems the most widely acceptable solution. It points to the reality that the short story embraces a wide variety of genres, but is itself a higher level category.

# Collections

Short stories often do not come to the reader alone. They exist in the context of other texts. Marie Louise Pratt writes of this matter as follows:

> A short story is always printed as part of a larger whole, either a collection of short stories or a magazine, which is a collection of various kinds of texts. Except in schools, perhaps, individual short stories are usually read as part of a larger reading experience.
>
> (Pratt 1994: 103–104)

Pratt argues that this "reinforces the view of the short story as a part or fragment" (104), but one can also suggest that this situation adds an extra dimension of meaning to the individual short story. It relates to the texts that surround it. In a discussion of short story collections and cycles, Thomas A. Gullason notes that Hemingway's highly elliptical "Hills Like White Elephants" achieves "movements, expansions, and ricochet effects" when read alongside the other narratives that make up *Men without Women* (1982: 225). The meanings added to an individual short story are very clear in obviously highly integrated collections of short fictions, often referred to as short-story cycles. Joyce's *Dubliners* and George Moore's *The Untilled Field* are well-known examples. More recently, Angela Carter's *The Bloody Chamber* comprises a closely linked collection of short fiction. Apart from Hemingway's *Men without Women*, Sherwood Anderson's *Winesburg, Ohio* and Tim O'Brien's *The Things They Carried* are notable examples of American collections of related stories.

As Pratt notices, short stories are, perhaps, read improperly in educational institutions, on their own or in historically or thematically organized anthologies. Indeed, not sufficient attention is paid, even in scholarly discussions,

*The British and Irish Short Story Handbook*, First Edition. David Malcolm.
© 2012 David Malcolm. Published 2012 by Blackwell Publishing Ltd.

to a story's textual environment. The degree to which a collection can add a semantic dimension to a short story can be illustrated by Kipling's *Traffics and Discoveries* (1904), not a short-story cycle, but a closely integrated collection of short fictions. The eleven stories in the collection illustrate the genre variety that is typical of Kipling's work. It contains three (much anthologized) pieces of war fiction: "The Captive," "A Sahib's War," and "The Comprehension of Private Copper." Indeed, military and naval subject matter runs through another five texts: "The Bonds of Discipline," "Steam Tactics," "The Army of a Dream," "Their Lawful Occasions," and "Mrs. Bathurst." These martial texts contrast (and that contrast bears meaning, surely) with quite different genres: supernatural story ("Wireless," "They," and "The Army of a Dream"); a utopia, employing the dream vision convention ("The Army of a Dream") (incidentally, this is a twentieth-century rarity); and beast fable ("Below the Mill Dam"). In addition, five texts have a very strong psycho-logical focus: the Sikh N.C.O.'s grief in "A Sahib's War," the complex feelings of the protagonist toward his Boer captor in "The Comprehension of Private Copper," Vickery's self-destructive obsession in "Mrs. Bathurst," Mr. Shaynor's hopeless love in "'Wireless,'" and the obtuseness and final deso-lation of the narrator in "They."

Despite this genre variety, the stories share a great deal. Most are substantially or completely first-person narrations, frequently, as in "The Captive," "The Bonds of Discipline," and "The Army of a Dream," contain-ing further first-person narrations within the overarching one. In addition, several of these narrations-within-narrations are given in non-standard English: the Sikh narrator in "A Sahib's War," Pyecroft in "The Bonds of Discipline" and "Mrs. Bathurst," for example. The stories are further integrated through recurrent motifs: technology and the figure of the expert (for example, "The Captive," "Their Lawful Occasions," and "Wireless"); the alien ("The Captive," "The Bonds of Discipline," and "A Sahib's War" – and it is important to note that both Private Copper and the Boer guerilla in "The Comprehension of Private Copper," Shaynor in "Wireless," and the narrator in "They," are out of their proper place). The motif of death runs through five of the stories: "A Sahib's War," "Wireless," "The Army of a Dream," "They," and "Mrs. Bathurst." Above all, stories are marked by an ambiguity. Private Copper does not like his Boer captor, but he understands his motivation. The bold Anglo-Sparta of "The Army of a Dream" is revealed as a consolatory vision born of loss. The whole collection, indeed, when read as a collection, becomes utterly ambiguous: the jolly japes of "The Captive" and "Steam Tactics" are balanced by the very dark notes of "Wireless" and "They"; the military stories concatenate with domestic ones; the stories that celebrate traditional order are juxtaposed with those that endorse insubordination and irregular dress and behavior. The collection ends with the humor and optimism of "Below the Mill Dam," but that story sits at the end of a sequence of four very dark tales ("Wireless," "The Army of a Dream," "They," and "Mrs. Bathurst"). The stories achieve further semantic amplitude by virtue of context, and one does them, and the author, a disservice to ignore that.

Kipling's collection is highly integrated, but Mary Lavin's volume of ten short stories *Tales from Bective Bridge* (1943), while less so, still contains stories that comment on each other. The very title – although Bective Bridge is never mentioned in any text – suggests a unity, like Anderson's *Winesburg, Ohio*. For example, "Sarah" and "A Fable" both deal with a provincial beauty, and the community's shifting response to her. In "Sarah," the protagonist is a peasant woman of loose morals who is destroyed by hypocrisy; in "A Fable," the gorgeous society lady of the big house is finally cherished by those around her. "A Fable" and "Miss Holland" both present outsider women; in the former story, the female figure is finally accepted; in the latter, she is rejected. The lady in the former is full of vigor and self-reliance; the lady in the latter is paralyzed by self-doubt. The young inland wife in "The Green Grave and the Black Grave" is similarly out of her place. It is not clear to what extent she wins or loses in her conflict with her environment, in this case the sea and her husband's dangerous and harsh life. "Brother Boniface," "At Sallygap," and "Love Is for Lovers" present entrapments and escapes. Brother Boniface manages to evade his environment; Manny Ryan in "At Sallygap" misses his chance to flee to Paris and is horridly trapped at the story's end (as is his gaoler, his wife); Matthew Simmins's avoidance of Mrs. Cooligan can be seen as a wise flight and a liberation or a return to a shabby provincial cage.

Stories juxtapose love in substantially different forms: the powerful, death-challenging love of "The Green Grave and the Black," the entrancing sensuality of "Sarah," and the grotesque threat and contrasting idealism of "Love Is for Lovers." Death runs through many of the stories, marking the wasting power of time in "Lilacs," taking the young and the vital in "The Green Grave and the Black Grave" and "Sarah," and tormenting the elderly in "The Dead Soldier." The middle story, (the much anthologized) "At Sallygap" concludes with a vision of utter despair, which is reflected in the mother's death's-head face at the end of the final story, "The Dead Soldier." The recurrence of motifs and themes in several stories allows Lavin to see her subjects in different aspects. In addition, that repetition generalizes characters' experiences and fates; they become not just a matter of individual crisis or joy, but part of a general pattern of human existence. The timelessness that Lavin overtly aims at in "The Green Grave and the Black" and "A Fable," is, in fact, integral to the whole collection.

The nine stories collected in J. G. Ballard's *Vermilion Sands* (1971) date from 1956 to 1969, and were originally published in journals such as *Science Fantasy*, *Fantastic Stories* and *Fantasy and Science Fiction*.[1] However, they form an integrated set of fictions, ones that do not contradict each other, as Kipling's and Lavin's do, but rather reinforce a vision of the world. Ballard's science fiction is of a particular kind, permeated by Gothic motifs. For example, the psychotropic houses of "The Thousand Dreams of Stellavista" are developments of the big houses with their dark secrets that mark Gothic fiction. The female protagonists of the stories owe their provenance to the vampires and *revenantes* of the Gothic. The stories are all first-person narrations, suggesting an unavoidable individuality of experience and impression. Four of the nine stories emphasize this individual and psychological focus by marking clearly that they are acts of recall, starting before the action proper and returning to a set of previous experiences ("Studio 5, the Stars," "The Screen Game," "Cry Hope, Cry Fury!," and "The Cloud Sculptors of Coral D"). Read in context, the stories become variations on a limited, but very suggestive, range of themes. The first-person narrator is drawn into a world of passion, desire, and madness or eccentricity, always by a glamorous and dangerous female figure – Jane Cyraclides, Lorraine Drexel, Aurora Day, and the rest. The narrator's experiences echo classical mythology (Melander and Corydon in "Studio 5, the Stars" is a myth invented by Aurora Day, but it echoes traditional myths and the narrator's acceptance of it illustrates his technology-induced ignorance) or canonical literature (Coleridge's "The Rhyme of the Ancient Mariner" in "Cry Hope, Cry Fury!"). The *femme fatale* is usually an intruder, formidably wealthy and formidably disturbed.

Settings are also unified. The time is the "Recess," a period of inertia and stagnation, presumably sometime in the human future. (Only in "Say Goodbye to the Wind" is there any attempt at vague dating.) The place is the lurid desert of the sand lakes and reefs around Vermilion Sands. Motifs of ruin and abandonment recur. Even Vermilion Sands itself is now de-populated and forgotten, the narrator tells the reader in "The Thousand Dreams of Stellavista." Material and psychological disintegration reinforce each other. The world of the stories is transgressive. Statues are organic and sing; clothes are alive and responsive to their wearers, as are houses to their owners; insects are jeweled ("The Screen Game"); the colors of the land are

---

[1] The context of the journal in which a short story appears is a legitimate area of study, and should reveal very interesting juxtapositions and concatenations. Many celebrated short stories appeared first in magazines with other texts. Can we see those other texts as part of the story's semantic environment? Short-fiction codilogical studies has a future, surely.

unfamiliar in most documented landscapes; seas are of sand and waves are thermal, and everywhere sand rays fly threateningly. Story materials are appropriate to this setting: they all involve destruction, death, passion, and departure.

Art and artists are central to the stories in *Vermilion Sands* – poets, sculptors, film makers, clothes designers. Even the pilots of "The Cloud Sculptors of Coral D" shape clouds with their gliders. The artistic motifs are reinforced by a self-referential tendency in the narrators' language. One should note, for example, the sound patterns (/d/, /s/, and /r/) of the opening of the highly literary "Cry Hope, Cry Fury!": "Again last night, as the dusk air moved across the desert from Vermilion Sands, I saw the faint shiver of rigging among the reefs, a topmast moving like a silver lantern through the rock spires."

In *Vermilion Sands*, the stories when taken together present a remarkably coherent and cohesive vision. Human life is a matter of destructive passion and of transgression, in which art plays a substantial and reinforcing role. Characters sail through deviant and dangerous landscapes, ruined and haunted, that reflect their disturbed and self-destructive psyches. Story after story emphasizes this vision; there is really no escape from Vermilion Sands. The dizzying, lurid, and perilous contraventions of the time and place draw characters and readers in alike.

Generalization of vision is also an effect of collection-context in William Trevor's *Lovers of Their Time and Other Stories* (1978). On their own, these stories are forceful and moving; combined, they have a power and vision that goes beyond each individual text. Only three of the stories have a first-person narrator, "Broken Homes," "Matilda's England," and "The Raising of Elvira Tremlett," but, in fact, these make up a sizeable part of the twelve-story collection, because "Matilda's England" consists of three parts covering approximately 50 pages in Trevor's collected *Stories* (1983). The other texts adopt either a unified point of view, like "Flights of Fancy" and "Attracta," or shift between points of view, as in "Another Christmas" and "Death in Jerusalem." As in the very different *Vermilion Sands*, the individuality of experience is emphasized thereby. Protagonists are very similar to each other. Although they may speak of childhood experience, almost all are middle-aged or older. Most are respectable – shopkeepers, teachers, businessmen, office workers; the relatively unglamorous little people of mid-century Britain and Ireland. All are isolated – by age ("Broken Homes"), by ethnic background ("Another Christmas"), by family loyalty ("Death in Jerusalem"), by religion ("Attracta"), by sexual orientation ("Flights of Fancy," "Torridge"), by an unhappy marriage ("Lovers of Their Time"), and by madness ("Matilda's England," "The Raising of Elvira Tremlett").

Experience may be individual, but individual stories and the collection contextualize and generalize that experience. Characters' isolation is a case in point. So, too, is the recurrent relation of characters' experiences and fates to war: the I.R.A.'s bombing campaign on mainland Britain in the 1970s ("Another Christmas"), the wastage of life in the two wars of the twentieth century ("Broken Homes," "Matilda's England"), and the Anglo-Irish War of 1919–1922 ("Attracta"). In addition, as the motif of war and its consequences suggests, characters' present lives are profoundly shaped by the past. Mrs. Malby's two sons died in the Western Desert in 1942, and her life has never been the same since ("Broken Homes"); Mrs. Ashburton's words to Matilda and the deaths of those she loves have similarly formed her ("Matilda's England"). The central characters of "Torridge" have denied their past; at the end of the story, Torridge returns to take his revenge. The past comes alive to the narrator of "The Raising of Elvira Tremlett," at first to offer him solace, and then to drive him into an asylum. The final story, "A Dream of Butterflies," stands out from the others in the collection. The characters seem less trapped by the past, able – despite reservations – to make a decision in a complex moral dilemma, and to free themselves from ties of the past.

Collections, thus, offer a context for reading short stories. They permit universalization of theme and vision. They also permit ambiguity and complexity. Stories reinforce and contradict each other, and the reader's experience is enhanced and broadened.

# Marginality

In *The Lonely Voice: A Study of the Short Story* (1962), Frank O'Connor argues that the short story has traditionally been principally concerned to depict "submerged population" groups. These groups change in time and with different authors; "it may be Gogol's officials, Turgenev's serfs, Maupassant's prostitutes, Chekhov's doctors and teachers, Sherwood Anderson's provincials" (O'Connor 1965: 18). "Always in the short story," O'Connor writes, "there is this sense of outlawed figures wandering about the fringes of society" (19). The short story is "By its very nature remote from the community – romantic, individualistic, and intransigent" (21). The short story is, thus, the form of fiction that flourishes in peripheral, fragmented, and unstable social worlds, such as nineteenth- and twentieth-century Ireland and the nineteenth-century U.S.A. (19–20).

O'Connor's argument has had a long afterlife in discussions of short fiction. V. S. Pritchett, for example, in 1986, describes the short story as being particularly appropriate to Southern U.S. and Anglo-Irish writers because both groups come from disintegrating and defeated societies. He contrasts the novel with the short story thus: "the novel depends enormously on the sense of a stable social structure and the short story does not really depend on there being a social structure at all" (Pritchett 1986: 16). Declan Kiberd boldly declares that "the short story flourishes on any cultural frontier, where solitary men daily confront the ambiguities of a changing society which is based on rival folk and cosmopolitan traditions" (Kiberd 1979: 20). Joseph Flora also reflects O'Connor's view, this time in a British context, when he writes: "The modern British short story is often the product of 'refugees' in exotic places and situations, exiles of culture, of class, of sexuality, or – the ultimate exoticism – of death" (1985: 37). (I must confess that the last phrase

*The British and Irish Short Story Handbook*, First Edition. David Malcolm.
© 2012 David Malcolm. Published 2012 by Blackwell Publishing Ltd.

of this quotation is obscure to me. How can the dead write? I presume Flora is referring to ghost stories.) Clare Hanson, too, insists that "The short story has offered itself to losers and loners, exiles, women, blacks – writers who for one reason or another have not been part of the ruling 'narrative' or epistemological/experiential framework of their society" (Hanson 1989: 2). She goes on to argue that the short form's elisions, its fragmentary shape, its disjunctions and its inconclusiveness allow it to offer "different *kinds* of knowledge, knowledge which may be in some ways at odds with the 'story' of the dominant culture" (6, 26). Mary Eagleton sees women writers as being interested in short fiction because of its tradition of presenting "non-hegemonic, peripheral, contradictory" characters (and also the traditional non-canonical status of the short-story writer) (Eagleton 1989: 62).

Much may be said to support O'Connor's position. One thinks of James Joyce's provincial Dubliners, Jean Rhys's *demi-mondaines*, Samuel Beckett's rejects and recluses, and William Trevor's Irish in England. Elizabeth Bowen, however, in her paean to the modernity and value of short fiction makes no such claims as O'Connor does (Bowen 1937). Adrian Hunter tellingly points out that O'Connor's argument that the short story is inherently a U.S. and Irish form might give us pause (Hunter 2007: 106). Indeed, O'Connor's argument is flawed for three reasons. First, it is unsound in terms of European literary history. Russian literature has many novels, not just Turgenev and Chekhov short stories, De Maupassant wrote novels as well as short fiction, and O'Connor himself admits he has no knowledge of German literature (20). Second, Joyce's, Rhys's, Beckett's and Trevor's novels (of which there are not a few), demonstrate a fascination with the disregarded similar to that found in those authors' short stories.

Third, while one can certainly point to a concern with socially discounted figures and experience in short stories – Kipling's Sikh N.C.O. in "A Sahib's War," A. E. Coppard's Old Dick in "The Old Venerable," Julian Maclaren-Ross's put-upon other ranks in *Just the Stuff to Give the Troops*, Gabriel Josipovici's immigrant Mobius in "Mobius the Stripper," George Mackay Brown's victim of brutal prejudice and hypocrisy in "Witch," Ian McEwan's child abuser and murderer in "Butterflies," John Berger's dwarfish outcast in "The Three Lives of Lucy Cabrol," and Lasdun's eccentric spiritualists in "Annals of the Honorary Secretary" – many short stories do not present such figures. Gabriel Conroy in Joyce's "The Dead" may be unhappy, but he does not intransigently inhabit a frontier. He is, in fact, a rather successful provincial intellectual. The narrator in Kipling's "They" is both part of a complex social order, and, by virtue of his bereavement, a complex existential one as well. Katherine Mansfield's Laura in "The Garden Party" may be at odds with her family, but it is hard to see her as belonging to a "submerged group." Something similar may be said even about the female protagonist of Angela Carter's "The Bloody Chamber." Anne in Frances Bellerby's "Pre-War" knows grief, but not marginality. Julian Maclaren Ross's egregious Adams in "A Bit of a Smash in Madras" survives disgrace precisely because he is not alone, but part of the tawdry fabric of the later British *Raj*. Sylvia Townsend Warner writes of the royals of Elfin, not about the serfs ("Five Black Swans" and "Queen Mousie," for example). J. G. Ballard's denizens of *Vermilion Sands* are not all by any means on a social margin. Most of the hugely destructive female figures are hugely rich women, not oppressed skivvies. (Indeed, where are the poor in *Vermilion Sands*?) The narrator of O'Connor's own "Guests of the Nation" is part of the winning side in a bitter colonial war; by the time O'Connor wrote the story, those men were running the Irish Free State (which is part of the point and bravery of the story). These are not submerged or marginalized figures.

The outsider figure, the peripheral, and the eccentric belong in twentieth- and twenty-first-century fiction generally, not just in its short stories. The reasons for the emergence of the short story in the U.S.A. and its tardy development in Britain have to do with the power of economics, institutions, and literary hierarchy, and not with a fragmentation or stability of society. O'Connor's argument, for all its charm, partial truth, and influence, is wrong.

# Canonicity

In Ireland the short story is a canonical form, integral to any discussion of Irish literature. Declan Kiberd notes that "For the past eighty years in Ireland, the short story has been the most popular of all literary forms with readers. It has also been the form most widely exploited by writers" (Kiberd 1979: 14). It has also long held scholars' attention: for example, see the general studies by Patrick Rafroidi and Terence Brown (1979), James Kilroy (1984), along with a host of discussions of the short fiction of writers such as James Joyce, Seán O'Faoláin, Mary Beckett, Edna O'Brien, John McGahern, William Trevor, Bernard MacLaverty, and Eilis Ní Duibhne. It is hard to write about modern Irish literature without writing about the short story. The situation is different in Britain.

Traditionally, the short story has been ignored and disparaged by commentators. G. K. Chesterton's and Arnold Bennett's disdain for the form is quite evident (qtd. in Shaw 1983: 17, 23). In 1964, Thomas Gullason published an important essay entitled "The Short Story: An Underrated Art." In it he documents the critical scorn that short fiction has garnered. "As a rule, the short story is produced in youth, while the novel is the product of experience," opined the editor of *The Critic* in 1887 (qtd. in Gullason 1964: 22). In 1934, Dorothy Brewster and Angus Burrell referred to it as a "subsidiary form of expression" (qtd. in Gullason 1964: 22). In a later essay, Gullason discusses Leon Edel's 1955 critique of Hemingway as a short-story writer. "The short story by its very nature demands simplification. . . . Hemingway is an artist of the small space, the limited view" (qtd. in Gullason 1982: 222). Other examples of such an attitude can be multiplied. There is a defensiveness in the title of T. O. Beachcroft's valuable study from 1968, *The Modest Art: A Survey of the*

*The British and Irish Short Story Handbook*, First Edition. David Malcolm.
© 2012 David Malcolm. Published 2012 by Blackwell Publishing Ltd.

*Short Story in English.* As recently as 2008, Stephen Millhauser sees it necessary to take issue aggressively with critical belittling in his essay "The Ambition of the Short Story," published in *The New York Times* (Millhauser 2008: 31).

For they really have been saying nasty things about short fiction for a long time. In *Punch* in 1964, Alan Coren writes of the "general critical contempt in which the genre is held in this country." "What overtones of dilettantism, of superfluous also-running that title [of short-story] writer carries in England," he exclaims (qtd. in Beachcroft 1968: 213–214). In the *Listener* in 1965, Hilary Corke asks: "Why is it [the short story] dying? Is it not just *because* the art is practically one with the craft? That one can write a perfect short story. (What on earth would a perfect novel look like?) That this art/ craft can be taught like tennis?" (qtd. in Beachcroft 1968: 213). In the *Journal of the Short Story in English* in 1983, Philippe Séjourné sees the situation in France as being even worse than that in the Anglophone world. His questions are rhetorical. "La nouvelle est-elle en général considerée avec suspicion? Genre mineur, ne peut-elle apporter que des satisfactions de second ordre? ... Ses détracteurs parfois vont plus loin. L'auteur est alors mis en accusation" (Is the short story generally looked at with suspicion? A minor genre, can it only offer satisfactions of a second order? ... Its detractors sometimes go further. Thus the author is put in the position of the accused) (Séjourné 1983: 13). "The short story is a subject that has been entirely neglected," V. S. Pritchett remarked (under prompting by his interviewer) in 1976 (Pritchett 1976: 425). It is, as Birgit Moosmüller tellingly puts it, "auch heute noch ein Stiefkind der Forschung" (even today still a step-child of scholarship) (Moosmüller 1993: 11).

This is no longer true. Substantial scholarly studies of British short fiction have been published in the last decade. Barbara Korte (2003), Arno Löffler and Eberhard Späth (2005), Cheryl Alexander Malcolm and David Malcolm (2006, 2008) have written or edited volumes on the form. Andrew Maunder's comprehensive and illuminating *Companion to the British Short Story* was published in 2007. Dominic Head's description of the short story as "neglected" (Head 1992: 8–9), and Clare Hanson's judgment that "the short story has been largely excluded from the arena of critical debate" (Hanson 1989: 1) may soon no longer be true. As Maunder suggests, "The acknowledgement of the short story's place in British literary history is one of the most striking developments of recent years" (Maunder 2007: v).

As Chapter 1 of this book has shown, the short story was a very important form in Britain in the 1890s, in the inter-war period, and during the Second World War. But even in, critically speaking, fallow times, major writers have devoted themselves to the form, or at least given it some serious attention. The Irish short story has always been taken seriously by critics. There is a chance now that British short fiction will be offered the same kind of sustained reflection.

# Institutions

Institutions – publishers, magazines, universities, and the economics of all these – play a role in shaping all printed literary texts. This is particularly true with regard to short fiction.

In Ireland, there have traditionally been many outlets for short stories of various kinds. As I noted in the Introduction, James Kilroy provides an impressive list of Irish journals in the nineteenth century that published short stories (1984: 10–13). This situation endures into the twentieth century. The *Irish Monthly* carried short stories between 1873 and 1954, *Dublin Magazine* between 1923 and 1958. *The Bell*, founded by Seán O'Faoláin in 1940, and edited by him until 1946, brought out short fiction until it ceased publication in 1954. David Marcus's *Irish Writing* also supported short fiction between 1946 and 1957. In 1968 the *Irish Press*, a major Dublin newspaper, started to devote a page every week to new Irish writing, including short stories. This policy particularly benefitted young writers, and several volumes of short stories in the 1970s drew on work first published in the *Irish Press* (Harmon 1979: 63–64).

In addition, U.S. journals, including *The New Yorker*, offered a lucrative and reliable outlet for short stories by Irish writers. Janet Egleson Dunleavy notes that "By the end of World War II, the Irish short story had become an established subgenre of twentieth-century literature," and that by the mid-1940s the *Atlantic Monthly* and *Harper's Bazaar* (in both U.S. and U.K. editions) "had begun to include an Irish short story in almost every issue" (Dunleavy 1984: 145). It is also worth noting that British publishers after 1945 demonstrate a willingness to publish short stories by Irish writers – for example, Faber published John McGahern, and The Bodley Head and Penguin published William Trevor – a willingnes they do not show with regard to British writers' short fiction.

*The British and Irish Short Story Handbook*, First Edition. David Malcolm.
© 2012 David Malcolm. Published 2012 by Blackwell Publishing Ltd.

The conditions for publishing short stories in Britain are more complex than in Ireland. (I have already commented on this subject in Part 1.) Harold Orel gives a long list of successful publications in nineteenth-century Britain that published short fiction, including *Blackwood's Edinburgh Magazine*, *Bentley's Miscellany*, and a host of others (Orel 1986: 8–10). Major writers certainly wrote for these, but such were the prestige and financial rewards of the longer novel that they seem not to have given the shorter form and its outlets (with the exception of *Blackwood's*) sustained attention. Much research remains to be done in the area of nineteenth-century short fiction before the 1880s, but the above does appear to be an accurate picture of short-story publishing for most of the century.

The situation changed in the *fin-de-siècle*. Short fiction became, as Henry James put it, "an object of almost extravagant dissertation" (qtd. in Shaw 1983: 3). This cultural shift was illustrated by, but also driven by institutional change. Barbara Korte and Adrian Hunter both document the explosion of periodicals, catering to a wide social and economic range of purchasers, willing, nay eager, to publish short stories in the 1890s: *The Strand Magazine*, the *National Observer*, *The Yellow Book*, *The Savoy*, the *Fortnightly Review*, and *Longman's Magazine* (Korte 2003 89–92; Hunter 2007: 6–7, 32–34). The period after the Great War and the inter-war period also offered both periodical and book publishing for short fiction (Hunter 2007: 44–49; Maunder 2007: xii–xiii). This was true of both avant-garde and popular writers. The modernists liked short fiction and wrote it and published it, and Somerset Maugham made large sums of money from it (Archer 1993: 3). The years of the Second World War were good for the short story too. *Penguin New Writing*, *Horizon*, and many other magazines and miscellanies published short stories (Bergonzi 1993: 40; Malcolm and Malcolm 2008: 10–11). Elizabeth Bowen and H. E. Bates both predicted a great future for the short story in the post-war world (Malcolm and Malcolm 2008: 11).

They were wrong. The years after 1945 have, by common consent, been very bad for short fiction in Britain, and the reasons are, predominantly, institutional. There is a sad litany of commentary on the period. Beachcroft in 1968 wrote: "Since the end of the Second World War, the outlets for short stories have altered. In the main, they have steadily diminished. Popular magazines as well as literary magazines have been disappearing" (216). In 1985, Joseph Flora painted an even darker picture. He suggests that

> many devotees of the genre [short fiction] have decried a steady decline in the genre in England since World War II, and some have concluded that the current state of the art is moribund. No single fact can account so decisively for the

waning of British achievement in the genre as the decline of publishing opportunities after World War II"

(Flora xv)

V. S. Pritchett, among many others, agrees. In 1976, he talks of "the general decline in the short story owing to the disappearance of periodicals" (Pritchett 1976: 424). In 1986, he says the same. "It is very difficult to find anyone to publish a short story" (36). There is some disagreement about this (Hanson 1985: 159), but Birgit Moosmüller painstakingly and carefully documents short-story writers' despair at finding journals to publish in, or publishers to take them seriously (Moosmüller 1993: 108–115). One of the few bright spots in short-story publishing in the U.K. since 1945 has been the role of the *The New Yorker* in supporting some short-story writers, for example Mollie Panter-Downes, Sylvia Townsend Warner, V. S. Pritchett, and William Trevor (*55 Stories from The New Yorker* 1952; Maxwell 2001: vii–xv; Bloom 2006). Another institutional aspect of the short-story in Britain since 1945 is broadcasting. In this period, the B.B.C. has been one of the principal outlets for and, indeed, commissioners of short fiction. Its role requires research, but is clearly of importance. (The BBC's role is mentioned briefly by Korte 2003: 173.)

Any attempt to establish reasons for the very different institutional situations of the short story in Ireland and Britain, especially since the Second World War, must be speculative. Perhaps, like U.S. publishers in the nineteenth century, Irish publishing interests have supported short fiction because of the prestige of British novels, as an act of post-colonial defiance. Perhaps Irish publishers simply, because they are cleverer and greater spirits, see the artistic and economic possibilities of the form. British publishers – despite protestations to the contrary – simply do not like short fiction, and have to be browbeaten by already established authors to consider publishing collections of short stories. Publishers' assertions that short-story collections do not sell are self-fulfilling (Taylor 2003; Linklater 2005). One suspects that they just do not try. In addition, in Britain the journals prepared to publish short stories are just not there.

Yet short stories *are* published, individually or in collections. This book does have both a British and an Irish subject. The economics and *mentalité* of British short-story publishing over the last sixty years cry out for serious research. I can do no more here, as at several points over the last few pages, than to point in the direction of an important topic in literary history and sociology.

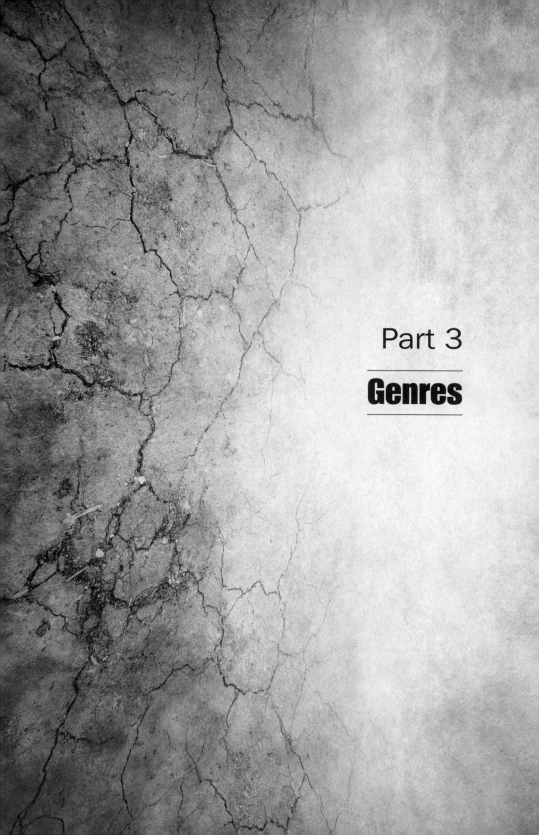

Part 3

**Genres**

This part considers the range of major genres current in the British and Irish short story from the 1880s through to the present. It attempts to give an overview of the genre preferences of British and Irish short-story writers during that period. It concentrates on genres that are substantial in terms of numbers of texts and status. Thus, espionage short fiction exists (for example, Maugham's *Ashenden* stories (1928), and Michael Moorcock's Jerry Cornelius tales (from the mid-1960s through to the 1980s), but espionage short fiction is finally a very minor type of short story (although it is important as a genre of the novel), and will be mentioned only in passing here.

In Part 2, I have discussed whether one can call the short story a genre. My conclusion is that it cannot be so called, being too large a category of text, and embracing, itself, a wide range of disparate traditional genres. In this part, genre is understood as a category of text, widely recognized by writers and readers (and publishers and bookstore proprietors), and having objectively verifiable markers. These markers may take any shape. In genres of prose fiction, they are usually characters, settings, kinds of action, and explicit thematic concerns. Each text offers a set of signs that informs the reader as to what kind of text he/she is dealing with, and what the appropriate expectations and pleasures are for that text. Not every text, of course, will manifest all the markers of its particular genre, but will be selective and configure them uniquely.

However, it must be stressed that genres are never fixed, but they evolve and develop. Writers choose different kinds of character, new settings, and innovative twists of events in order to keep their text fresh and alive, while all

*The British and Irish Short Story Handbook*, First Edition. David Malcolm.
© 2012 David Malcolm. Published 2012 by Blackwell Publishing Ltd.

the time staying in touch with the basic contemporary matrix of the genre. Over time, genres may develop in quite radical ways, so that what one means by a specific genre at one moment may be very different after a hundred years, or less. However, the steps of development should be observable to the literary historian. In addition, it is important to note that few (if any) examples of any one genre are pure in terms of genre. Any individual text is likely to be polyvalent with respect to genre, and to show features of other genres. Sometimes this is of no more than passing interest – the other genre is fleetingly alluded to, or is in any case very close to the text's dominant genre in its markers. In other cases, there is a radical mixing of widely differing genres. This is semantically very heavily loaded, and the recognition of such genre concatenation is very important in the analysis and interpretation of the text in question.

# The Ghost Short Story, the Supernatural Short Story, and the Gothic Short Story

These closely related genres are among the oldest and the most persistent in the history of the British and Irish short story. Their genre markers have remained set for over two hundred years: the figure of the ghost or other supernatural entity (of the devil, boggart, *Doppelgänger*, or vampire sort), a sinister atmosphere, and (often) a setting that involves a large, dark building or castle, with cellars and gloom-laden passages, or some variant of that (for example, a labyrinthine London of rookeries and back alleys).

Some of the earliest short fiction (if not yet, by consensus, short stories) belongs to this genre. Daniel Defoe's "The True Relation of the Apparition of One Mrs. Veal" (1705) relates a supernatural encounter with a *revenante*, and, further, with a device that is very common in the genre, surrounds the tale with verisimilar authentication. Stories of supernatural encounters are the stuff of Romantic short fiction: John Polidori's "The Vampyre" (1819) and Scott's "Wandering Willie's Tale" (embedded in the novel *Redgauntlet* (1824)) are only two of the most celebrated canonical examples. Later in the nineteenth century, Dickens wrote supernatural short fiction, for example, "The Signalman" (1866). Hardy, too, produced supernatural short fiction, "The Withered Arm" (1888) for example. J. Sheridan Le Fanu is most noted for his ghost stories, and Stevenson's "Dr. Jekyll and Mr. Hyde" (1886) and "Markheim" (1887) are central texts in the ghost-supernatural-Gothic genre matrix. These genres have retained the interest of writers and readers throughout the twentieth century. Henry James ("The Turn of the Screw"

*The British and Irish Short Story Handbook*, First Edition. David Malcolm.
© 2012 David Malcolm. Published 2012 by Blackwell Publishing Ltd.

[1898]), the short stories of M. R. James, many short stories by Kipling (including "They" [1904], one of the best short stories ever written in English), H. H. Munro's "Gabriel-Ernest" (1910), Walter de la Mare's "Seaton's Aunt" (1922), Elizabeth Bowen's "The Demon Lover" (1941), Jean Rhys's "I Used to Live Here Once" (1976), Muriel Spark's "The Portobello Road" (1958), Angela Carter's "The Erl-King" (1979), Patricia Duncker's "Stalker" (2003), and James Lasdun's "Annals of the Honorary Secretary" (2009), all illustrate the vitality and enduring power of a very old set of genres.

What is striking about the ghost-supernatural-Gothic cluster is the way in which its markers have remained constant, and in which the device of the verisimilar framing or envelope is recurrent. The genres do evolve, however. There is an increasing amount of psychological matter in many examples of the supernatural story since the late nineteenth century. Not only is an exciting, and even deeply unsettling, story told, but that story is designed to open up areas of obscure and complex psychological experience. The supernatural matter of James's "The Turn of the Screw," Kipling's "The Phantom Rickshaw" (1888), "At the End of the Passage" (1891) and "The Wish House" (1926) and Bowen's "The Demon Lover," for example, is clearly meant to expose mental and spiritual disturbance in the protagonists, with social implications in the case of Kipling and Bowen. James aims to raise epistemological questions, as well as psychological ones. The psychological focus of the ghost story or Gothic short fiction has, in any case, been present from the inception of the genres, and endures into the present. Other genres borrow from the cluster, too. Ballard's *Vermillion Sands* stories, for example, "The Thousand Dreams of Stellavista" and "Cry Hope, Cry Fury," manifestly annex Gothic motifs.

# The Science Fiction Short Story and the Fantasy Short Story

Science fiction short stories and fantasy short stories belong to two genres closely related to each other, and also related to the Gothic-ghost-supernatural cluster. They, too, propose a set of norms for reality quite at odds with the conventions of realist fiction: technology unknown at time of writing and publishing, space travel, undocumented societies and universes, and the human possession of powers unattested in realist fiction.

Science fiction as a genre belongs firmly to the period 1880 through to the present. It has retained its vigor to the present, although in Britain it fell out of favor, too, for a substantial part of the twentieth century. Many of Wells's short stories are clearly examples of proto-science fiction. The term "science fiction" itself was not used until 1929 (by the American editor and writer Hugo Gernsback), but the roots of the genre in Britain can be seen in stories like "The Time Machine" (1895), "The Argonauts of the Air" (1895), and "The War of the Worlds" (1898). "A Story of the Days to Come" (1899), and "The Land Ironclads" (1903), and the uncollected "A Tale of the Twentieth Century," illustrate the closeness of science fiction to the genre conventions of utopia/dystopia. It is striking how little science fiction there is among Wells's short stories – supernatural stories, psychological fiction, stories of exotic adventure, and historical fiction predominate, although there are frequent scientific motifs within the examples of some of those genres. Kipling's contribution to proto-science fiction in this period is worth noting. "With Night Mail" (1909), "As Easy As A.B.C." (1917), and "Unprofessional" (1932) are strong pieces of science fiction.

*The British and Irish Short Story Handbook*, First Edition. David Malcolm.
© 2012 David Malcolm. Published 2012 by Blackwell Publishing Ltd.

Commentators see the early decades of the twentieth century as being a period in which little science fiction, and certainly little science fiction short fiction, was produced in Britain, and the genre enjoyed negligible status. The critical consensus, however, points to the re-emergence of the genre in the 1960s, with a "new wave" science fiction produced by Brian Aldiss and J. G. Ballard (Rosenberg 2007: 373; Lewis 2008: 372). Critics note a seriousness and literariness in this "new wave" science fiction: the psychological interests of science fiction short stories bring it closer to "mainstream" fiction. Ballard trails his literary credentials through his short stories; as I have pointed out in Chapter 2, *Vermillion Sands* is permeated by allusions to other literary texts, and is marked by a self-referentiality in language. The work done in the 1960s and 1970s in Aldiss's and Ballard's *New Worlds* to renew and ennoble the genre of science fiction has been continued by the journal *Interzone* from the 1980s to the present (Lewis 2008: 380–383). The genre has approached realist psychological fiction (still the dominant genre in British fiction), and, indeed, some mainstream writers, such as Martin Amis in *Einstein's Monsters* (1987), have approached science-fiction motifs. Other writers, such as China Miéville and Michel Faber are able to crossover, and be taken very seriously by critics and readers whose primary interests lie outside science fiction.

Fantasy is often not distinguished from science fiction, and, indeed, the two genres are closely related and overlap in some texts. The lack of motifs of traditional science should be taken as indicative of a different set of genre conventions from those of science fiction. Fantasy clearly draws on the repertoire of romance, folk tale, and legend: magic, the muscular masculine warrior, the sword of power, the witch, the alternative universe beyond or in place of the documented one. Nonetheless, the genres clearly blur into one another, and an author such as Michael Moorcock mixes them in his output as a whole, and, at times, in individual stories (for example, "The Stone Thing: A Tale of Strange Parts" (1974).

The fantasy short story is widely regarded as a phenomenon of the period after 1960. Moorcock's numerous fantasy stories, centered on heroic warrior figures like Elric of Melniboné ("The Dreaming City" [1961], "The Singing Citadel" [1967]) or Earl Aubec, demonstrate the genre's possibilities and, it must be said, attractions. "Earl Aubec" (1993) is a typical heroic fantasy short story, in which Aubec, a mighty warrior, sets out on behalf of Queen Eloarde of Klant to conquer Castle Kaneloon, which lies on the edge of Unformed Chaos. In the castle he defeats monsters of his own imagining, plus a terrible Golem. Here he also encounters Myshella, the Dark Lady. She offers to sleep with him; he resists; she persuades him to enter chaos to win new lands. The unabashed escapist excitement of such stories is difficult to resist.

A less heroic brand of fantasy is represented by the work of the distinguished novelist and short-story writer Sylvia Townsend Warner. Her *Kingdoms of Elfin* stories (1977), several of which were published in *The New Yorker* (which also published many of her non-fantasy stories), posit an elfin world, cheerfully cruel, violent, and enigmatic, that runs parallel to and at times intersects with the human. Angela Carter's *Bloody Chamber* stories (1979) and China Miéville's stories in *Looking for Jake and Other Stories* (2005) are often identified with fantasy. However, while both work in non-realist genres, in Carter's case the genre identification seems more appropriately to be legend and fable, while Miéville's texts seem more aligned with science fiction or Gothic stories. The short stories of Neil Gaiman, however, draw frequently and clearly on variants of the fantasy genre. *Smoke and Mirrors* (1999) contains "Chivalry" in which the elderly Mrs. Whitaker finds the Holy Grail in her local Oxfam shop and is visited by Galaad of the Round Table who wishes – most courteously – to acquire it of her. In the same volume, "One Life. Furnished in Early Moorcock" is an act of *homage* to fantasy writers, and "Bay Wolf" reworks the Beowulf story material via Raymond Chandler and Venice Beach. The degree of self-referentiality and the comic elements in Gaiman's stories are features typical of a thoroughly developed genre, indeed one in need of radical deautomatization.

# The Fable

One of the non-realist genres of the short story that has a long, if intermittently active, career in the twentieth century is the fable. Fables are marked by clearly allegorical/symbolic figures (this frequently being marked by type names, or baroquely improbable ones), often in the form of anthropomorphic talking animals (or, in Kipling's case, machines), a highly streamlined action, not at all bound by the conventions of realism (humans can change shape, beasts can talk, witches and wizards perform magic), all tending to a moral, either stated or implied at the conclusion. It needs to be stressed that the symbolism of character can be complex, as can the moral. The latter can even be enigmatic, but it is still present. The fable is an ancient genre, and is common in the Middle Ages and the neo-classical period; however, it has drawn the interest of some important British and Irish short-story writers in the nineteenth and twentieth centuries.

Oscar Wilde's *The Happy Prince* (1888) contains the title story, and, among others, fables such as "The Rose and the Nightingale," "The Selfish Giant," and "The Remarkable Rocket." Kipling tackled the fable (with varying morals) throughout his career from "The Children of the Zodiac" (1893), *The Jungle Books* (1894, 1895), *The Just-So Stories* (1902), ".007," "A Walking Delegate," and "The Ship That Found Herself" (all 1898), to "The Mother Hive" (1909), and "The Bull That Thought" (1926). T. F. Powys published a volume in 1929 entitled simply *Fables*, but the earlier *The House with the Echo* (1928) also contains examples of the genre (with very enigmatic morals at times): the title story, "The Badger Hunters," and "I Came As a Bride." Fables can also be found in A. E. Coppard's work: "Olive and Camilla" (1926), "Silver Circus" (1928), "The Green Drake"

*The British and Irish Short Story Handbook*, First Edition. David Malcolm.
© 2012 David Malcolm. Published 2012 by Blackwell Publishing Ltd.

(1931), "Doe" (1933), and "Speaking Likenesses" (1937). D. H. Lawrence's "The Man Who Loved Islands" and "The Rocking-Horse Winner" (both 1926) manifest genre markers of the fable. More recently, Angela Carter's enormously successful collection *The Bloody Chamber* (1979) reworks the genre in "The Courtship of Mr. Lyon," "Puss-in-Boots," "The Snow-Child," and "The Company of Wolves." Salman Rushdie's *Haroun and the Sea of Stories* (1990) is another revisiting of the genre by a major late twentieth-century writer, and one feels the pressure of the genre in Ian McEwan's collection *The Day Dreamer* (1994), while Neil Gaiman's "Troll Bridge" (in *Smoke and Mirrors* [1999]) is a fine moral fable set in contemporary suburbia.

# The Short Story of Exotic Adventure

The realist genre that is closest – in the colorful attractions it offers its readers – to the non-realist genres of the ghost-supernatural-Gothic cluster and the science fiction and fantasy genres is the story of exotic adventure. It is also a genre of the short story that explodes into British literature in the 1880s and remains a very powerful genre right through to the 1930s. It is set in lands far from Britain, often in distant parts of the British Empire, and frequently involves traditionally heroic and violent (and masculine) action, often in defense of that empire. Stories can also center on clashes between indigenous cultures and European/British agendas in tropical forests and dusty plains.

The short story of exotic adventure is closely linked to British imperial ideology and power. In fact, many examples of the genre, now little read, serve wholly as British imperial propaganda. Several are directed largely at an adolescent audience. Many stories, however, often published alongside explicitly propagandist pieces, are critical of European imperial ambitions, and colonists' purposes and attitudes toward indigenous peoples. Conrad's "An Outpost of Progress" (1898), with its equally hapless and vicious Belgian colonial agents, is one of such short stories most obviously hostile toward the colonial project. Indeed, Conrad shows a very complex picture of both exotic cultures and their intricate relationships with Europeans, for example in "Karain, a Memory" (1898). The same is true of Stevenson's exemplary exposé of colonial nastiness, "The Beach of Falesá" (1892). The exotic setting and the adventure of the sea and distant lands are also used by Conrad to analyze generalized existential illusions and psychological development in a range of stories, such as "Youth" (1902), "Freya of the Seven Isles" (1912), and "The Planter of Malata" (1915).

*The British and Irish Short Story Handbook*, First Edition. David Malcolm.
© 2012 David Malcolm. Published 2012 by Blackwell Publishing Ltd.

But even stories with an evident imperial propagandistic intent are often richly complex in their presentation of empire. Kipling's stories are particularly so. *Plain Tales from the Hills* (1888), for example, presents British India as gossipy, cynical, backbiting, place-seeking, and sexually promiscuous. "To Be Filed for Reference," the last of the *Plain Tales*, a story of the social, racial, moral, and physical degeneration in India of McIntosh Jellaludin, ex-classical scholar, practically inverts the genre's traditional story material. In other stories in other volumes, that India is also haunted by phantoms and inhabited by neurotic overachievers. The British are not nearly as clever or as civilized as they think themselves. The whole framework of Empire is much more rickety than it appears. "The Strange Ride of Morrowbie Jukes" (1888) is a good example of how fragile colonial authority can be. Mariadele Boccardi points out that even John Buchan's colonial short stories (and Buchan was an imperialist, albeit a Scottish one), such as "The Grove of Ashtaroth" (1910) and "The Green Wildebeeste" (1928), point to disabling instabilities in the identities of colonists and the social and political order they represent (Boccardi 2008: 28). The groundwork is already laid for Somerset Maugham's cynical reprises of colonial adventure motifs in the 1930s in stories like "Footprints in the Jungle" (1933). Julian Maclaren-Ross presents a tawdry late Empire in his reverse stories of exotic adventure, "A Bit of a Smash in Madras" and "The Hell of a Time" (1945).

The genre does not entirely die with decolonization. Doris Lessing's *African Stories* (1964, 1973) cannot but refer to earlier examples of the short story of exotic adventure, but in her stories the whole colonial enterprise is bedeviled by loneliness, lies, and bad faith. Lessing gives a voice to the expropriated and disenfranchised indigenous people of southern Africa in her short story "The Old Chief Mashlanga." Naomi Mitchison's *Images of Africa* (1980), a collection of stories set in southern Africa, are inversions of the traditional story of exotic adventure, written as they are from the point-of-view of black Africans and black African culture. The stories, too, of the Caribbean-British writer E. A. Markham invert the traditional perspective of the exotic adventure story (*Ten Stories* [1994] or *Taking the Drawing Room through Customs* [2002]). The distant land is now seen by black West Indians, or Britain itself is viewed as the exotic locale by West Indian immigrants.

# The Detective and Crime Short Story

The detective and crime short story has its roots in nineteenth-century crime narratives (by Poe in the U.S.A. and by Dickens in Britain), but Arthur Conan Doyle's Sherlock Holmes stories (five collections of short stories between 1887 and 1927, along with four longer narratives between 1886 and 1915) make the genre both prominent and respectable. They also establish markers that define the genre in the twentieth century. These are: the eccentric, partly outsider, mostly unlikely, detective; the pattern of action (problem-investigation-solution); and the importance of the city as a setting for the genre. *Mutatis mutandis*, much detective-crime short fiction in the twentieth century reworks these basic genre elements. G. K. Chesterton's Father Brown (five collections of short stories between 1911 and 1935) is an unassuming but fiercely intelligent Catholic priest; Agatha Christie's Hercule Poirot is a dandyish Belgian detective (in collections between 1924 and 1951), and her Miss Jane Marple is an elderly rural spinster (her exploits are recounted in, for example, *The Thirteen Problems* [1932]); Dorothy L. Sayers's Lord Peter Wimsey (first seen in *Lord Peter Views the Body* [1928], but present in collections from 1933 and 1939) may be an aristocrat, but he, too, is a figure out of step with his times (and guilt-ridden as a result of his actions in the Great War); and Margery Allingham's Albert Campion (in stories published in *The Strand Magazine* in the 1930s, collected in *Mr. Campion and Others* [1939]) similarly plays the role of a fool while penetrating to the heart of a crime (see: Nyman 2008: 65–80).

The detective-crime genre achieved such success that attempts were made to codify its conventions in the 1920s, by Ronald A. Knox in 1929, for example. Knox attempts "to elevate the genre into a chess-like intellectual

*The British and Irish Short Story Handbook*, First Edition. David Malcolm.
© 2012 David Malcolm. Published 2012 by Blackwell Publishing Ltd.

pastime" (Nyman 2008: 71). For the detective-crime story has always, since Holmes, been a vehicle for serious social and psychological concerns. Conan Doyle's, Christie's, Sayers's, and Allingham's detectives police the city and decent society against foreign schemes and inner corruption. They are defending a traditional England, but at the same time explore the viciousness behind the facades of that very tradition. It is important, too, to note that the detective figure himself or herself can be rendered very complex. Holmes is utterly eccentric and his relationship with Watson is markedly homoerotic. In any case, as Nyman points out, the detective-crime story, in the period from 1880 to 1945, frequently addresses definitions of masculinity and English masculinity in particular (2008: 68, 75).

In the course of the twentieth century, especially after 1945, the detective-crime novel has become the dominant vehicle of the genre, but detective-crime short stories are still produced, at least as spin-offs from novels. Iain Rankin's *A Good Hanging* (1992) and *Beggars* [sic] *Banquet* (2002), for example, collect stories involving the author's complex and flawed detective Rebus, who – in the manner of Raymond Chandler's Philip Marlowe – stalks the dark streets of a Gothic Edinburgh, solving gruesome murders that expose the seamy side of modern Scotland (and Britain). Major British crime writers continue to write short stories. Ruth Rendell's *Piranha to Scurfy, and Other Stories* was published in 2000 (and her *Collected Stories* in 1987 and 2008). Peter Lovesey has published numerous collections of short fiction, including *Butchers, and Other Stories of Crime* (1985), *The Sedgemoor Strangler, and Other Stories of Crime* (2002), and *Murder on the Short List* (2009). Val McDermid's collection *Stranded* appeared in 2005. Anthologies are published regularly, like *The Detection Club Anthology*, edited by Simon Brett (2006), containing stories by Colin Dexter, P. D. James, H. R. F. Keating, Lovesey, and Michael Ridpath. The Crime Writers' Association has offered a short story award since 1995. The crime-detective short story provides the traditional satisfactions of the genre, plus increasingly anguished and complex detectives, substantially more hideous misdemeanors, an increasingly flawed social order, and more exotic locations (for example, Rankin's Edinburgh and the Bombay of Keating's collection *Inspector Ghote: His Life and Crimes* [1989]).

# The Historical Short Story

The historical novel has been one of the major novel genres of the nineteenth and twentieth centuries. Thackeray, Dickens, George Eliot, and Hardy all tried their hands at historical fiction. In the twentieth century, despite periods of absence, the historical novel has never vanished from the literary system. Robert Graves, Sylvia Townsend Warner, Sybille Bedford, and Mary Renault all produced distinguished historical novels in the mid-twentieth century. Since John Fowles's *The French Lieutenant's Woman* (1969), the genre has enjoyed unparalleled popularity among mainstream British novelists – William Golding, Salman Rushdie, Timothy Mo, Kazuo Ishiguro, Ian McEwan, William Boyd, Hilary Mantel, Angela Carter, Jeannette Winterson, Rose Tremain, Eva Figes, Anita Brookner, and many others – a popularity that continues into the present. Yet, the historical short story is a minor genre of the short story. It is important primarily because Kipling produced several important pieces of historical short fiction, although more recently John McGahern has produced major stories with strong historical components. Perhaps the short story is just too short to perform the reconstructionist task that the historical novel has always set itself.

Wells dabbled in historical short fiction, in stories such as "A Story of the Stone Age" (1897) and "The Grisly Folk" (1921), but Kipling produced historical short fiction consistently throughout his career. The collections *Puck of Pook's Hill* (1906) and *Rewards and Fairies* (1910) are best known, but his late volume, *Limits and Renewals* (1932), also contains a substantial historical short story, "The Church That Was at Antioch." One of the most striking stories in *Rewards and Fairies* is "The Knife and the Naked Chalk." The conceit underlying Kipling's two historical collections is that the spirit

*The British and Irish Short Story Handbook*, First Edition. David Malcolm.
© 2012 David Malcolm. Published 2012 by Blackwell Publishing Ltd.

Puck calls up figures from England's past (prehistoric, Roman, medieval, Elizabethan, and eighteenth-century) to inculcate a sense of Englishness in two modern children. Here the figure is a prehistoric shepherd from the Weald of Sussex, living at the cusp of the Flint and Iron Age, who sacrifices his body and happiness to secure iron weapons for his people to use against marauding wolves. Clearly, the story has a modern agenda (but what historical fiction has not?) to do with the need and cost of self-sacrifice, but a credible, if historically unverifiable, historical milieu and mentality are created in select details. Prehistoric and classical pasts are the subjects of Scottish writer Naomi Mitchison's historical short fiction in collections such as *Black Sparta: Greek Stories* (1928), *Barbarian Stories* (1929), and *The Powers of Light* (1932). Mitchison continued to write historical short fiction into the 1950s. Her non-canonical status is a sad reflection on contemporary literary studies. The Scottish contribution to historical short fiction is, in fact, striking. George Mackay Brown's "Witch," "Master Halcrow, Priest," and "The Story of Jorkel Hayforks" (all 1967) are major exercises in historical imagination in the short-story form.

John McGahern's stories are often set in a relatively close past, but in three stories in his last collection of short fiction, *High Ground* (1986), he attempts the temporal sweep and reconstruction of historical fiction. All three are centered on Anglo-Irish Protestant families and their interaction with the Catholic majority after independence. "Oldfashioned" moves from the Irish Free State of the 1930s through to the modern Ireland of the 1980s, focusing on the relationship of a young Catholic boy with the wealthy Anglo-Irish Sinclairs, who return from England after the Second World War. The gradual integration of the Protestant Kirkwood family into an independent Ireland, and the cost of that integration, form the subject of "Eddie Mac" and "The Conversion of William Kirkwood." However, historical short fiction is not a major part of the large body of twentieth-century Irish short stories, which remains stubbornly focused on contemporary psychological and social issues.

Historical subject matter is present in recent British short fiction by John Arden (*The Stealing Steps* [2003]), in the title story of Rose Tremain's *The Darkness of Wallis Simpson* (2005), and Patrick McGrath's *Ghost Town: Tales of Manhattan* (2005). But the short story form seems to be largely inimical to the historical imagination, despite the fact that some major writers (Wells, Kipling, Mitchison, Mackay Brown, and McGahern) have taken it on.

# The Realist
# Social-Psychological Short Story

The dominant genre in British and Irish short fiction is the realist social-psychological short story. This has been the case since the 1880s and shows no sign of changing. The realist social-psychological short story focuses on more or less complex human characters in their social relationships. It does so within the conventions of realism: the fictionality of the created world of the text is not stressed; the contemporary material-social world is fundamental; characters may believe in a metaphysical realm but no visitors from it call (except, subjectively, to those characters); places are documented, or very like documented ones; technology is recognizable; and figures have no powers (flight, time-travel, lycanthropic metamorphosis) that are not attested to in *Middlemarch*. These are not negative observations. The realist text is a powerful and very satisfying kind of fiction; its conventions allow a wide range of interventions in the world. A fondness for and estimation of its achievements and potential do not preclude a deep respect for other genres. For the purposes of this volume, one must simply note that it is, fundamentally, the way British and Irish writers do the short story. Indeed, two genres already discussed, the story of exotic adventure and the historical short story, do not deviate from the basic conventions of realism. Setting alone allows us to distinguish them as discrete genres.

Let me risk a hypothesis. The vast majority of the major (and canonical and frequently anthologized) British and Irish short stories of the late nineteenth century, the twentieth century, and the twenty-first century are

*The British and Irish Short Story Handbook*, First Edition. David Malcolm.
© 2012 David Malcolm. Published 2012 by Blackwell Publishing Ltd.

examples of the social-psychological genre: Hubert Crackanthorpe's "Profiles" (1893), Henry James's "The Beast in the Jungle" (1903), Joseph Conrad's "Amy Foster" (1903), "George Moore's "The Wedding Dress" (1903), H. H. Munro's (Saki's) "Sredni Vashtar" (1911), D. H. Lawrence's "Odour of Chrysanthemums" (1914), James Joyce's "The Dead" (1914), Rudyard Kipling's "Mary Postgate" (1917), Katherine Mansfield's "The Garden-Party" (1922), A. E. Coppard's "The Higgler" (1925), Frank O'Connor's "Guests of the Nation" (1931), V. S. Pritchett's "Handsome Is As Handsome Does" (1938), Elizabeth Bowen's "Mysterious Kôr" (1945), Seán O'Faoláin's "Lovers of the Lake" (1957), Alan Sillitoe's "The Loneliness of the Long Distance Runner" (1959), Muriel Spark's "The Gentile Jewesses" (1967), John McGahern's "Korea" (1970), William Trevor's "The Ballroom of Romance" (1972), Jean Rhys's "On Not Shooting Sitting Birds" (1976), Edna O'Brien's "A Rose in the Heart of New York" (1978), John Berger's "An Independent Woman" (1979), James Kelman's "Forgetting to Mention Allende" (1987), Bernard MacLaverty's "Walking the Dog" (1994), and Hanif Kureishi's "We're Not Jews" (1997). The list could go on.

There are clear discriminations to be made among such short fiction, but these are distinctions of theme not of technique. The Irish, working-class, the anti-colonial, the feminist, the immigrant, or the Anglo-Jewish subject matter of various stories certainly makes them distinct, but it does not constitute a genre differentiation.

A distinction is often made between realist and modernist short fiction. Modernist short fiction is said to be less plot-driven, to have less developed story materials, and to focus on the movements of consciousness and an epiphanic moment (Hanson 1985: 55–81; Head 1992: 15, 16, 34, 36; Jarfe 2010: 85–139). This is in some measure true. However, short fiction generally has limited amounts of story material (for reasons of space), and many texts other than those classed as modernist short fiction build toward a moment of psychological development or insight. The distinction between modernist and realist short fiction obscures the fact that, despite undeniable differences, the conventions (outlined above) hold good for stories that are usually seen in both categories. Joyce's "The Dead" and Mansfield's "The Garden-Party," on one hand, and Rhys's "On Not Shooting Sitting Birds" and McGahern's "Korea," on the other, do not differ by a hair's breadth in the conventions they employ. The social-psychological short story shows no signs of a falling-off of interest among major writers. Most of the stories in Colm Tóibín's *Mothers and Sons* (2007), William Boyd's *The Dream Lover* (2008), James Lasdun's *It's Beginning to Hurt* (2009), and Kazuo Ishiguro's

*Nocturnes: Five Stories of Music and Nightfall* (2009) exemplify the genre.

However, there is a group of short stories in twentieth-century British short fiction that does reject the conventions of the realist social-psychological short story (or realist conventions *tout court*), and these are the subject of the following sub-section of this chapter.

# The Metafictional/Experimental
# Short Story

All art is in some measure experimental, in that a text never exactly repeats all
the features of its predecessors and models. All fiction is to a degree self-
referential and metafictional. Readers are simply accustomed to being blind
to certain conventions. Such conventions are apparent even within realist
texts. An omniscient third-person narrator is about as conventional a convention as one can imagine. Yet readers choose not to worry about it. The
same holds true for the supposed accuracy (either in form or content) of
recorded direct speech, and the semantic weight of fictional landscape.
Although one can, thus, argue for the deep conventionality of all literature,
in the twentieth century critics have identified a substantial body of texts that
advertise their self-referentiality, and, in an explicit manner, address issues
connected with the problems and purposes of writing fiction. This kind of
writing is apparent in short fiction in Britain over the last 100 years. It is noted
as part of modernist fiction (Hanson: 1985: 55–81; Korte 2003: 127–137).
Further, Clare Hanson (1985: 140–172), Birgit Moosmüller (1993:
119–364), Barbara Korte (2003: 148–162), and Günther Jarfe (2010:
187–229) have written with insight on experimentality in what may be called
postmodernist short fiction (a term which, like Hunter (2007: 98), I find
remarkably unhelpful, if almost unavoidable).

Their arguments are flawed at certain points as they wish to include as
experimental a choice of provocative subject matter (Ian McEwan's interest
in incest and fetishism in his short stories from the late 1970s, for example) or
affiliation to non-realist genres (Angela Carter's use of fable in *The Bloody
Chamber*, for instance). While such moves may be innovative, I find it difficult

*The British and Irish Short Story Handbook*, First Edition. David Malcolm.
© 2012 David Malcolm. Published 2012 by Blackwell Publishing Ltd.

to see them as experimental. McEwan, in "Homemade" (1975) or "Dead As They Come" (1978), may be pushing at the limits of acceptable subject matter (although even that can be questioned), but most of his short stories are technically well within the conventions of realism ("Reflections of a Kept Ape" [1978] aside). Carter is rewriting folk tales and beast fables in *The Bloody Chamber*, but that is a matter of reversion to older genres, rather than experiment *sensu stricto*.

Virginia Woolf's "Kew Gardens" (1921) is often seen as a paradigmatic experimental and metafictional short story. One can see why this is so. It abandons anything that could be described as a traditional story material. It refuses to establish character in conventional ways. It radically shifts and limits point of view. Its language has markedly poetic features. Thus, conventions are both breached and laid bare, and something novel is produced. However, one should also note that the text has a clear psychological focus; it aims to expose consciousness and consciousnesses, according to a non-realist model, but its subject is the movement of a mind. Further, as Stef Craps has argued, "Kew Gardens" is also concerned with the dislocations of war and social constraints on women, traditional subjects of social-psychological fiction (Craps 2008: 197–198).

In Part 1 of this book, I have discussed Samuel Beckett's *Texts for Nothing* (1958, 1962–1967), stories certainly identified as experimental and metafictional. Once again, as with Woolf's "Kew Gardens," the texts' experimentality lies in abandoning so much that is seen as belonging to stories and to fiction in general: established characters and story material, clear and coherent settings. Like Woolf's work, Beckett's prose text also takes on strictly poetic features (for example, on the level of sound orchestration). A similarly radical *expérimenteur* among short story writers is Gabriel Jospipovici. His collection *Mobius the Stripper* (1974) contains a range of stories that more or less radically deviate from and question the norms of traditional realist narratives. For example, "The Reconstruction" consists only of direct speech (Ronald Firbank had done something similar in the novel *Vainglory* [1915]). There is no narrator, only a dialogue between an unnamed questioner and an unnamed answerer. There is no setting, although one can infer an interrogation or a session with a psychiatrist. There are frequent breaks in the dialogue. The answerer is being asked to recall the past and is not making a very good job of it. The text shockingly diverges from the conventions of realism, and also problematizes the business of producing a narrative, of giving an account.

There is certainly, a determined and very interesting, if small, body of experimental and metafictional short-story writers: Brigid Brophy, Christine Brooke-Rose, B. S. Johnson, Clive Sinclair, and Ronald Frame, among others.

But despite deliberate and stimulating deviances from realist conventions, one should note that all the above three stories by Woolf, Beckett, and Josipovici, present human minds in complex fashion, and that in all cases, too, the stories are not without social resonance. For example, one of the speakers in "The Reconstruction" is clearly from elsewhere, an immigrant from another land and another language, trying to recall a distant past elsewhere. Beckett's isolated, muttering, disheveled outcasts can be met with on the streets of any large European city. Even at its most experimental, the short story carries traces of the social-psychological text that is dominant in twentieth-century British and Irish fiction.

Part 4

# Key Authors

# Richard Aldington (1892–1962)

Aldington is much better known as a novelist than as a writer of short stories. His novels *Death of a Hero* (1929) and *All Men Are Enemies* (1933) are important fictional examinations of the Great War and its consequences. Aldington was also a serious literary critic, writing, *inter alia*, substantial appreciations of Maugham (1939) and Lawrence (1927 and 1935). Yet Aldington's collection of short stories *Roads to Glory* (1930) is an important text in the post-1918 questioning of the Great War. "Meditation on a German Grave" deals with the post-war experiences of a demobbed officer who attempts to survive the peace, eventually returning to his memory of sitting by a German soldier's grave in a desolate war-ravaged landscape in October 1918. He recognizes the German soldier as a brother and he resolves to try to avert another war even if this is hopeless. "Killed in Action" and "A Bundle of Letters" present the Great War in an utterly unheroic light. In "Victory," set on the night before the war's end, the protagonist Ellerton, cold, fatigued, and in a desolate landscape, reflects that victory is the "victory of death over life," and that the twentieth century is "A lot of cheering idiots in an unlimited cemetery."

*The British and Irish Short Story Handbook*, First Edition. David Malcolm.
© 2012 David Malcolm. Published 2012 by Blackwell Publishing Ltd.

# J. G. Ballard (1930–2009)

Ballard was born in Shanghai in China and spend formative and traumatic years in a Japanese prisoner-of-war camp. He is of great importance in the development of post-war science fiction, both in his novels (such as *The Drowned World* [1962]) and his short fiction. His *Complete Short Stories* (2001) contains ninety-six texts. His first short story was published in 1956.

Ballard was associated with the journal *New Worlds* in the 1960s, for which, along with Michael Moorcock, he produced some of the most innovative and controversial science fiction of the century. His stories form a glittering exploration of the possibilities of science fiction, largely with strong emphasis on dystopian and apocalyptic motifs. "The Terminal Beach" (published in 1964 and discussed in detail in the next chapter) is one of the most powerful and representative texts of this aspect of his *œuvre*. In addition, his work shows a debt to cosmopolitan twentieth-century avant-garde fiction. Always intensely literary in style and replete with references to past literature, texts frequently draw attention to their own fictiveness and become virtuoso exercises in fabulation. A notable example is "The Assassination of John Fitzgerald Kennedy Considered as a Downhill Motor Race" (1966), which is influenced by Alfred Jarry's "The Crucifixion Considered as an Uphill Bicycle Race" (1911). His work aims at an ennoblement of science fiction, making it more like canonical mainstream and high-status fiction, while keeping its speculative excitement.

There is a hard political edge to Ballard's short fiction. He is in horror at the military-industrial-inspired degradation of the planet, at the terrible possibilities of media technology and its power ("The Subliminal Man" [1963]), and at the urban wastelands that modern Western society has built ("The Concentration City" [1957]). The title of the story "Why I Want to

*The British and Irish Short Story Handbook*, First Edition. David Malcolm.
© 2012 David Malcolm. Published 2012 by Blackwell Publishing Ltd.

Fuck Ronald Reagan" (1968) says it all. In the introduction to *The Complete Short Stories*, Ballard recalls that his early science fiction stories were criticized because "they weren't science fiction at all." He also notes that his work has also been censured for not envisaging the actual future that has in the meantime happened. He answers this by saying that his fiction is not set in the future, "but in a kind of visionary present – a description that fits the stories in this book and almost everything else I have written."

# Samuel Beckett (1906–1989)

Beckett was born in Dublin (of Protestant middle-class parents), but lived for much of his life in France, including the years of the Second World War, the German occupation, and the collaborationist Vichy Government. He knew some of the twentieth century's nastiness from within. Firmly a member of the inter- and post-war avant-garde, Beckett lived in obscure self-imposed exile in Paris until the success of his plays *Waiting for Godot* (1952/1954) and *Endgame* (1957/1958) won him international fame. He was awarded the Nobel Prize for Literature in 1969. Beckett's work is unusual in that he wrote both in French and English. The French versions of most of his fiction pre-date the English ones, and often there are noticeable and meaning-filled differences between the two. Beckett published his first piece of short fiction, "Assumption," in 1929, and he continued to work in the short form until shortly before his death. The three stories in *Stirrings Still* were published in 1988. His most celebrated pieces of short fiction include the *Stories and Texts for Nothing* (published in 1955, although several stories date from earlier), "Ping" (1966), "Lessness" (1969), and *Fizzles* (1973–1975).

Beckett's work is ferociously difficult. The conventional elements of the short story, setting, character, and action, are attenuated and obscure, in a way that makes very considerable demands on the reader. In "Lessness," the substance of the text is determined by a mathematical exercise. His texts are usually the voices of lonely and isolated figures, themselves not entirely sure who or where (or when) they are. Beckett's prose is often marked by deviant punctuation, word order, and ellipses. It is often also remarkably beautiful. The language (full of phonological, lexical, and syntactic parallelisms and repetitions) offers a faint glimmer

*The British and Irish Short Story Handbook*, First Edition. David Malcolm.
© 2012 David Malcolm. Published 2012 by Blackwell Publishing Ltd.

of hope in a desolate world of exile, abandonment, uncertainty (Beckett's readers are at a loss as much as his characters), inertia, and physical desolation. Beckett's and J. G. Ballard's characters often inhabit similar spoiled and abandoned worlds.

# Frances Bellerby (1899–1975)

Despite enormous personal difficulties (her only brother died in the Great War; she was, as a result of an accident, a cripple from 1930; her mother committed suicide in 1932), Bellerby published three volumes of short stories during her life, *Come to an End* (1939), *The Acorn and the Cup* (1948), and *A Breathless Child* (1952). In an excellent discussion and contextualization of Bellerby's short fiction, Sabine Coelsch-Foisner writes: "Bellerby is interesting for the debate about women's short fiction, because her handling of the genre reflects an ambivalent desire to tell and to withhold stories. . . . Springing from her own tragic life, Bellerby's stories focus on exceptional experiences and events too large or formidable to understand: the traumas of war, pain, and bereavement" (Coelsch-Foisner 2008 a: 103). Certainly motifs of death, pain, loss, division between characters, and marginalization run throughout Bellerby's short fiction.

Death haunts the stories of *Come to an End*. In the title story, Jill, the daughter of Hugh and Stella, has died in an accident. Now Hugh must go to pick up his eleven-year-old son from school and tell him of his sister's death. The story gives Hugh's impressions and thoughts before and after telling his son. He realizes "yet this moment would not ever pass." In "Pre-War," Anne, who is nine, suddenly has a vision, while playing with her brother, of death and transience, of her brother's not being. The date is 1 January 1911. By 1917, the brother will be eighteen years old. In "The Carol," the protagonist, "he," looks round his bedroom, reflects on the past and the sounds of the present moment. He whistles his favorite carol, and then realizes that he is dead, killed in the Great War.

*The British and Irish Short Story Handbook*, First Edition. David Malcolm.
© 2012 David Malcolm. Published 2012 by Blackwell Publishing Ltd.

# John Berger (born 1926)

For large parts of his career, Berger has worked in self-imposed isolation from literary and artistic circles in Britain, living in the French Alps since the early 1970s. He is an art critic, novelist, poet, and short-story writer. He has also written numerous film scripts. A political commitment, explicitly Marxist, has run throughout his writing. He is, above all, dedicated both to embedding literature and art in its economic and social matrix and to focusing on the experience of the poor, the marginal, the exploited, and the displaced. His work in short fiction includes the collections: *Pig Earth* (1979), *Once in Europa* (1987), *Lilac and Flag* (1990) (these three volumes gathered together in 1991 in *Into Their Labours*), *And Our Face, My Heart, Brief as Photos* (1984), *Keeping a Rendezvous* (1991), and *Photocopies* (1996).

*Into Their Labours* is an ambitious gathering of three volumes. The stories deal with rural life among peasants, but also the impact of the advent of mechanized capitalist farming on their lives. The stories in *Lilac and Flag* deal with the lives of migrant workers in the city. The stories in *Pig Earth* are of particular interest. They set out in grim detail the experiences of peasants in the French Alps. Cows and pigs are slaughtered, ditches are dug, animals are brought together to copulate, cows are cared for and milked, tractors come to the locality. Through all this, people work, have relationships, endure death, harsh conditions, and the intrusions of the state. The temporal scope is considerable. The war and the German occupation are living memories. Although the subject matter and Berger's austere and informal language suggest an affiliation with Zola-esque social realism, the stories are not completely limited to the here and now or to the conventions of realism. The long short story "The Three Lives of Lucy Chabrol" contains a sequence

*The British and Irish Short Story Handbook*, First Edition. David Malcolm.
© 2012 David Malcolm. Published 2012 by Blackwell Publishing Ltd.

where the dead of the locality gather to help build a house. Imagination and memory are also part of the reality of the villages and farms of the Jura.

In his introduction to *Into Their Labours*, Berger argues strongly that to be interested in the experience of French peasants is not to commit oneself to political and intellectual irrelevance. The "peasant experience of survival," embodied in the stories of *Pig Earth*, he suggests may offer us better models of how to meet the brutal exigencies of modern capitalism than traditional left-wing politics.

# Elizabeth Bowen (1899–1973)

Bowen is a very influential figure in the development of the British and Irish short story, and is legitimately claimed by both national traditions. Hunter points out that "Elizabeth Bowen's is a name to conjure with in the history of short story criticism" (Hunter 2007: 112). Born in Dublin and daughter of the owner (and ultimately the owner herself) of a large southern Irish house and estate in County Cork, she was brought up and educated in England, but maintained a strong connection with her property in the Irish Free State and later the Irish Republic. Bowen is an important novelist. *The Heat of the Day* (1949) is a remarkable novel about obsession and treachery set in war-time London and southern Ireland. She was also a strong advocate of short fiction throughout her career, and her *Collected Stories* (1980) contains seventy-nine fictions. She published collections of short stories between *Encounters* in 1923 and *The Good Tiger* in 1965.

Most of her stories work within realist conventions, and are social-psychological pieces, usually employing omniscient narrators, often focusing on upper and upper-middle-class lives. She writes frequently of childhood experience, and supernatural stories figure prominently in her output. She is, thus, seen to be at odds with the modernists of the 1920s, although it is hard to see how her work differs radically from that of Katherine Mansfield or Jean Rhys. Her most celebrated stories date from the period of the Second World War and shortly afterwards: "Green Holly," "Ivy Gripped the Steps," "Mysterious Kôr," and the much anthologized "The Demon Lover."

Several of these combine supernatural motifs with a complex evocation of the sights and sounds of war-time Britain, and human responses to the place and the time. "Mysterious Kôr," is not a supernatural story, but gives the reader a sense of what that dislocated and disorienting London of the early

*The British and Irish Short Story Handbook*, First Edition. David Malcolm.
© 2012 David Malcolm. Published 2012 by Blackwell Publishing Ltd.

1940s must have been like, at least for some. "The Demon Lover" gives the reader some of the sinister qualities of that time of deaths and brief encounters. Angus Wilson insists that there are "only two writers who convey what life in blitzed London was like – Elizabeth Bowen and Henry Green" (Wilson 1980: 7). Bernard Bergonzi claims that "Mysterious Kôr" is "one of the finest of all the stories to come out of the Second World War" (Bergonzi 1993: 44).

Bowen was a vigorous advocate of the short story. *The Faber Book of Modern Stories* (1937), which Bowen edited and for which she wrote an introduction, is a very important collection of both British and Irish short stories, including stories by Bowen herself, A. E. Coppard, E. M. Forster, James Hanley, James Joyce, D. H. Lawrence, Walter de la Mare, Frank O'Connor, Seán O'Faoláin, and Liam O'Flaherty. Bowen's introduction argues for the modernity of short fiction; it breaks with the *longueurs* of the novel; like the cinema it is free from an over-weighty tradition, and it can cut from scene to scene with rapidity; it is short, taut, and lively. There are "free" stories, not bound by commercial demands; they can be great art. For Bowen, the short story was the true, the modern, form. She concludes: "The present state of the short story is, on the whole, healthy: its prospects are good." In the short term she was right; the period of the Second World War was good for short stories. In the long term, in Britain at least, she was wrong.

# Angela Carter (1940–1992)

Carter became very famous in the course of her career, and her reputation has grown even more since her death. Her novels *The Infernal Desire Machines of Doctor Hoffmann* (1972), *Nights at the Circus* (1984), and *Wise Children* (1991) are among the most interesting pieces of post-war British fiction. *The Bloody Chamber* is one of the most famous and widely discussed and taught collections of British short fiction. She published three volumes of short stories during her life, and two more came out after her death. *Fireworks: Nine Profane Pieces* as published in 1974, *The Bloody Chamber, and Other Stories* in 1979, and *Black Venus* in 1985. The two posthumous volumes are *American Ghosts and Old World Wonders* (1993) and *Burning Your Boats* (1995).

Carter's short fiction is deeply literary. Legends, folk-tales, fairy tales, and myths are reworked and often appropriated for feminist purposes. Supernatural motifs abound. Her characters are shape-shifters, talking cats, werewolves. The Gothic is plundered for characters, situations, and settings. Carter adores the picaresque. Allusions are rife to major works, not just from British but from world literature: Dickens, Dostoyevsky, Flaubert, Pérrault. Carter is, in addition, fascinated with violence and emotional and sexual extremes. Rape, enslavement, passion, death, fetishism – these are her subjects. Her work, like that of several contemporaries (Patricia Duncker, for example), shows affinities with pornography. Carter's language veers dizzyingly between the informal and demotic and the elevated, producing a baroque style that is part of the fascination of her work. Her texts are virtuoso fabulations attesting to the power of language and the human mind, and to the richness of the world. They also, most of them, are powerful examples of feminist *littérature engagée*.

*The British and Irish Short Story Handbook*, First Edition. David Malcolm.
© 2012 David Malcolm. Published 2012 by Blackwell Publishing Ltd.

The stories in *The Bloody Chamber* will surely be her most enduring short fictions. The traditionally anti-woman legend of Bluebeard, designed to inculcate obedience in difficult wives, is rewritten in the title story, to produce a text that acknowledges, undermines, and ultimately rejects male power and its glamour. Ambiguity marks many of the texts in the collection. The narrator of "The Erl-King" both loves and fears the innocent wild man whom she ultimately kills. Stories like "The Tiger's Bride" and "The Company of Wolves" are disturbingly ambiguous, like authentic legends and myths, their rough edges and strange turns of action designed to provoke thought. Carter will long intrigue readers by virtue of her panache in fusing a deep traditionality (folk tales, beast fables, gothic fiction) with a contemporary fascination with the pornographic and a rigorous but thoughtful feminist agenda.

# Arthur Conan Doyle (1859–1930)

Although not as talented as Stevenson, Conan Doyle is the other great *fin-de-siècle* Scottish writer, along with Stevenson and J. M. Barrie inventing some of the central figures of world culture in the twentieth century. Holmes and Watson are as all-pervasive as Jekyll, Hyde, Long John Silver, and Peter Pan. His first published short story for which he was paid was "The Mystery of Sasassa Valley," an imperial adventure story, which appeared in *Chamber's Journal* in 1879. It is for his Sherlock Holmes stories that Conan Doyle is best remembered. They began to be published in *Strand* from 1891, with compelling illustrations by Sidney Paget, and were enormously popular and commanded increasingly (indeed, dizzyingly) high fees. These softened Conan Doyle's reluctance to keep writing Holmes stories. Conan Doyle confessed his debt to Poe in *Through the Magic Door* (1907), but the Sherlock Holmes stories go far beyond Poe's detective fiction in quantity and complexity. Like much detective fiction, they reveal the unstable side of their society, here late nineteenth-century Britain. The borders of decent society are constantly threatened from within and without, and Holmes's task seems to be to police them constantly, without any hope of winning a final battle. Holmes himself, for all that his genius and eccentricity are mediated by his colleague and the narrator, the amiable and ex-colonial Dr. John Watson, is himself a marginalized and deviant outsider. The instability of identity is further suggested by Holmes's skills in disguise (a motif taken up by John Buchan later in the Richard Hannay novels, and by Conrad in *The Secret Agent*). One can only speculate why the adventures of a drug-taking misfit, which involve brutal crimes and an exposure of the inner rot of good society, have so intrigued generations of readers in Britain and elsewhere.

*The British and Irish Short Story Handbook*, First Edition. David Malcolm.
© 2012 David Malcolm. Published 2012 by Blackwell Publishing Ltd.

Conan Doyle wrote much more short fiction besides Holmes stories – historical short stories (for example, *The Exploits of Brigadier Gerard* ([1896]), stories centered on doctors (*Round the Red Lamp* [1894]), and early science fiction stories (*The Maracot Deep, and Other Stories* [1929]). But he gave Sherlock Holmes and Dr. Watson to world literature and world culture, and that ensures him a kind of well-deserved immortality.

# Joseph Conrad (1857–1924)

Conrad is one of the greatest writers of fiction in the English language. His achievement is all the more remarkable because English was neither his first language (Polish) nor his second language (French), nor was his life remotely like that of any other British writer before or since. He was born into a Polish patriotic and gentry family Korzeniowski, spent some of his childhood in internal exile with his parents (because of his father's involvement in political activities against Tsarist Russia), and, fleeing Poland and all its complexities, in his youth led an adventurous life in the Mediterranean and the Caribbean. He joined the British Merchant Navy in 1878 and became a British citizen and a Master Mariner in 1886. He traveled widely in Asia and in Africa. He started to publish fiction in 1896, adopting the (for a Pole) culturally loaded pseudonym of Conrad.[1] A series of extraordinary and influential novels followed, including *The Nigger of the "Narcissus"* (1897), *Lord Jim* (1900), *Nostromo* (1904), *The Secret Agent* (1907) (a magnificent piece of espionage fiction *avant la lettre*), and *Under Western Eyes* (1911).

Throughout his career, Conrad wrote and published short fiction, usually stories of colonial adventure, but texts that question in a sophisticated fashion the very premises of European colonial expansion. "An Outpost of Progress" (1897), "Karain: A Memory" (1897), "Amy Forster" (1901), "Youth" (1902), "The Secret Sharer" (1910), "Freya of the Seven Isles" (1912), "The Planter of Malata" (1915), and "The Shadow Line" (1917) are or should be at

---

[1] Conrad is an Anglicized version of one of Conrad's middle names. It is also an allusion to the protagonist of Adam Mickiewicz's poetic narrative *Konrad Wallenrod* (1828) or to one of the central characters in the same author's drama *Dziady* (Forefathers' Eve) (published in various parts between 1823 and 1860). Both are extremely complex figures, psychologically and in their relations to Poland.

*The British and Irish Short Story Handbook*, First Edition. David Malcolm.
© 2012 David Malcolm. Published 2012 by Blackwell Publishing Ltd.

the center of the British short-fiction tradition, and have generated a wealth of analysis and interpretation. They are marked by a psychological and existential complexity that makes Conrad a very great and ambiguous writer. Conrad's "Heart of Darkness" (1902) is a text that inhabits a borderland between short story and novel, and can legitimately be discussed as either. Such formal indeterminacy is part of the text's deeply unsettling quality. "Prince Roman" (1911) is the only short story that explicitly addresses Polish issues, although Yanko Goral, the protagonist of "Amy Foster," has to be some kind of Pole. Nevertheless, one feels the pressure of Polish history and culture – the demand for commitment to a Romantic nationalist cause, its glamour and its curse – behind some of Conrad's fiction. One must also remember that, when Conrad wrote of colonialism and imperial expansion in "An Outpost of Progress" and "Heart of Darkness", he belonged to a nation that had been wiped off the face of Europe by three imperial powers. One must remember, too, that he knew the pains and freedoms of immigration from the inside. He spoke English with a Polish accent all his British life, but his writing is the immigrant's revenge. He does it as well, if not better, than the natives themselves.

# A. E. Coppard (1878–1957)

Although little discussed and read at present, Coppard was an important writer of short stories and highly regarded by some knowledgeable readers. Frank O'Connor devotes a chapter to him in *The Lonely Voice* (1962), and speaks very approvingly of him. "Coppard knew Chekhov and Maupassant backward," he writes,

> but he never settles for one convention rather than the other, or indeed for any convention other than his own need to grip the reader by the lapel and make him listen. As a result his formal range is remarkable – greater I should say than that of any other story teller.
>
> (O'Connor 1965: 173–174)

In an introduction to a collection of Coppard's stories, Doris Lessing writes: "These short stories are as fine as any we have" (Lessing 1972: vii). Major collections include: *Adam and Eve & Pinch Me* (1921), *Clorinda Walks in Heaven* (1922), *The Black Dog* (1923), *Fishmonger's Fiddle* (1925), *The Field of Mustard* (1926), *Silver Circus* (1928), and *Nixey's Harlequin* (1931).

There is, indeed, considerable range in Coppard's fiction. "Fifty Pounds" (1926) is a detailed study of deceit, love, and money, in which Lally's noble gesture is betrayed by her lover, the rather shifty writer Phil. "The Old Venerable" (1926) is a Maupassant-like tale in which an old poacher's dreams of comfort are deliberately ruined by a new and officious gamekeeper. In "The Field of Mustard," two agricultural laborers, Dinah and Rose, both in their forties, rest by a field of mustard while waiting for a companion. They talk of Dinah's sick husband and of children and families. Their lives seem without joy or beauty, and they are aware of that. They start to speak of a

*The British and Irish Short Story Handbook*, First Edition. David Malcolm.
© 2012 David Malcolm. Published 2012 by Blackwell Publishing Ltd.

handsome gamekeeper, and it turns out they both had affairs with him. "We was all cheap to him . . . cheap as old rags," murmurs Rose. But the story ends with some hope. As they return through the wind, Dinah reaches out to Rose, saying "I like you, Rose. I wish you was a man."

Coppard is concerned to capture psychological states – of guilt and outraged respectability in "Nixey's Harlequin" (1931), and erotic bedazzlement in "Dusky Ruth" (1921). One of Coppard's most anthologized stories, "The Higgler" (1925) (discussed in the Key Works chapter of this book) presents a complex study of its protagonist, torn between two women, not sure what choice is in his best interests. But Coppard has other less traditional social-psychological studies, and also stories that breach realist conventions. "Speaking Likenesses" (1937) has four talking pictures and a talking pea plant; "The Green Drake" (1931) has a garrulous duck; and in "Silver Circus" (1928), two men battle each other in a Viennese circus, one in a tiger skin, the other in a lion skin, each convinced that the other is a wild beast.

# Hubert Crackanthorpe (1870–1896)

Although now little discussed and little known, Crackanthorpe was an important short-story writer in the 1890s, and a writer whose work has lasted very well. His life was cosmopolitan, short and colorful, as if he were living out a *fin-de-siècle* cultural model of the bold experimenter, cut down with his promise unfulfilled. Associated with the avant-garde of the 1890s, the periodicals the *Yellow Book* and the *Savoy*, he published two volumes of short stories in his lifetime, *Wreckage: Seven Studies* (1893) and *Sentimental Studies, and A Set of Village Tales* (1895). *Vignettes: A Miniature Journal of Whim and Sentiment*, a collection of prose impressions of people and landscapes in Europe and England, was published before his death in 1896. *Last Studies* was published posthumously in 1897. It contained an "Appreciation" by Henry James.

Crackanthorpe's work was heavily influenced by his reading of French literature, particularly Zola and Maupassant, at least in his choice of subject matter and his unillusioned and at times raw depiction of male–female relations. Crackanthorpe's narrators do not judge but present their often flawed, unrespectable, and self-serving protagonists. He is particularly good in his presentation of female characters, manipulated and used by men ("A Commonplace Chapter" [1895]), but also shows male characters being knocked off balance by the women they court ("In Cumberland" [1895]). He is good at regional stories, too, and pieces like "A Dead Woman" (1893) and "Anthony Garstin's Courtship" (1897), echo Hardy's work and anticipate Lawrence's, both in subject matter and in language. It is tempting, also, to see some stories, for example "Wreckage" (1893), as anticipating Rhys's fictions of the *demi-monde*. James thought highly of Crackanthorpe. In his "Appreciation" of 1897, he writes in mannered but firmly positive language.

*The British and Irish Short Story Handbook*, First Edition. David Malcolm.
© 2012 David Malcolm. Published 2012 by Blackwell Publishing Ltd.

"He [Crackanthorpe] had an almost precocious glimpse of the charm of the technical problem," and his work is "an experiment both modest and resolute . . . of significant examples and distinguished successes" (xvii–xviii). Crackanthorpe is a very powerful short-story writer, and was seen as such in the mid-1890s. He was dead by the age of twenty-six, and one can only speculate what he might have done, had he lived longer. His small body of work certainly deserves to be much better known.

# Walter de la Mare (1873–1956)

Although well-known as a poet, de la Mare's short fiction has been long neglected. Yet he published short stories in journals from 1895 (at first under the pseudonym Walter Ramal). He brought out stories in major periodicals such as *The Cornhill*, *The Pall Mall Gazette*, and *Black and White*. He also began publishing collections of his short stories in 1923 (*The Riddle, and Other Stories*) and continued to do so until the 1950s. He wrote many stories for children, and the two volumes of his adult stories (1996 and 2001) contain over eighty pieces.

De la Mare specializes in stories of the sinister and macabre, often told from a child's point of view. Such is "The Almond Tree" (1909) and most celebratedly "In the Forest" (1904). The latter is a disturbing story of a young boy's amoral cruelty and selfishness, set against a background of adult violence. It is both English and universal, and anticipates some of the horrors of the twentieth century, as much as Wells's *The War of the Worlds* (1898) or Conrad's "Heart of Darkness" (1902) do. It reads like a mixture of Poe and Ian McEwan. The strange atmosphere and part-human characters of "The Creatures" (1920) makes it a very unsettling text, and "An Ideal Craftsman" (1905) is a powerful evocation of nightmare. However, de la Mare had other subjects, and "The Three Friends" (1913) couples comedy and a description of banality with an existential darkness.

*The British and Irish Short Story Handbook*, First Edition. David Malcolm.
© 2012 David Malcolm. Published 2012 by Blackwell Publishing Ltd.

# Hugh Fleetwood (born 1944)

Fleetwood's work is an example of the (to a large extent ignored) strength in depth of the British short story since the Second World War. He is a prolific writer whose work has been published by major presses and respectfully reviewed; yet he certainly counts as a non-canonical novelist and short-story writer. His standing demonstrates the blindness of the canon. Alongside fifteen novels, he has published four volumes of short fiction: *The Beast* (1978), *Fictional Lives* (1980), *A Dance to the Glory of God* (1983), and *The Man Who Went Down with His Ship* (1988). Fleetwood's themes are frequently disturbing – hatred, adultery, deception, and savage physical violence often among the cultured, wealthy, and cosmopolitan in glamorous settings – all recounted in a sophisticated syntax and lexis that match settings and characters and that make the topics all the more disturbing. "The Power of Love?" (from *Fictional Lives*) is a typically dark story of art as revenge. Fran Niebauer, very rich and a patroness of writers, is informed by a protegé, David Chezzel, that he is writing a novel about a rich woman who is being poisoned by her husband. Fran suspects her husband Gerhard of doing just this to her, in order to get her money and live with his French mistress. Fran does indeed fall ill, and the author continues to write her death. Her pains grow worse, but her son Cyrus destroys the manuscript of the novel and she recovers. The writer later declares that he has chosen to love rather than to hate, and has written a story that parallels exactly the action of "The Power of Love?" Fran herself interprets the episode as "a parable of oppression," but is reconciled with the writer.

"The Man Who Went Down with His Ship" (from the collection of the same name) is equally ambiguous and sinister. The Jewish writer, Albert Albers, has survived a shipwreck and, despite the fact that he is rumored to

*The British and Irish Short Story Handbook*, First Edition. David Malcolm.
© 2012 David Malcolm. Published 2012 by Blackwell Publishing Ltd.

have behaved very badly during the incident, has enjoyed a very successful career since then and has been lionized and cosseted by the social and literary world. However, when he makes it known that he is considering telling the truth about the shipwreck, in which he played a heroic role as opposed to the other passengers' rampant cowardice, he is both threatened and ostracized by his former supporters. He must decide whether to tell lies about the night the ship went down or reveal the truth. Like "The Power of Love?", "The Man Who Went Down with His Ship" works within realist conventions, but is a dark fable of human turpitude and bravery. Fleetwood's work is substantial and deserves to be much better known than it is.

# Graham Greene (1904–1991)

Greene may have been disparaging about short fiction and have thought of his short stories as minor appendices to his novels (Greene 1985: 14–15), but he wrote some major short stories during the sixty years of his career. His first adult short story, "The End of the Party" was published in 1929. His *Twenty-One Stories*, containing work from the 1920s through the 1950s, was published in 1954, *A Sense of Reality* in 1963, *May We Borrow Your Husband?* in 1967, and *The Last Word, and Other Stories* in 1990. His short fiction is as wide-ranging as his longer work. "The Destructors" (1954) is disturbing and bitterly comic examination of resentment and violence. "The Blue Film" (1954) is a moving study of loss and a failed marriage. "Across the Bridge" (1938), comically and sadly at the same time, looks at the wasteland of the U.S.-Mexican border and sets up existential and religious echoes in its action. Religious themes also run through "The Hint of an Explanation" (1948) and "A Chance for Mr. Lever" (1936), the latter a dark reworking of the story of colonial adventure. "The Basement Room" (1936) is told from a child's point of view, one who views the adult world and collaborates with it, until he can stand no more and betrays his idol, Baines the butler and murderer. The distinguished film *The Fallen Idol* (1948) was based on this short story. "May We Borrow Your Husband?" (1967) is a thoroughly nasty comedy of sexual manners. "The Lieutenant Died Last: An Unrecorded Victory in 1940" (first published in book form in *The Last Word*) details a German invasion of England, and is the basis for the memorable war-time film *Went the Day Well* (1942). "An Appointment with the General" (1990) sets out a journalist's encounter with a Latin American dictator. The dark humor and ironies of Greene's work may be well represented by "A Shocking Accident" (1967), one of the few short stories in which the protagonist's

*The British and Irish Short Story Handbook*, First Edition. David Malcolm.
© 2012 David Malcolm. Published 2012 by Blackwell Publishing Ltd.

father has met his death by a pig's falling on him from a balcony in Naples. As has been noted above, Greene's short fiction was used to make good films. The outstanding example of this is his short novel, or long short story, *The Third Man* (1949), which derives from the screenplay Greene wrote for one of the great movies of the post-war British cinema, Carol Reed's *The Third Man* (1948).

# Thomas Hardy (1840–1928)

Hardy is most unusual. He is a major novelist and a major poet. *The Mayor of Casterbridge* (1886), *Tess of the d'Urbervilles* (1891), and *Jude the Obscure* (1895) are central to the tradition of the British novel, and Hardy's poetry was greatly admired by Auden and Larkin, and is perhaps among the most influential *œuvres* in twentieth-century British verse. Hardy wrote short stories throughout the first long phase of his career, but his first collection, *Wessex Tales*, dates from 1888. He also published short stories in the collections *A Group of Noble Dames* (1891), and *Life's Little Ironies* (1894). In the mid-1890s he abandoned fiction for poetry, but published a collection of short fiction in 1913 entitled *A Changed Man, and Other Tales* (1913). This volume included stories written between 1881 and 1900.

Hardy wrote stories set in the historical past, often in the early nineteenth century. His favored spatial settings are, as in the novels, the fictionalized Dorset that is his Wessex. Hardy continually attempts to give a circumstantial density to his stories, to record a rural way of life in all its complexities. Often, too, his stories echo folk tales and ballads that would be part of the rural culture of which he writes, and which it is manifestly his intention to record. Dialect is used in direct speech. Story materials are frequently melodramatic and have marked supernatural or Gothic elements. Narration is third-person omniscient. Yet, with his short fiction, Hardy, as with his longer fiction, frequently ran into severe problems because of the controversial and shocking nature of his story materials; sex, adultery, and illegitimacy being still difficult for publishers to swallow. "The Three Strangers" and "The Withered Arm" (both from *Wessex Tales*) are frequently discussed as typical of Hardy's short fiction. The former, set in the early nineteenth-century, is an ironic tale in which three strangers arrive at an isolated cottage: an escaped convict, the

*The British and Irish Short Story Handbook*, First Edition. David Malcolm.
© 2012 David Malcolm. Published 2012 by Blackwell Publishing Ltd.

hangman who is to execute him, and the convict's brother. The first two strangers interrupt a christening party, but it is the second stranger who most disturbs the gathering. The third stranger, the brother, flees on arrival and is arrested, while his sheep-stealing brother escapes.

"The Withered Arm" is a dark and ironic story with supernatural motifs. Gertrude Lodge's withered arm appears to be the unwilled consequence of her husband's lover's unconscious animosity toward her. Rhoda, who has had an illegitimate son by Lodge, does not hate Gertrude, but tries to help her by bringing her to a local folk-healer Conjurer Trendle. He reveals that a hidden enemy has brought about the withered arm, and Rhoda leaves the village sure that Gertrude knows who is responsible for her disfigurement. Some time later, Gertrude tries to cure her withered arm by placing it on the neck of a newly hanged criminal. The executed man turns out to be her husband's illegitimate son. Everyone ends the story unhappily: Gertrude dies; Lodge lives and dies alone; Rhoda ages wretchedly. Even the young man was unlucky to be hanged.

Hardy's short fiction has been criticized for its traditional technique, its motifs of social determinism, its reliance on coincidence, and its melodramatic and predictable story materials (Hunter 2007: 15–19). However, this seems unfair. Hardy was not trying to write modernist enigmas. His traditionality is consistent, and his attempts to celebrate and to preserve the lives and experiences of part of rural England are worthy of considerable respect.

# Henry James (1843–1916)

It is legitimate to discuss James in the context of the British short story. Although he was an American and very much an American writer, he was *also*, like T. S. Eliot, a part of the literary world of Britain in the late nineteenth and early twentieth centuries. He published in Britain and many of his short stories have no American characters at all. In addition, the expansion of short-fiction publishing in Britain in the 1880s and 1890s gave James outlets for his shorter pieces. He was admired by young writers like Crackanthorpe and reciprocated that admiration.

James's fiction, long and short, has been so extensively discussed that it is redundant to add to that impressive body of analysis and interpretation. A few words are, however, in order. As Hunter points out, James was a tireless advocate of short fiction, and, above all, adamant that short stories were not boiled-down novels, but a form that had its own possibilities and challenges (Hunter 2007: 7–8). He published short fiction – in periodicals and in collections – from 1864 onwards, and his total output of short stories is around a hundred titles. "An International Episode" (1878), "Daisy Miller: A Study" (1878), "The Aspern Papers" (1888), "The Real Thing" (1892) "The Altar of the Dead" (1895), "The Beast in the Jungle" (1903), and "The Jolly Corner" (1903) are among the most interesting and sometimes the most challenging short fictions in English. "The Turn of the Screw" (1898) (in which there is not a single American character or setting) is a very disturbing Gothic story, in which the complex narrational organization (a story about someone telling someone else's story, which leaves the reader at three removes from the central events) only adds to the examination of obsession and evil lurking beneath fair surfaces. "The Beast in the Jungle" remains, even after a

*The British and Irish Short Story Handbook*, First Edition. David Malcolm.
© 2012 David Malcolm. Published 2012 by Blackwell Publishing Ltd.

century, a difficult and experimental text, couched in very difficult language, about a life spent (or misspent) waiting for a moment of revelation or purpose.

James's output of short fiction is rich: the international subject matter of European-U.S. relations (never better written of); psychological complexity; a formidable sense of the dark hollows of existence, of the failures and lost chances of love; the excitements of the artistic life (and *mirable dictu* of the scholarly life in "The Aspern Papers"); and a language that is at once serpentine and difficult, and strikingly modern and colloquial. It seems churlish of Americanists not to wish to share him with their British counterparts.

# Gabriel Josipovici (born 1940)

Josipovici is the most widely discussed experimental short-story writer working in Britain. His highly self-referential and auto-thematic texts (advertising their fictionality and addressing issues connected with the production of fictions) bear comparison with contemporary work in the U.S.A. by John Barth, Donald Barthelme, William H. Gass, and John Edgar Wideman. His writing also has affiliations with that of Beckett, the French *nouveau roman*, and other English experimentalists like B. S. Johnson and Christine Brooke-Rose. His short stories have appeared since the early 1970s in four collections: *Mobius the Stripper: Stories and Short Plays* (1974), *Four Stories* (1977), *In A Fertile Land* (1987), and *Steps: Selected Fiction and Drama* (1990). The last volume contains previously published work only. He is an important writer whose work has not had the critical and scholarly reception it deserves. A notable exception is Günther Jarfe's work (Jarfe 2006: 121–127, and Jarfe 2010: 202–212). Generally, Continental European scholars give Josipovici more attention. Hunter does not mention him; Barabara Korte offers an intelligent reading of "Mobius the Stripper" (Korte 2003: 151–158).

Josipovici's short stories deviate decidedly from the norms of realist and non-realist narrative. Character and story material are not clearly set out; there are frequently ellipses and radical disruptions of logical-chronological narrative. The processes and difficulties of creation and writing are foregrounded. "Contiguities" (from *Four Stories*) exemplifies many of the challenges and rewards of Josipovici's fiction. Forty short sections are presented. The reader is asked to work out how to link these and who is involved in the scenes. As in "The Reconstruction" (from *Mobius the Stripper*), a questioning, indeed an interrogation, is taking place. Jarfe argues that the "you" of

*The British and Irish Short Story Handbook*, First Edition. David Malcolm.
© 2012 David Malcolm. Published 2012 by Blackwell Publishing Ltd.

"Contiguities" is a writer figure, barely able to formulate sentences, "who has lost his audience and leads an existence seemingly cut off from society without any assured meaning" (Jarfe 2006: 124).

Josipovici's methods may appear arcane and his concerns obscure. But they are not. Traditional narrative, with its linear development and cohesiveness, does somewhat simplify the confusions and obscurities of reality. How we make sense of the world and try to say what is difficult to say – these are not issues of irrelevance to anyone. In an essay "Egypt and After," Josipovici argues that "Only fiction, in the right hands, can awaken in us the sense of how little we know of ourself and the world, and how intense is our desire to change that condition" (qtd. in Jarfe 2006: 126). Further, Josipovici, born in France and brought up there during the Second World War, and, after that, educated in Cairo, the child of Jewish emigrants/immigrants, often presents foreign protagonists, out of place, questioning and questioned. Stories like "Mobius the Stripper" or "Reconstruction" are not so distant from brute realities as one might think.

# James Joyce (1882–1941)

Joyce is one of the most important short-story writers in English in the twentieth century (and beyond), an un-ignorable presence in British and Irish short fiction. Yet that importance is based on one collection of fifteen stories, *Dubliners*, written before 1906, and rooted deeply in the concerns and methods of late nineteenth-century European realism/naturalism. But Joyce's notion of "epiphany" (see Part 5 Key Works) has proved influential in the writing and interpretation of short fiction in English, in Britain, Ireland, and the U.S.A. (This is striking because, in fact, many short stories do not have much in the way of an epiphany.) Further, the explicitly linked nature of the stories in *Dubliners* is exemplary for that kind of collection, and emphasizes the way in which the context of an individual short story is crucial for its interpretation.

*Dubliners* is a rich and fascinating exposure of the paralysis of late colonial and provincial Dublin. The stories move from stories of childhood through to those with older protagonists. First-person narrations become third-person ones. Characters seem utterly trapped in a constricting world, partly of their own, partly of others' making. The religious lexis that permeates the narrators' language only serves to emphasize the degraded nature of their existence. One of the most anthologized and accessible of the *Dubliners* stories is "Araby." A nameless young boy, the narrator, falls in love with his friend Mangan's sister. He carries his devotion to her, ecstatically and shaped by religious longings, through the coarse vulgarity, cold weather, and dead-end streets of Dublin. He offers to get something for her from an itinerant bazaar, Araby, that is coming to the city. However, he is delayed in reaching the bazaar and when he does get there, he finds it about to close. In the darkness, he recognizes "a silence like that which pervades a church after a

*The British and Irish Short Story Handbook*, First Edition. David Malcolm.
© 2012 David Malcolm. Published 2012 by Blackwell Publishing Ltd.

service." A shop girl flirts in banal fashion with two men with English accents. The narrator leaves the bazaar full of self-contempt. Joyce was concerned that he had misrepresented the citizens of the city that imaginatively he could never leave, but despite the chilly distance to their often banal concerns and failures, the collection as a whole invites compassion and thoughts about the reader's own hemiplegia.

# James Kelman (born 1946)

Kelman is a provacative, politically committed novelist and short-story writer, continually at odds, as he sees it, with the metropolitan, snobby, blinkered, bourgeois literary establishment of Britain. He is part of a group of proletarian Scottish writers from southern Scotland who have – paradoxically, in the light of Kelman's disdain for the prejudices of the contemporary literary world – been very successful in Britain since the 1980s: Alasdair Gray and Irvine Welsh. His short fiction is published in the following major collections: *An Old Pub near the Angel, and Other Stories* (1973) (first published in the U.S.A.), *Not Not While the Giro, and Other Stories* (1983), *Lean Tales* (1985) (written in collaboration with Gray and Agnes Owens), *Greyhound for Breakfast* (1987), *The Burn* (1991), *The Good Times* (1998), and *If It Is Your Life* (2010).

Kelman's subjects are the vicissitudes of working-class life in the late twentieth century, a grim life spent in ill-paid labor or paralyzing unemployment, time passed in repetitive and meandering conversations, in killing time or in loathsome and dangerous work. The landscapes are brutalized urban ones, ugly, hostile, ravaged. The language is often proletarian demotic with a strong southern Scottish flavor. Kelman's aim is to make the lives of the marginal and despised a fit subject for literature, their thoughts, their experiences, their jokes. He tries to speak for his people from the inside. Their language takes over the narration; free indirect and free direct speech are rife; dialogue and monologue outweigh narration. Often stories are very brief, enigmatic fragments of the urban comedy or nightmare. Often they have next to no traditional story material. Often they have the shape of working-class anecdotes. Many of them are deeply moving and very provocative, enigmas that force the reader to reflect. "Acid," from *Not Not*

*The British and Irish Short Story Handbook*, First Edition. David Malcolm.
© 2012 David Malcolm. Published 2012 by Blackwell Publishing Ltd.

*While the Giro*, tells of father's being forced to kill his son, the victim of a dreadful and grotesque industrial accident. "Samaritans," from *Greyhound for Breakfast*, is a *tour-de-force*, laconic, demotic, and enigmatic. Kelman's claims about literature in general are suspect (as his own critical and financial success suggests), but his uncompromising and resourceful insistence on the interest and importance of working-class life, his lack of sentimentality, and his dark vision of a brutalized world, are worthy of great respect. He is not without optimism: Tommy McGoldrick in "Forgetting to Mention Allende" (see the Key Works part of this book) does the best he can under difficult circumstances, keeps on painting his flat, and, after all, knows about Allende and what he stood for.

# Rudyard Kipling (1865–1936)

Kipling published some seventeen collections of short stories between 1885 and 1932. His output of short fiction is over 250 stories. He only wrote two novels (although he wrote a lot of travel writing and history). One of the most remarkable features of his work is its genre range. The largest part of his short fiction works with realist conventions. Social-psychological fiction dominates, but he also wrote a lot of war fiction, historical fiction, stories of colonial adventure, and detective stories. Kipling was also fascinated by non-realist genres: supernatural stories, beast fables, and early science fiction. He even attempted that rarest of twentieth century genres, a utopia ("The Army of a Dream" ([904])). He wrote a great deal for children and young readers.

This genre restlessness is matched by a technical resourcefulness and innovation. Kipling frequently frames his stories so that they are told by narrators who relate others' stories. Thus, there is a distancing and an ambiguity to his texts that critics have not always valued. This is coupled with an increasing inclination to narrative ellipses, to silences that make his texts even more difficult. Further, he is a writer who frequently has his characters and narrators speak non-standard English, either narrators from the Indian sub-continent, or English working-class soldiers and rural laborers.

Kipling is frequently accused of racism, imperialism, and love of war, gratuitous violence, and writing up boring practical jokes, and his non-literary utterances are certainly filled with intemperate utterances on the first four of those. Yet the stories are usually much more complex and nuanced than many critics acknowledge, especially when read in the context of their collection. Any Kipling enthusiast will have a set of favorite stories, but, at his best, Kipling wrote stories that are unrivalled for their technical brio, their

*The British and Irish Short Story Handbook*, First Edition. David Malcolm.
© 2012 David Malcolm. Published 2012 by Blackwell Publishing Ltd.

psychological depth, their imaginative invention, and their fascination with the strange and other. "To Be Filed for Reference" (1888) is a fascinating inverted story of imperial adventure. "Without Benefit of Clergy" (1891) is a moving tale of love across racial lines, and, from the same volume, "The Courting of Dinah Shadd" is a masterpiece of working-class tragedy. "William the Conquerer" (1898) can almost convince the reader that the British Empire was not wholly bad, while "A Sahib's War" (1904) and "Mrs. Bathurst" (1904) are moving psychological studies set against an imperial background. ("Mrs. Bathurst" is celebrated, too, for its narrative enigmas and its early references to cinema.) "A Centurion of the Thirtieth" (1906) and "The Church That Was at Antioch" (1932) are remarkable feats of historical imagination. "Mary Postgate" (1917) and "A Madonna of the Trenches" (1926) are unusual and deeply unheroic – and yet heroic, disturbingly heroic – war stories. "The Wish House" (1926) is the most sinister and poignant of supernatural stories, while "They" (1904) is the best and saddest ghost story in the language. *The Jungle Books* (1894 and 1895) delight readers at all ages. How the same writer produced the utter and boring nastiness of the *Stalky & Co.* stories (1898) must remain a mystery. But in the great stories – "On the City Wall" (1888), or "They," or "The Bull That Thought" (1926) – Kipling is beyond compare.

# Hanif Kureishi (born 1954)

Kureishi is a celebrated novelist (*The Buddha of Suburbia* [1990]) and film scriptwriter (*My Beautiful Laundrette* [1985]). His work, for example *Intimacy* (1998)) has been successfully filmed. Indeed, his work often trans-fers well to other media – film and theater. His three volumes of short stories are *Love in a Blue Time* (1997), *Midnight All Day* (1999), and *The Body* (2002). Especially, *Love in a Blue Time* has provoked considerable critical discussion. Kureishi's *Collected Stories* was published in 2010, and includes hitherto uncollected stories.

Kureishi is a chronicler of inner-city and suburban desolation. His char-acters are often young, of immigrant families, having to deal with the complexities of being Asian-British in the late twentieth century. Kureishi is a specialist, too, in presenting the sexual confusions of late twentieth-century British cities, with gender roles, ethnic identities, and sexual choices in bewildering disarray – all set against vividly captured urban ugliness. Apart from "We're Not Jews," which is discussed in the chapter of this study on Key Works, two stories from *Love in a Blue Time* particularly seize the reader's attention. "My Son the Fanatic," first published in *The New Yorker* in 1994 and filmed in 1998, is a study of a generation clash within an immigrant family in Britain. Parvez is an Indian Muslim from the Punjab. His son Ali, who has grown up in England, is studying to be an accountant. Ali starts to shed all the trappings of his English identity, suits, electronic equipment, music CDs. He even starts to keep his room tidy. Parvez suspects him of taking drugs, but discovers that his son has become a practising Muslim. Parvez is non-religious. He drinks alcohol and eats bacon sandwiches; he has a close friend, Bettina, who is a white prostitute. The generational and cultural gap between father and son erupts in bitterness. Parvez has worked all his life to

*The British and Irish Short Story Handbook*, First Edition. David Malcolm.
© 2012 David Malcolm. Published 2012 by Blackwell Publishing Ltd.

have some kind of decent existence in England. Ali bitterly, and reasonably, condemns Western society; he insults Bettina; Parvez resorts to physical violence. "So who's the fanatic now?" demands Ali.

The complexities of lives lived partly in the Indian sub-continent and partly in England make up the story material of "With Your Tongue Down My Throat." Nina is the daughter of a white English mother and a Pakistani father. Her father is wealthy and well-connected in Pakistan. Although her mother, Deborah, is a school teacher, she and Nina live in a rough housing estate in London. Nina takes drugs, steals, earns money by prostitution, and has had an abortion. Her half-sister, Nadia, visits from Pakistan. Nadia experiences the unsettling desolation of Nina's life. She also seduces Nina's mother's boyfriend, the writer Howard. Nadia's visit to London is paralleled by Nina's visit to Pakistan, which she finds horrifying. Her father's family despise her. She is disturbed by the wealth and evident corruption of her father's associates from the military and business establishment. She finds a companion and sexual companion in Billy, a Canadian–Pakistani youth of her own age, equally displaced. She returns to London. The last section of the story reveals that, in fact, Howard has written this story about Nina, Deborah, and all the rest, based on what Nina has told him, thus raising the issue of the appropriateness of a male writer's assuming a female voice. The revelation also makes his account of Nina's life problematic. Nina visits him, dismisses his fiction – "and no one reads the shit you write anyway except a lot of middle-class wankers" – and heads off majestically in the rain, to Hackney, where Billy, she says, will join her. Howard, the "I" of the final section is left at a loss without Nina, "but the place still smells of her."

Kureishi is an important voice in Anglo–Asian writing in Britain. But, even if Asian themes are prominent in his writing, he also speaks directly to the experiences of the young (and not so young) and displaced and uncertain in Britain's metropolis. After all, *London Kills Me* (1991) is the title of one of his screenplays.

# James Lasdun (born 1958)

Lasdun is a fine poet, an intriguing novelist, and a widely admired short-story writer. His first collection of short fiction, *The Silver Age,* was published in 1985, his second, *Three Evenings, and Other Stories,* in 1992. *The Siege, and Other Stories* was published in 1999, but contains no new stories. "The Siege" was filmed in 1998 by Bernardo Bertolucci as *Besieged.* Lasdun won the National Short Story Award in 2006 for his story "An Anxious Man." This is one of the stories published in his recent collection, *It's Beginning to Hurt* (2009).

Most of the stories in *The Silver Age* involve disturbing and degrading experiences that change the lives of the characters. For example, in "Property" the narrator visits his wealthy grandmother, and watches the old lady being driven into mental confusion and death by packages and messages from a former nurse or servant. Motifs of material excess and decay and narrative enigmas fuse to make this a very unsettling story. "The Siege" is part political fable and part reworking of a classical story of a god's seduction of a beautiful mortal woman. Mr. Kinsky sells all the marvelous artifacts he possesses to win the love of his servant Marietta. He aims to do this by converting his property into cash that will help to free Marietta's husband, who is imprisoned by an unnamed foreign dictatorship. Kinsky (who behaves with considerable refinement throughout) succeeds, and the story ends with Marietta (moved by her employer's devotion and service to her, aware as she is of "the treacherous magnanimity of the powerful") in his bed, and her freed husband at his door.

Lasdun, who lives and works in the U.S.A., has increasingly turned to American subjects in his short fictions, very often reworking the Jamesian topic of the confusions of British-U.S. encounters. These subjects are apparent

*The British and Irish Short Story Handbook*, First Edition. David Malcolm.
© 2012 David Malcolm. Published 2012 by Blackwell Publishing Ltd.

in *Three Evenings, and Other Stories*, and also in *It's Beginning to Hurt*. The prize-winning story, "An Anxious Man", shows Lasdun returning to and developing his work in earlier volumes. The central character, Joseph, whose point of view is used throughout the text, is mesmerized by the privilege, wealth, and amoral selfish power of the confident moneyed elite of the contemporary U.S.A. An inheritance of his wife Elise has allowed her and Joseph to play the stock market, and Joseph is psychologically and emotionally in thrall to its vagaries and to the reports of those vagaries. Although not without skills (he is a successful antique dealer), he is a weak man morally at sea in a world of glitter, power, and unashamed amoral selfishness. When Joseph believes that his daughter has been abducted by rich neighbors, he promises to amend his ways. But when he discovers that his fears are unfounded, the reader sees him once again preparing to listen to a stock market report on the radio. Lasdun's evocation of his central character's shifting feelings about the second gilded age that is early twenty-first-century America is absorbing and provocative. As always, he is a disturbing and ambiguous moralist.

# Mary Lavin (1912–1996)

In her long career, Lavin produced more than one hundred highly-regarded short stories, focusing on the restrictions of mid-century Irish life, very often as they affect women. She was a frequent contributor to *The New Yorker*. Her major collections are: *Tales from Bective Bridge* (1942), *Long Ago, and Other Stories* (1944), *At Sallygap, and Other Stories* (1947) (which reprints texts from the earlier volumes, as well as new stories), *A Single Lady, and Other Stories* (1951), *The Patriot Son, and Other Stories* (1956), *The Great Wave, and Other Stories* (1961), *In the Middle of the Fields, and Other Stories* (1967), *Happiness, and Other Stories* (1969), *A Memory, and Other Stories* 1972), *The Shrine, and Other Stories* (1977), *A Family Likeness, and Other Stories* (1985), and *In a Café* (1995) (which reprints earlier work). In a tribute to Lavin on her death, William Trevor wrote: "Lavin's stories eschew self-importance and that shrillness which is the bane of the form. They are subtle without making a palaver about it, beautifully told, no pat endings, no slickness; and as in life, nothing is resolved" (qtd. in Winston 2006a: 164).

One of the best introductions to Lavin's short stories is Greg Winston's entry in the *Dictionary of Literary Biography* (Malcolm and Malcolm 2006: 151–164). Lavin's fiction returns again and again to the domestic, to marital relations, to personal loneliness, and to tensions and regrets among parents and children. She frequently writes stories with religious and church-related motifs and characters. Her settings are small Irish towns, Bective Bridge for example, or the poorer suburbs of Dublin. Her stories span the twentieth century in time settings. Women's experience predominates, although Lavin also writes of male characters. She rarely writes of Irish politics – although an important exception is "The Patriot Son" (1956).

*The British and Irish Short Story Handbook*, First Edition. David Malcolm.
© 2012 David Malcolm. Published 2012 by Blackwell Publishing Ltd.

But if there is one of Lavin's collections that impresses above all, it is her first, *Tales of Bective Bridge* (discussed in Part 2 of this book). Stories of small-town Irish life interweave with stories such as "The Green Grave and the Black Grave" and "A Fable," that aim for a universality directly. "The Green Grave and the Black Grave" is, in addition, a prose text, the language of which takes on marked poetic features. "At Sallygap" captures the paralysis of mid-century Irish life with complete humanity and sympathy, and "Love Is for Lovers" is a humorous and yet psychologically acute and moving picture of emotional fear and caution. "Brother Boniface" is a fine story of religious vocation. In "Miss Holland," Lavin presents social and emotional alienation as well as Trevor ever does. Lavin has her place among the great Irish short story writers of the twentieth century.

# D. H. Lawrence (1885–1930)

Lawrence, despite the vicissitudes in his reputation, is a great novelist. He is also a substantial poet. He is, however, an unambiguously great short-story writer, of considerable range and technical and topical daring. His short fiction lacks the sometimes dull repetitions and over insistence of his novels. He published his first short story in the *Nottinghamshire Guardian* in 1907, and in his lifetime brought out five collections of short fictions: *The Prussian Officer, and Other Stories* (1914), *England, My England* (1922), *The Lady-bird, The Fox, and The Captain's Doll* (1923), *St Mawr* (1928), and *The Woman Who Rode Away, and Other Stories* (1928). Posthumous volumes of short fiction were also published in the 1930s.

"The Odour of Chrysanthemums" (from *The Prussian Officer*) is one of Lawrence's most anthologized stories. It has story material familiar from Lawrence's novel *Sons and Lovers* (1913). The text centers on the clash of the aspiring working-class Elizabeth Bates (her father is a locomotive driver, an aristocrat of labor) and her husband, who is a mere coal miner, and satisfied to be such. Her house is tidy and clean; she only has two children. Her neighbors have many more children and their houses are untidy. She is a profoundly disappointed woman, first seen in a scrappy garden. Whatever led her to marry Bates (the story is silent on this) has now worn away. Bates regularly drinks away his wages and returns drunk. In the course of the story, she waits for him to return from a shift. He is late; she becomes angry. Then his body is brought back; he has been suffocated in a mining accident. His body, still beautiful, is laid out by his wife and mother. Elizabeth realizes the gap between them, and the dark emptiness of life (this last is a recurrent Lawrentian motif). This story has much that runs through Lawrence's short fiction: a meticulous sense of social class distinctions and their effects on characters; a careful use of

*The British and Irish Short Story Handbook*, First Edition. David Malcolm.
© 2012 David Malcolm. Published 2012 by Blackwell Publishing Ltd.

setting; an ability to capture the movements of human consciousness; and a deep sense of the psychological and emotional disruptions that torment his characters. The language he uses in "The Odour of Chrysanthemums" is simple but eloquent, a language that his characters themselves might, in part, use and understand. This, too, is a feature of many of his short stories.

Dislocation among characters is a recurrent motif in Lawrence's short fiction. In "The Daughters of the Vicar" (*The Prussian Officer*), the Lindleys are separated from the mining community, in which they perforce live, by social class and regional background; Mary needs to find a husband and, for the family's sake, chooses the terrifying Mr. Massy, powerful and domineering despite his diminutive size; Louisa chooses to marry out of her class and takes up with a miner's son, Alfred. But there is no place for them in England; perhaps emigration to Canada will help bring happiness. "The Prussian Officer," a remarkable feat of imagination on Lawrence's part, presents a conflict between an officer and his orderly set in the pre-Great War Imperial German Army. The officer cannot confess his clearly homosexual longing for his servant; the only way he can bridge the institutionalized chasm between them is to torment the orderly mentally and physically. Finally, the young servant is driven to kill his superior, and, fleeing punishment, dies himself.

"Tickets, Please" (which is discussed in Part 5 Key Works) is one of the stories in *England, My England* (1922). It deals with sexual conflict (indeed, rage) and gender roles during the First World War. In the story, young women who feel ill-treated by the lothario of the tram company for which they work, band together to beat the offender. Their act of violence, surprising, still shocking to readers, and very complex, is embedded in the lawless freedoms of wartime. "The Horse-Dealer's Daughter" (from *England, My England*) also shows an independent-spirited female protagonist, Mabel, who rejects the inertia of her brothers and her family's hopeless lot by attempting suicide. She is saved by a young doctor, and, for both, the act of saving her from death by drowning leads to kind of resurrection through mutual passion. Later Lawrence short stories, such as "The Rocking-Horse Winner" and "The Man Who Loved Islands" (both from *The Woman Who Rode Away*), show Lawrence moving beyond the conventions of realism. Both are strongly moral tales. "The Rocking-Horse Winner" is a supernatural story in which a young boy destroys himself for his mother's sake. He can predict racing winners by riding his rocking horse. He rides himself to death to satisfy his mother's insatiable need for money. "The Man Who Loved Islands" is a complex story about human isolation and withdrawal from the world, unsettlingly at the borders of realist text and moral fable.

# Doris Lessing (born 1919)

Lessing's first collection of short stories, *This Was the Old Chief's Country* (1951), contains ten stories set in a lightly fictionalized Southern Rhodesia. She also wrote of Africa in her collection *Five Short Novels* (1953). The subjects of these revisionist stories of colonial adventure are white life in southern Africa, black-white relations, and personal coming of age in a colonial context. Only one of these texts, "Hunger" (1953), is set largely within the black majority population of the colony. Of the African stories (later collected as such in 1964 and 1973), "The Old Chief Mashlanga" is often singled out for commentary, as a complex exposure of the thrills (for the young white protagonist) and deep unexamined injustices of colonial Rhodesia, experienced through the mind of a young female protagonist. The unnamed central white character, however, comes to see the invidious nature of the colonial world. Her attempt to bridge the divisions between white and black cannot succeed, and the story ends with the shameless injustice of white expropriation of black property. Other stories, such as "Winter in July" and "A Home for Highland Cattle," dissect the follies, emptiness, and sadness of the lives of white colonists. Lessing is a didactic writer, and her aim is to expose the wrongness of colonialism in southern Africa. Her didacticism has not gone without criticism (Adams 2008: 441, 446–447).

Didacticism is also part of Lessing's short fiction with English settings. Her task, which she accomplishes with verve, is to dissect and display the consequences of male fear, arrogance, and power in relations with women. *A Man and Two Women* (1963) contains some of the most representative and powerful of such stories, set not just in England, but also in Africa. "To Room Nineteen" shows the increasing emptiness of Susan Rawlings's life in "successful" marriage and parenthood. Simply needing to be alone, she

*The British and Irish Short Story Handbook*, First Edition. David Malcolm.
© 2012 David Malcolm. Published 2012 by Blackwell Publishing Ltd.

begins to rent a hotel room. Her husband assumes she is having affair. She says she is, and kills herself in her room 19. "A Woman on a Roof" depicts the casual sexism of men, a response to women that leaves neither women nor men satisfied. "One Off the Short List" is a damning depiction of pointless philandering by the central male character. In both these last stories, the female characters behave with some independence, especially in the latter.

Lessing is a highly regarded novelist, and won the Nobel Prize for literature in 2007. Her work in science fiction is especially worthy of note: *The Canopus in Argos: Archives* (published between 1979 and 1983). In her *œuvre*, only "Report on the Threatened City" (1972) is a science-fiction short story however. Didactic Lessing may be, but her feminist agenda produces trenchant and memorable fiction, especially in "To Room Nineteen" and "One Off the Short List."

# George Mackay Brown (1921–1996)

"I am not an isolated storyteller writing in the late twentieth century, Mackay Brown wrote of himself in 1975. "I draw from a treasury of narrative written and unwritten out of the islands' past; many voices speak through me; I am part of a tradition" (Mackay Brown 1977: x). The islands are the Orkneys, an archipelago of small islands off the north coast of Scotland, where Mackay Brown spent most of his life. Both where he chose to live and work, and what he chose to write about put Mackay Brown in a marginal position, away from the urban centers of mainland Scotland, positioning himself in an archaic tradition of local story telling that aspires to universal, even "mythic," status.

Mackay Brown produced several notable volumes of short stories, alongside widely admired poetry and novels. His most celebrated volumes include: *A Calendar of Love* (1967), *A Time to Keep, and Other Stories* (1969), and *Hawkfall* (1974). The place settings of his short fiction (like most of his work) are his native Orkneys; the time settings are usually in the past, often the distant past, most notably the period of Viking invasion and settlement of the islands (from the eighth century CE onwards). However, Mackay Brown's stories also go even further back into the Pictish past of the Orkneys, and touch upon more recent, but still hidden, periods in Orcadian history – the time of the Reformation, for example. He also, despite his unhappiness in writing about the present, can in "The Seller of Silk Shirts" (1967) move to more contemporary times. In this story, the narrator and protagonist is a Sikh seller of cloth goods who has penetrated to the far and alien north to find customers.

In an excellent introduction to Mackay Brown's short fiction, Gavin Miller points to ceremony and ritual as being at the heart of Mackay Brown's stories (and, indeed, much of his other work). His characters attempt to find in the

*The British and Irish Short Story Handbook*, First Edition. David Malcolm.
© 2012 David Malcolm. Published 2012 by Blackwell Publishing Ltd.

everyday patterns, symbols, experiences that transcend but incorporate the here and now. He is particularly interested in the cyclic shape of fundamental human experiences and of nature itself (Miller 2008: 472–479). Miller also – surprisingly – relates Mackay Brown's work to that of more urban Scottish writers like George Friel, Alasdair Gray, and James Kelman, in terms of its interest in strangers and newcomers, in its insistence on the importance of the non-metropolitan, and in its championing of a demotic language.

Mackay Brown's stories range widely within the compass of the Orkney Islands, from the Viking period, through the Reformation, to the twentieth century. Perhaps his most fascinating and moving stories are set in times where the historical record is defective. "The Story of Jorkel Hayforks" (1967) is a laconic and at times darkly humorous account of a journey from Bergen to the island of Hoy, in which much goes wrong. "Master Halcrow, Priest" (1967) movingly brings alive the disruption of the Reformation on a local and individual level. The narrator is the elderly Catholic priest of Stromness, who in 1561 finds himself utterly disinherited and displaced by the currents of history for "There is a new kirk in the land." "Witch" (1967) is a searing account of the trial and execution of a young woman in late sixteenth-century Orkney. Mackay Brown's stories are often impressive feats of historical imagination, movingly making the past alive and the effects of history on individuals. The settings may be peripheral (although that term begs questions – peripheral by whose criteria?), but the stories never are. His work is a constant reminder that there is no one Scotland, but many, and that the urban wasteland of Kelman's work is not all there is to say of a culture and a nation.

# Julian Maclaren-Ross (1912–1964)

Maclaren-Ross is a fascinating figure in the history of the British short story. He wrote three considerable volumes of short fiction – *The Stuff to Give the Troops* (1944), *Better Than a Kick in the Pants* (1945), and *The Nine Men of Soho* (1946) – as well as one substantial novel, *Of Love and Hunger* (1947). A volume of miscellaneous prose, *The Funny Bone* (1956), contains several short stories, as well as literary parodies and memoirs. Although his promise was never fulfilled, he was taken very seriously by critics, and especially his war-time stories deserve wider recognition.

Maclaren-Ross's short fiction falls into three main groups: army stories, childhood stories (usually set in the South of France, where Maclaren-Ross did, indeed, spend much of his childhood and youth), and "Soho" stories (largely set in the bohemian milieu of the pubs and clubs in that seedy area of central London). Army stories make up the whole of *The Stuff to Give the Troops*, but Maclaren-Ross returned to wartime subjects in stories in *The Nine Men of Soho* and in *The Funny Bone*. *Better Than a Kick in the Pants* also contains a miscellaneous group of stories that deal with pre-war life: Indian stories and those presenting an existence on the margins of social respectability (and at times outside them). Of this group, "Action Nineteen-Thirty-Eight" is a sobering account of a meeting with two lumpen pre-war British fascists, while "I'm Not Asking You to Buy" offers material about working as a vacuum-cleaner salesman later incorporated in *Of Love and Hunger*. *The Nine Men of Soho* contains one unusual story, a lightly fictionalized account of Maclaren-Ross's father's and mother's lives, entitled "My Father was Born in Havana," a highly innovative condensed family-saga novel, in which copious fabular material is covered breathlessly in thirteen pages.

*The British and Irish Short Story Handbook*, First Edition. David Malcolm.
© 2012 David Malcolm. Published 2012 by Blackwell Publishing Ltd.

Maclaren-Ross's best fiction focuses on life largely among ordinary soldiers in the British Army during the Second World War. The stories are profoundly cynical and funny, yet at times touch on darker notes. Bergonzi writes that Maclaren-Ross "presents the military-medical bureaucracy as something out of Kafka rewritten by the Marx brothers" (Bergonzi 1993: 43). Narrated in a breezy and informal language, texts like "They Put Me in Charge of a Squad" and "They Can Have It" are comic, but "Death of a Comrade" and "The Tape" much less so (all from *The Stuff to Give the Troops*). Among Maclaren-Ross's best stories are two set in pre-war India, "A Bit of a Smash in Madras" and "The Hell of a Time" (both from *Better Than a Kick in the Pants*). These stories reek of authenticity and present the late stages of the Raj in utterly tawdry colors. They are inverted Kipling, all the more remarkable because Maclaren-Ross never visited India.

# Bernard MacLaverty (born 1942)

MacLaverty was born in Belfast in Northern Ireland and lived there until 1975, when he moved to Scotland. He is a widely admired novelist. Among his novels, both *Lamb* (1980) and *Cal* (1983) have been filmed. He has produced five volumes of short stories: *Secrets, and Other Stories* (1977), *A Time to Dance, and Other Stories* (1982), *The Great Profundo, and Other Stories* (1987), *Walking the Dog, and Other Stories* (1994), and *Matters of Life and Death* (2006).

Although Northern Ireland and its troubles are MacLaverty's central topic, he has many stories that are set elsewhere and deal with characters and situations that have nothing to do with the sectarian complexities and violence of Ulster. Many stories are set in Scotland; many involve purely personal encounters untainted by the bitter politics of MacLaverty's native place. He often writes about marginal figures, children, the old, the poor. MacLaverty is particularly given to writing (and writing very well) of women's experiences. He often uses children's perspectives. Both of his early volumes, *Secrets* and *A Time to Dance* open up the dark unhappiness of characters' lives: a son's realization of his father's limits ("The Exercise"), a hidden romance ("Secrets"), and a priest's loneliness ("St. Paul Could Hit the Nail on the Head"). Some stories from *A Time to Dance* stand out from the others. The title story gives a young boy's half-knowing, half-unknowing perspective on his mother's work as a strip-tease dancer. The boy and his mother are Northern Irish immigrants in Scotland, which only adds to their social marginality. "My Dear Palestrina" is a story of a young boy whose musical gifts are encouraged by the mysterious immigrant, Miss Schwartz. Both are outsiders in their world. "The Daily Woman" is a terrible tale of sexual exploitation, loneliness, and sectarian friction in Belfast. *Walking the*

*The British and Irish Short Story Handbook*, First Edition. David Malcolm.
© 2012 David Malcolm. Published 2012 by Blackwell Publishing Ltd.

*Dog* contains some of MacLaverty's best stories about Ulster and its politics. In "Walking the Dog", the protagonist, a Northern Irish everyman, is picked up by a murder team. He does not know whether they are Catholics or Protestants. They do not know which side he belongs to. The story is both comic and terrifying as both sides try to discover who is who. "A Silent Retreat," discussed in the Part 5 Key Works, is a sad evocation of sectarian conflict on a personal level between two young men, a sectarian conflict nuanced by factors of social class, for MacLaverty is always a subtle commentator on the political and psychological cruxes in which his characters find themselves.

# Katherine Mansfield (1888–1923)

Mansfield was the author of five collections of short stories, two of which were published after her death. The volumes published in her lifetime were: *In a German Pension* (1911), *Bliss, and Other Stories* (1920), and *The Garden Party, and Other Stories* (1922). Her husband, John Middleton Murry, supervised the publication of posthumous volumes in 1923 and 1924. Mansfield is a major short-story writer, and her canonical status has been made firm by her position as a woman writer, a colonial writer (she was born in New Zealand and lived there until 1903, leaving the country permanently in 1908), and as a woman with a colorful biography played out against the background of the early twentieth-century cosmopolitan avant-garde.

In *a German Pension* contains a sequence of stories satirizing contemporary German mores, stories from which Mansfield sought to distance herself later in life. *Bliss, and Other Stories* includes the long autobiographical story "Prelude," set in New Zealand, and published separately by the Woolfs in the Hogarth Press in 1917. "*Je ne parle pas français*" was also first published privately, and then in a cut form in *Bliss*. The narrator, Raoul, is a French writer, promiscuous, bisexual, and cynical. The action plays out in the bohemian *demi-monde* of Paris, involves homosexual infatuation, and is centered on tensions between English and French mores. *The Garden Party, and Other Stories* contains some of Mansfield's best-known fictions. "The Daughters of the Late Colonel" is a complex study of the consequences of patriarchy on two middle-aged women, the eponymous daughters of a dominating father. Like many of Mansfield's stories, the story material is limited and the text is an evocation of character, mood, and place. Among Mansfield's most anthologized stories is "The Garden Party," the title story from her 1922 collection. It is an evocation, largely through free indirect and

*The British and Irish Short Story Handbook*, First Edition. David Malcolm.
© 2012 David Malcolm. Published 2012 by Blackwell Publishing Ltd.

free direct speech and thought, of a young girl's consciousness on the splendid sunshiny day of a garden party. In the course of the story she learns of the death of a young man in the poor houses near to her own family's grand home. Her encounter with death – for she visits the man's family with bounty from the garden party – is utterly ambiguous ("'Isn't life,' she stammered, 'isn't life . . . ' "), and, despite its slender frame, leaves the reader to think about the complexities of youth, pleasure, curiosity, idealism, responsibility, death, and social divisions. The ambiguity of experience is central to Mansfield's work, illustrated well by the story "The Stranger" (1922), about as good a study of a complex marriage as one can get, which is discussed in Part 5 Key Works.

# E. A. Markham (1939–2008)

Born on Montserrat in the West Indies, Markham came to Britain in 1956, and from the 1970s established himself as a major British short-story writer. He also published poetry under pseudonyms (including that of an invented white Welsh woman writer, Sally Goodman). His collections of short fiction include: *Something Unusual* (1986), *Ten Stories* (1994), and *Taking the Drawing Room through Customs* (2002). The last volume includes both new and previously published fictions. In his thorough introduction to Markham's work, Greg Winston writes that "recurrent themes emerge in his fiction, ranging from black male identity, transatlantic migration, family dynamics, and island boyhood, to meditations on contemporary international travel, romantic relationships, and the pressures of being a writer" (Winston 2006 b: 200).

However, West Indian experiences and immigrant experiences and their complexities are Markham's subject to which he returns in all his collections of short stories. The much anthologized "Mammie's Form at the Post Office," from *Something Unusual*, recounts a West Indian woman's unsuccessful attempt to remit money to the West Indies, a story that tellingly examines race relations and the psychological legacy of empire in modern Britain. "Now What Was That All About?" is a remarkable story in which a white woman takes a kind of revenge on an immigrant man (his origin is uncertain) for his sexist attitudes. The story becomes a complex and disturbing examination of gender and racial roles. *Ten Stories* contains some of Markham's most ambitious fictions. "NJK Holt" is a scrutiny of black male identity. "A Short History of St. Caesare" offers a history of an invented Caribbean island, an elaborate hoax in the story, but one that allows Markham to examine both colonial history and the power of fictions, and the relationship of the two.

*The British and Irish Short Story Handbook*, First Edition. David Malcolm.
© 2012 David Malcolm. Published 2012 by Blackwell Publishing Ltd.

"Life before the Revolution" is set among West Indian immigrants to Britain, and presents their memories, their complex attitudes to Britain, and one character's experience of a return to the Caribbean.

Markham also played an important role in bringing Caribbean short fiction to a world audience. He edited *The Penguin Book of Caribbean Short Stories* in 1996.

# W. Somerset Maugham (1874–1965)

Maugham was a very successful novelist and playwright, as well as one of the most important, prolific, and well-paid British writers of short fiction in the twentieth century. A much-traveled man, his stories frequently have non-British, exotic settings, and he can be seen as major reviser of the tradition of the story of colonial adventure. His espionage short fiction, the *Ashenden* stories of 1928, has proved very influential in the development of an important twentieth-century genre. But Maugham's reputation has not lasted, and negative commentary is now common (Malcolm 2008: 227–228). He has lost the canonical status he once had. Maugham's own bluff disdain of innovative fiction probably has something to do with the decline of his literary standing. Stanley Archer writes of Maugham's short fiction that "his astonishing popularity and success, along with his tendency to deprecate his stories as commercial, combined to produce a largely negative reaction from serious critics" (Archer 1993: xi). The same critic adds, nonetheless, that "an examination of his [Maugham's] stories reveals that his own narrative techniques are not always so simple and straightforward as he claims" (9). Even if many are conservative in technique, Maugham's stories are bleak and cynical exposures of human greed and hypocrisy. Maugham's view of the world is without illusions and at its center dark indeed. The volumes of short stories are: *Orientations* (1899), *The Trembling of a Leaf* (1921), *The Casuarina Tree* (1926), *Ashenden* (1928), *Six Stories in the First Person Singular* (1931), *Ah King* (1933), *Cosmopolitans* (1936), *The Mixture As Before* (1940), and *Creatures of Circumstance* (1947). But omnibus collections of Maugham's short fiction have had a long and successful publishing life since 1947.

*The British and Irish Short Story Handbook*, First Edition. David Malcolm.
© 2012 David Malcolm. Published 2012 by Blackwell Publishing Ltd.

"Rain," from *The Trembling Leaf,* is one of Maugham's most successful and typical fictions. Archer calculates that Maugham made around a million dollars from the story; from the text itself, and from its dramatized version and three film versions (3). The story is a lurid one. It is about the tensions among a group of white European and American travelers unable to leave a Pacific island, a U.S. colony, for two weeks during the rainy season. The unremitting rain adds to the unpleasant pressures of the situation. The story is told largely from the point of view of Dr. Macphail, a veteran of the Great War, on his way to a posting on another Pacific island. On board ship and later in Pago-Pago, he and his wife fall in with zealous American missionaries, the Davidsons. Mr. Davidson takes exception to the behavior of an American prostitute, stranded like them. He attempts to change her ways and when that meets with derision, through social and legal pressures he brings her to submission. However, in the end, he is seduced by her, or has lusted after her all along (it is not clear), and commits a grotesque suicide. Sadie, the prostitute, is triumphant and contemptuous. All men are "filthy, dirty pigs! ... Pigs! Pigs!" she cries in scorn. This story deserves serious revaluation. It is a powerful indictment of a colonial mentality, of religious zeal, and of the hypocrisies of the respectable. The Davidsons' missionary ardor and their institutional power are presented as disturbingly oppressive. But the text is complex in its treatment of its characters. Davidson has a kind of impressive vigor despite his terrifying self-confidence. Macphail may disdain his companion and his actions, but cannot do anything against him, or lacks the will to do so. Sadie is an outrageous hussy, and sin is painted in very unsavory colors (including a passage directly from the narrator about the red light district of Honolulu). The story is dark and, ultimately, dispiriting.

Maugham's *Ashenden* stories are equally somber. The work of a spy is drab. There is much waiting and shabby manipulation of others. Settings are unglamorous and populated by dingy characters. The protagonist himself has no illusions about what he is doing and, indeed, considerable sympathy with his enemies. There is betrayal, deception, blackmail, and broken lives. The wrong man is killed. These astringent stories deserve wide readership and discussion, just as Maugham's short fiction as a whole deserves wider recognition, and not just for its literary-historical importance.

# Ian McEwan (born 1948)

McEwan is one of the most important contemporary novelists in Britain. However, his career began with two volumes of short stories, much praised and the cause of much controversy. These are *First Love, Last Rites* (1975) and *In Between the Sheets* (1978). The stories in these volumes were widely commented on at the time of their publication for their gruesome and macabre story materials, touching upon taboo subjects with a gusto that many reviewers and readers found distasteful, but others saw as robustly fresh. *First Love, Last Rites* stakes out the terrain for McEwan's short fiction (and for some of his novels too). "Homemade" is narrated by a young, very articulate and sex-obsessed boy who persuades his younger sister to have sexual intercourse with him. "Butterflies" is told by a child molester and murderer. "Disguises" is a tale of child transvestism. *In Between the Sheets* maintains the earlier collection's interest in the taboo. In "Pornography," there is sexual exploitation, the careless spreading of venereal disease, and the protagonist's willing acquiescence in the excision of his penis by his irate girlfriends. "Reflections of a Kept Ape" involves species miscegenation. In "Dead As They Come," the narrator falls in love with a shop-window mannequin and lavishes care and affection on it until he is sure that his beloved is betraying him with the chauffeur, whereupon he feels compelled to kill her.

The last story indicates the serious purpose underlying McEwan's unsavory subjects. "Dead As They Come" is a striking and darkly comic exposure of male desires for and attitudes toward women, as is "Pornography." "Homemade" and "Butterflies" explore disturbing psychological territories. The brouhaha concerning McEwan's short fiction should not obscure, however, the fact that many stories have much less controversial subject

*The British and Irish Short Story Handbook*, First Edition. David Malcolm.
© 2012 David Malcolm. Published 2012 by Blackwell Publishing Ltd.

matters, and that technically McEwan mostly stays within the conventions of realist fiction, and has a firmly psychological-social focus on character and action.

McEwan may be seen as a short-story writer *manqué*. His first two novels, *The Cement Garden* (1978) and *The Comfort of Strangers* (1981), are very short novels. Further, throughout McEwan's novels one often has a sense of discrete episodes that would make fine free-standing short stories (Malcolm 2002: 17–19). The dismemberment of Otto's body in *The Innocent* (1990) and June's climactic encounter with the dogs in *Black Dogs* (1992) are cases in point. In fact, McEwan returned to short fiction in the children's stories of *The Daydreamer* (1994), and a recent novel, *On Chesil Beach* (2007), seems like an expanded short story.

# John McGahern (1934–2006)

McGahern was one of the greatest and most respected of twentieth-century Irish novelists, although his career was not without controversy, and his second novel *The Dark* (1965) was banned in the Irish Republic and its author effectively forced into exile in Britain and the U.S.A. for several years. However, *The Barracks* (1963), a story of a woman's dying in rural Ireland, is one of the finest novels in English, while *Amongst Women* (1990) has persistently been seen in Ireland as one of the novels that best handles common Irish experience in the mid-twentieth century (Maher 2003: 117). McGahern was also a dedicated writer of short stories. His three collections are *Nightlines* (1970), *Getting Through* (1978), and *High Ground* (1985). *Collected Stories* (1992) contains one major new story, "The Country Funeral."

The stories in *Nightlines* are set in the 1950s and 1960s, mostly in rural Ireland. The stories together aim at a universality as, like those in Joyce's *Dubliners*, they cover childhood, adolescent, and adult experience. Family conflicts are rife, sexual initiation and adult sexuality are disturbing and cheerless, and life for adults and children alike seems poisoned by paralysis and disappointment. When stories move outside Ireland – to London in "Hearts of Oaks, Bellies of Brass" or to Franco's Spain in "Peaches" – things are no better. One of the most celebrated stories from *Nightlines* is "Korea," an initiation story in which a young man becomes convinced that his father wishes him to emigrate to the U.S.A. so that he may be drafted and killed in Korea, and thus his parents will receive compensation from the U.S. government. *Getting Through*, as the collection's title suggests, indicates that human life will be largely unsuccessful and the best we can do is somehow make it to the end. "Swallows" and "The Wine Breath" are two remarkable

*The British and Irish Short Story Handbook*, First Edition. David Malcolm.
© 2012 David Malcolm. Published 2012 by Blackwell Publishing Ltd.

stories of passing time, mistaken but perhaps unavoidable choices, and failure. In *High Ground*, McGahern expands his range. "Oldfashioned," "Eddie Mac," and "The Conversion of William Kirkwood" are outstanding for their historical sweep and for their attempt to consider the experiences of Protestants in a post-1922 independent Ireland. Not all McGahern's short fiction is bleak. Just as his last novel, *That They May Face the Rising Sun* (2002), is a meticulous and affectionate examination of the strengths as well as the failings of a small Irish rural town, so "The Country Funeral" is a complex meditation on the relationship of rural and urban Ireland in the late twentieth century.

McGahern is usually seen as a committed realist, and while this is true, the language of his fiction, short and long, often has highly self-referential features and comes close to the language of poetry. In addition, his created worlds, for all their verisimilitude and documented places, eerily echo the paralyses and despairs of Beckett's fictional universe.

# Michael Moorcock (born 1939)

Moorcock is a very influential editor (*inter alia* of the science-fiction magazine *New Worlds* from 1964 to 1971, and from 1976 to 1996) and one of the most prolific and varied writers working in Britain. His stories and novels belong to a wide range of genres: science fiction, heroic fantasy, dystopia, detective fiction, espionage fiction, historical fiction, and (not least) social-psychological fiction. His "mainstream" fiction – novels like *Byzantium Endures* (1981), *The Brothel in Rosenstrasse* (1982), and *Mother London* (1988) – is ambitious and worthy of respect. Parts of his output are satiric attacks on political and social duplicity, hypocrisy, and greed. His work can be comic. As a whole, it builds into a vast self-referential whole, parading the powers and the possibilities of fiction.

Mitchell Lewis identifies "three key elements that inform" much of Moorcock's short fiction from the early 1960s. These are the figure of the Eternal Champion, the Battle between Law and Chaos, in which he participates, and the multiverse: "Moorcock's nonlinear fictional world of infinite, simultaneously existing, often interconnecting universes" (Lewis 2006: 249). Certainly, Moorcock's stories build into cycles involving a number of central characters: the stalwart warrior Eric of Melniboné, the secret agent Jerry Cornelius, the languid immortals of the End of Time sequence of stories, and the von Bek family and all their busy cosmopolitan descendants.

The variety and quantity of Moorcock's work makes it very difficult to sum up. It is impossible here to list even his major collections of short fiction, and for a full bibliography (and trenchant discussion), the reader is referred to Lewis's introduction to his work (Lewis 2006: 245–256). *Earl Aubec, and Other Stories* (1993) also offers an accessible introduction to

*The British and Irish Short Story Handbook*, First Edition. David Malcolm.
© 2012 David Malcolm. Published 2012 by Blackwell Publishing Ltd.

the variety of Moorcock's short fiction, with a robustly revealing preface from the author. Moorcock's short fiction fascinates by its sheer bravura, its inventiveness, and, indeed, its serious purposes. He has never received the close critical attention of his contemporary J. G. Ballard, but he deserves it.

# H. H. Munro ("Saki") (1870–1916)

Munro worked in a Wildean tradition of witty and urbane stories about the upper echelons of society, but combined this in many texts with a widespread use of supernatural motifs and motifs of extreme cruelty and violence, the latter all the more sinister for the unemotional reporting of deeds of unusual savagery. He is one of the funniest of British short-story writers, but his is a humor, often quite beyond the limits of good taste, that makes one uneasy and prompts reflection on human callousness.

Munro is best known for his short-fiction collections, *Reginald* (1904), *Reginald in Russia* (1910), *The Chronicles of Clovis* (1911), and *Beasts and Super-Beasts* (1914), but he also published novels, including *When William Came: A Story of London under the Hohenzollerns* (1913), which imagines Britain under German occupation. He was also a much-traveled and experienced foreign correspondent. The Reginald stories are slim satires on contemporary social life, centered on the amoral, cynical, and dandyish Reginald, full of Wildean *bons mots* and paradoxes. "To have reached thirty ... is to have failed in life," Reginald wearily opines ("Reginald on the Academy").

*Reginald in Russia* includes the first of Munro's sinister supernatural tales, "Gabriel-Ernest," a tale of lycanthropy. Like several of Munro's supernatural stories, the central motif is one of transformation, here of boy into wolf. There is a clear suggestion in such stories of a savagery underlying polite exteriors, a suggestion that is made clear in the case of "The Unrest-Cure" (*The Chronicles of Clovis*), in which a proposed massacre of local Jews is part of a trick played on the staid Huddles. Munro's humor often has a biting and eerily prophetic edge, as in the Baroness's *sang-froid* when she reflects on an escaped hyena's devouring of a gypsy child ("Esmé" [*The Chronicles of Clovis*]).

*The British and Irish Short Story Handbook*, First Edition. David Malcolm.
© 2012 David Malcolm. Published 2012 by Blackwell Publishing Ltd.

Domineering women are often the victims of cruel vengeance, as in "Sredni Vashtar," "The Music on the Hill" (both from *the Chronicles of Clovis*), and "The Lumber Room" (from *Beasts and Super-Beasts*). "Sredni Vashtar" is discussed in Part 5 Key Works. However, women are also very forceful and admired figures in many of Munro's texts (the Baroness in "Esmé," for example). Indeed, one of Munro's funniest stories is "The Open Window," in which an imaginative young girl terrifies a male guest with her consummate story-telling ability, a story in which Munro reflects on his own cruel, resourceful, and necessary art.

# Frank O'Connor (1903–1966)

Frank O'Connor was the pseudonym of Michael Francis O'Donovan. As O'Connor, he became one of the most influential writers of post-independence Ireland. He fought both in the war against the British (1919–1922), and then, on the anti-Treaty side, in the Irish Civil War (1922–1923). Besides his fiction, he published English translations of poetry in Irish, and a biography of the Irish guerrilla leader Michael Collins. Productive and often at odds with the authorities in the Irish Free State and the Irish Republic, he frequently published his work in Britain and the U.S.A., and had a twenty-year long relationship with *The New Yorker* from 1945 to his death. From 1952, he taught at a series of prestigious U.S. universities. His *The Lonely Voice: A Study of the Short Story* (1962), with its argument that the short story flourishes in unstable societies, on borderlands, giving voice to "submerged population groups" (O'Connor 1965: 18–19) – an argument that is both right and wrong simultaneously – has long been an important piece of generalized reflection on short fiction.

He published his first fiction in the 1920s, and his first collection *Guests of the Nation* was published in 1931. Other major collections include *Bones of Contention* (1936), *Crab Apple Jelly* (1944), *Traveller's Samples* (1951), and *The Stories of Frank O'Connor* (1952). The *Collected Stories* (1981) does not contain all his short fiction, but does offer a solid *œuvre* of 67 fictions. O'Connor is best known for his tales of small-town Irish life, very often seen from a child's point of view. Although he was far from blind to the constrictions of Irish life in the first decades after independence, his stories lack the dark savagery of O'Faoláin's and McGahern's work. Stories like "The Majesty of the Law" (1936), "First Confession" (1951), and "The Long Road to Unmera" (1944) seem to play too much to Irishry stereotypes. "The

*The British and Irish Short Story Handbook*, First Edition. David Malcolm.
© 2012 David Malcolm. Published 2012 by Blackwell Publishing Ltd.

Shepherds" (1944), "A Story by Maupassant" (first published in book form in 1969), and "The American Wife" (first published in book form in 1969), however, are as good an evocation of mid-century Irish malaise as any written, and "My Oedipus Complex" (1952) is a surprisingly astringent study of father-son relations. But it is to the harsh vision of "Guests of the Nation" that many readers return. Here O'Connor is at his best, as in the political and historical ambiguities of "Eternal Triangle" (1951).

# Seán O'Faoláin (1900–1991)

Seán O'Faoláin was born John Francis Whelan and adopted the name O'Faoláin as an act of political and cultural self-identification. Like O'Connor, he fought in the war against the British (1919–1922) and, on the anti-Treaty side, in the Irish Civil War (1922–1923). He was a novelist and the founder and first editor (from 1940 to 1946) of the journal *The Bell*, which continually questioned and challenged what O'Faoláin saw as the neutral Irish Republic's cultural and mental parochialism and its insulation from the struggle against Fascism in Europe. In his long career, he published seven volumes of new stories. These include: *Midsummer Night Madness, and Other Stories* (1932), *A Purse of Coppers* (1937), *Teresa, and Other Stories* (1947), *I Remember! I Remember!* (1962), *The Heat of the Sun* (1966), and *Foreign Affairs, and Other Stories* (1976).

O'Faoláin's collection of war stories, *Midsummer Night Madness*, is an extraordinary gathering of disillusioned, unheroic fictions. The struggle against the British for Irish freedom is seen in a thoroughly unglamorous light, and the Civil War (in "The Patriot") as a matter of shabby uniforms, hiding and freezing in bleak landscapes, officer incompetence, and humiliating surrender on the anti-Treaty side. The collection was banned in the Irish Free State. A disappointed, if comic, questioning of independent Ireland and its institutions continues in stories such as "A Broken World" (1937) and "The Man Who Invented Sin" (1947). "The Sugawn Chair" (1962) captures in one brief domestic action the central transition in twentieth-century Irish experience from country to city, with its attendant gains and losses. "Lovers of the Lake" (1957) and "The Faithless Wife" (1976) are humane examinations of human love and sexual feelings against the conservative background of mid-century Ireland. "The Heat of the Sun" is a dark tale of

*The British and Irish Short Story Handbook*, First Edition. David Malcolm.
© 2012 David Malcolm. Published 2012 by Blackwell Publishing Ltd.

transience and inertia. O'Faoláin could hit surprisingly dark notes in his work, for example in the disturbing "I Remember! I Remember!"' His is a powerful, original, and brave voice in mid-century Irish writing. His example and his work help to make the even bleaker, although not braver, short stories of John McGahern possible.

# Mollie Panter-Downes (1906–1997)

Panter-Downes was one of those privileged British and Irish authors who had a "First Reading Agreement" with *The New Yorker*, which meant that the U.S. magazine had first option on anything she wrote. This entailed regular and good fees and a very large audience. Between 1938 and 1987, Panter-Downes wrote extensively for *The New Yorker*, writing a weekly 'Letter from London' from 1939 to 1984. She published thirty-six short stories in the magazine, mostly during the Second World War. They were not reprinted until Gregory LeStage's collection *Good Evening, Mrs. Craven: The War Stories of Mollie Panter-Downes* was published by Persephone Books in London in 1999. Panter-Downes published novels before and after the war, but it is her short fiction from the war years that has started to engage critics' attention. She is still, however, an unjustly unknown author of some of the most interesting British fiction of the Second World War.

Panter-Downes's subject is the home-front, a place of social and personal change and danger. Although her stories are quite different, in language and in their firm adherence to realist conventions, from those of Elizabeth Bowen, the same sense of dislocation and unease is apparent in both writers' fictions about the war years. "Fin de Siècle" (1941), for example, depicts the changes wrought by the war on a couple; artists and pacifists before its outbreak, now altogether more conformist and conservative, and also happy that Ernestine, now that Don is in the Army, can draw her wife's allowance every week. The stories are complex studies of psychology and material circumstances in wartime. The characters are mostly middle-class or upper middle-class (very different people from Maclaren-Ross's other ranks), but that makes their experiences no less interesting, nor, in many cases, less moving. "Good Evening, Mrs. Craven" (1942) is a study of the despair of a woman, uncertain

*The British and Irish Short Story Handbook*, First Edition. David Malcolm.
© 2012 David Malcolm. Published 2012 by Blackwell Publishing Ltd.

about what has happened to her married lover. How can she find out about him? "The War Office doesn't have a service for sending telegrams to mistresses, does it?" she attempts to joke. In "The Hunger of Miss Burton" (1943), the protagonist, a French teacher at a private boys' school, simply feels hungry – for decent food, for chocolate, for her dead pre-war German lover, for some warmth and escape from the drab hardships of the time. In "The Danger" (1944), the middle-class Mrs. Dudley has had enough of the colorful and raucous working-class evacuees billeted on her, so that once they are gone, she lies to a family friend who wishes to move in with her to be close to her soldier husband. Mrs. Dudley (understandably) just wants her home to herself, but her action brings her no happiness. Some of Panter-Downes's main characters are men, also on the home front, and in the case of Mark Goring in "Year of Decision" (1944) bemused that he is having a good war, while others he knows have been killed. The title of one of Panter-Downes's last war stories, "The Waste of It All" (1944), says it all.

# T. F. Powys (1875–1953)

The author of the highly regarded novel *Mr. Weston's Good Wine* (1927), Powys wrote some 150 short stories from around 1910 through to the 1930s. His first collection was *The House with the Echo* (1928), and other collections include *Fables* (1929), *No Painted Plumage* (1934), and *Bottle's Path, and Other Stories* (1946). An anthology of his stories, *God's Eyes A-Twinkle*, was published in 1947.

Powys's stories are different from most British short fiction in the twentieth century. They are moral and religious fables, although morals are lacking and any conclusions are enigmatic. The settings are rural, but Norman Nicholson described them as a "nightmare landscape halfway between Bedlam and Hell" (qtd. in Orlet 1996: 309). "These stories treat of the general and unalterable," writes Charles Prentice in a preface to *God's Eyes A-Twinkle*. Earlier he notes that "It would be a mistake to attribute to Powys any systematic theory, either theological or metaphysical," but he emphasizes the religious and metaphysical topics and, above all, the ethical and philosophical "antimonies" that organize his short stories (Prentice 1947: xv, xii–xiii).

"Mr. Pim and the Holy Crumb" (from *No Painted Plumage*) shows Powys's short fiction at its enigmatic and fabular best. Mr. Pim, a holy fool, an innocent, who although he has worked as church clerk has never heard of transubstantiation and never taken the sacrament, finally learns "the tale of the holy feast." This, however, unleashes a set of coherent but strange occurrences. Mr. Pim seeks "to confer" with a snowflake, but cannot for it has melted. He then proceeds to talk over matters with a dead friend, a suicide, who lies in the churchyard, and who asks Mr. Pim to talk to the bread that is the body of the Lord, and ask that he be left alone on the Day of

*The British and Irish Short Story Handbook*, First Edition. David Malcolm.
© 2012 David Malcolm. Published 2012 by Blackwell Publishing Ltd.

Judgment and not raised from the dead. Mr. Pim accordingly addresses a crumb of the host that has fallen on the church floor, asking that he, too, may be allowed to rest in the earth on the last day. The crumb, of course, answers. Surprised by Pim's request, it urges him and his friend to reconsider, because "I had hoped you would have wished to dwell with me, for, to tell you a truth, I made heaven glorious for you and for John Toole." Mr. Pim urges God to join him and his friend in the earth, whereupon the holy crumb declares, "Mr. Pim, Mr. Pim, you are exactly what I meant myself to be. When I consider the troubles I have caused... I almost wish I had entered into a mouse instead of a man." A church mouse creeps from beneath the altar and eats the crumb. The story has a wonderful freedom of action and an enigmatic lucidity. Mr. Pim sensibly worries about the implications of the doctrine of transubstantiation. His concerns about heaven and the end of things are germane. His innocence has all the wise and perceptive simplicity of holy fools in many cultures. Powys is an original in the history of the British short story, resolutely resisting in his own manner the blandishments of realism, as much as Ballard and Moorcock do. Powys's only fellows in their fabular ambitions are, surprisingly, Kipling and Angela Carter.

# V. S. Pritchett (1900–1997)

It is one of the scandals of the canon of British literature that it finds so little space for the work of V. S. Pritchett. Even an otherwise excellent book, Andrew Maunder's *Companion to the British Short Story*, gives Pritchett a very brief entry, and there is no extended discussion of his stories. Yet Pritchett's *Complete Short Stories* (1990) contains over eighty fictions. He published eleven collections of short fiction between 1938 and 1989. Perhaps Pritchett's relative neglect is evidence of the disdain in which the short story, the form that he devoted himself to throughout a long career, has been held by British critics and scholars in the second half of the twentieth century. Andrzej Gąsiorek writes of Pritchett that "it is impossible in a short space to do justice to Pritchett's gifts as a writer of stories. . . . they range widely in theme and technique. But his greatest contribution . . . surely lies in his even-handed representation of ordinary people in all their glorious multiplicity" (Gąsiorek 2008: 429).

This is an acute observation. His characters are usually the relatively humble, working-class, but above all lower-middle-class. They live and work in the unglamorous districts of London and its environs. But their lives, like those of Kelman's Scottish proletarians, are presented with insight and sympathy. Their voices and their experiences fascinate. "Sense of Humour," from Pritchett's first collection *You Make Your Own Life* (1938), establishes many of the features of the Pritchettian created world. It is narrated, in a racy and demotic 1930s idiom, by Arthur Humphrey, an astute and successful traveling salesman. The settings are provincial towns and pre-war highways. The son of an undertaker, Humphrey is doing very well, drives a company car, and has lots of samples. He takes up with the receptionist at the hotel where he sometimes stays. Unfortunately, she has a boyfriend already, the rather

*The British and Irish Short Story Handbook*, First Edition. David Malcolm.
© 2012 David Malcolm. Published 2012 by Blackwell Publishing Ltd.

moony Colin, who takes to following Humphrey and Muriel around on his motorbike. A climax of the story comes when Colin is killed in an accident near Arthur's home. He and Muriel drive the corpse back in one of Arthur's father's hearses. As they return, all three together, bystanders take off their hats in respect. "It's like being the King and Queen," Muriel laughs.

Characters and settings are unglamorous, without even the literary attraction of being poor. Humphrey and Muriel are both sensible and materialistically aware of their own interests. The language of dialogue and narration are theirs. Yet, the text touches on psychological complexities. Humphrey clearly loves Muriel. He both despises and feels sorry for Colin, and, in fact, puts business his way. Muriel needs to get away from town, hotel, and boyfriend, but when Colin dies she is genuinely upset. She and Humphrey have sex together only in the immediate aftermath of the accident. The story is also comic. Colin's constant following of the couple, yet claiming they are following him, is funny. Arthur's father is comically *distrait*. The trip back in a hearse through small 1930s ribbon-development towns, the lovers side by side in front of Colin's coffin, is darkly hilarious. Yet Humphrey also has a peculiar respect for Colin, especially dead, and pride in Muriel. He is also, the while, thinking of the cost of railway fares and his savings, and whether Muriel might be pregnant.

"You Make Your Own Life" (1938) is a miniature masterpiece of sinister ambiguity. The setting is a barber shop in a boring provincial town somewhere in the south of England. "It was a small town in a valley with one long street, and a slow mud-coloured river moving between willows and the backs of houses." The narrator has to wait for his haircut; the barber has another customer. The customer is well-dressed, almost dandyish for that town, and darkly handsome; the barber is pale and balding. The customer does not pay for his shave and shampoo. While he is cutting the narrator's hair, the barber tells slowly, in short bursts, the customer's story. He is consumptive and once fell in love with the barber's girlfriend. He tried to win her, but without success. Indeed, jealous, he tried to poison the barber once, and attempted to gain the young woman's affection by cutting his throat. However, the barber got the girl, and now the customer comes over to play with their children. Despite all his successes, the customer has no steady girlfriend and after his suicide attempt does not care to shave himself. "I never charge him," says the amused barber.

Once again the circumstances are unglamorous. The barber's story is punctuated with his actions as he cuts the narrator's hair. But the story is one of lurid passion. It is also uncorroborated, just a story that might or might not be true. The saturnine customer seems healthy, successful, and well satisfied with himself. The barber is "a dull young man with pale blue eyes and a look of ironical stubbornness in him." His smile is "like claw marks at the corners of his lips." The story's excellence lies in its reticence. True? Partly true? Compensation for the barber's own inadequacy and failure? The reader can only speculate. But under the drab provincial lower-middle-class surface, there is passion and complexity enough.

# Jean Rhys (1890–1979)

By the end of her life, Rhys was widely recognized as a major writer, but, for a substantial part of that life, she vanished from public and critical view. Nevertheless, her work in the novel – *Voyage in the Dark* (1934) and *Wide Sargasso Sea* (1966) – is now highly regarded. Her short story collections have also received critical attention: *The Left Bank, and Other Stories* (1927), *Tigers Are Better Looking* (1968), and *Sleep It Off, Lady* (1976).

*The Left Bank, and Other Stories* focuses on life in Paris after the First World War, very often among women who inhabit a *demi-monde* of modeling and semi-prostitution. Settings are urban. Story materials are attenuated. Narrators and central characters are usually female. The language is often informal, and sentences are short, frequently sentence fragments. The impression is of a language of intense subjectivity, and one appropriate to the characters involved in the texts. (Later, in "Let Them Call It Jazz" (1968), Rhys attempts, with success, black West Indian English.) Narrational technique is often first-person or is that of limited omniscience with a particular point of view. These features of Rhys's fiction, present in *The Left Bank* stories, are constant throughout her later novels and short fictions, although she does have some male narrators (in "In the Luxemburg Gardens" [1927] for example).

Rhys's aim is to give voice to outsiders, figures peripheral to, disdained by, and often exploited by, good society: call girls, models, mistresses, the old, immigrants, ghosts. In "Hunger" (1927) a hard-up woman talks of the experience of not eating anything for five days. "Vienne" (1927) is narrated by a woman riding high, temporarily and precariously, on a wave of post-war money in a poverty-stricken central Europe. In "I Spy a Stranger" (not published until 1969) an eccentric woman visitor is destroyed mentally and

*The British and Irish Short Story Handbook*, First Edition. David Malcolm.
© 2012 David Malcolm. Published 2012 by Blackwell Publishing Ltd.

emotionally by a hostile English community during the Second World War. In "On Not Shooting Sitting Birds" (1976) a white West Indian girl, on her own in pre-First World War London, destroys her chances with a possible patron by not understanding English ways. In "Let Them Call It Jazz," the black West Indian Selina in post-1945 London falls foul of landlord, neighbors, and the law, and ends up in Holloway Prison. An acquaintance even appropriates the song she makes up for herself while in prison. The narrator of "I Used to Live Here Once" (1976) is that ultimate outsider, a revenant, who can touch no one and whom no one can see. Despite their usually bitter fates, the women in many of Rhys stories are far from passive. They try to make a living, to do the best they can in a world that is controlled by men and their money. The protagonist in "On Not Shooting Sitting Birds" is not crushed by her failure. "Some other night perhaps, another sort of man," she reflects. "I buy myself a dusty pink dress with the money," says Selina, defiantly, at the end of "Let Them Call It Jazz."

# Alan Sillitoe (1928–2010)

In a long and productive career, Sillitoe wrote – besides novels, screenplays, and essays – short stories. His major short-story collections include: *The Loneliness of the Long-Distance Runner* (1959), *The Ragman's Daughter, and Other Stories* (1963), *Guzman, Go Home, and Other Stories* (1968), *Men, Women and Children* (1973), *The Second Chance, and Other Stories* (1981), *The Far Side of the Street: Fifteen Short Stories* (1988), and *Alligator Playground: A Collection of Short Stories* (1997). A *Collected Stories* and a *New and Collected Stories* appeared in 1996 and 2005.

Sillitoe's work is much concerned with poverty, class divisions, exploitation, and rebellion. His characters in his most widely read and anthologized fiction are from the East Midlands working class, from which Sillitoe himself came. The picture of life that emerges from his stories is often dark indeed, and offers a vision of human life not entirely dependent on social class. "The Fishing Boat Picture" (1959), for example, is a bleak account of a life of hard work and marital failure and disappointment. Sillitoe's great achievement in short fiction is "The Loneliness of the Long-Distance Runner." The central character and narrator is Smith, a lumpen proletariat everyman (he is not working-class, and has no intentions of being anything but a criminal), and yet also an individual of fierce views and complex character. In a series of analepses he recounts his life up to the story's present. He is a young criminal, haunted by memories of a dead father, burning with a hatred of the great, good, respectable, and powerful of his world. He is caught by the police for a burglary and placed in a borstal, a prison for young offenders. Here his abilities as a runner are discovered, and the governor of the borstal seeks to use him to win a trophy in cross-country running for the institution. He is given privileges; the governor has great hopes for him. Smith, however, has no

*The British and Irish Short Story Handbook*, First Edition. David Malcolm.
© 2012 David Malcolm. Published 2012 by Blackwell Publishing Ltd.

intention of letting himself be used by "them." Demonstrating that he could win if he wished, he deliberately throws the race. The governor makes the rest of Smith's stay in the borstal unpleasant, but Smith does not mind. His fellow inmates work out what he has done and why. The pleurisy he catches in borstal keeps him out of the Army. The end of the story sees him happily pursuing his chosen life of crime. "The Loneliness of the Long-Distance Runner" is a challenging story. Smith's fierce defiance is at once political and perfectly understandable, and yet it can never be assimilated to any movement of social amelioration or change. In the end, he is a petty crook. But his running and his defiance of authority are memorable, and the story is an essential one. It and the film version, directed by Tony Richardson and scripted by Sillitoe himself, with Tom Courtney's gaunt face staring out at one, are central to the consciousness of many who grew up in 1960s Britain.

# Muriel Spark (1918–2006)

Although best known as a novelist, Spark's *The Collected Stories* (1990) contains twenty-nine stories. *All the Stories of Muriel Spark* (2001) contains forty-one stories. Many of her stories were published in *The New Yorker*, and her major collections include *The Go-Away Bird, and Other Stories* (1958), *Voices at Play* (1961), and *Bang-Bang You're Dead, and Other Stories* (1983).

Spark's short fiction, like her novels, is mischievous, witty, and never quite what it seems. The superficial acknowledgement of realist conventions is often subverted, and the stories become metaphysical. Supernatural motifs permeate her stories. As Robert E. Hosmer Jr. points out: "Crucial and axiomatic to all Spark's fiction is an understanding that this world and the world beyond, the temporal and the spiritual, the quotidian and the transcendent, are inseparably integrated. No parallel reality theories ever captivated Spark" (Hosmer 2008: 457). He goes on to insist that "Everything in Spark's short fiction takes place *sub specie aeternitatis*" (458). One might also add that Spark constantly stresses the fictionality of all her fictions, just as she emphasizes the insubstantiality of the material world.

"The Seraph and the Zambesi," Spark's first published story (it won the Christmas story competition in the *Observer* newspaper in 1951) illustrates Spark's procedures. The central mortal character is a fiction, borrowed from a Baudelaire novella, yet here running a garage and a rooming house in Africa in the 1940s. The story derives much comedy from this fabular improbability, as it does from the blank and panicked incomprehension that greets the Seraph's coming to take over a Christmas pageant. The Seraph is literally that, an angelic presence, who defies the constraints of the material world and the ambitions of the mortal. The narrator records the insubstantiality and

*The British and Irish Short Story Handbook*, First Edition. David Malcolm.
© 2012 David Malcolm. Published 2012 by Blackwell Publishing Ltd.

tawdriness of the material world, the banality and abraded quality of the mortals. The Seraph is everything the mortal and material world is not, and cannot be accommodated to conventional understandings of it. But he is unambiguously there.

"The Portobello Road" (1958) again brings together the material and the metaphysical. It is an unusual ghost story, being narrated by the ghost Needle, murdered by George. Meeting by chance with her murderer on the Portobello Road, Needle continues to haunt him cheerily till he emigrates to Canada. Just like "The Seraph and the Zambesi," "The Portobello Road" puts the importance of the material world in question. Characters age, youthful confidence turns to disappointment and shabby compromise, mighty civilizations collapse, and the Portobello Road is full of antiques, the detritus of others' lives. Needle herself lives almost as a ghost even before her murder, detached from other people, uncommitted, happiest in an empty house. Once again, Spark combines wit and humor with an uncompromising challenge to the readers' beliefs in the solidity of the here and now. She also attests to the vitality and possibilities of the ghost-story genre.

"The House of the Famous Poet" (1967) is a difficult story. Like some of Bowen's stories, it is an eerie war-time story, set in the summer of 1944, as the V-1 flying bombs fall on London. The circumstantial details of the text have a convincing ring – a crowded and delayed train, sleeping passengers, a smoking private soldier, an overgrown garden, a poet's house in Swiss Cottage, the sound of the sirens as the bombs come in, the characters' terrible fatigue. Indeed, much of the story works within realist conventions. However, these break down when the narrator encounters the private soldier again. He sells her "an abstract funeral." She meets him again on the train, and again even after he has just got off it, now "only a notion" of himself. He is clearly not quite of this world, a spirit, an invention. For the narrator makes it clear that she is telling a story. She addresses the reader. "You will complain that I am withholding evidence. Indeed, you may wonder if there is any evidence at all." Once again, the insubstantiality of the material world is foregrounded in the story. People die in air raids; buildings are destroyed. Our funerals, abstract and not, are real. "The angels of the Resurrection will invoke the dead man and the dead woman," but only stories can save experience and things. Spark is a religious fabulist of great wit and resource. The only writer her work echoes is T. F. Powys.

# Robert Louis Stevenson (1850–1894)

Novelist, poet, and essayist, Stevenson wrote some major short fiction in his brief life. Just as *Treasure Island* (1883), *Kidnapped* (1886), and *The Master of Ballantrae* (1889) are ground-breaking novels, so stories like "The Strange Case of Dr. Jekyll and Mr. Hyde" (1886) and "The Beach at Falesá" (1893) are important modern short stories. Stevenson's great contribution to short fiction was in the genre of the supernatural story and of the story of colonial adventure (although, like Conrad, Stevenson revises the principles of the genre). He is also a major, exemplarily cosmopolitan, and influential Scottish writer. His major short-story collections are: *New Arabian Nights* (1882) (which contains the thrilling "The Pavillion on the Links"), *The Merry Men, and Other Tales and Fables* (1887), and *Island Nights' Entertainments* (1893).

Stevenson's most famous supernatural stories include "Thrawn Janet" (1881), a tale of obsessive madness and witchcraft that is written partly in Scots. "Markheim" (1885) – discussed in the chapter on Key Works in this book – is a study of the mind of a man in the few hours after he has killed someone. The second half of the story involves a sinister dialog with a diabolic visitor whose blandishments to further evil Markheim rejects in a bold assertion of free will. "The Bottle Imp" (1891) is a happier tale of the supernatural, a story of a cursed but magic bottle that must be sold always for less than the purchaser paid for it. Despite its fortunate outcome for the Polynesian protagonists, Keawe and Kokua, prosperity and success carry a terrible price in this story. "The Strange Case of Dr. Jekyll and Mr. Hyde" offers the twentieth century one of its central story materials. The noble and good Dr. Jekyll transforms himself into the bestial and ruthless Mr. Hyde, and starts to enjoy the freedoms that the transformation brings. The story sold in

*The British and Irish Short Story Handbook*, First Edition. David Malcolm.
© 2012 David Malcolm. Published 2012 by Blackwell Publishing Ltd.

large numbers in both Britain and the U.S.A. It is one of a trio of fin-de-siècle texts – James's "The Turn of the Screw" (1898) and Conrad's "Heart of Darkness" (1899/1902) are the others – that somehow predict the terrors and evil seductions of the twentieth century.

Like Conrad's later story, Stevenson's "The Beach at Falesá" is a savage exposure of the cruelties and hypocrisies of European colonial power. The beautiful island of Falesá is a site of theft, corruption, intrigue, and a battle for material success that leads to murder. The racism that underpins exploitation is vividly rendered in the narrator Wiltshire's assumptions of racial superiority, all the more questionable because of his own shoddy English.

# Sylvia Townsend Warner
# (1893–1978)

Townsend Warner wrote some good historical novels – for example, *Summer Will Show* (1936), *The Corner That Held Them* (1948), and *The Flint Anchor* (1954) – and a substantial body of short fiction. Yet she is a barely canonical writer. Eleanor Perényi claims that Warner's anomalous and marginalized position within British fiction is related to the difficulty commentators have in categorizing her.

> Feminist, Marxist, historical novelist, social comedian, teller of fairy tales – she was all these, and none of them to a degree that would ultimately define her; and this is her disadvantage. If a convenient pigeonhole could be found for her ... no doubt we would be in the flood of a Warner revival.
>
> (Perényi 1985: 30)

Fourteen collections of Townsend Warner's short stories were published between 1929 and her death, and another three after it. Approximately 150 stories were published by *The New Yorker* during her long association with the magazine. Warner's stories are usually divided into two groups: stories that depict English life, often that of eccentric and peripheral characters, within realist conventions, and her *Kingdoms of Elfin* stories (collected in 1977). It is the latter group that seem most radically innovative (and deeply traditional at the same time). The conceit in the Elfin stories is that there exist complex and elaborate Elfin kingdoms that run alongside, and at times overlap with, human life. These Elfin kingdoms appear to range (in human terms) from medieval through to eighteenth-century costumes and mores.

*The British and Irish Short Story Handbook*, First Edition. David Malcolm.
© 2012 David Malcolm. Published 2012 by Blackwell Publishing Ltd.

The Elfins are like humans but not quite, and their world is marked by a peculiar mixture of amorality and firm standards. The world of Elfin, as is often the case in such fictions, is intended to provide a distanced and ironic commentary on human behavior. But the Elfin stories also have a sheer verve and gusto of their own that make them entertaining and provocative texts.

Stories are often extremely enigmatic, like "Queen Mousie" (not published until 1984). Many are marked by a cheerful violence and cruelty, like "Five Black Swans," in which the Elfin Queen, Tiphaine, recalls her mortal lover. The stories are comic, but with a dark edge to them, as in "The Revolt at Brocéliande," which tells of the complex adventures of two human eunuchs at the cruel court of Queen Melior. "The One and the Other" is a changeling story, in which Adam (elfin) and Tiffany (human) are exchanged for each other. The story recounts their differing lives in the human world and in Elfhame. Adam, who is cold and calculating, does not know he is an elfin, and eventually kills Tiffany, thinking the latter is one. Townsend Warner deserves to be much better known than she is. Her non-realist short fiction is especially interesting, and indicates the endurance of traditional short genres, here the fairy tale, into the late twentieth century. Her stories also offer a context for the much better-known work of Angela Carter.

# William Trevor (born 1928)

Trevor is a major Irish novelist, with eighteen highly regarded novels to his credit. His short stories, however, are also seen as a major part of his *œuvre*, and he certainly made his reputation first as a short-story writer. His most important collections include: *The Day We Got Drunk on Cake, and Other Stories* (1967), *The Ballroom of Romance, and Other Stories* (1972), *Angels at the Ritz, and Other Stories* (1975), *Lovers of Their Time, and Other Stories* (1978), *Beyond the Pale, and Other Stories* (1981), *The News from Ireland, and Other Stories* (1986), and *The Hill Bachelors* (2000). Omnibus collections of his stories appeared in 1983, 1993, and 2009.

Trevor has spent most of his adult life in Britain, and his stories deal both with English and Irish topics and characters. They also deal with the Irish in England, as in the memorable "Another Christmas" (from *Lovers of Their Time*), which is discussed in Part 5 Key Works. One of Trevor's most celebrated Irish stories is "The Ballroom of Romance", which evokes with great sympathy the Joycean paralysis of the life of Bridie, an unmarried woman caring for an invalid father on an isolated southern Irish hill farm. Her life is made up of hard labor with little companionship. She goes to Mass on Sundays and once a month shopping to the local town. On Saturdays she cycles seven miles to a wayside dance hall, ironically called *The Ballroom of Romance*. For it is anything but that. Despite its bright colors, the dance hall is a gimcrack affair, the dance band middle-aged, conversations repetitive and banal, the men useless or drunkards or both, and the girls aging and increasingly desperate. Bridie, a woman of courage and intelligence, is left thinking of her dismal present and her dismal future with Bowser Egan, one of the unattractive men who attend the dances. She decides not to return to the Ballroom again.

*The British and Irish Short Story Handbook*, First Edition. David Malcolm.
© 2012 David Malcolm. Published 2012 by Blackwell Publishing Ltd.

In "Lovers of Their Time," life in London in the early 1960s is scarcely brighter. As in "The Ballroom of Romance," Trevor's sympathy for the unglamorous grey, little people of the world produces a comic and moving tale of dreams and their dismantling. Forty-year-old Norman works in a travel agent's in west London. He is married to the lubricious and rather repellent Hilda. He falls in love with Marie, who works in the local pharmacy, and is twelve years younger. They meet regularly, but the only place they can meet to make love, and that after much waiting, is a luxurious bathroom in the Great Western Royal Hotel in Paddington Station. It is an act of bold intrusion, for they are not guests there, a brave insistence on the rights of love over property, a sign of the decade. For three years this is their place of romance, their place of escape from the tawdry restrictions of their life. But when Norman tries boldly to free himself and Marie, their life together founders in two rooms in Kilburn (the bathroom, ironically, shared with fifteen other people) and in Marie's mother's house in Reading, and on poverty and maintenance payments to Norman's wife. They are defeated and part. Norman returns to Hilda. But for Norman "as the decade of the 1960s passed, it trailed behind it the marvels of his love affair with Marie."

Trevor's work is varied. He faces the nightmare of Ireland's history and present, in "Attracta" for example, and the nightmare of England's history too, in "Matilda's England" (both from *Lovers of Their Time*). His stories of Irish paralysis are matched by those of English unhappiness. In his comic but humanely sympathetic portrayal of little people, the old, the lower middle-class, the unglamorous, the suburban, he continues the tradition of Pritchett's exemplary fictions.

# H. G. Wells (1866–1946)

Wells's contribution to the development of the short story in Britain is second to none. Some of his major novels – *The Time Machine* (1895) and *The War of the Worlds* (1898) – are very short, and could even be seen as long short fictions. In the crucial years for the sudden burgeoning of British short fiction, Wells published his major collections: *The Stolen Bacillus, and Other Incidents* (1895), *The Plattner Story, and Others* (1897), *Tales of Space and Time* (1899), *Twelve Stories and a Dream* (1903), and *The Door in the Wall, and Other Stories* (1911). Most of his short fiction was also published in journals, such as *Pearson's Magazine, Pall Mall Gazette*, and *The Strand Magazine*. Wells's development of early science fiction in his short stories has always been recognized, but the genre range of his short stories is remarkable. He tried his hand at stories of colonial adventure ("Aepyornis Island" [1894] and "The Empire of the Ants" [1905]), supernatural stories ("Pollock and the Porroh Man" [1895]), historical fiction ("A Story of the Stone Age"[1897]), dystopia ("A Story of the Days to Come" [1899]), and war fiction (with a dose of science fiction) ("The Land Ironclads" [1903]). As is common in the fin-de-siècle, Wells's stories are often wrapped in a complex narrational packaging that problematizes truth and raise issues of the nature of story-telling and giving accounts of things. In this he is both of his own time and of the late twentieth century.

Wells's short stories often involve an encounter with an unexpected other (the enigmatic "The Valley of Spiders" [1903] is exemplary). In "Aepyornis Island" – a traveler's yarn told by Butcher to an unnamed frame narrator – the protagonist is swept on a drifting boat in the Indian Ocean far beyond civilization, with little but some ancient but preserved Aepyornis eggs for company. Two he eats; the third hatches. Initially, friendship develops

*The British and Irish Short Story Handbook*, First Edition. David Malcolm.
© 2012 David Malcolm. Published 2012 by Blackwell Publishing Ltd.

between prehistoric bird and the man. Butcher even calls him Friday, in an echo of Defoe's *Robinson Crusoe*. Their rapport, however, degenerates after two years, and open hostility breaks out between them. In the end, Butcher manages to slay the great bird. He is picked up by a yacht and returns to civilization with only bones. At one level, the story is a comic and outrageous traveler's tale. At another, it is a colonial parable, a tale of colonial exploitation, in which the avian Friday quite rightly turns on his Crusoe, appropriately named Butcher (he has, of course, devoured two of the bird's siblings without compunction, as well as shooting a Malagasy bearer).

An encounter with what is other is also central to "The Country of the Blind" (1904). Nunez arrives by chance in an isolated valley where all the inhabitants are blind. He assumes that the old proverb – "In the country of the blind the one-eyed man is king" – will be validated. It is not. The blind in their own environment are much more competent in every way than he. His talk of a world outside the valley makes no sense to them. They have no notion of blindness itself. Finally they propose to excise his troublesome eyes for his own good. He acquiesces, but at the last minute flees. It is not clear whether he escapes the valley, but he climbs and lies contentedly high in the snows. The story works as a moral fable, but one also feels in Nunez's humbling both the questioning of cultural superiority that underlies colonialism, and also the scrutiny of the claims of the visionary. The blind have a perfect and rather suburban environment; Nunez comes with wild tales of another reality. The artistic focus of the story is emphasized by the splendid descriptions of mountain scenery at the end, and by the whole narrational framing of the text. The narrator is at pains to establish the story's credibility at the beginning, but withdraws from this strategy at the end, giving no indication as to how Nunez's story has been transmitted to the world at large.

"The Door in the Wall" is a story in which, again, two realities meet: the character Wallace's successful career, and the "immortal realities" that lie behind the mysteriously shifting door that invites him to enter. As in the previously discussed stories, the narrator is careful to suspend his judgment as to the reality of Wallace's experiences behind the door. Wallace has rejected the door, time and again, for a dizzyingly successful career. He is now full of regrets and looks ceaselessly for the door. His body is found at the base of a deep shaft near East Kensington Station. He has passed through an unlocked door in a hoarding and fallen to his death. Was that his door, the narrator asks? Did his dream mislead him? "By our daylight standard he walked out of security into darkness, danger, and death. . . . But did he see like that?"

# Oscar Wilde (1854–1900)

Wilde's output of short fiction was slight, and overshadowed by *The Picture of Dorian Gray* (1891) and his plays, but it is important, if for no other reason than it is, by anybody's standards, very good. "The Canterville Ghost: A Hylo-Idealistic Romance" (1887) is a superb comic reworking and revitalization of the conventions of the supernatural story, and a fine comic study of Anglo–American relations. It also plumbs emotional and psychological depths in Virginia's freeing of the unfortunate revenant. As always in Wilde's fiction, there is a meta-artistic focus, for the ghost is a performer, whose artistry now no longer works on its audience. "Lord Arthur Savile's Crime: A Study of Duty" (1891), with its wildly improbable story material, satirizes so much of late Victorian society and culture: faddishness, a sense of duty, moral uprightness, selfless dedication, class pride, and melodrama. Its morally inverted world – murder is a path to rectitude – is comic but also challenges that of the reader. "The Portrait of Mr. W.H." (1889) is a study of obsession, an epistemologically astute consideration of the claims of those who claim to know, and, by implication, of the cause of Irish nationalism. It is also very funny. (For a fuller discussion of this text, see Part 1.) The stories in *The Happy Prince, and Other Stories* (1888) are deeply moving children's stories, not without resonances for adult readers. (Part 5 Key Works discusses one of these stories, "The Selfish Giant.")

*The British and Irish Short Story Handbook*, First Edition. David Malcolm.
© 2012 David Malcolm. Published 2012 by Blackwell Publishing Ltd.

# Virginia Woolf (1882–1941)

Although Woolf's short fiction is inevitably overshadowed by her work in the novel, the short story was important for her. In her lifetime, she published eighteen short stories, but *The Complete Shorter Fiction* (1985) contains forty-six short stories (and twelve incomplete ones). Woolf wrote short fiction from 1906 to her death in 1941. It was part of her struggle with the legacy of the nineteenth-century novel, although some of her short fiction, "A Society" (1921), "The Duchess and the Jeweller" (138), and "The Shooting Party" (1938), work within nineteenth-century conventions. *Monday or Tuesday* (1921) contains Woolf's best-known short stories. "A Haunted House" is that unusual thing, a benign ghost story, in which the spirits seem to cherish the living inhabitants of an old house. The text is fascinatingly elliptical, and thoroughly deautomatized, a supernatural story in which the story material is only hinted at. The language is poetic – phonologically, lexically, and syntactically repetitive – like much of Woolf's fiction, short or long.

"Kew Gardens" (discussed in Part 5 Key Works) is a highly innovative short story, with fragmentary and elliptical presentation of story material, radical shifts in point of view (and to that of a snail!), and a markedly poetic language. It does not lack, however, both social and historical resonance. "The Mark on the Wall" is perhaps even more radical, action reduced to memories and associative thoughts, as the narrator meditates on a strange mark on the wall. It finally turns out to be a snail again. None of these experiments is frivolous (and who are we to say what experiments are frivolous anyway?). The meditation on the mark on the wall takes place in time of war, the reader learns. The text can be read as the setting out of a mind desperately trying to stay half-sane in a time of carnage and hopelessness.

*The British and Irish Short Story Handbook*, First Edition. David Malcolm.
© 2012 David Malcolm. Published 2012 by Blackwell Publishing Ltd.

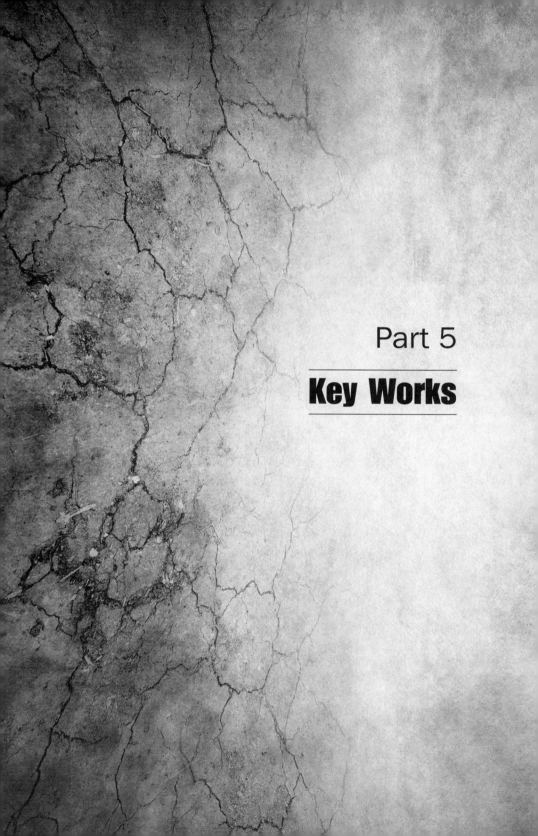

Part 5

# Key Works

# Robert Louis Stevenson, "Markheim" (1885)

Published in the anthology *The Broken Shaft: Tales of Mid-Ocean* (1885)
and in Stevenson's own collection
*The Merry Men and Other Tales and Fables* (1887)

"Markheim" is a complex and sophisticated short story, drawing on Gothic tradition, and also showing clearly the influence of American short fiction, not of Poe but of the much greater Nathaniel Hawthorne. Underlying "Markheim" are surely Hawthorne's fictions such as "Young Goodman Brown" (1835) and "Rappaccini's Daughter" (1844), complex moral and psychological tales set out in stark (but never simple-minded) metaphors and symbols, and in absorbing and often sinister actions.

The story material of "Markheim" is, however, simple. On Christmas Day, Markheim visits an antique dealer with whom he has had dealings in the past. His intention is to murder the dealer and steal his money. He stabs him. The murderer is immediately stricken by fears of detection. He also has a strong, but inexplicable, sense that he is not alone in the dealer's house. He goes upstairs to attempt to find his victim's money. While Markheim tries to decide which key will open a cabinet, a stranger enters the room. The affable visitor appears to be a supernatural, and seemingly diabolic, figure who wishes to help Markheim accomplish his end. Markheim resists his overtures, although the stranger argues that he is really lost already. The dealer's maid returns. Markheim, in an act intended to defy the stranger, descends the stairs and announces that he has murdered her master.

The narrator is a third-person one, but Markheim's mind is the only one the narrator has access to, and Markheim (eponymous hero into the bargain) is the central focus of the text. In addition, on several occasions, the narrator

*The British and Irish Short Story Handbook*, First Edition. David Malcolm.
© 2012 David Malcolm. Published 2012 by Blackwell Publishing Ltd.

employs free indirect speech to capture Markheim's thoughts almost directly. For example, as the protagonist surveys his victim's body, the narrator comes very close to the movements of Markheim's reflections and feelings. "There must it lie; there was none to work the cunning hinges or direct the miracle of locomotion; there must it lie till it was found. Found! ay, and then? Then would this dead flesh lift up a cry that would ring over England, and fill the world with he echoes of pursuit. Ay, dead or not, this was still the enemy."

The story material of "Markheim" may be simple, but its organization is not, and is very suggestive. There is no exposition. The reader is thrust into the world of Markheim and the antique dealer with no preparation. Indeed, the story is remarkable for its omissions. Readers are told very little about the protagonist, his past, and his circumstances. He refers to his mother at one point. At another, in the only extended analepsis in the text, he recalls a childhood experience in which he sees gruesome pictures of murders and murderers at a fair. The affable stranger reminds him that he has participated in revivalist meetings a few years previously. Markheim plays the Stock Exchange and has lost money there. This is little indeed. What has driven Markheim to murder (he claims to have an explanation, but does not give it)? What has driven his moral decline over so many years? Is he, in fact, a thief, who has not emptied a rich uncle's collection, but obtained the antiques he has dealt in by other means? This is a story of ellipses, a feature emphasized by the text's abrupt and, to a degree, open ending.

Further, the story material is organized to emphasize the motions of Markheim's mind. The protagonist's conversation with the dealer and his murder of the latter occupy a brief opening section of the text. Thereafter follows a much longer section (nearly half the story) that focuses on Markheim's worries, regrets, and fears. A slightly shorter, but still lengthy, section follows that consists largely of Markheim's dialogue with the visitor. The story's focus is clearly on the intricacies of Markheim's thoughts and feelings, his dialogue both with himself, and a projection of himself (for the stranger at times bears a resemblance to Markheim). His decision to free himself from his downward progress in turpitude is the story's climax. Setting, too, helps to place the focus of the text on Markheim. It is, physically, London, England, sometime in the nineteenth century, but beyond that it is difficult to say much. Markheim is isolated in the empty shop and house, empty that is apart from a corpse and a supernatural visitant. The fact that the time setting is Christmas Day, around three o'clock in the afternoon, further isolates Markheim. When much of London is involved in a communal celebration of goodwill, he is alone, first with the unlovely dealer, and then with the prince of darkness. Time is important in the story in another way also. Clocks are everywhere in the antique dealer's shop. The devil emphasizes that for Markheim time is running out. He has become worse and worse with the years. The maidservant is returning. If he does not act, he will be caught.

Markheim is the only named character in the text, and one could argue that the two other characters are, at least partly, his shadows. Like his customer, the dealer has isolated himself from the rest of humanity. He counts his money on Christmas Day. He, like Markheim, is a materialist with no human ties. The satanic visitor is partly *Doppelgänger*, partly an inverted guardian angel who has observed Markheim for many years and who knows his "moral horoscope." On a literal level, there is a murder and a conversation with a supernatural power, but, on another level, Markheim is talking to himself. The motif of the mirror that runs throughout the text confirms this. For Markheim, a mirror is "this damned reminder of years, and sins and follies – this hand-conscience." After the murder, "In many rich mirrors... he saw his face repeated and repeated, as it were an army of spies."

The dialogue with the aimiable demon is the core of the story. It is complex. The demon argues that he knows Markheim. Markheim denies this and declares that he is not summed up by his acts. His interlocutor tempts him to further evil, arguing that all acts end in death anyway. The core of the tempter's argument is that clearly Markheim's path has been determined and there is no escape. "Then," he urges, "content yourself with what you are, for you will never change; and the words of your part on this stage are irrevocably written down." Despite its seeming logic, the dialogue between murderer and demon has marked inconsistencies and irresolutions. Markheim's companion, at one moment, argues that motive is irrelevant, and act is all. At another, he declares that he is not interested in Markheim's acts but in who Markheim is. The devil's whole aim is to convince Markheim that he has no choice.

Markheim's concluding act denies this. He refuses to go further on the downward path of evil. He does not murder the maid, as his Mephistopheles urges him to do. One of the story's final ambiguities (apart from its open ending) is the response of the tempter to Markheim's decision to defy him. "The features of the visitor began to undergo a wonderful and lovely change: they brightened and softened with a tender triumph, and, even as they brightened, faded and dislimned." How is the reader meant to interpret this sentence? Was a benign power in the universe trying to pull the strings, to push Markheim to goodness through proposing evil? Is the visitor really the part of Markheim that now triumphs in his taking charge of his life? The ambiguity is part of the richness of this accomplished story, not a shrunk novel, but a text that employs its shortness to powerful and suggestive effect. Stevenson's story draws on past native traditions (of the Gothic), and on American models, and points the way to the future.

# Oscar Wilde, "The Canterville Ghost: A Hylo-Idealistic Romance" (1887)

Published in *The Court and Society Review* (1887) and in book form in
*Lord Arthur Savile's Crime, and Other Stories* (1891)

"The Canterville Ghost" is a comic supernatural story, and has nothing to do
with Ireland. Mr. Hiram B. Otis, the U.S. Ambassador in Britain, buys for
himself and his family the ancient house of Canterville Chase, despite
warnings from the owner Lord Canterville that the place is haunted. Almost
immediately on taking up residence, the Otis family (mother, father, an eldest
son, a daughter, and two younger twin sons) encounters the ghost. It is that of
Sir Simon de Canterville, a man of evil life, who murdered his wife in the
library in 1575, and, having been tortured to death by her brothers (the body
has never been discovered), must haunt his old home. His hauntings are,
however, defused, defeated, and dispelled by the materialism and enterprise
of the American family. In the end, Sir Simon's ghost is liberated by the
courage and pity of Virginia, the Otis daughter. As her reward, she is given
wonderful old jewels by the ghost, and herself marries an English aristocrat.
The U.S. family, despite their professed austere republican principles, is
integrated into English society.

The story material draws heavily on a tradition of ghost stories, while
playing with the genre's conventions. It also offers another version of the
Anglo–American subject matter that runs through James's and Kipling's short
fiction, and that turns up much later in James Lasdun's short stories. The
paradoxes of the story's action are marked: the supernatural, rather than – as
convention usually has it – troubling and defeating the material and materialist, is roundly trounced by them; the naïve New World discomfits the

*The British and Irish Short Story Handbook*, First Edition. David Malcolm.
© 2012 David Malcolm. Published 2012 by Blackwell Publishing Ltd.

sophisticated Old; the brisk Amazon daughter of the materialist Americans turns out to be the most feeling and idealistic of all the characters. Much of the story's humor derives from such inversions of convention and expectation.

The narrator is very knowledgeable (when he chooses to be) and witty (throughout). For example, early in the story, the reader meets with a traditional and almost classic narrational intervention on the subject of the differences between British and American English. "Indeed, in many respects, she [Mrs. Otis] was quite English, and was an excellent example of the fact that we really have everything in common with America nowadays, except, of course, language." There is a nod to the frame convention of the supernatural story, and the device of indicating where knowledge comes from (the narrator cites Mr. Otis as an informant), but these are insubstantial allusions to standard features of the genre, and as the narrator knows what the ghost thinks and feels, they are not meant to be taken seriously. The narrator is inclined to long and increasingly baroque lists, usually of the circumstances and victims of the ghost's depredations, but also of the usual subject matters of "the ordinary conversation of cultured Americans of the better class." Mostly, his language is marked by an elegant interplay of rather long complex sentences, with numerous parentheses, and relatively short, sometimes indeed simple, sentences.

His organization of his story material is strange. The bulk of the story follows the main subject matter, the conflict between ghost and family. The exposition, setting out the negotiations and conversations between Otis and Canterville, and giving details of the Otis family, are perhaps longer than one might expect; the conclusion, around a quarter of the story, comprising sections 6 and 7, and detailing the exhaustive search for Virginia, her return, the dilemma of the jewels, Sir Simon's funeral, and Virginia's marriage and presentation at court, is certainly much more protracted than seems necessary.

The text, however, is organized around very clear oppositions (signaled in the subtitle: "hylo" is a prefix meaning related to matter): the U.S.A. and England; materialism and the spiritual; the modern and the ancient. The Otises are contrasted with Lord Canterville; the central conflict of the text is between their robust this-worldliness and the ghost's supernatural nature; the Otises are modern (and carry stain remover, lubricant oil, and a revolver when necessary), while the ghost is a Renaissance one, dresses in antique clothes, and often speaks mock Elizabethan. As with the text's paradoxes, much of its humor lies in these juxtapositions, as when Washington Otis flings himself on the ancient bloodstain on the library floor with Pinkerton's Champion Stain Remover and Paragon Detergent. Even without the Otises, however, the unfortunate ghost experiences the recalcitrance of the material world, when, for example, he vows terrible vengeance before Chanticleer crows twice, and the local cock does not oblige.

Paradoxically, it is the Otises' daughter, Virginia, who embodies the Wildean themes of the power of innocence and the value of sacrifice. It is she who eventually talks to and listens to the ghost, and who saves him, by putting herself at sinister risk. She also comes out of it all not just with jewels, but with a knowledge and an experience she is reluctant to impart to anyone, even to her husband. The story achieves a seriousness here, as when Sir Simon himself speaks of his desire to rest, to be at last at peace. Expiation for sin is also a Wildean theme. The syntactic parallelism and repetitions of the ghost's words carry considerable power. "Death must be so beautiful. To lie in the soft brown earth, with the grasses waving above one's head, and listen to silence. To have no yesterday, and no tomorrow. To forget time, to forgive life, to be at peace. You can help me. You can open for me the portals of Death's house, for Love is always with you, and Love is stronger than Death is."

Along with its other features, social-national satire, wit and humor, a concern with vice and forgiveness, "The Canterville Ghost" is also a self-referential, metafictional text. First, it is an exposition and revitalizing of the conventions of the ghost story. The genre's markers – the (lightly alluded to) informant, the old house, the weather's and nature's answering of sinister action, the dark secret (Sir Simon's skeleton in the hidden reaches of the mansion), the figure of the child, and a child at risk – are all set out, exposed, and revitalized by the humorous clash with the Otises. Second, the ghost is, in a real sense, a performer. He adopts roles to haunt, and has done so for centuries, his most successful manifestations being a list of parts with appropriate costuming and make-up. "With the enthusiastic egotism of the true artist he went over his most celebrated performances, and smiled bitterly to himself as he recalled to mind his last appearance as 'Red Reuben, or the Strangled Babe,' his *début* as 'Gaunt Gideon, the Blood-sucker of Bexley Moor,'..." Later he considers appearing "in the character of 'Dumb Daniel, or the Suicide's Skeleton,' a *rôle* in which he had on more than one occasion produced a great effect, and which he considered quite equal to his famous part of 'Martin the Maniac, or the Masked Mystery'." But he is an artist whose performances are no longer effective, disrupted, derided, and humiliatingly disdained by the materialist temper of the Otises. The old plots no longer work. Indeed, the text embodies this in its slight displacement of narrative focus. The last quarter of the story has little to do with the ghost story material, but is social in its ambit. On one level, this section reinforces a message of the importance and possibility of social cohesion. American, aristocrat, household servants, and gypsies all combine to search for Virginia; the American girl marries her English lord and is presented to the Queen.

But, also, this section emphasizes that the glamorous gules of ghost story, romance (the story's subtitle is a "Hylo-Idealistic Romance"), and ballad will be replaced by the sober materialism of a different kind of narrative. Only Virginia's modest blush at the story's end suggests there may be another kind of story that will surface in the future.

# Oscar Wilde,
# "The Selfish Giant" (1888)

Published in *The Happy Prince, and Other Stories* (1888)

The fables contained in the volume *The Happy Prince, and Other Stories* are among Wilde's most important contributions to British and Irish fiction generally, and to short fiction in particular. The remarkable feature of Wilde's output is that he did so little and, yet, achieved so much of such quality in drama, in the novel, in verse, and in the short story. The fable (as I suggested in Part 3) is a resilient genre. Wilde's moral tales are echoed in Carter's feminist fables ninety years later.

"The Selfish Giant" has all the features of the fable: the simplified, clearly symbolic characters and action, the presence of figures drawn from folk tale and legend and unattested to in realist texts, the relatively simple story material leading to a moral *pointe*. The eponymous Giant banishes "the children" from his "large lovely garden" with its twelve peach trees; the garden is seized by relentless winter, by the characters Snow, Frost, the North Wind, and the Hail. Summer never comes until the children break through a hole in the garden wall and climb the trees. All the trees blossom except one, for one child is too small to climb it. The Giant lifts the child up, and the tree blossoms, and birds and flowers return to the garden. The Giant, realizing his selfishness, casts down his wall and gives it over to the children. The small boy he has lifted to the tree, however, does not return until the Giant's death, when his identity as Christ is made clear.

The text is centered on its oppositions: the lovely garden frozen by selfishness, bitter egoism redeemed by selflessness, and the cruelty of the world (the small boy's wounds) balanced by the possibility of grace. The moral of the text could not be clearer. The Giant dies transformed and happy,

*The British and Irish Short Story Handbook*, First Edition. David Malcolm.
© 2012 David Malcolm. Published 2012 by Blackwell Publishing Ltd.

"all covered with white blossoms," no longer selfish. Wilde's delicate poly-syndeton (repeated use of "and") is biblical without being heavy-handed. This fable both enlivens the genre and recasts Christian story material (it clearly echoes both Matthew 18.3 and Mark 10.14) in a fresh manner reminiscent of John Bunyan at his best. The fable, too, carries a suggestiveness beyond its immediate subject matter. The Giant's joyless authoritarianism, redeemed by generosity, can serve as a metaphor for varieties of social and political bone-headedness. One is tempted to read the Giant as a socially exclusive landlord, as England, or, indeed, as a straight, joyless, repressive social order.

# Arthur Conan Doyle, "The Adventure of the Engineer's Thumb" (1892)

Published in *The Strand Magazine* (1892) and
*The Adventures of Sherlock Holmes* (1892)

Conan Doyle's "The Adventure of the Engineer's Thumb" may not be, as Dr. Watson points out, a completely typical "problem" for Sherlock Holmes, but it does contain many of the elements that make the Sherlock Homes stories so engaging and popular. It also exemplifies the sources of the story materials of detective fiction and points to later developments of the genre. In addition, it has the rich suggestiveness of many of Conan Doyle's crime stories.

Dr. Watson's practice is near Paddington Station and the railway officials are among his patients. One brings to him a young man, just arrived in London that morning, who seems badly hurt. He is a gentleman, a Mr. Victor Hatherly, a hydraulic engineer, but he is in a state near hysteria. Watson inspects his wounded hand and finds that his thumb "had been hacked or torn right out from the roots." This is, Hatherly reveals, the result of a "murderous attack" on him. Watson proposes a visit to Holmes. Over breakfast in Baker Street, Hatherly tells his tale, Holmes interrupting him with questions only occasionally. Hatherly is an unsuccessful young hydraulic engineer, only recently having set up business on his own. He is visited by an austere and emaciated man with a German accent who calls himself Colonel Lysander Stark. He offers Hatherly a huge fee to inspect a piece of machinery in the country near Reading. The commission must be conducted in utter secrecy (Stark explains that it has to do with a scheme secretly to extract fuller's earth from neighbors' land) and that very night. Although repelled by Stark, Hatherly thinks of his fee and accepts the job. He travels into the country, is picked up at the railway station in a carriage with frosted windows, and

*The British and Irish Short Story Handbook*, First Edition. David Malcolm.
© 2012 David Malcolm. Published 2012 by Blackwell Publishing Ltd.

whisked to an old house in the country. There, Hatherly encounters a mysterious, well-dressed, and attractive woman with a foreign accent who later advises him to flee the place. He stays, however, and inspects Stark's, and an associate's, machinery. It is a powerful hydraulic press that has been constructed inside a small room. Hatherly works out what the problem is – " one of the india-rubber bands which was round the head of a driving-rod had shrunk so as not quite to fill the socket along which it worked." The engineer sees that Stark's story is "the merest fabrication" and returns to the room to inspect the press. He is discovered there by Stark who calls out: "Very well. . . you shall know all about the machine." The villain then starts the machinery, and the ceiling of the room starts to descend on Hatherly. At the last moment, a small panel is opened in the wall, Hatherly rolls out and discovers he has been saved by the mysterious woman. They are pursued through the house to the lady's bedroom. As Hatherly climbs out the window, his thumb is severed by a cleaver-wielding Stark. He flees and faints in the garden, but wakes up near the local railway station.

Holmes, Watson, and Hatherly go to the police, and then with Inspector Bradstreet of Scotland Yard, travel to Eyford. When they get there, they see a nearby house in flames. It is Stark's house, which has caught fire when Hatherly's lamp was crushed in the press. Holmes and Bradstreet reveal that Stark and his associates are forgers, using the press to make half-crown coins. The criminals have made their escape. Hatherly has been saved by the woman and by Stark's English associate. Hatherly bemoans the loss of thumb and fee, but Holmes reminds him that he now has an enthralling story to tell.

Like all the Sherlock Holmes stories, "The Adventure of the Engineer's Thumb" is driven by the complex and exciting story material. As Watson says, the narrative fascinates "when the facts slowly evolve before your own eyes, and the mystery clears gradually away as each new discovery furnishes a step which leads on to the complete truth." The participants and settings clearly derive from Gothic fiction: the dark, ancient, and lonely house; the menacing and alien stranger; the mysterious and attractive woman; the brutal violence. The hydraulic press itself is the descendant of the murderous blade in Poe's "The Pit and the Pendulum" (1842). The element of Stark's foreignness also points to the development of the crime-story genre into espionage fiction, a genre that was evolving already in the 1890s (for example, William le Queux's *A Secret Service* [1896]; also relevant is the same author's *The Great War in England in 1897* [1894]).

But like much popular fiction, especially from the *fin-de-siècle*, "The Adventure of the Engineer's Thumb" carries a suggestiveness beyond the excitements of its story material. As Mariadele Boccardi points out, Holmes is a figure policing the borders of late Victorian society, a society (in Conan

Doyle's fiction) under threat both from deviance within and foreign threat (Boccardi 2008: 26–27). In "The Adventure of the Engineer's Thumb," Hatherly is moved to accept a dubious professional commission because he needs the money. If he accepts Stark's story, he is conniving at an act of fraud. Stark, himself, with his thinness and his murderous violence embodies a late Victorian fear of the foreign, especially of Germany. It is notable that the criminals are forging the currency of the realm, and that they are not captured and punished. They escape with their forged coins. Indeed, in this story Holmes does very little, and seems impotent to protect society from its enemies.

The psychological and sexual ramifications of the text's story material should also be noted. Hatherly is a bachelor and an orphan. Stark is clearly a kind of castrating father figure, older and murderous when provoked. The scene of savage mutilation takes place in the bedroom of a woman who has defied his authority. The crushing force of paternal and senior authority could scarcely be better represented than in the small room the ceiling of which descends to obliterate Hatherly. Further, the phallic connotations of Colonel Stark's machinery cannot be ignored. Like a penis, it is powered by hydraulics. It has become defective, and he needs young engineers to fix it. Holmes points out that Hatherly is not the first victim of the undernourished Colonel. Another young engineer has gone missing about a year ago. "Ha!" Holmes exclaims. "That represents the last time that the colonel needed to have his machine overhauled, I fancy." The central part of the story takes the form of a narration in which Hatherly sets out his traumatic experience and partially recovers from it. Finally, all he is left with is "experience," and a story to tell.

# Hubert Crackanthorpe, "Modern Melodrama" (1895)

Published in *Sentimental Studies, and A Set of Village Tales* (1895)

Like Stevenson, and Henry James, Crackanthorpe produced stories in which brevity and economy are celebrated and their potential exploited. This is evident in "Modern Melodrama." Here, the grandiloquent title, suggesting colorful and complex action, is ironically denied by the austere paucity of the text.

The action occupies a very short period of time, barely an hour. Daisy is dying of tuberculosis. The doctor visits her and offers a hopeful if cautious prognosis. However, Daisy persuades her servant to listen to the following private conversation between the doctor and her lover, Dick. The servant tells Daisy that the doctor, in fact, gives her only a few months to live. Daisy subsequently tells Dick that she knows she will die soon. The story ends with her asking her lover if the doctor's verdict is to be trusted.

The action is a fragment, torn from a longer implied story material. Elisions are obvious. The reader knows next to nothing about Daisy's past or the status of her relationship with Dick (although much is implied). The text ends inconclusively with Daisy's clutching at the hope that perhaps the doctor is wrong. Selectivity is apparent also in the story's narration. The narrator is a third-person one who economically sets the scene and gives the dialogue that makes up considerable parts of the text. For example, the room in which all the action takes place is rendered in a few telling details.

> The pink shade of a single lamp supplied an air of subdued mystery; the fire burned red and still; in place of door and windows hung curtains, obscure,

*The British and Irish Short Story Handbook*, First Edition. David Malcolm.
© 2012 David Malcolm. Published 2012 by Blackwell Publishing Ltd.

formless; the furniture, dainty, but sparse, stood detached and incoordinate like the furniture of a stage scene; the atmosphere was heavy with heat, and a scent of stale tobacco; some cut flowers, half-withered, tissue paper still wrapping their stalks, lay on a gilt, cane-bottomed chair.

The pink lamp shade, the shapeless curtains, the stage-like furniture, the heavy, stale air, and the abandoned and never unwrapped flowers vividly create a scene. They also suggest Daisy's profession (an actress of some kind?) and her indifference to life (the flowers have not been unwrapped, and what does that say about her attitude to the lover who has brought them?). The unappetizing doctor and lover are similarly rendered in a descriptive short-hand. For example, the lover is first presented largely through a series of sentence fragments.

Clean-shaved; stolid and coarsely regular features; black, shiny hair, flattened on to his head; undersized eyes, moist and glistening; the tint of his face uniform, the tint of discoloured ivory; he looked a man who ate well and lived hard.

The narrator is equally economical in the rendering of dialogue. Considerable parts of the story are made up of characters' words to each other, without substantial intervention on the narrator's part. For example, the story ends thus. One should note here both the narrator's reticence, and also the relative informality and modernity of narrator's and characters' language.

"You clumsy fool!" she exclaimed.
She drank the wine off at a gulp.
"Daisy," he began.
She was staring stonily at the empty glass.
"Daisy," he repeated.
She tapped her toe against the fender-rail.
At this sign, he went on –
"How did you know?"
"I sent Liz to listen," she answered mechanically.
He looked about him, helpless.
"I think I'll smoke," he said feebly.
She made no answer.
"Here, put the glass down," she said.
He obeyed.
He lit a cigarette over the lamp, sat down opposite her, puffing dense clouds of smoke.
And, for a long while, neither spoke.
"Is that doctor a good man?"
"I don't know. People say so," he answered.

From the moment Daisy is left alone by the doctor and her lover, the narrator shifts to her point of view. This becomes very marked once Daisy has learned she will die. The next two and a half pages offer the reader the motions of her anguished thoughts and feelings. Both direct speech and free indirect speech are employed to do so. For example, here, free indirect speech is used to render Daisy's despair and shallow defiance.

> The end of February – she was going to die – it was important and exciting – what would it be like? Everybody else died. Midge had died in the summer – but that was worry and going the pace. And they said that Annie Evans was going off too. Damn it! She wasn't going to be chicken-hearted. She'd face it. She had had a jolly time. She'd be game till the end.

The narrator is self-effacing here, as he is in providing details of the context of the scenes he presents. He also offers no moral commentary on character or action. This is all the more striking because the hints given in the story suggest strongly that Daisy is an actress or chorus-girl or demi-mondaine, or a combination of all three. Dick is in evening dress, hinting at wealth, and perhaps a previous or subsequent engagement for that evening. The room is not his home (he does not know where the paper is kept), yet he stands in proprietary fashion before the hearth. The fact that he (or Daisy) keeps champagne in the cupboard caps one's impression that the story deals with a roué, although one with feelings, and his kept woman. (Crackanthorpe's fictional worlds often anticipate those of Jean Rhys.) Further, the narrator offers no commentary on Daisy's behavior. She is no languid invalid, transfigured and redeemed by her suffering, but a testy and desperate woman who does not want to die.

Crackanthorpe's death at the age of twenty-six cut short a career that was not simply promising, but had achievements to show. "Modern Melodrama" is a powerful, innovative, and elegantly laconic story. In it, Crackanthorpe comes closest to some of the fiction of one of his masters, Guy de Maupassant.

# Henry James, "The Altar of the Dead" (1895)

Published in *Terminations* (1895)

Although James was an American, it is appropriate (indeed, necessary) to include him in any account of the development of short fiction in Britain. Settled for most of his life in England, James played an important role in the literary life of Britain, especially in the 1890s during the period of the most rapid and energetic development of the short story there. Many of his short stories are set in England and have few or no American characters. "The Altar of the Dead" is an example of one of these. The piece was first published by Heinemann in London (although a U.S. edition followed in the same year). The action takes place exclusively in London, and the only American character is the minor, if strident, second Mrs. Creston. Although James fretted at the constrictions of the shorter short story, and preferred what he called the longer "nouvelle," those fictions can most readily be understood as longer short stories, but well within any consensual understanding of the form. At 13 000 words, "The Altar of the Dead" is twice the length of Stevenson's "Markheim," and much longer than Crackanthorpe's "Modern Melodrama" or Saki's "Sredni Vashtar," but it is about the same length as Conrad's "Youth" and shorter than the same author's "Karain: A Memory."

Every year since her death, George Stransom has visited the grave of the woman, Mary Antrim, to whom he was engaged to be married. At the age of fifty-five, he has experienced the death of many other people important to him, and has kept their memory alive out of a sense of responsibility toward them. Returning from his visit to Mary Antrim's grave in a cheerless London suburb, Stransom enters by chance a Catholic church ("a temple of the old

*The British and Irish Short Story Handbook*, First Edition. David Malcolm.
© 2012 David Malcolm. Published 2012 by Blackwell Publishing Ltd.

persuasion"). There, he conceives the idea of establishing and funding an altar in a chapel of the church, which secretly, to him alone, will be an altar commemorating his dead. Apart from the death of Mary Antrim, one of the most bitter experiences of his life has been his quarrel with a close male friend, Acton Hague. Although Stransom learns of Hague's death just before he thinks of the idea of his altar, such is the estrangement between the two that Hague is to have no candle on it.

As Stransom regularly attends his chapel with its altar, he notices that a lady is regular in attendance too. He meets her by chance, and over several years a limited acquaintance develops between them. Stransom hopes that after his death, she will maintain the altar and his memory. After some time, the lady brings Stransom to her home where he discovers that her room is a shrine to the memory of Acton Hague, with whom she had a relationship and who clearly abandoned her. This shakes Stransom's and the lady's liaison. She asks him to include a candle to Hague on the altar; he stubbornly declines to do so. This impasse endures over several months and through Stransom's steady decline in health. Finally, Stransom recovers from a final illness enough to go to the church on his own, to wander "the fields of light" of his altar. He has a vision of his dead fiancée and decides to include a candle for Hague on his altar. He now notices that the lady is by his side. He tells her of his decision. She tells him that she has come back to the altar to respect the dead it commemorates and that she does not expect a candle for Hague. Stransom dies before the altar. Is it, the reader asks, his candle or Hague's that must be added to the array?

This odd and sinister story material sounds odder and more sinister in summary (and part of the oddness lies in its teasing playing with and never fully realizing ghost story conventions), but the story is a complex and moving meditation on the power of memory and the ability of individual human beings to give meaning to their lives and losses through imagination and outward signs. The story is deeply indebted to Hawthorne. The stark metaphor/symbol of the altar to the dead, literal and concrete, and yet shimmering with complex meanings ("multiplied meanings," Stransom says), would be in place in Hawthorne's fiction.

Part of the text's oddness lies in its narration. The narrator is a traditional third-person one, but is oddly configured. He is limited to Stransom's point of view among the characters, but can also make general remarks about life and society. He can be distant from Stransom ("If occasions like this had been more frequent in his life, he would have been more frequently conscious. . ."). Yet, often the text operates through free indirect speech (and, at times, something that is nearly free direct speech) to give a strong and almost immediate sense of the movements of Stransom's consciousness ("That new woman, that hired performer, Mrs. Creston?"). However, at still other times, the narrator takes on what is almost a storyteller persona, as if the narrative is being delivered to a group of specific listeners. This is suggested by the "poor Stransom" in the story's first sentence, and by the references to a narrator-listener "we" and to Stransom as "our friend." At times, one is far from certain what point of view is employed: the narrator's or Stransom's. For example:

> These things made their whole relation so impersonal that they had not rules or reasons people found in ordinary friendships. They didn't care for the things it was supposed necessary to care for in the intercourse of the world. They ended one day (they never knew which of them expressed it first) by throwing out the idea that they didn't care for each other. Over this idea they grew quite intimate. ...

What is certain, however, is that the act of narration is foregrounded in this text. The storyteller narrator is not placed in time and space; there is no mechanism for transmission established (how does the narrator know about Stransom?). The persistent shifts between quasi-omniscience, focalization, free indirect speech, and even free direct speech underline the narration as a performance. I will return to this topic later.

Space is limited in "The Altar of the Dead." The story is set in London, but only intermittently in a fashionable London. The jeweler's shop in front of which Stransom meets the Crestons presumably belongs to that London, as does the concert in St. James's Hall. But the bulk of the story takes place in a shabby, dismal London suburb. Here, however, there is also the church with its blazing altar, offering a remedy to the cheerless environment. The contrast is central to the text. Time markers emphasize the *longue durée* of the action, as befits a story of memory and its maintenance through time. Mary Antrim's death happened long before the action starts. Stransom and the lady are not young when they meet. Stransom's quarrel with Hague occurred ten years before the December day he learns of his death. The lady's and Stransom's relationship develops over years. In the end, Stransom outlives all his possible dead. The period between the discovery that the lady has been connected with Hague and Stransom's death is stretched out over many months.

The text is centrally and most extensively an exposure of Stransom's complex psychology. In this respect, it is striking how much is excluded from the account. Stransom's work and his public life are alluded to only fleetingly, only sufficiently to mark their occlusion. The same is true of the other worshipper at the altar. The lady's name is not given by the narrator.

The story has narrowed its focus only to the central (and complex enough) concern, Stransom's and her relation to the past and to memory of that past. Stransom's devotion to his dead is at the heart of the story. On one level, this is presented as admirable, a maintenance of memorial to those who cannot speak for themselves, a loyalty to those who have been close to him. Creston's rapid remarriage stands in opposition to Stransom's lifelong devotion to a lost love. Yet, on another level, Stransom's engagement with the past must give the reader pause. He comes to prefer the company of his dead to the living. The very idea of "his" dead seems oddly and inappropriately proprietary. In any case, Stransom is not quite as faithful as he makes out. He is undeniably interested in his handsome fellow habitué of the altar. He is capable of a jealousy toward the memory of Hague that she cherishes. His desire that his be the one last candle added to the altar, and that, after his death, the lady devote herself to his memory too, smacks of egoism. Yet his final vision before the altar is ecstatic and begets in him the generous gesture he makes to include Hague among the cherished dead.

Two central motifs run through the text: light and secrecy. The light of the altar is glorious, and contrasts with the tawdry splendor of shop windows. Secrecy, as well as light, also shapes the text. What was the nature of Stransom's quarrel with Hague? The lady does not tell Stransom of Hague, nor once he learns of her relationship with him, does she explain what Hague did to her. She never talks of Stransom to her aunt, and only invites him to her home once she is dead. Stransom's altar has one function for the church and its authorities, and another function for him. For a story about light, there is much that is occluded.

The central metaphor/symbol of the glowing altar, "the fields of light" that recall the dead, is similarly both blazingly concrete and mysterious. It is an enactment of memory, a tribute, however flawed and partly selfish, to those who are gone. It is an attempt to give meaning and shape to the losses of life, and offer some consolation for them. It is the center of a meaning-filled ritual in a secular world. But it is also "a mystery of radiance in which endless meanings could glow." It also suggests art. Stransom creates something beautiful that can have meaning for him, but that also bears significances for others. At one point, Stransom thinks of it as "the shining page." He talks of its "multiplied meanings." The story itself advertises its status as a verbal artifact, a work of art – in its coincidences (the lady at St. James's Hall, her relationship with Hague), in its division into sections (especially the move-ment from section vi to vii, which interrupts an action), in the half-heard and never realized allusions in the text to ghost-story conventions, and in the fact that Stransom first speaks to his fellow-worshipper at a concert. Like other of

James's short fictions, for example, "The Lesson of the Master" (1888) and "The Real Thing" (1892), "The Altar of the Dead" takes on a metafictional focus. It reflects, indirectly, on the role of art for the artist, and for others. It is one of James's most complex and fascinating short stories, a moving and intricate reflection on loss, memory and secrecy, and also a consideration of the power and possibilities of art.

# Joseph Conrad, "Amy Foster" (1901)

Published in *Illustrated London News* (1901)
and in book form in *Typhoon, and Other Stories* (1903)

"Amy Foster" is a story of shipwreck, strangeness, and utter isolation. The central figure is not the eponymous Amy (and this is one of the story's odd features), but a Slavic (the narrator calls him "Sclavonian") emigrant/immigrant from somewhere in Galicia, in the eastern part of the Hapsburg Empire. The ship in which he is sailing to America sinks off the southern coast of England. He alone survives. Treated as a dangerous lunatic by the English country folk he first encounters, he is saved by Amy Foster, an unattractive and stolid local servant girl, who is attracted to him, and by an elderly farmer, Swoffer, who eventually provides him with a job and a home. He is given the name of Yanko Gooral, a corruption of his name in his own language, Janko (little Jan), and the Polish word for someone who lives in a mountainous region, "*góral.*" Despite learning English and becoming a fixture in the local community, he remains an object of deep suspicion and hostility to most of its members. He courts Amy, they marry, and they have a son. However, Amy's fascination with Yanko turns to distaste for him and his foreign tongue and ways. Yanko falls ill. In a fever, he calls out for water in his own language. Amy is terrified by him and leaves him. He is found by the local doctor the next morning and dies soon after.

This sad story material is set in an English countryside that is presented in considerable and circumstantial detail. The story clearly gives the appearance of the landscape, distances between places, and the principal points of orientation (Colebrook, Eastbay, Brenzett, and so on). The whole story, too, is embedded in verisimilar particularity, that of mass immigration from Central Europe in the late nineteenth century, and that of rural life in the

*The British and Irish Short Story Handbook*, First Edition. David Malcolm.
© 2012 David Malcolm. Published 2012 by Blackwell Publishing Ltd.

eastern lands of the Habsburg Empire in the same years. Yanko's account of his travels through Europe to reach Hamburg and of conditions on the ship that is to take him to America (filtered through the narrators of the text) is very powerful and disturbing. "Amy Foster" is also a searing account of the consequences of difference, both for the immigrant and for the community in which he finds himself. Yanko is "taken out of his knowledge" in the Kentish countryside. Initially, he cannot speak English. He does not understand why people treat him as a dangerous figure, and is terrified by the rude treatment he receives. The customs of the English who surround him seem impenetrably strange. For the farmers, shepherds, and gentry who encounter this stranger, his difference gives little but offence. His voice, his religious observances, and his songs alienate and disturb, even when he learns English, cuts his hair, and dresses in local garb. When he celebrates the birth of his son in the local inn, he is ejected because his singing irritates the other patrons. Even Amy, who, fascinated by him, is kind to him, and marries him, is, in the end, repelled and abandons the poor man when all he needs is care and water. Yanko is, it appears, forgotten after his death, a death which his father-in-law sees as something of a blessing.

But, yet, of course, he is not entirely forgotten. His story is told. The narration of the text has an organization that is typical for Conrad's work, both in shorter and in longer fiction. An unnamed narrator, of whom the reader knows little (although something), tells a story about someone, in this case a country doctor called Kennedy, telling him a story. As always, this narrational organization is crucial for an understanding of the text. Conrad highlights the process by which stories are made and told. The reader is reminded of the situation in which the tale is related. Visiting his friend Kennedy in the country, the overall narrator sees Amy Foster and elicits part of her and Yanko's story from Kennedy, as they continue the doctor's rounds. Later that evening, Kennedy, "breaking a spell of moodiness that had come over him," tells the remainder by an open window looking out over the sea.

The whole process of storytelling is further foregrounded by the non-chronological arrangement of parts of the story material in Kennedy's account. Although his story does move from Yanko's arrival in England to his death, Kennedy moves freely around in time, going backwards to explain the procedure by which Yanko ends up on an immigrant ship from Hamburg. He also acknowledges when he abbreviates his account ("I can't follow step by step his development"). Further, Kennedy intimates the process by which he has gathered information about Yanko, what the stranger himself has told him and over what period of time, who has told him other parts of the material, and what he has seen for himself.

However, if one reads attentively, it is striking how much is, if not exactly invented by Kennedy, then certainly imaginatively recreated by him. The responses of the farmer Smith to Yanko are presented very closely, without Kennedy's making it clear how he (Kennedy) knows his (Smith's) feelings and actions in such detail. The same is true of his account of Amy's first meeting with Yanko, although he reveals that she told Mrs. Smith something of what happened. Some of Kennedy's presentations of Yanko's feelings are similar. Even though it is apparent that Yanko has talked a great deal to the doctor, the degree of identification of narrator and character is remarkable, and the border between character's words and narrator's intuitions is blurred.

> ... an overwhelming loneliness seemed to fall from the leaden sky of that winter without sunshine. All the faces were sad. He could talk to no one, and had no hope of ever understanding anybody. It was as if these had been the faces of people from the other world – dead people – he used to tell me years afterwards. Upon my word, I wonder he did not go mad. He didn't know where he was. Somewhere very far from his mountains – somewhere over the water. Was this America, he wondered?

The degree to which Kennedy is imaginatively recreating others' experience is apparent in the climactic sequence of Yanko's illness and abandonment. "I believe... I suppose," Kennedy says at one point. The detailed presentation of the events of that evening seem to go beyond what Kennedy could have been told by either of the participants.

The fact that the provenance of parts of the story is emphasized and questioned simultaneously is very important. Yanko's story is one of difference and abandonment, but it is told by a particular narrator under particular circumstances. Kennedy is an outsider, just as Yanko is. He is a traveler, an explorer, a scientist whose "penetrating power of mind" has acted "like a corrosive fluid" on his life. He collects information and he likes to find "a particle of general truth in every mystery." He might be speaking of himself as much as of Yanko when he remarks: "It is indeed hard upon a man to find himself a lost stranger, helpless, incomprehensible, and of mysterious origin, in some obscure corner of the earth." His audience, the overall narrator, is an outsider too. He has been abroad; he is visiting his friend in the country. An outsider tells a story of an outsider telling a story about an outsider.

Kennedy also interprets Yanko's fate. He sees it as exemplifying general patterns and continually relates it to cultural and literary models. Thus, Amy's love of Yanko is "love as the Ancients understood it: an irresistible and fateful impulse – a possession!" Yanko's isolation is related to that of many others, shipwrecked and abandoned in strange lands. The development of Yanko's and Amy's relationship is presented in terms of abstract forces:

"I wondered whether his difference, his strangeness, were not penetrating with repulsion that dull nature they had begun by irresistibly attracting." Yanko's cry of "Why?" after his abandonment seems to Kennedy the "voice of a man calling to a responsible Maker." Kennedy's, too, is the interpretative conclusion: "A gust of wind and a swish of rain answered." When Kennedy looks at Yanko's son, he sees him, too, as a snared bird (he had earlier talked of Yanko in this way), and he sums up the father's (and, in his mind, the son's) fate - "cast out mysteriously by the sea to perish in the supreme disaster of loneliness and despair."

The overall anonymous narrator, it should be noted, shares this pattern of thought. The ploughed land seems to gleam with the blood of generations of ploughmen. A passing wagon against a red sun assumes the dimensions of legend and heroic effort "on the background of the Infinite." He sees the landscape through which he and Kennedy travel (and where Kennedy relates part of Yanko's story) thus:

> With the sun hanging low on its western limit, the expanse of the grass-lands framed in the counter-scarps of the rising ground took on a gorgeous and sombre aspect. A sense of penetrating sadness, like that inspired by a grave strain of music, disengaged itself from the silence of the fields. The men we met walked past slow, unsmiling, with downcast eyes, as if the melancholy of an over-burdened earth had weighted their feet, bowed their shoulders, borne down their glances.

None of this undermines the essential veracity of Kennedy's account of Yanko's life and death in England, but it does complicate it. The reader is aware of how the story material is gathered, where it is told, by whom and to whom, and is asked to think about what parts are, if not invented, then creatively interpreted. Someone like Kennedy, who is an outsider in his world, *would* tell a story like this to his outsider friend. Yanko's life is interpreted as well as told. Conrad's greatness lies in his ability to write of the foreign, the strange, and the outcast, and simultaneously to make it clear how stories are made and why and to whom they are told. The story is more mysterious than it seems at first glance, and one cannot be sure of it – just as Yanko cannot fully understand or be sure of what is going on in England around him. The title is - strangely - "Amy Foster," not "Yanko Gooral." One wonders why. Is there another story that Kennedy is not telling – Amy Foster's? Are there actions and occurrences his account elides? Amy is an enigma – passion and fascination, followed by repulsion and fear. Her presence in the title marks some irresolvable and irreducible enigma at the heart of this text. "Amy Foster" is one of the most moving and subtle stories about the immigrant/emigrant experience in English literature.

# George Moore, "Home Sickness" (1903)

Published in *The Untilled Field* (1903)

Like all the stories in *The Untilled Field*, "Home Sickness" deals with socially humble rural life in (roughly speaking) contemporary Ireland. *The Untilled Field* itself is an important collection of short stories precisely because of its relatively unvarnished depiction of the social and personal relations current in Irish villages of the time.

The protagonist of the text, James Bryden, returns to Ireland after thirteen years in the U.S.A., where he works in a bar in the Bowery slums of New York. His doctor, treating him for "blood poisoning," advises a sea trip and perhaps a return to his native land. Three weeks later, he is in Cork and makes the journey to his home town of Duncannon, a poor village on a peninsula on a lake. Once in his former place, Bryden observes the local community. His feelings range from boredom and fear to enchantment and a desire to stay. He meets a young woman, Margaret Dirken, starts to walk out with her, and agrees to marry her early the next year. This cements his desire to stay in Duncannon, despite coming into conflict with the parish priest, and despite his alienation from many of the ways of his neighbors. He has money, riches beyond what is usual in the township, and plans a life there. However, a casual letter from an acquaintance in New York makes him long for the smell of his bar and his life in America. As abruptly as he decided to return to Ireland, he now decides to escape back to America. He brushes Margaret off with lies and leaves. The last paragraphs of the text sum up his life in New York. He prospers, marries, has children, but toward the end of his life recalls with regret the attractions of the distant Irish village, Margaret, and the landscape of his visit.

*The British and Irish Short Story Handbook*, First Edition. David Malcolm.
© 2012 David Malcolm. Published 2012 by Blackwell Publishing Ltd.

The story is given in logical, chronological sequence. It moves from Bryden's visit to the doctor to his old age reveries. However, the emphases of the narrative are interesting. Nothing is said of Bryden's life in Ireland before he emigrates to New York. Very little, indeed, is given of his life in America. The reader knows that he works in an insalubrious bar, but that is all. Similarly, Bryden's stay in Duncannon is rendered economically through synecdotal scenes: the first day in the new circumstances, his boredom and horror at the people around him and their lives, his encounters with Margaret, and his shifting attitude toward landscape. Bryden's many years after his return to New York are passed over in a paragraph. Details of time and place are similarly economical. No year is given, and the season of Bryden's return to Ireland must be inferred from the detail that Michael Scully is setting off to mow grass the day after Bryden moves into his house. Bryden and Margaret intend to marry after Christmas. The reader cannot be sure when Bryden actually makes the decision to go back to America. He mentions August as a new marriage date, but there is no indication of how far away that is. In one sense, space is clearly marked. There is New York, and to get to Duncannon, Bryden must pass increasingly further away from it, using increasingly less grand means of transport; to Cork, and then by train to a rural station, and from there, by horse-drawn car, lie five miles to Duncannon, the last part of which he walks. On the other hand, space is generic. Duncannon is a typical rural place of small farms, a lake, ruined castles, a big house. Bryden returns to a generic rural Ireland, and the vague time scheme of the story augments the text's generality.

The story is narrated by a third-person omniscient narrator who makes a general observation (further generalizing the text) at the story's conclusion ("There is an unchanging, silent life within every man that none knows but himself. . . ."). However, for most of the story the narrator's point of view is limited to Bryden's, often deploying free indirect and even free direct speech.

> . . . he was not affected when he heard that Mary Kelly, who used to go to do the laundry at the Big House, had married; he was only interested when he heard that she had gone to America. No, he had not met her there; America is a big place. Then one of the peasants asked him if he remembered Patsy Carabine, who used to do the gardening at the Big House. Yes, he remembered Patsy well.

The result is that the reader encounters the world almost exclusively through Bryden's impressions, thought, and feelings. He is the story's center. One never really learns what Margaret thinks or what becomes of her.

This restriction to Bryden's point of view is marked by the limited use of names in the story. Some of the characters in Duncannon have names

(Margaret and Michael Scully, for example), but many do not. In the conversation at Scully's on the first night, Bryden's interlocutors are referred to collectively as "peasants"; only the absent, it seems, have names. Similarly, one never learns the name of the priest, nor Margaret's uncle. The landlord of the Georgian Big House has no name, nor do the dancers at Bryden's party. Partly, this suggests that they are functions of a community, rather than individuals, but it also suggests Bryden's egoism, perhaps even his American immigrant's lack of a sense of connection with others. Certainly, he ditches Margaret almost as soon as he starts to feel trapped in the village.

Like the other stories in *The Untilled Field*, Moore's narrator in "Home Sickness" uses an informal language. Sentences are not simple, but are frequently compound. There is a proliferation of polysyndeton, that is, a recurrent use of "and" to link clauses and phrases. Polysyndeton is deployed to give a sense of a relatively uneducated and unsophisticated rural community. (How accurate that is, is another matter.) It is also used – with its biblical rhythmic and lyric echoes – to capture the beauty and charm of what Bryden feels he has lost when he reflects, in old age, on Duncannon and Margaret.

> The bar-room was forgotten and all that concerned it, and the things he saw most clearly were the green hillside, and the bog lake and the rushes about it, and the greater lake in the distance, and behind it the blue line of wandering hills.

One of the striking motifs that run throughout the text is that of decline. The village appears poorer and more shoddy to Bryden when he first returns; his new neighbors constantly complain of their circumstances; once he receives the letter from New York, he is overwhelmed by sense of the dilapidation and poverty of the land and the village. Rural Ireland seems not a pastoral idyll (as the homeland is often seen in emigrant fiction – see, for example, E. A. Markham's stories of the West Indies), but a miserable place slipping into decay.

"Homesickness" is a complex treatment of the complex theme of emigration and return. Bryden both longs for the old world, and yet abandons it at a moment's notice, almost on a whim. In later years, his memories of it are of a lost paradise (which it did not seem to him at the time), and are, finally, both cloyingly sentimental and completely genuine. A major theme of the twentieth-century English-language novel and short story has been the cost of displacement, emigration, and exile. At the beginning of the twentieth century, Moore presents a subtle and moving account of the dilemmas of the emigrant.

# H. G. Wells, "The Valley of Spiders" (1903)

Published in *The Strand Magazine* (1903) and in book form in
*Twelve Stories and a Dream* (1903)

In his autobiography, Wells remarks that in the 1890s and early 1900s, he
"became dextrous in evolving situations and anecdotes from little possibilities
of a scientific or quasi-scientific sort" (qtd. in Coelsch-Foisner 2008 b: 175).
The range of his short fiction is extraordinary, from the exotic adventure of
"Aepyornis Island" (1894) and "The Country of the Blind" (1904) to the war
fiction cum science fiction of "The Land Ironclads" (1903), from the fantastic-
supernatural of "Pollock and the Porroh Man" (1895) and "The Door in the
Wall" (1906), to the historical fiction of "A Story of the Stone Age" (1897),
and the dystopia of "A Story of the Days to Come" (1899). His inventive verve
is matched by the elegance and memorability of his prose and the resourcefulness and boldness of his technique (the latter features often-forgotten
discussions that focus on Wells's ideas).

One of the richest and most enigmatic of his short fictions, a story that
exploits the possibilities of the form's brevity to the full, is "The Valley of
Spiders." The story's action is limited to a few hours. Three riders, without
names, identified only as a "leader" and "master" and the "man with the
silver bridle," and two subordinates, "the gaunt man with a scarred lip" and
"the little man on the white horse," enter a wide valley, "at the very limits of
the world" they know. They are in pursuit of two or more fugitives, one of
whom is a "half-caste girl" who is running away from the master. Once they
enter the barren valley, a wind rises. They see a dog running before the wind.
One of them notices wild hogs galloping down the valley. Their horses
become agitated. Then they see drifting globes in very large numbers coming

*The British and Irish Short Story Handbook*, First Edition. David Malcolm.
© 2012 David Malcolm. Published 2012 by Blackwell Publishing Ltd.

toward them. They are attacked by spiders that float in these balls and enmesh their prey with threads that they shoot from them. The gaunt man saves his master. He is then himself attacked and overpowered by the spiders. The master and the little man bolt in terror. The leader falls from his horse and takes refuge in a ravine. The little man also survives, but when he returns to find his master, he (the little man, who has previously entertained suspicions of his lord) upbraids him with cowardice, whereupon his master kills him and takes his horse. At the end of the text, the only survivor leaves the valley. It is indicated that the fugitives have, in fact, escaped him.

The story ends with the enigmatic utterance of the "man who had once possessed the silver bridle," now reduced simply to "he." "'Spiders,' he muttered over and over again. 'Spiders! Well, well... The next time I must spin a web'." What does he refer to? Another attempted liaison with a girl, only one that allows the victim no escape? A story that he will tell the next time he is caught out in cowardice? The reader does not know. Indeed, the enigmas of this text are a key organizing component of the story. The story material itself is incomplete. Why are the three in pursuit of the fugitives? Apart from the girl, how many fugitives are there? Why is it so important and so annoying that the little man rides a white horse? Do the fugitives escape the spiders and cross the valley? What happens after the text ends? Even a central item of action, the little man's death, is presented indirectly.

Setting is at once concrete and undefined. The action takes place between midday and sunset, but the historical period is unclear. That the men carry swords, not firearms, is the only temporal indicator of this kind. The valley is presented in concrete detail: its colors, its aridity, its spaciousness, the mountains and forest that mark its borders. The reader knows that it is four days ride from the hunters' base, and "at the very limits of the world." However, country and continent remain unknown, just as historical period does. There are hints of South America in a period of Spanish colonization – the silver bridle, the swords, the reliquary that the leader carries, the suggestion of the limitless power of a *latifundista*, the silk bandana that the little man wears. But these are only hints. The characters, too, are nameless, and are designated only by minimal physical features and by their social relations.

The story's enigmatic quality is further connected with its indeterminacy in terms of genre. It is, partly at least, a story of exotic adventure, involving "white men" in an exotic and hostile environment, pushing at the limits of their civilization. It has elements of historical fiction, signaled exiguously (but this is a very short story) in the characters' swords. It is a fantastic tale, in which the protagonists meet with phenomena beyond their knowledge that surprise and disturb them. Finally, there are overtones of medieval romance. The party is on a quest in a desolate land. The leader's sword is broken in his flight from the spiders, "as though" the narrator notes, "Chance refused him any longer as her Knight." Point of view is also disjointed in "The Valley of Spiders." The story is narrated by an omniscient third-person narrator, but in the first half of the story, until the full arrival of the spiders, the narrator takes the point of view of the little man on the white horse, even employing free indirect speech to do so. Once the spiders arrive, the point of view changes to that of the leader, and it is his experience of the battle with the spiders and his escape that is offered to the reader.

Thus, the whole text becomes an enigma, intriguing the reader, demanding attention, unsettled and unsettling. This links closely with a recurrent motif in the story: rebellion, rejection and critique of authority. The man with the silver bridle is a person of great power and authority. The little man asks himself why his master is so obsessed with the girl he is pursuing. "And the man had whole cityfulls of people to do his basest bidding – girls, women!. . . It was the way of the master, and that was all he knew." The little man starts to question his leader's authority. "Why should it be given to one man to say 'Come on!' with that stupendous violence of effect. Always, all his life, the man with the silver bridle has been saying that. If I said it – !" The little man speculates that the gaunt man with the scarred lip is "as stalwart as his master, as brave and, indeed, perhaps braver, and yet for him there was obedience, nothing but to give obedience duly and stoutly." After the battle with and escape from the spiders, the little man returns to blame the leader for his cowardice. The master had left his servant to be consumed by the spiders. "Why are you our lord?" demands the little man. His master then kills his servant with a broken sword and steals his horse. The man with the silver bridle, established authority and power, reveals himself as a self-serving and treacherous rat.

"The Valley of Spiders" is a rich text, a subtle rewriting of the story of exotic adventure, and a complex mixture of genres. It brings together some major concerns of Wells's fiction, the power of the natural world, the vast possibilities of the universe, and the tenuous legitimacy of traditional authority. It also relates an exciting adventure story, the unresolved enigmas of which make it all the more fascinating. It exploits the possibilities of the short story's brevity with a panache that has rarely been equaled.

# M. R. James, "Canon Alberic's Scrap-Book" (1904)

Published under a different title in the *National Review* (1895) and in book form in *Ghost-Stories of an Antiquary* (1904)

The supernatural story, especially its ghost story variant, is an enduring and important genre in British short fiction. M. R. James is one of the most influential and highly regarded writers (by H. P. Lovercraft among others) of supernatural fiction in twentieth-century Britain. One of James's earliest and best ghost stories is "Canon Alberic's Scrap-Book."

The story material stands in contrast to the innocent sound of the "scrap-book" in the title. The narrator is an unnamed friend of the protagonist, Dennistoun. The narrator offers an account of Dennistoun's experiences over a day and a night in a "decayed town on the spurs of the Pyrenees not very far from Toulouse." Dennistoun is an archaelogist (a typically scholarly Jamesian protagonist) who visits St. Bernard de Comminges in order to examine and document the local church. He is accompanied during his examination of the ancient building by the sacristan, an elderly man who gives evidence of being afraid of something. In the church, Dennistoun hears various strange noises. The sacristan refuses to leave him alone. In the late afternoon, once he has completed his inspection of the church, the sacristan invites him to his home where he sells him a large folio volume from the seventeenth century, assembled by the canon of the church, Albéric de Mauléon, containing priceless pictures and manuscripts, but also a sepia drawing from the late seventeenth century of Solomon in combat with a terrifying demonic figure. As Dennistoun departs with his prize, the sacristan's daughter gives him a cross to wear. While he reads the marvelous folio, the very demon depicted in the picture appears behind him. He is saved by the cross and the intervention

*The British and Irish Short Story Handbook*, First Edition. David Malcolm.
© 2012 David Malcolm. Published 2012 by Blackwell Publishing Ltd.

of his landlady's servants. Later, the sacristan reveals that he too has seen the demon and been tormented by the sight throughout his life.

The action follows the ironic pattern of much supernatural fiction. The protagonist does not know what he is involving himself in. The preliminary signs and mysterious events are interpreted rationally. The sacristan is a hen-pecked husband or perhaps a monomanic. The strange noises in the church are simply those that arise in any old building. Conversations are only half heard and their real meaning (it is good that stout servants will be in the inn that night) is missed.

The apparatus of plausibility that the narrator establishes for this story is one of its most striking features, and one that belongs to the very beginnings of the genre. The narrator is at pains to frame his story of the supernatural within a network of credible details. Thus, the reader receives Dennistoun's story from an informed but non-participant speaker. Dennsiton himself is that stereotype of a sensible trustworthy figure, a Scottish Presbyterian, unsus-ceptible by definition to Franco-Catholic hocus-pocus. The narrator informs the reader in detail of the setting of the story, locating it in relation to documented places. A fairly precise date is given (the spring of 1883). In addition, both the narrator and Dennistoun are scholarly men, given to making fine distinctions. For example, the narrator prefers to call the elderly church servant a sacristan rather than a verger. Dennistoun himself oozes expertise and competence in his field. He can roughly date manuscripts and pictures at a glance, knows what he is doing in the church, and (along with the narrator) has the necessary command of foreign and high-status tongues. The story even has footnotes that make scholarly points or add details of what happens after the story's events to the sacristan's daughter. There is an energetic attempt throughout the story to make the supernatural credible, including information as to where the scrap-book can now be found and that, although the sepia picture has been destroyed, there exists a photograph of it.

The sinister (but verisimilar) setting is established throughout the text too, the decayed town in Southern France, the ancient church full of old and fascinating artifacts, the early evening, and the sacristan's old and partly closed-up house. The props that the setting contains also contribute to the reader's sense of dark mystery, especially the late seventeenth-century folio, full of priceless documents, brought out from an antique chest under a tall crucifix. The human inhabitants, too, add a layer of the sinister; above all, the haunted, terrified sacristan, but also, in the past, Canon Albéric himself, whose death has been recorded in an unusual fashion and who has clearly trafficked with what he should not. The unnamed creature, referred to only as "demonis nocturnus" (demon of the night) in a note attached to the terrifying sepia picture, is quite vile, a creature of grave cloths and hairy skeletal, spider-like limbs, inhabiting a border between the human and the bestial. This is how it appears to Dennistoun.

> The shape, whose left hand rested on the table, was rising to a standing posture behind his [Dennistoun's] seat, its right hand crooked above his scalp. There was black and tattered drapery about it; the coarse hair covered it as in the drawing. The lower jaw was thin – what can I call it? – shallow like a beast's; teeth showed behind the black lips; there was no nose; the eyes of a fiery yellow, against which the pupils showed black and intense, and the exulting hate and thirst to destroy life which shone there, were the most horrifying features in the whole vision. There was an intelligence of a kind in them – intelligence beyond that of a beast below that of a man.

It is the European nightmare of the other, what is not white, European, and human. "Canon Alberic's Scrap-Book" takes an honorable place among a large number of texts of *fin-de-siècle* unease, from Bram Stoker's *Dracula* (1897) through H. G. Wells's *The War of the Worlds* (1898), from Henry James's "The Turn of the Screw" (1898) through Conrad's "Heart of Darkness" (1899/1902). It is also a very skillful and frightening romp through the repertoire of conventions and techniques of supernatural fiction.

# H. H. Munro ("Saki"), "Sredni Vashtar" (1911)

Published in *The Chronicles of Clovis* (1911)

"Sredni Vashtar" stands out even among Munro's other short fictions by virtue of its brevity, economy, sinister suggestiveness, and satisfying cruelty. Conradin, the young protagonist, is being slowly destroyed, emotionally and physically, by his cousin and guardian, Mrs. De Ropp, for no other reason than it is her duty as a respectable, middle-class woman to thwart him, a male child, "for his own good." Conradin resists through his imagination, especially once he discovers the possibilities of the toolshed in Mrs. De Ropp's dismal garden. He turns it into a cathedral for his imaginary faith, with a hen and a polecat-ferret (the latter of which he has secretly purchased and which he names Sredni Vashtar). As part of her almost disinterested thwarting of the boy, Mrs. De Ropp has the hen removed, and then herself investigates the hutch at the back of the shed. Seemingly in response to Conradin's ecstatic prayer, the polecat-ferret kills the guardian. The triumphant Conradin now has a chance to live.

The story writes mostly of Conradin's experiences and feelings, but the language is that of an adult, and there is a degree of distance from the boy, for example, in the humorous approach to the faith he establishes, especially with regard to his Anabaptist Houdan hen. Conradin has no idea what an Anabaptist is, but hopes it is "dashing and not very respectable." The narrator can also, on occasion, enter Mrs. De Ropp's mind to explain her almost disinterested intent to crush her ward. The story is very brief and utterly streamlined. There is the bare minimum of exposition. What has happened to Conradin's parents, for example? Conradin's life with Mrs. De Ropp is summed up in a few papargraphs. The creation of the new religion of Sredni

*The British and Irish Short Story Handbook*, First Edition. David Malcolm.
© 2012 David Malcolm. Published 2012 by Blackwell Publishing Ltd.

Vashtar and its rituals are given a centrality that they deserve. Then follows a comparatively long section detailing the climactic events of the story: Mrs. De Ropp's final trip to the toolshed, Conradin's prayer, feeling of certain defeat, and then triumph, followed by the glorious and sinister appearance of the polecat-ferret itself. The story ends with Conradin's victory as he prepares himself the hitherto forbidden fruit of toast.

The story is organized round a tension of characters and motifs. On one hand, there is Mrs. De Ropp, her "silky and effete" doctor, her "sour-faced" maid, and her obedient servants. Hers, too, is the dismal garden, overlooked by panopticon-like windows, and its almost barren fruit trees. Hers is the church (which Conradin calls the "House of Rimmon") and all the restrictions of female respectability and authority. On the other, there is Conradin's imagination, which allows him to survive, the toolshed where he can be alone (and unobserved) and construct his fierce faith that stands for everything the Woman, as he calls his cousin, rejects. Sredni Vashtar is its embodiment, a product of fancy, and in that fancy gloriously savage. He, like Conradin, is male, and the opposition of male and female is central to the story. In the end, an unrestricted male fury overcomes pursed female respectability.

The gender hostility of the story is clear (and unashamed), and the phallic overtones of the polecat-ferret unmistakable. From the "tool-shed" (the meaning of "tool" as "penis" is well-attested to throughout the nineteenth and twentieth centuries) emerges "a long, low yellow-and-brown beast, with eyes a-blink at the waning daylight, and dark wet stains around the fur of jaws and throat." The story ends with Conradin, toasting fork in hand, doing exactly what he has been forbidden, by a woman, to do. Further, "Sredni Vashtar" fascinates because, like much of Saki's work, is entails a violence against the established order, and a celebration of that violence, which in the terms of the world of those fictions is quite just. Sredni Vashtar is "a god who laid some special stress on the fierce impatient side of things." The tensions of the *fin-de-siècle* in Britain and Europe, and the explosions of an avant-garde impatient with the old ways are echoed in this short story. Perhaps, too, it predicts the enthusiastic welcome given to the outbreak of the First World War in 1914, in which a fierce god of slaughter claimed, among others, Munro himself.

# James Joyce, "An Encounter" (1914)

Published in *Dubliners* (1914)

Joyce wrote the stories in *Dubliners* over several years in the early twentieth century. The stories were mostly finished by 1906. Several were published in Irish journals before the First World War. However, Joyce was not able to find a publisher for a book edition until Grant Richards brought them out in London in 1914. It is important to remember the stories' approximate dates of composition, because, as Hunter (2007: 50–52) points out, Joyce's later identification with avant-garde modernist experimentation obscures the fact that the stories in *Dubliners* are imbued with the conventions and the interests of realist fiction, and are contemporary with the work of Moore.

So much has been written about *Dubliners* that it seems redundant to add more. However, this handbook would be incomplete without some discussion of Joyce's work in the short story, for although he only published fifteen short stories, these stories in the twentieth century assumed a canonical status that has never been challenged. In addition, Joyce's writing about his short fiction, especially his notion of an epiphany, a moment of realization and judgment that the story should build toward, has been very influential, both in short story criticism and in the writing of short fiction. (For recent discussion of the term "epiphany," see Korte 2003: 129, Hunter 2007: 57–58, Greaves 2008: 165, and Jarfe 2010: 122–123.)

Joyce insisted that the stories in *Dubliners* expose a hemiplegia or paralysis that has seized the Irish capital, a moral, intellectual, and social paralysis that is associated with the city's colonized status (Maunder 2007: 215–217). Although the idea that Dublin and Dubliners are irredeemably paralyzed has met with some questioning (Greaves 2008: 165–166), it is easy to see why the term seems to sum up exactly what the stories demonstrate. "An Encounter," the second story in the collection, is a powerful analysis of the desire to escape

*The British and Irish Short Story Handbook*, First Edition. David Malcolm.
© 2012 David Malcolm. Published 2012 by Blackwell Publishing Ltd.

and the difficulty of doing so. Characters seem utterly trapped in an unappealing world. The stories of *Dubliners* are grouped in a chronological progression, from childhood through adolescence to middle age. "An Encounter" deals with childhood experience. The anonymous first-person narrator tells of playing truant from school in early June. He and his companions in crime plan to spend a day going across the river to "the Pigeon House." One associate does not turn up, and the narrator and his companion Mahony wander the streets of industrial and commercial Dublin, eventually resting in a field. There they have an encounter with a sinister older man, who seems to delight in discussing sexually suggestive matters with the narrator. The story ends with the narrator calling on his friend to return home.

In a story marked by inconsequence, the narrator's language is appropriately strange. The story material is given from the point of view of a relatively young boy, without any full adult understanding of some of the events he narrates, such as the boisterous and rough Joe Dillon's decision to become a priest, or the nature of the evidently perverted old man he meets. Nonetheless, the narrator's language is marked both by an informality (for example, "a day's miching," meaning playing truant), and a very marked degree of formality. For example, when he talks of Western adventure stories, he declares:

> But when the restraining influence of the school was at a distance I began to hunger again for wild sensations, for the escape which these chronicles of disorder alone seemed to offer me. The mimic warfare of the evening became at last as wearisome to me as the routine of school in the morning. . . .

It stretches the reader's credulity that a young boy, no matter how bookish, uses lexis like "the restraining influence of school," "hunger for wild sensations," "chronicles of disorder," and "mimic warfare."

The narrator's lexical inconsequence is matched by a degree of inconsequence on the level of narrated action. Why does Joe Dillon become a priest? The old man is himself very inconsequential, at one point "liberal," as the narrator notes, in his views, subsequently violently repressive. The narrative itself has odd elisions. There is a lack of substantial exposition: we know little of the narrator's family or circumstances. The ending is open, and, indeed, enigmatic. Why has the narrator "always despised" Mahony "a little"? What is the old man doing in the field as Mahony watches? Is he urinating, defecating, or even masturbating? Further strange features of the narrative deserve some mention. As in several of the stories in *Dubliners*, the narrative is one of aimless wandering, quite without any traditionally understood story material, and, if indeed an epiphany (or any kind of more traditionally understood climax) is to be expected in the text, where is it in "An Encounter"?

What has the narrator seen and understood? Is it in the boys' failure to reach their goal? Is it the old man's monologue? Is it in the narrator's moment of realization at the end that he has despised Mahony? The epiphanic moments in stories such as "Araby" and "The Dead" seem clear-cut in comparison.

The story's oddness is evident, too, on the level of genre. Clearly a story of psychological initiation (however ambiguous), "An Encounter" possesses echoes of the Gothic or the supernatural. The narrator pays close attention to the foreign sailors he sees, for he is looking for one with green eyes. He is reticent about what he associates with green eyes (one of the text's silences), but it is clearly sinister. The old man's "pair of bottle-green eyes peering at me from under a twitching forehead" are suggestively diabolic, and, further, the narrator is afraid, as he walks away, "that he would seize me by the ankles," in the time-honored tradition of a bogey-man. The text is as unsettling as the experience it recounts.

Inconsequence builds to be a recurrent motif in the text, as does the central aimlessness of the boys' wandering. The old man's monologue about girls suggests to the narrator that "magnetized by some words of his own speech, his mind was slowly circling round and round in the same orbit." This motif recurs when the old man changes tack to talk of whipping boys who are interested in girls. Just as Mahoney and the narrator can never reach the Pigeon House, so the old man can never leave his obsessions. Indeed, escape and its impossibility are central to this story, as to many others in *Dubliners*. The stories of the Wild West, the Indian games, and the day's truancyare all attempts to break with the dullness of life. That the grand expedition does not achieve even its modest aim, and leads the boys to the "Vitriol Works" on the North Strand Road, or to grocers' shops in Ringsend in which "musty biscuits lay bleaching," is sadly ironic. The only moment of happiness for the narrator occurs as he is waiting for Mahoney on the Canal Bridge in the sunshine of a June morning.

Part of the strangeness of "An Encounter" lies in the way, common to the stories of *Dubliners*, that religious lexis permeates the drab quotidian world of the city. Here, the word "mystery" recurs when the narrator talks of the old man's monologues on girls and chastisement. He speaks "mysteriously" and "as if he were unfolding some elaborate mystery." The narrator says that "he led me monotonously through the mystery." However, the meaning of the presence of such religious lexis is not clear. It is not just that the religious is debased by its context, nor that the religious term establishes some contrast with a debased material world. The ambiguity of the presence of such lexis with regard to an old pervert is central to the story. What is the reader to make of it? As in so much else, the text leaves one to work it out for oneself.

# D. H. Lawrence, "Tickets, Please" (1919)

Published in *The Strand Magazine* (1919), and later in book form in *England, My England* in the U.S.A. in 1922 and in Britain in 1924.

Different versions of this story exist, and although the changes are interesting, they are not substantial. One that may cause confusion among readers is that in an earlier version, the male protagonist is called John Joseph Raynor, while in a later version, he is called John Thomas Raynor. His character, however, remains the same.

Set during the Great War in the English Midlands, "Tickets, Please" is a story of love and vengeance among the employees of a tram company. It is war-time, so the tram company is staffed by young women and by men who cannot serve in the armed forces. Annie is a conductor on a tram-service that runs from an industrial city for two hours through countryside and smaller towns. John Thomas Raynor is a handsome young inspector. He is something of a local Casanova and plays fast and loose with her affections. She and the other girls whom he has toyed with get together and severely beat him, humiliating him, and insisting that he choose one of their number. He chooses Annie, but this gives her no satisfaction.

Despite the serious and violent subject matter and action, the story is narrated in a jaunty and demotic manner. The narrator's language is informal, and close to the language that characters themselves use (although they occasionally speak in dialect to each other too). The narrator speaks of "we" when recounting events, employing a device typical of spoken narratives. He uses present tense at times, when the literary text would more usually use past tenses ("The inspector's name is John Thomas Raynor. . . ."). He deploys clichés on occasion – "Trams that pass in the night," "pastures new," "on the *qui-vive*" – and his lexis is on occasion strikingly demotic – "his face... was ruddy and smiling and handy as ever," "drew her a little nearer to him, in a very warm and cuddly manner," "he had a wonderfully warm, cosy way of holding a girl with his arm, he seemed to make such a nice fit." The narrator frequently employs free indirect speech to give Annie's thoughts and feelings almost directly. "A fine cock-of-the walk he was," she reflects of John Thomas. "She could sum him up pretty well." "Well, it was fun, it was exciting to be at the Statutes [fair] with John Thomas." The narrator, however, is still an omniscient third-person one, who is able to offer considerable exposition, and to comment on characters' behavior and thoughts from outside them. The language at these points shifts up a few degrees in formality. For example, of Annie's feelings toward John Tomas, he writes, "But with a developing acquaintance there began a developing intimacy. Annie wanted to consider him a person, a man; she wanted to take an intelligent interest in him, and to have an intelligent response. She did not want a mere nocturnal presence, which was what he was so far." "[D]eveloping intimacy," "intelligent response," and "nocturnal presence" are not phases Annie would use herself.

The organization of the narrative is striking. A section of exposition covers perhaps a quarter of the text. The development of Annie's and John Thomas's "walking-out" takes up approximately another quarter. Almost half the text consists of an account of the girls' act of vengeance on the man who has toyed with them. Thus, the story's focus is substantially on this act of insubordinate violence. Much of this part of the story is narrated via dialogue, although there is also a full account of the violence the women do to John Thomas. The story's climax is, indeed, recounted in detail; the violence is almost dwelled on with a kind of quasi-pornographic satisfaction. Despite its resounding climax, the text ends without closure. John Thomas has chosen Annie, but that seems to satisfy no one. Even the violence, satisfying though it be, seems to leave no one very happy. John Thomas leaves and the women get ready to go their separate ways into the night.

Annie's character is the most explored in the story. She experiences a mélange of attraction and affection toward John Thomas, desire for a different sort of relationship with him, outraged pride when he shies away from her, and a hot drive for vengeance, which, once realized in her humiliation of the offending man, turns to a bitter distaste and disdain She gets very angry at her lover. "You ought to be *killed*, that's what you ought," she hisses. "You ought to be *killed*." The narrator notes "a terrifying lust in her voice." All other characters are shown vividly but superficially, including the gigolo of the tramlines John Thomas himself. In the absence of large numbers of men, who have gone for soldiers, he is very glamorous, and clearly knows how to deploy his charms. There cannot be much more to him, because he is, indeed, a superficial and handsome rogue. Only once he has been outrageously thrashed by the usually acquiescent and accommodating young women, does a complex spitefulness rise in him.

> There was a pause. Again he averted his face. He was cunning in his overthrow. He did not give in to them really – no, not if they tore him to bits.
> "All right," he said, "I choose Annie." His voice was strange and full of malice.

Linked motifs run throughout "Tickets, Please." The tram's journey through the countryside is presented as an "adventure." "The ride becomes a steeple chase. Hurray! We have leapt in a clear jump over the canal bridges – now for the four-lane corner. With a shriek and a trail of sparks we are clear again. To be sure, a tram often leaps the rails – but what matter!" This wild boldness is echoed in the fair rides that John Thomas takes with Annie ("Round they spun and heaved, in the light"). This wildness is further echoed in what the story sees as the derangements of wartime. The narrator speaks of the "lawlessness of wartime," meaning the disruption of established social patterns occasioned by the war. Young women are conductors on trams, controlling crowds of unruly passengers in verbal and physical conflict. They wear short skirts and boots. A group of women feel confident enough to get together and thrash the man who has been using them. John Thomas's "official" admonitions do not stop them.

Indeed, the story becomes very violent in its second half. The women fall upon John Thomas like so many irate Bacchantes, tear his clothes, strike him, pin him down, humiliate him.

> He went forward rather vaguely. She [Annie] had taken off her belt, and swinging it, she fetched him a sharp blow on the head with the buckle end. He sprang and seized her. But immediately the other girls rushed upon him, pulling and tearing and beating him. Their blood was now thoroughly up. He was their sport now. They were going to have their own back, out of him. Strange, wild creatures, they hung on him and rushed at him to bear him down.

Yet the vengeance seems to bring little satisfaction. Annie declares she does not want the humiliated man. Her feelings are of "bitter hopelessness," "something was broken in her," and she speaks "fiercely, as if in torture." As John Thomas slinks off into the night, the women deride him, but the story ends on a hesitant and ambiguous note. "The girls were all anxious to be off. They were tidying themselves hurriedly, with mute, stupefied faces."

"Tickets, Please" is a remarkable text. The narrator's language is informal and shadows his characters' language closely. The text's presentation of wartime and its lawless possibilities is fascinating. Further, the story's account of female rebellion against male exploitation is frank and complex at the same time.

# Virginia Woolf, "Kew Gardens" (1919)

Published privately in 1919, and subsequently in
*Monday or Tuesday* (1921)

"Kew Gardens" is one of Virginia Woolf's best known and most highly regarded short fictions. The story is set on a summer's day in Kew Gardens in south-west London. The action, such as it is, takes place during the Great War of 1914–1918 (one character refers to "this war"). The text starts with a close and objective description of a flower bed in the gardens. Four groups of characters pass the flower bed, and their thoughts and words are given as they do. A family group passes, made up of a husband and wife and their two children. A couple of men walk by, followed by two "elderly women of the lower middle class." Finally, a young couple pause by the flower bed. The names of some of the characters are given, although not in full. The married couple are called Eleanor and Simon (their children are Caroline and Hubert). One of the men, the younger, is called William. The young girl in the fourth group is called Trissie. However, the older man, the two lower middle-class women, and the young man are unnamed. The characters reflect on the past, talk agitatedly about spiritualism, remain silent, talk of sugar and mutual acquaintances, or consider the fact that today is a day when one can enter the park for free. Two groups think about taking tea.

These fragmentarily known characters and their fragmentary conversations and thoughts are interwoven with descriptions of the flower bed they pass, and of a snail that is attempting to make its (the text has "his") way somewhere across the earth and leaves. The snail has a chance encounter with a "singular high stepping angular green insect" that (the text has "who") passes in the opposite direction.

The story material of "Kew Gardens" is clearly very distant from that of most short stories before or since. Adrian Hunter calls it one of Woolf's "most important and experimental stories" (Hunter 2007: 63), and Stef Craps

*The British and Irish Short Story Handbook*, First Edition. David Malcolm.
© 2012 David Malcolm. Published 2012 by Blackwell Publishing Ltd.

discusses how it has been seen as an "ur-text" for Woolf's radically innovative longer fictions (Craps 2008: 194). The piece is, indeed, a convention-busting tour de force, but before I discuss those aspects of the story, it is important to point out, too, how conventional and traditional "Kew Gardens" is. The narrator is a third-person omniscient one, who, with the educated, formal-leaning language and self-confidence of the nineteenth-century tradition, looks into the minds and overhears the words of the wide range of characters. For example, of the two lower middle-class women, the narrator firmly remarks that "Like most people of their station they were frankly fascinated by any signs of eccentricity betokening a disordered brain, especially in the well-to-do." The narrator is free to shift point of view from that of the human characters to the snail. The reader is told of the snail at one point: "He had just inserted his head in the opening [between leaf and earth] and was taking stock of the high brown roof and was getting used to the cool brown light when two other people came past outside on the turf." This is omniscience indeed.

The devices by which the text exposes its characters are traditional: narrational comment, free indirect speech, and dialogue. The narrator also offers detailed description of setting, character, and action: of the flower bed, of the light in the park, of the behavior of William and his older companion. In addition, the text has something of the social range of traditional realist fiction, from the firmly middle-class groups to the two lower middle-class women. The story, too, as Craps points out (Craps 2008: 196–197) has strong social resonances. Part of the setting is the Great War, and William's companion's interest in spiritualism is very much of that time and shaped by the losses of the conflict. The elderly women talk not just of family and acquaintance, but also of foodstuffs, including rationed sugar. Even the tea room that two groups of characters direct their paths to has political and social echoes. The Kew Garden tea pavilion was burned down by suffragists in 1913. As Craps argues, Woolf's adoption of a non-human perspective is relevant to a time in which the War demonstrated human frailty and insubstantiality. The largely aimless wandering of the characters perhaps also suggests a society and culture that has lost its way. Even the film-like movement to extreme long shot at the story's end belongs to a Victorian tradition (see Dickens's *Little Dorrit*, for example). People and the park are seen against the backdrop of the great city.

Nonetheless, "Kew Gardens" is a highly innovative story, and its innovations stand out more clearly against the traditional devices and techniques that it also deploys. Story material is deviant. The human action is fragmentary and completely elliptical. Readers know little about the human characters and their lives beyond the syncopated moment in which they pass the flower bed. Whole swathes of story material are implied behind the words and conduct of these human characters, but they are not given. Further, to make a snail's progress across a flower-bed one of the major sequences of action in the text is a bold step indeed. Even here, the reader knows so little. Does the snail make it wherever it is going? The close attention to minute detail that one finds in the paragraphs about the flower bed and the snail is also unusual. The opening paragraph meticulously, and objectively, describes flowers and light, in a passage that goes beyond the non-human, but animate, perspective of the snail, for here there are mostly only elements of nature, plants, light, water, and even the snail is just a shell.

In addition, the language of "Kew Gardens," as one might expect in Woolf's fiction, goes beyond the conventional transparence and modesty of fictional prose. As the story goes on, figurative language becomes more prominent. In the last paragraph, the garden is described thus:

> How hot it was! So hot that even the thrush chose to hop, like a mechanical bird, in the shadow of the flowers, with long pauses between one movement and the next; instead of rambling vaguely the white butterflies danced one above another, making with their white shifting flakes the outline of a shattered marble column above the tallest flowers; the glass roofs of the palm house shone as if a whole market full of shiny green umbrellas had opened in the sun; and in the drone of the aeroplane the voice of the summer sky murmured its fierce soul.

Here, simile alternates with metaphor in a density that makes the prose self-advertising.

In "Kew Gardens," Woolf pushes beyond the traditional borders of the short story and of realist prose. The text is a powerfully innovative one, yet remains in touch with techniques and genre-markers of less exploratory work. The innovations, too, have much sense. One's experience of life and others often is fragmentary and inconclusive. We are surrounded, in part, by strangers. There are so many points of view. Further, the story makes the point with vigor that there is a world that is not human, of elements, of colors, of light, and, indeed, of snails. In times of state and human arrogance, then as now, such observations are never out of place.

# Katherine Mansfield, "The Stranger" (1921)

Published in *London Mercury* (1921) and in book form in *The Garden Party,* and *Other Stories* (1922)

Mansfield's work is often seen as offering an innovative inconclusive kind of story without substantial plot (Head 1992: 16; Hunter 2007: 72–73). It is certainly true that Mansfield had a disdain for much contemporary short-story writing, and saw her stories (and good stories, like those of Chekhov) as abandoning traditional plots and asking questions rather than answering them (Hunter discusses this fully [2007: 72–73]). While her fiction is, indeed, elliptical, open-ended, and ambiguous, it stays firmly within the conventions of the realist text, and the degree to which it abandons traditional story material can be exaggerated. "The Stranger" is a good example of Mansfield's work: a psychological study that ultimately challenges the reader's assumptions, a bravura exercise in point of view writing, and a highly ambiguous examination not just of a psychology, but of a marriage.

The story material is simple, but not without complexities. John Hammond (referred to by the narrator as Mr. Hammond or Hammond) is waiting for his wife to return from a voyage to Europe. The time and place of setting are never specified clearly, but characters' clothes sound contemporary to the 1920s, and the two references to towns (Salisbury and Cooktown) sound as if they might be fictional versions of cities in Mansfield's native New Zealand (the setting of several stories in *The Garden Party*). The large ocean liner's docking is delayed. A doctor has been called on board. Eventually, the vessel comes in. Hammond goes aboard and meets his wife Jane (he calls her Janey), whom he clearly loves intensely. He wishes to carry her off so that they can be alone together, but is faced with frequent delays as she bids farewell to her fellow first-class passengers (she has clearly, as always, been extremely popular), the stewardess, and the doctor. They leave the ship and travel to a hotel, where once again Hammond is in an emotional stew to have his wife alone. He has always felt that she is not quite his. Once they are alone, Jane tells her husband that the ship's docking was delayed because a man died, and that he died in her arms. The nature of the dead man's relationship with Jane is obscure, but Hammond is broken by the news and feels that the dead man will, from now on, always come between him and his wife.

The story material echoes Joyce's "The Dead," and is not without its lurid and even melodramatic aspects (and is none the worse for that). It is, indeed, a reprise of the very traditional story material of the doting older husband and the younger wife. The text is narrated by a third-person narrator, but one who sticks very closely to Hammond's point of view. In fact, very little of the story is not filtered through the protagonist's consciousness. The story's second paragraph in which he is introduced is the only substantial exception. Even the first paragraph, in which the arriving liner is described, is presented from the point of view of the waiting crowd on the wharf, of which Hammond is part. From the third paragraph on, and then throughout the story, the reader experiences Hammond's thoughts and feelings through an extended use of free indirect speech. "But what a fool – what a fool he had been not to bring any glasses! There wasn't a pair of glasses between the whole lot of them." Thereafter, the narrator's direct task is limited to indicating characters' actions and marking who speaks in dialogue.

Thus, the reader is limited almost entirely to Hammond's mind. The picture offered of this character is complex and, finally, surprising. Hammond is a middle-aged business man, well-dressed, self-confident in most matters, genial, bossy, and forceful. He is the leader of the crowd waiting for the liner. He knows the harbor-master. He gets on the vessel first ("As to 'ladies first,' or any rot like that, it never entered his head"). He has reserved the best room in the hotel for him and his wife. The manager greets them, as people of consequence. He travels first-class on trains. He is an embodiment of male power, social and financial adeptness, and control. He clearly loves his wife to distraction. He wonders if she has been able to get a cup of tea while the ship is waiting to come in. He is inarticulate when he meets her. He "groaned for love" when she suggests his appearance has improved during her absence. His one driving impulse in the text is to be alone with her.

Yet he is never sure of her. "And again, as always, he had the feeling that he was holding something that never was quite his – his. Something too delicate, too precious, that would fly away once he let go." He has been distressed during her absence. "The strain was over. He felt he could have sat there for ever sighing his relief – the relief of being rid of that horrible tug, pull, grip on his heart. The danger was over. That was the feeling. They were on dry land again." When he tells her he is "glad" to have her back, and she replies that she feels the same, Hammond still reflects that he "never knew – never knew for dead certain that she was as glad as he was." He longs to make her "so much part of him that there wasn't any of her to escape."

This last quotation points to the oppressive nature of Hammond's love of his wife. He wants "to blot out everybody, everything," apart from him. He is even resistant to her reading letters from their children. He treats her like a child. He puts her on his knee and bounces her up and down (which she does not care for). He holds her as he held the young girl on the wharf while waiting for the liner.

Part of the story's complexity resides in Jane's resistance to Hammond's benign control. She has a "cool little voice." She calmly insists on fulfilling her social duties to fellow passengers, and to others. She does not respond to his baby talk and withdraws her hand from his in the taxi as they drive through bright-lit streets. She clearly has an attractiveness to others and an ability to manage her own affairs, independent of her older husband's ministrations. She is Jane, not just Janey. Indeed, on her return Hammond reflects that "there was no need to worry about anything. She was here to look after things. It was all right. Everything was."

However, the story's end when Jane reveals her relationship with the dead man on the vessel, her coolness and self-assurance seem insensitive. She is an accomplished manipulator of her husband, and knows how to control him physically and emotionally ("She stepped over the rugs, and came up close, touched his breast, and looked up at him. . . . The gentle pressure of her hand was so calming that he put his over hers to hold it there"). Her revelation disturbs Hammond profoundly. She insists that her relationship with the dead man has "nothing to do with you and me," but Hammond feels his uncertainty about her return and that her experience on board the ship will forever divide them. The reader's sympathy must surely be meant to become nuanced here. Hammond becomes child-like in his distress.

"The Stranger" is a text of considerable subtlety and complexity. Hammond's capable, bossy bonhomie is presented from different angles, at once intrusive and also a sign of deep love, and yet of insecurity too. His devotion to his wife is at once a powerful and benign emotion, yet also crushingly and demeaningly oppressive. His wife is part ideal and part little doll. One can understand Jane's cool resistance to his suffocating attentions. But the story's conclusion must modify that already complex picture. Is Jane being cruel? She reminds her older husband that the dead man was young. Is she putting Hammond in his place? Or does she not really care? Whatever the answer, his grief at the story's conclusion is powerful. The reader's sympathy surely must shift slightly.

The fact that the reader is obliged to ask questions at the end of "The Stranger" is central to the text, for it is elliptical and ambiguous. The reader is not told certain crucial things. Why has Jane been in Europe? What is the nature and source of Hammond's worries about her during her absence? What was her relationship with the man who died in her arms, alone with her? Hammond certainly suspects infidelity. The narrator is reticent, but the overtones of an affair are present.

Mansfield's story is a powerful and modern story. In a modern neutral language, with a highly consistent deployment of free indirect speech, it is a very intelligent portrait of a complex emotional state (Hammond) and of an ambiguous psychology (Jane). The text is sexually quite frank: Hammond holds Jane on his knees, and he is clearly longing to have her in bed. (Like the floppy boot in Joyce's "The Dead," Hammond's overcoat, flung over the hotel's "blind bed" "like some headless man saying his prayers" suggests that he will not have his wife sexually tonight or any other night.) The reader's responses to the characters and their situations cannot but be intricate. He/she is invited to examine a traditional marriage and think about the relations and tensions, the resistances and cruelties of that institution.

# A. E. Coppard, "The Higgler" (1925)

Published in *Fishmonger's Fiddle* (1925)

"The Higgler" is one of Coppard's best-known stories, and one often anthologized. Remaining within the conventions of realism (which not all Coppard's stories do, see, for example, "Adam and Eve and Pinch Me" (1921), "The Green Drake" (1931), and "Speaking Likenesses" (1937)), the story is reminiscent of Hardy's narratives of rural English life and their bitter ironies (for example, "The Withered Arm" [1888] or "The Son's Veto" [1894]). It also echoes some of Lawrence's contemporary short fiction, such as "The Fox" (1918/1921) or "You Touched Me" (1922).

A higgler is an itinerant trader who buys agricultural produce from farmers and then sells it on to customers. He/she may also barter goods. The word is derived from the verb 'haggle', and, as the story makes clear, suggests a certain amount of craftiness and cunning. Harvey Witlow is, nonetheless, an "honest higgler." He has been a soldier in the Great War, as recently as a year previously, and is now trying to make a living in the higgler's trade. Business is not good. However, while crossing a high upland moor for the first time, he comes upon the farm of Mrs. Sadgrove and her daughter Mary. He is able to do very profitable trade with Mrs. Sadgrove and is attracted to the red-haired, cultivated daughter. Witlow starts to visit the Sadgrove farm frequently, for commercial reasons, but also because of Mary (this, despite his semi-engagement with Sophy Daws, a girl in his village). He is invited to Sunday dinner and at that time Mrs. Sadgrove asks if he will marry Mary, stressing the considerable wealth that the girl will inherit from her mother. Witlow is tempted. He loves Sophy, but loves Mary, too. However, he fears a trap. How could such a superior person want to be married to him? Why is the mother marrying off her daughter in this way? Is she defective in some way; do they have debts?

*The British and Irish Short Story Handbook*, First Edition. David Malcolm.
© 2012 David Malcolm. Published 2012 by Blackwell Publishing Ltd.

Accordingly, he marries Sophy instead, cutting off all intercourse with the Sadgroves. His business starts to fail; marriage to Sophy turns out to be difficult. He determines to ask Mrs. Sadgrove for a loan. When he arrives at the farm, on a wild March evening, he finds that Mrs. Sadgrove has died that day and Mary is alone. He helps her lay out the corpse, and learns that it was Mary who wished to marry him, against her mother's advice. Witlow leaves Mary at the story's end, but thinks that he could return and work as her bailiff now she is alone, although he knows his wife Sophy will not be happy about such an arrangement.

The narrative is largely logical and chronological, although Witlow relates an earlier episode from his time in the war to the Sadgroves. The narrative is, however, oddly digressive. As he is getting dressed to go to visit the Sadgroves, Witlow observes two neighbor children perform a parody of a church service, or rather of the circulation of the collection plate in church. While he is picking fruit in Mrs. Sadgrove's orchard, Witlow kills a mouse. He tells a grotesque story about killing a mad pig while in France. Sophy's grandmother and her third husband come to Sophy's and Harvey's wedding, and the old lady bickers with her present husband, and also talks of the gentleman who, she claims, was her real father. The reader also sees Harvey on his wedding night demonstrating real gentleness toward the rather distressed Sophy. In addition, the narrative is open-ended. What will happen next? Will Harvey become Mary's bailiff, and how will that end?

The digressions are functional. The children's parody of church custom suggests the materialism that drives the world of the story (Witlow's financial problems, Mrs. Sadgrove's casting marriage in the light of a business proposition, Harvey's erring calculations as to what lies behind her offer). The killing of the mouse parallels Harvey's abandoning Mary (for she is in the orchard when he does it). His anecdote about killing the pig illustrates his "bucolic" humor and, thus, his inappropriateness for Mary, while Sophy's grandmother's story of her origins also touches upon the problems of misalliance and the theme of male cruelty toward women. Harvey's behavior on his wedding night, however, puts him, at least, in a positive light. Further, one can argue that these narrative digressions point to the existence of a world beyond that of the protagonists, a whole context of life in which their experiences are only a part of a larger whole.

The narrative's open-endedness is crucial to the text's meaning. Harvey is calculating (higgling?) with the future. How can he survive and prosper? Will Mary take him back in some measure? Will he have to break with Sophy? He is weighing up his options. Indeed, the time organization of the narrative reinforces the text's lack of final resolution. The story starts on a windy and cold day in April. It concludes on a wild evening in March. The protagonists are, in a sense, back where they started, perhaps ready to begin a relationship again.

As the narrative in "The Higgler" is complex, so, too, is the narration. The narrator is a third-person one, although one almost completely limited, among the characters, to Harvey's point of view. There is extensive use of free indirect speech, free direct speech, and interior monologue. For example, when Harvey is introduced in the second and third paragraphs of the story, narration moves from third-person generalization to Harvey's point of view to free direct speech, and then to direct monologue.

> Higglers in general are ugly and shrewd, old and hard, crafty and callous, but Harvey Witlow though shrewd was not ugly; he was hard but not old, crafty but not at all unkind. If you had eggs to sell he would buy them, by the score he would, or by the long hundred. Other odds and ends he would buy or do, paying good bright silver, bartering a bag of apples, carrying your little pig to market, or fetching a tree from the nurseries. But the season was backward, eggs were scarce, trade was bad – by crumps, it was indeed! – and as he crossed the moor Harvey could not help discussing the situation with himself.
>
> "If things don't change, and change for the better, and change soon, I can't last and I can't endure it. . . ."

The complex movements between narrator and character are well illustrated by the following passage. Harvey is reflecting on his relationship with Mary.

> Too beautiful she was, too learned, and too rich. Decidedly it was his native cunning, and no want of love, that inhibited him. Folks with property did not often come along and bid you help yourself. Not very often! And throw in a grand bright girl, just for good measure as you might say. Not very often!

Most of this passage is not just written from Harvey's point of view, but via free indirect and direct speech, which are more or less in Harvey's words too. The exception is the sentence "Decidedly it was his native cunning, and no want of love, that inhibited him," in which the lexis is clearly not that of Harvey. There are many such instances in "The Higgler." The narrator is very close to Harvey, but also keeps a certain distance, although at times the narrator adopts a very informal lexis and syntax that bring him close to the central character once more. "A high upland common was this moor. . .," the reader is told in the first paragraph. The inversion sounds like that of an oral storyteller, as does the same device at various points in the text: "Beautiful she was. . .," the narrator informs of Mary; "She was worth money was Mrs. Sadgrove. . .," he tells the reader; and later "Very bright and green it was, and very blue the sky. . . ." These are all cases where the point of view is not clearly that of Harvey, but yet his language has permeated the narrator's. Coppard maintains a shifting distance to and closeness with his protagonist.

The narrator also withholds information. The story's irony and climax depend on the narrator's not revealing that it is Mary who really wants to marry Harvey, although her mother has reservations. The hints of Mary's oddness – her silence, her walking in the orchard, her being educated beyond her station – all suggest that perhaps Harvey is right to be suspicious of Mrs. Sadgrove's offer.

The story's main interest is Harvey's character and the difficulties that it leads him into. He is a complex figure. He is a bold entrepreneur among higglers. He has survived the war and means to make a go of the business if he can. Charming and handsome, he has a robust sense of humor. On one hand, self-assured, he also cannot overcome his sense of his own unworthiness of the educated and refined Mary. He is a decent and honest tradesman, yet his craftiness undoes him, for he sees a trap in Mrs. Sadgrove's proposal where there is none. He leaves Mary without a word, yet shows great tenderness toward Sophy. He can help Mary when she has practical and emotional difficulties, particularly in dealing with her mother's corpse. He is clearly calculating at the end what his chances are for the future.

Harvey is ultimately misled by signs. Of these, there are several in the text: that painted on his wagon; a notice attached to a telegraph pole on Shag Moor; the one painted on Mrs. Sadgrove's wagon; the picture the French hussar draws of a pig; the weather signs that the guests to Harvey's and Sophy's wedding discuss. Some of these are hard to interpret: the pig picture and the weather signs, particularly. Above all, Harvey completely misreads the signs given out to him by Mrs. Sadgrove. His craftiness interprets her frankness as deception, and Harvey's fortunes go askew thereafter. One wonders how well he interprets Mary's responses to his help with her mother. How will Harvey's "haggling" with Mary and Sophy prosper?

# Rudyard Kipling, "The Gardener" (1926)

Published in *McCall's Magazine* and in
*The Strand Magazine* (both 1925),
and in book form in *Debits and Credits* (1926)

"The Gardener" is one of Kipling's stories about the Great War of 1914–1918. Like all of these stories, it is not about the war as such, but about the effects of the war on combatants and non-combatants. Like "Mary Postgate" (1915/1917), it looks at the war from the point of view of a woman; unlike that savage and disturbing study of cruelty and suffering, "The Gardener" focuses on suffering alone and offers some hope of peace or remission from pain. However, again like "Mary Postgate," it offers a vision of the war that is far from traditional military heroics.

"The Gardener" is a story that is radically different the second time one reads it, for the ending reveals information that the narrator has withheld through the rest of the text. Helen Turrell, "thirty-five and independent," lives in an English village. She belongs, one must assume (although details are scant), to the rural upper middle-class, well-off, servant-employing, and utterly respectable. Her scapegrace brother George has managed to father an illegitimate child on the daughter of a retired N.C.O. in India, and then to die in an accident. Helen takes charge of the child and brings him up. She does not deny his illegitimacy to the world, but her respectability, honesty, and bravery mean that this is never held against the child, whom she names Michael. They have a close and loving relationship (he even calls her his mother in private). He follows a normal (and successful) path for one of his class and time (preparatory school, public school, scholarship to Oxford). He is, however, of the generation that must fight in the Great War, and

*The British and Irish Short Story Handbook*, First Edition. David Malcolm.
© 2012 David Malcolm. Published 2012 by Blackwell Publishing Ltd.

eventually, sometime between late 1915 and mid-1916 (by internal dating in the text), is killed by a "shell-splinter dropping out of a wet dawn." Helen lives through the various stages of grief, and after the Armistice travels to the military cemetery where Michael is buried. Confronted by a "merciless sea of black crosses," she asks help of a gardener to find her nephew's grave. The gardener says he will show her where her son is buried.

The ending is a surprise one, and one that has provoked much controversy among commentators (Matthews 1926: 341; Russell 2007: 164). Only on a second reading, does one see that the narrator has presented the circumstances of Helen's adoption and raising of Michael with complete fairness toward the reader, but has withheld the crucial information that Michael is Helen's illegitimate son, not her brother's. By this ending, too, the narrator also gives the story a metaphysical dimension, inasmuch as the gardener is clearly a Christ-figure. Helen is a Magdalene, an adulteress. Like her Biblical prototype, she encounters a gardener in a cemetery. The story ends with Helen's not realizing who the gardener is – "and she went away, supposing him to be the gardener." This precisely echoes the King James Bible. In John 20.15, Mary Magdalene, having discovered that Christ's tomb is empty, meets Jesus and at first mistakes him, "supposing him to be the gardener." The subject is a common one in Christian iconography.

The narrator configures the story material of "The Gardener" in an intriguing fashion. Most importantly, he withholds the information about Michael's true parentage until the story's end. However, he also withholds and never reveals who the boy's father is. In a sense, it is irrelevant, for the focus of the story is on Helen's conduct after her affair and on her dealing with the loss of her child. But a second reading encourages one to think about the boy's father. His features are those of the Turrells, but, although Helen insists "that little Michael had his father's mouth to a line," this is a smokescreen, for the narrator indicates that, in fact, "His mouth was somewhat better cut than the family type." Does this suggest an aristocratic liaison? Whatever the case may be, appropriately to a story about secrets, the reader is never told who the father is. Helen's resolution and courage is apparent here as well as in other parts of the text.

The narrator's organization of the story material further indicates the text's focuses. Helen's and Michael's life before the war takes up approximately a quarter of the text; Michael's involvement in the war occupies perhaps an eighth; and Helen's response to her son's death, in its immediate aftermath, and then after the Armistice, is presented in the remainder. Her journey to Hagenzeele Third Military Cemetery itself, in fact, takes up more space than her and Michael's life before the war. Traditional military heroics have no place in the story. Michael does not die in battle, but almost by chance, he and his body eliminated with a technological, a mechanical impersonality and neatness.

The story is, centrally, a study of Helen Turrell. The first section of the story, both on first and subsequent readings, depicts her as a courageous, resilient, and loving woman, respectable, but able to conduct herself bravely and independently within most of the conventions of her world. She, of course, cannot reveal Michael's true parentage; in late nineteenth-century England anywhere that was simply impossible. She does the best she can under the circumstances. The only time the story moves away from Helen is in its brief account of Michael's war, and even there events are related in part to her. For example, Michael has written to her just before he dies. Thereafter, the focus is firmly on Helen and the stages of her bereavement, moving from going through all the procedures established to find out whether her son, officially missing, is in fact alive or not. Once all hope (which she has never entertained) has run out, she enters a period of numbness and loathing of the surviving, which endures after the Armistice. The longest part of the story deals with her journey to Hagenzeele, her half-indifferent, half-horrified response to the whole apparatus surrounding travel to the cemetery, lodging, and the people she meets en route. Her encounter with the sheer enormity of a British Great War cemetery is memorable.

> She climbed a few wooden-faced earthen steps and then met the entire crowded level of the thing in one held breath. She did not know that Hagenzeele Third counted twenty-one thousand dead already. All she saw was a merciless sea of black crosses, bearing little strips of stamped tin at all angles across their faces. She could distinguish no order or arrangement in their mass; nothing but a waist-high wilderness as of weeds stricken dead, rushing at her. She went forward, moved to the left and right hopelessly, wondering by what guidance she should ever come to her own.

The above quotation indicates one of the central motifs of "The Gardener": the industrial, mechanical, non-human nature of the Great War. Michael's death is presented as almost devoid of human agency. A piece of shrapnel kills him when it drops from the sky, and a second shell "neatly" buries his body. As she goes through the official procedures to establish Michael's fate, Helen feels that she, like the shells in a munitions factory, is "being manufactured into a bereaved next of kin." The "official intimation" that Michael's body has been found and interred, comes "backed by a page of a letter to her in indelible pencil" (presumably Michael's last letter to her), "a silver identity-disc, and a watch." Things survive. The technology of the indelible pencil outlasts the body.

Further, Michael's cemetery has a number, "Hagenzeele Third Military Cemetery," and the whole process of getting there is a branch of the modern transport and hotel system, almost the tourist industry. Helen's encounter with the military cemetery quoted above clearly points not just to its extent but its mechanical uniformity. It seems an industrial product, mass manufactured like shells.

In this impersonal system, the reader encounters other human figures besides Helen, most notably women deeply damaged by the war. These are the deranged, hopelessly lost mother, who cannot find her son, and whose ignorance of his enlisted name and his body's whereabouts means that she will never find him. Equally damaged is the Mrs. Scarsworth whom Helen meets on her journey to Hagenzeele. Appropriately named, Mrs. Scarsworth hides under a ghoulish cheer, firm disclaimers ("*I* haven't lost anyone, thank God"), and a cover of commerce (she takes photographs of graves for bereaved families – technology again) the secret that she – like Helen, one understands on a second reading – is visiting the grave of someone whom she can never acknowledge; a lover, one suspects, for whom she cannot publicly grieve.

It is part of this story's austerity, lack of sentimentality, and ambiguity, that when Mrs. Scarsdale reveals the truth to Helen, she also comments on the peculiarity of Belgian hotel decor ("What extraordinary wall-papers they have in Belgium, don't you think?"), and clearly misunderstands Helen's compassion. Helen's final encounter with the Christ-figure similarly avoids sentimentality and is also ambiguous. The gardener is a gardener. There is no hint of Christ physically about him. The "infinite compassion" in his eyes might be human only. His words are simple to the point of austerity. "Come with me. . . and I will show you where your son lies." Further, Helen seems not to register his calling Michael her son. She leaves the cemetery without realizing that this is Christ. Only the narrator's words indicate that he might be so.

But the connection is firmly made. The gardener can be read as Christ, and the story hovers between the two identifications – a simple gardener and Christ. In either case, the reader is offered a glimmer of hope in a world of machines and deceit. Someone has guessed. Even if it is a slip of the tongue, there is a moment of truth. If the gardener is, indeed, Christ, there is some chance that there is more than this stupid waste of life. Maybe the soldiers' graves are "his young plants." However, that metaphysical hope is very fragile, set against the bleak mechanisms, the desolate landscape ("a board and tar-paper shed on the skirts of a razed city full of whirling lime dust and blown papers"), and the hideous ranks of crosses in Hagenzeele Third.

# Jean Rhys, "Mannequin" (1927)

Published in *The Left Bank, and Other Stories* (1927)

"Miss Rhys cut[s] down to essentials with a vengeance.... There is no nonsense about her – she goes right for her point," wrote Conrad Aiken in a review of *The Left Bank, and Other Stories*, in the *New York Evening Post* in 1927. He compared her work favorably to that of Katherine Mansfield and Ernest Hemingway, praising all these writers' economy (qtd. in Malcolm and Malcolm 1996: 118–119). "Mannequin" is a story that embodies many of Rhys's concerns and much of her technique in her output as a whole. It is a good representative of her work in *The Left Bank* collection.

The story is quite without traditional plot materials (much more so than most of Mansfield's short fiction). Anna – an early Rhys woman *par excellence*, young, uncertain, hard-working, ill-paid – has just started work as a mannequin in a very ritzy Paris fashion house (in the Place Vendôme, no less), modeling clothes for buyers from "big shops all over Europe and America," and for individual purchasers. She has been hired by the owner, spent an hour putting on her make-up, and has modeled a coat for a buyer from the U.S.A. Now she is on her way through the labyrinthine corridors behind the glamorous sales rooms to take her lunch. She meets her fellow mannequins. She meets some of the other personnel that populate her new world. She spends five hours in the afternoon being fitted for a dress and then modeling it for a range of clients. At six in the evening, she leaves work. In the darkness, for it is spring, the mannequins emerge from all the shops on the Rue de la Paix and disperse into the city.

The text is a fragment. There is little exposition, and the text really has no closure. Anna will return to work the following day, but the reader does not even know where she is going that evening. Much of the text is written

*The British and Irish Short Story Handbook*, First Edition. David Malcolm.
© 2012 David Malcolm. Published 2012 by Blackwell Publishing Ltd.

from Anna's point of view and frequently through free indirect speech. For example:

> About five o'clock Anna became exhausted. The four white and gold walls seemed to close in on her. She sat on her high white stool staring at a marvellous nightgown and fighting an intense desire to rush away. Anywhere! Just to dress and rush away anywhere, from the raking eyes of the customers and the pinching fingers of Irene.

But there is also a narrational distance from the main character. The narrator gives information about place setting, about Anna's appearance, and about the customs of the fashion-house. "Aspirants for an engagement," the reader learns, "are always dressed in a model of the house." Later, there is information about Anna's fellow mannequins.

> There were twelve mannequins at Jeanne Veron's: six of them were lunching, the others still paraded, goddess-like, till their turn came for test and refreshment. Each of the twelve was a distinct and separate type: each of the twelve knew her type and kept to it, practicing rigidly in clothing, manner, voice and conversation.

The narrator's language is modern and largely neutral in stylistic level. There are several short sentences and, indeed, short paragraphs. There are fragments. The story's opening paragraph is simply: "Twelve o'clock. *Déjeuner chez* Jeanne Veron, Place Vendôme." Although Rhys does not avoid simple sentences, she does not (any more than Hemingway does) avoid longer and complex ones. But a paragraph like "She was Madame Pecard, the dresser" gives a laconic immediacy to the story, a pared down linguistic configuration that is appropriate to Rhys's unsparing and unsentimental view of women's lives in the great capitalist cities of Europe.

Indeed, the glamorous world of the fashion-house is deglamorized bit by bit in the course of "Mannequin." Upstairs are the gold and white "decorative salons" where clothes are modeled by "goddess-like" mannequins. Downstairs are "the regions of utility and oilcloth," the bare corridors and stairs, the shabby backstage to splendor. The mannequins' dressing-room may have "an extraordinary and distinctive atmosphere of slimness and beauty," "silken lingerie" and "the smell of cosmetics," but it is a "depressing room, taken by itself, bare and cold."

It is a world of women (there are almost no male characters, except among the clientele), but the mannequins, who are at the text's heart, are carefully prepared products, dressed uniformly when off duty, carefully made up, and fixed in specific roles: "blonde *enfant*," "*femme fatale*," "*garçonne*," "chic of the devil," and Anna's "*jeune fille*." Other women, also, are part of the fashion-house; sewing women and sales women, they, too, dressed appropriately and were playing a part as cogs in a commercial machine. Though the mannequins' work has glamour, it is also hard. After four hours work, Anna is exhausted and near to quitting. One of the sales women's words comfort her. But relations among women in this world are far from universally friendly. There is some affection and solidarity, but much jealousy, sly antagonism, and hostility too.

The mannequins and especially Anna are the story's central focus. Anna is beautiful, young, frail, and vulnerable. The mannequins generally are seen as "flowers," both near the start of the text and at its end, when the reader realizes that Anna is not just one among many women models at Jeanne Veron's, but part of an even larger industry. The Paris night swallows up the mannequins "as gay and beautiful as beds of flowers." Female beauty is insubstantial. How long will Anna keep her beauty? How long will she be able to stand the modeling hour after hour?

Rhys's greatness (and she is a great, and an undervalued short-story writer, overshadowed by her contemporaries Mansfield and Hemingway) lies in her ability to present the lives of women in economical, unsentimental, and austere stories. She shows the show girl, the *demi-mondaine*, and the mannequin doing their best to keep alive, parlaying their transitory beauty and charm into some kind of living within a world of commerce, hard-faced calculating women, and male power. "Mannequin" is a clear-eyed exposure of a world where female beauty and capitalism meet.

# W. Somerset Maugham, "Footprints in the Jungle" (1927)

Published in 1927 and in book form in *Ah King* (1933)

"Footprints in the Jungle" is a mixture of (late) story of imperial adventure and detective fiction. The narrator is the kind of figure so favored, in stories of imperial adventure, by Conrad, Kipling, and Maugham himself: the visitor to whom a friendly acquaintance relates an interesting tale in the tropical night. In "Footprints in the Jungle" the setting for the narration is the charming settlement of Tanah Merah, in colonial Malaya, once very important, but now marked by "vanished grandeur." The narrator is staying with the head of the colonial police force there, a Major Gaze. At the club on a Wednesday evening, when the rather faded and staid institution becomes at least a little livelier than usual, the narrator makes the acquaintance of the Cartwrights, during a bridge session, in which he makes up a four with the them and his friend Gaze. The narrator finds Mrs. Cartwright both a formidable card player and an interestingly intelligent and forceful woman, who clearly dominates her rather lackluster husband. He and Gaze are roundly outplayed by the husband and wife, who are a couple very much at ease with each other and happy in their marriage. The narrator also encounters the Cartwrights' daughter, who bears, he notes, a resemblance to Mr. Cartwright. After they leave the club, Gaze slowly tells the Cartwrights' story to the narrator. Although he denies he is much of a storyteller, Gaze carefully, and only when the two white men are alone, reveals what he is certain happened some twenty years ago in another part of British Malaya.

It is a tale of adultery and murder. Mrs. Cartwright was then married to a man called Bronson, a successful rubber planter. Made unemployed by a fall in the price of rubber, Cartwright moves in to the Bronsons' home on their

*The British and Irish Short Story Handbook*, First Edition. David Malcolm.
© 2012 David Malcolm. Published 2012 by Blackwell Publishing Ltd.

plantation. Bronson is murdered while returning home with a large sum of money from a bank in another town. Gaze is called upon to investigate the murder. Theft is immediately assumed to be the motive for the murder, and the culprits are assumed to be Malays or Chinese. Gaze notes the footprints of the victim on either side of his bike tracks. He has stopped to talk to someone and been killed as he rides away. Gaze's investigations lead nowhere, however. Four months after her husband's death, Mrs. Bronson is delivered of a child, the Olive that the narrator meets much later at the club in Tanah Merah. Within a year, she and Cartwright marry, in a manner that Gaze calls "very natural." At about the same time, a Chinese man is arrested for trying to pawn Bronson's watch. The watch has been clearly lying in the jungle for more than a year. Gaze institutes a search of the area round the spot where Bronson was murdered. He discovers the dead man's pocket book, still full of rotted banknotes. Although he cannot find the rest of the money (silver coin) Bronson was carrying, Gaze decides that theft did not lie behind Bronson's murder. He starts to work out another interpretation. He concludes, as the narrator has, that Cartwright and Mrs. Bronson fell in love, she became pregnant, and they together murdered Bronson, as the only way out of their situation. "I held my tongue and the Bronson murder was forgotten," says Gaze.

"I'm afraid I'm telling you this story very badly," says Gaze to the narrator. This is one of two acts of narrational disingenuousness in "Footprints in the Jungle." The narrator himself toward the end of the text expresses his admiration for detective fiction and regrets "that I have never had the skill to write one." Both Gaze and the narrator are misleading their interlocutors. Gaze reveals the Bronson-Cartwright story gradually and with great skill, marking off the sub-climaxes with some verve ("Bronson was killed," "And then a Chinaman was caught trying to pawn poor Bronson's watch") and offering all the clues as to the real criminals as he goes along. The narrator, of course, has, when he professes lack of skill, presented his readers with an artfully organized detective story, and one with a surprise ending, for the murderers, while known to Gaze, are not prosecuted, nor indeed even condemned by the policeman. The narrator and Gaze both practice a deceit just like the murderers.

Mariadele Boccardi calls "Footprints in the Jungle" "exemplary in its disturbance of the surface of colonial life" and discusses it as part of the revision of the story of imperial adventure that takes place after the First World War, but which had been implicit in the genre from its beginnings (Boccardi 2008: 31). The story is, certainly, far from any glorification of the colonial enterprise. The colonial setting for the narration, Tanah Merah, is well past its time of glory. The British club is dull and often empty. Gaze frequently remarks on the wearing down of characters by the action of time and climate. Most importantly, the criminals are white, not the Malays and Chinese that Gaze initially blames. Further, those criminals, although Gaze has known their crime for two decades, are still part of the colonial world and described by the policeman as "very nice people" (which in 1920s British discourse, especially abroad, was a high complement).

The revision of the genre is made even clearer in Gaze's description of Bronson. Big and healthy, much given to sport and sweating, Bronson "was about thirty-five when I first knew him, but he had the mind of a boy of eighteen. You know how many fellows when they come out East seem to stop growing." The narrator confirms Gaze's words. He knows the type well. "You might almost think that no idea has entered their heads since they first passed through the Suez Canal," he remarks. He is a good manager, a "typical public schoolboy," the kind of character celebrated in so many tales of British colonial expansion, but yet stupid and not what Mrs. Cartwright wants. He also does not appear to be able to give her children.

"Footprints in the Jungle" carefully dismantles any moral or cultural capital of the colonial world. The Empire is seen as a commercial interest, as indifferent to its white agents as it is to its Malayan or Chinese subjects. In times of crisis, Singapore, Gaze tells the narrator, is full of British plantation managers in dire financial straits. This is not Empire as civilization, but as capitalist enterprise. The story's crime – performed as Christmas, a great feat of white British solidarity, is coming on! – is committed by respectable and "nice" white people. The agent of law, Gaze, refuses to prosecute them, and indeed cannot. Further, he will not condemn the Cartwrights. The whole text is imbued with motifs of transient life, glory, and beauty. In his closing words, Gaze speaks of Judgment Day, the end of things as we know it, the end of the existing order. The footprints in the jungle are vanished. All this, too, will pass.

# T. F. Powys, "John Pardy and the Waves" (1929)

Published in *Fables* (1929) and *No Painted Plumage* (1934)

Powys's work demonstrates the resilience of non-realist short fiction throughout the twentieth century. His marginality in most discussions of twentieth-century literature, however, also points to the selectivity of the canon at every level: form, genre, and author. Like many of his short stories, "John Pardy and the Waves" has much in common with fable, parable, and allegorical fiction. Non-realist motifs abound in his work. In "Mr. Pim and the Holy Crumb" (1929), for example, a dead friend converses amicably with the eponymous Mr. Pim. Later in the story, a crumb of communion bread speaks to him too. Mr. Pim is not surprised by these events, nor is John Pardy when toward the end of the text he engages in a conversation with the waves by the seashore.

"John Pardy and the Waves" is an idiosyncratic reworking of Christ's parable of the Prodigal Son (Luke 16: 11–32). The text is replete with other biblical echoes. For example, John Purdy's sores recall those of the prodigal in Luke 16: 21. Pardy's impulse to count the hair on a servant's head echoes Matthew 10: 30 and Luke 12: 7. Revelations is referred to explicitly when Pardy counts 1500 waves on the shore. The narrator informs that it is "the same magic number that the angel reached to when he measured with his rod the city of the Lamb." (This echoes Revelations 21: 15–17, although the mathematics seem wrong, or at least different from the biblical measurements, in Powys's story.)

John Pardy is one of three children of a hard-working master-carpenter. When the three other children declare that they will be successful in the future, John makes it clear he intends to be idle. Accordingly, when his father dies,

*The British and Irish Short Story Handbook*, First Edition. David Malcolm.
© 2012 David Malcolm. Published 2012 by Blackwell Publishing Ltd.

he leaves John nothing. Thanks to a kind aunt, however, who pays his fare to America, John travels as a hobo in America for the next thirty years. These travels are dealt with in summary fashion, although the reader is told that John has looked for happiness among the people of America and found it nowhere. On his return to England, he seeks out his siblings. Rejected by both brothers (one is a successful grocer, the other a wealthy farmer), he finds refuge with his sister, Agnes. She soon wants rid of the beggarly brother, even attempting to poison him. John continues his search for happiness, and spies on Agnes's husband, a rich farmer. He sees him counting his money and assumes that it is the counting that gives him pleasure. John, thus, considers counting the rats in the barn where he sleeps (but cannot do so for want of light) and the hairs on a servant's head (the servant, warned against him, flees). He finally settles on counting the waves on the shore. The waves speak to him and explain why his brothers have treated him so, that his sister has tried to poison him. They also explain that they are immortal, part of a vast sea that exists independent of human sight and concern. John enters the ocean having been told that he will find pleasure in destroying others. "You may sink a ship," the waves tell him, "and with good luck you may become a tidal wave that will drown a city."

The story operates with the conventions of fable, parable, and allegory. The characters are simplified figures representing moral and religious principles – idleness, materialism, lack of charity. Non-human entities can speak (in this story, waves). But the meaning of the text is (like that in many fables, parables, and allegories) ambiguous and unclear. The text's narrative is, in any case, strangely off-center. Mr. Pardy the elder's death is caused by a chance hornet sting. John's thirty years in America are passed over most succinctly. Logical chronological sequence is not always observed: readers learn of John's search for happy people in America after they have learned of his return to England. John himself is a peculiarly naïve figure. When he sees Agnes's husband counting money, he assumes it is the counting, not the money, that brings happiness.

Ambiguities run throughout the text. John is not part of the materialist world of his siblings. He loves the beauty of nature. His search for happiness uncovers the baseness of much human life. In the American South he sees the lynching of a black man, but cannot see that anyone is happy. He later enters

a rich man's palace, where he watched a frolic during which, after a huge feast, the monkeys were sent to tickle and tease the women, who wore no clothes. When John left the house he was obliged to own to himself that neither the onlookers, the monkeys, nor the girls had been happy.

His visits among the dying do not uncover any happiness either.

But John is also an unapologetic ne'er-do-well and a freeloading leech. The reader is asked at least to think about why his siblings should take him in after his thirty years absence. Those siblings, however, are scarcely admirable. The waves reveal the futility of the grocer brother's this-worldliness; the sister Agnes is prepared to poison her brother; and the brother Walter's relationship to his pigs, it is more than hinted in the text, is an amalgam of the sinister and the perverse. John, too, for all he is a means of exposing human nastiness and hypocrisy, is a vile fellow, covered in sores, prepared to take food from the cat's dish, and one who has never done a day's work in his life. He goes to his death in the ocean looking forward to sinking ships and inundating cities. The waves themselves are cheerfully hostile to human life. They simply do not care much for human beings, but are a kind of eternal and strange other, which John joins in the end. They seem to embody a vision of the divine – or is it only nature? – as something unutterably and irreducibly alien to human life.

> We, who are waves, know you, who are men, only as another sea, within which every living creature is a little wave that rises for a moment and then breaks and dies. Our great joy comes when we break, yours when you are born, for you have not yet reached that sublime relationship with God which gives the greatest happiness to destruction.

Powys's short stories illustrate the power of fable, parable, and allegory to confuse and to provoke thought. His texts are imbued with Christian references, yet the divine is disturbingly unaccommodating and unaccommodatable, decidedly not anthropocentric, the harsh, ambiguous, and disturbing God of many of Christ's parables. John Gray writes of Powys: "Vey few twentieth-century authors have a knack of writing convincingly of first and last things. A religious writer without any vestige of belief, Theodore Powys is one of them" (Gray 2001: 55).

# Seán O'Faoláin, "Midsummer Night Madness" (1932)

Published in *Midsummer Night Madness, and Other Stories* (1932)

Like Frank O'Connor, O'Faoláin was one of the major prose writers and writers of short fiction in post-independence southern Ireland. *Midsummer Night Madness, and Other Stories*, O'Faoláin's first collection of short fiction, was published by Jonathan Cape in London in 1932. A U.S. edition came out in the same year. The collection consists of seven short stories set during the Anglo-Irish War of 1919 to 1922, and, in the case of "The Patriot," the last story in the volume, during the Irish Civil War of 1922 to 1923. To an extent, the stories interweave. Characters recur – for example, Stevey Long is one of the protagonists in "Midsummer Night Madness" and is the central figure in "The Death of Stevey Long." The Rory who is killed by the British in "The Fugue" is possibly the same Rory who is one of the Irish guerrillas who execute the Anglo–Irish Bella in "The Small Lady." The stories are all marked by their unglamorous, and usually utterly unheroic, depictions of warfare. Much time is spent hiding from British patrols (or, in "The Patriot", Free State ones). The protagonists in "The Bombshop" are confined, in deep boredom, to a few rooms, making bombs of various kinds to use against the British. Conflict between them even causes the accidental death of their protector, an old lady in the rooms below. Stevey Long, in "The Death of Stevey Long," escapes from a British goal, with the help of his Black and Tan warder, only to turn on him and allow him to be shot, despite promises to help him, once he has served his turn.

"Midsummer Night Madness" is narrated by John (the reader never learns his surname), an I.R.A. officer, sent from a city (Cork, it would appear from the text) into the country to investigate the inactivity of a local battalion.

*The British and Irish Short Story Handbook*, First Edition. David Malcolm.
© 2012 David Malcolm. Published 2012 by Blackwell Publishing Ltd.

For the narrator, this is a return to the land of his childhood. He is to stay in the large country house of a local Anglo–Irish landowner, Henn, as this is a safe place that the Black and Tans (British irregular counter-insurgency forces) will scarcely think of searching. He remembers Henn from his childhood and from stories his mother told him of a wildly eccentric figure, noted particularly for his sexual excesses and rampant promiscuity. Once he reaches Henn Hall, John immediately realizes that he has stepped into a complex sexual triangle involving his acquaintance, the inactive battalion commander, Stevey Long, the proprietor of Henn Hall himself (now eighty years old, decrepit, drunken, and still fierce), and a beautiful tinker woman, called Gypsy. His arrival is a catalyst for an eruption of a conflict among the three, which also involves political, social and historical disputes. As the madness of a midsummer night develops, Long and a band of incendiaries set fire to another local Anglo–Irish landowner's big house, and Long threatens to do so to Henn Hall if Henn will not marry the pregnant Gypsy. Henn agrees to wed her, although it is far from certain who is the father of her child. John, who has striven hard to keep Long's (in his view useless) violence within bounds, demotes his inept and idle battalion commander *in absentia*, and returns to the city. In a coda, the reader learns that the ill-matched pair of Henn and Gypsy, now presumably married, have departed from Cork for Dublin and Paris.

The story is narrated from John's point of view in linear fashion, although with one substantial analepsis, in which the narrator recalls one of his mother's stories about Henn and his own memories relating to the landowner. The text hinges on juxtapositions of space and character. John leaves the city for the countryside, looking back at the cityscape as he does so. He "turned to the open fields and drew in a long draft of their sweetness, their May-month sweetness, as only a man could who had been cooped up for months past under one of those tiny roofs." He returns to the contrast of town and country later in the text. The rural world is presented as beautiful, full of plant growth, fine smells, and the enchanting sounds of birds and water. Even after the disturbing events of the night, the next day is radiant in the sun of a summer morning. The city is for John, and others, a place of danger, policed by violent British irregulars, and a place of confinement, as they hide from those. But despite its lush charms, the rural world is also violent and dangerous. After his first encounter with Gypsy, the narrator realizes that he will not be able to escape conflict in the area around Henn Hall; he sees that it has "an unpleasant real life of its own." Indeed, the story sets out this "unpleasant real life": the sexual conflict between the protagonists, the bitter disputes of Irish history, and the violence that these take on in the 1920s. The paradox (natural and rural beauty juxtaposed with human violence) is underlined by the narrator when he remarks that the fire in the Blakes' house across the valley has roused the songbirds and "the night was sweet with their music."

The central characters – the narrator, Henn, Stevey, and Gypsy – are involved in an intricate set of contrasts and affiliations. Henn stands out against the other three. As the narrator remarks, he is "one of the class that had battened for too long on our poor people," his house "one of those thousand unofficial blockhouses of the English on Irish soil." He speaks differently from both the narrator and all those around him. He has long been an ogre-like creature for the narrator and for two generations of children. His home is one of the big houses, owned by the Anglo–Irish, embedded, the narrator reminds the reader, in the memories of the Catholic peasantry around them, as sites of oppression and cruel neglect (at the time of the Famine of the 1840s and 1850s, for example). In class solidarity, the Blakes, whose house has been burned out, know that they can come to Henn's, even though they have not been on good relations for decades.

Stevey and the narrator represent a very different Ireland, an Ireland now in rebellion, in what the narrator calls "revolution." Stevey despises and bullies the old Henn; he threatens to have his house burned down, and is quite capable of doing so. The narrator, too, is provoked into argument with the old landowner. O'Faoláin allows the voice of the *ancien régime* to speak its mind about Irish fecklessness (although there is a complex identification with, as well as rejection of, Ireland in Henn's diatribe). The narrator answers back, pointing out that Henn's family money comes from commerce. But the narrator also appreciates the old man, is polite to him, and defends him against Stevey and the incendiaries. The narrator even feels that Stevey is coarse in comparison to the old roué of Henn Hall. The beautiful and sensual Gypsy's response to her master is tangled too. She has a strongly sexual relationship with Stevey (indeed, he may be the father of her child) and is repelled by Henn's age, but she is also drawn to and indulges Henn's devotion to her (a physical devotion, it must be noted). Like the narrator, she protects him, and in the end leaves with him, to be his wife.

Complex affiliations and contrasts run throughout this story. Stevey and Henn represent two opposed poles of the Irish dispute, but in their hothead-edness and violence are similar to each other. The narrator and Gypsy reject the Ireland of the big house, but identify themselves with its representatives, particularly with Henn, but also with the Blakes when they arrive. Time setting is crucial in this intricate set of relations. Underlying the whole story are centuries of vexed inter-Irish conflicts, which are themselves very intricate. It is clear, for example, that the narrator's father has been a policeman, or agent at least of the colonial dispensation, and has participated in evictions on the landowner's side. The particular historical moment is also crucial in the text. There is still "enough romance left in the revolution" for the narrator, suggesting that later there will not be (and, indeed, other stories in *Midsummer Night Madness* offer a most disenchanted view of the war to free Ireland). The conflict with the Tans is at an early stage; "reprisals" like burning down landowners' houses is not the norm; the narrator can stop the incendiaries now, but even "six months later" he would neither have wanted to nor been able to.

The motif of madness (the madness in the title) of various kinds runs through the text. Sexual passion burns in the triangle of Henn–Gypsy–Stevey. The Tans roar through village and city in their armored vehicles, weapons blazing indiscriminately, drunk, and bent on revenge. The local incendiaries retort with their own violence. Stevey rages at Henn, and he at Stevey. The fire at the Blakes' house reflects this human violence. (The motif of fire is repeated throughout the text, from the city's "furnace-glow" to the blazing fire in Henn's hearth.) At the center of the text is ruin: the human ruin that is Henn and the dilapidation of his home. The walls around it are fallen, and his drawing room, like his farm yard, is full of what is cracked, broken, and bare. Ireland is madness and ruin, and only nature retains any beauty and benignity.

"Midsummer Night Madness" is an intricately knotted, but never confused, historical and political text, attempting to deal with the tangled relations, the human snarls of a time of rebellion and change, itself the result of centuries of antagonism and mistrust. It does nothing to glamorize the dispute, and gives both sides their full voices. It brings conflict down to a human level, which it views with complexity, austerity, and humanity. In post-independence southern Ireland it is a brave text, part of O'Faoláin's lifelong critique of his land, its myths, its politics, and its mores.

# V. S. Pritchett,
# "Handsome Is As Handsome Does"
# (1938)

Published in *You Make Your Own Life* (1938)

"Handsome Is As Handsome Does" is a complex picture of a complex English
marriage. It is set in the 1930s in what looks very like the south-west of
France. Julia and Tom Coram are an ill-matched and yet perfectly matched
couple. She comes from not very wealthy country gentry; he has educated
himself out of the working class in the English Midlands, and has risen
(although by the standards of a class-bound 1930s, not very high) to become
an industrial chemist. Both have broken with their social origins: Julia by
marrying someone of working-class background and who (for this is the
1930s) is in commerce and industry; he by education and by marrying Julia.
Both are, thus, very dependent on each other, socially and personally isolated.
Both are ugly by conventional standards, although Julia by intelligence and
charm can appear beautiful. They have no children. While holidaying by the
ocean in France (it is Tom's first trip outside England), they mix with the
owner of their *pension* and the only other guest. The owner, Monsieur Pierre,
is a fussy, foppish elderly man. The other guest, Alex, is a young and
extremely handsome Jew (or, at least, that is what the Corams call him) of
mixed French and German parentage, educated in England, multilingual,
cosmopolitan, sophisticated.

Julia is articulate and intelligent; Tom is "uncouth" and tongue-tied. She
continually covers up his boorishness and gauche behavior. Tom is antag-
onistic toward the rich and, for him, exotic landscapes of southern France;
Julia likes the people she meets and the heat. Tom distrusts M. Pierre and,

to a lesser extent, Alex. Julia, however, childless and aware of her husband's clumsy unattractiveness is drawn physically and emotionally toward Alex. All the tensions of years of marriage and a stressful holiday come to a head during an afternoon's expedition to a nearby beach. M. Pierre is in danger of drowning; Tom refuses to go to his rescue; Alex saves the older man. Later, on their return to the *pension*, Julia visits the young man in his bedroom. She strips to her underwear before him, although she now feels no desire for him. She realizes that she wishes to abase herself, just as she feels her husband has by his cowardice on the beach. The story's complexities do not end there, however. Later, in the evening, when it comes to recounting the day's events, Julia, in the presence of M. Pierre and Alex, insists that it was Tom who saved the older man. "The Corams against the world," the story ends.

The fact that, in recounting the story material, one has to spend considerable time providing details of the two central characters, is indicative of the way in which this story is fundamentally a study in character and psychology. The climactic events of the story, Alex's rescue of M. Pierre, and Julia's encounter with Alex in his bedroom, are exciting enough, but the story's real interest lies elsewhere. Indeed, one might even argue that the story's climax proper is the final section of the text in which Julia Coram lies about her husband's conduct that afternoon. The importance to the story of the background to the events of that afternoon is signaled by the fact that approximately half the text is given over to a presentation of the Corams, their marriage, and their relationships with M. Pierre and Alex.

Place setting also plays an important role in "Handsome Is As Handsome Does." For Tom, it is an utterly alien environment; Julia has spent a large part of her life abroad and is drawn to it. The physical environment is hot and colorful. The town is described by the narrator as "like a pink flower opening by the peacock sea." M. Pierre guides the Corams (in their car) to "the torrid towns raked together like heaps of earthenware in the mountain valleys, the pale stairways of olives going up hills where no grass grew and the valleys filled with vines." There is "fixed unchanging sunlight" and "sudden sights of the sea in new bays more extravagant in color." "At noon," the reader learns, "the mountains of the coast seemed to lie head down to the sea like savage, panting and silver animals," and "in the evening... the sea became like some murmuring lake of milky opal." The landscape is not merely beautiful and passive, but dynamic too. At the beach where M. Pierre almost drowns, "the sea was not the pan of enameled water they had known but was open and stood up high from the beach like a loose tottering wall, green, wind-torn, sun-shot and riotous." This setting contrasts markedly with England, which is Tom Coram's industrial Midlands. England is a place of "villas and chemical factories... where the air was like an escape of gas and the country brick-

bruised and infected." Later he thinks of England again as a place of factories and rain.

Each of the Corams responds differently to the landscape. "All this was too beautiful," Tom feels. The setting's beauty "had made a wound in him." "The beauty of this country was a fraud, a treachery against the things he had known.... The emeralds and ultramarine of this sea and the reddened, pine-plumed coast, made him think of those gaudy *cocottes* he had seen in Paris. The beauty was corruption and betrayal." At the beginning of the text, the reader learns that while Julia lies at ease in the sun, Tom sits hunched and defiant and wearing his thick tweed jacket. He swims only once, and then badly. Julia responds to the landscape erotically. "Movement came to her blood from the sight of the blowing vines and the red soil of the olive fields and out of the wind-whitened sky." It is, however, surprising that she never swims in the sea. "I'm not allowed," is all she says on the matter. At one moment, too, she realizes that so taken up is she with her relationship with her husband, that she has not clearly seen the town in which they live. The two other major characters, M. Pierre and Alex, both fit into the environment. Both are alone and seem self-sufficient in different ways. Both swim, and swim well. Alex's rich complexion is even associated with the southern landscape. He is "like some fine statue centuries old that had worn and ripened in the sun," his skin "burned to the color of dark corn." He goes off on his own to see paintings in nearby churches; he immediately knows the locality and can return from walks by unknown paths. Alex in his beauty, youth, and cosmopolitan charisma contrasts markedly with the inhibited and blocked English couple. Even the foppish, old-maidish M. Pierre is much more self-confident and at one with himself than they are.

A further sign of the story's psychological focus is its use of free indirect speech. The narrator is a third-person one, but remains limited to Julia's and Tom's point of view. The narrator can look into Tom's mind and understand the intentions of this very tongue-tied man. With Julia, the narrator goes even further, representing her thoughts and feelings almost directly. She watches her husband undressing.

> Her questions went on silently in her mind. Twenty-two? And she was forty. What did he think of her? What did he think of her husband? Did her husband seem crude and vulgar? Did he seem slow-minded? What did the young man think about both of them?

As she looks at Alex swimming, she exclaims to herself: "To be young like that and lie in the sea in the sun!" (which is really an example of free direct speech). Throughout the text, the narration often hovers between free indirect and free direct speech. For example, when Julia thinks of her husband's past, the text is as follows.

> She saw it clearly; he was mean. Men of his class who had worked their way up from nothing were often mean. Such a rise in the world was admired. She had once admired it. Now it amused her and made her contemptuous. Mean! Why had she never thought of that before? She had been blind.

The reader is, thus, introduced to Julia's consciousness, and, in the text as a whole, is made privy to the intricacies of her feelings about her husband and their marriage, about the other characters in the story, and the events of the afternoon on the beach and its aftermath. Similarly, the text also exposes Tom's conflict-ridden emotions about his life and his marriage. He is constantly at odds with the world and his wife, because of his social origins, because of his inarticulacy, and because they are here in a glorious southern landscape that hurts him by its alien qualities. The narrator calls him "uncouth." His wife suggests he is a "vulgar" boor. For him, everything that is beyond him is a "fraud." Yet he is also fascinated by commercial frauds, of which he speaks at length with Alex. It is striking, however, that at his moment of cowardice on the beach, the narration remains firmly with Julia, and only Tom's actions are noted. The narrator, however, clearly aims to garner considerable sympathy for Tom, despite his boorishness. He appears trapped in his own unattractiveness, his own past, his own sense of what is right, and his own resentments of what is different from him. He will never be able to overcome the bars set by these, incapable of courage and generosity.

In Julia, Pritchett offers a compelling and complex depiction of unhappiness. She feels herself aging. (Her feelings are presented with a considerable directness.) She has not been able to have a child by her husband. She longs for and desires intensely the young Alex, with his cosmopolitan substance and charm, his physical beauty, his youth. Like her husband, she has been scarred by the barbed wire of the social worlds she moves in, the dull minor country gentry, the dim army officers she is meant to marry, her socially unacceptable and coarse husband (whom she has married to offend and break with her family). Her own self-loathing comes to a climax in Alex's bedroom when she offers herself (but yet does not) to him, not out of desire now, but out of a desire (she finally realizes) to bring herself as low as her husband has. At the story's end, she returns to the role she has played for much of her married life, that of her husband's protector, a buffer between his failures and the world. "Her life was full of pretences, small lies and exaggerations which she contrived for her husband's sake," the narrator reveals early in the text.

The end of the text is marked by a substantial pretence. Tom saved M. Pierre not Alex, and that said in front of all the participants in the afternoon's events. "[T]hey were an ugly pair," declares the narrator when first introducing the Corams. Their physical unattractiveness and their social oddity have made them into a discrete unit throughout their married life, for all their tensions and quarrels with each other. At the end they are a pair once more, defying the world that neither likes nor needs them. As a surprising, frank, and very complex picture of relations within a marriage, "Handsome Is As Handsome Does" stands out as a major piece of fiction, all the more striking because it deals with the unglamorous and unattractive with very considerable sympathy. Pritchett's relative neglect as a major British writer is at times dispiriting to his admirers.

# Mollie Panter-Downes, "Goodbye, My Love" (1941)

Published in *The New Yorker* (1941)

"Adrian's mother welcomed them as though this was just an ordinary visit," begins "Goodbye, My Love." But this is late autumn 1941, and neither the time nor the visit is ordinary. The story is narrated in the third person, but mostly from Ruth Vyner's point of view. Ruth's husband Adrian is to be sent abroad in four days time with the British Army. No one knows where, although there is speculation that he will be sent to the Middle East. Ruth and Adrian visit his parents in the south-west of England, where his father is a Church of England clergyman. They arrive and find Adrian's mother gardening. She asks him calmly when he is leaving. He and his father pour over an atlas, "quiet and contented," working out where Adrian might be sent. They attend church the next day. On Monday, they return to London. On the Wednesday of Adrian's departure, they say goodbye in the cramped hall of their apartment, scarcely finding words to express their feelings. For the next two days, Ruth fights to come to terms with her husband's departure. She has "terrible" dreams, in one of which she sees Adrian struggling in an oil-covered sea after his ship has been sunk. On the third day after Adrian's leaving, "Ruth woke up feeling different. It was a queer feeling, exhausted but peaceful, as though her temperature had fallen for the first time after days of high fever." She feels, "The end of something had been reached, the limit of some capacity for suffering." She feels resilient and even happy again. Then late in the day, her husband calls to say that his departure with his unit has been postponed, and he has a week or ten days leave. He will be with her very soon. Ruth's response is unexpected. She bursts into tears of grief.

*The British and Irish Short Story Handbook*, First Edition. David Malcolm.
© 2012 David Malcolm. Published 2012 by Blackwell Publishing Ltd.

Panter-Downes's stories are usually reports on the Second World War from an upper-middle-class perspective and from the Home Front. Most of her protagonists are women. The stories offer often surprising and unexpectedly off-center accounts of the conflict, full of carefully placed and convincing details of life in London and the home counties in the early 1940s. They are subtle in their balance of sympathy and astringency in relation to their central characters. In "Goodbye, My Love," Ruth observes other characters' reactions to her and her husband's situation. She watches her husband's family deal with his departure and finds their superficial calm and matter-of-factness extraordinary and finally disturbing. She recalls her French governess's rage at English *sang-froid*. She is vexed by the retired Major Collingwood's bluff, old-soldiery encouragement. Friends in London treat her as an invalid who must be coddled. She is not only struck by others' responses, but by Adrian's too. He calmly discusses a long war with her. He wants her to go out with an old admirer while he is abroad. But she, too, maintains an emotional steadiness throughout. She will not let Adrian express his love for her as he leaves.

> Language was inadequate, after all. One used the same words for a parting which might be for years, which might end in death, as one did for an overnight business trip. She put her arms tightly round him and said, "Good-bye, my love."
> "Darling," he said. "I can't begin to tell you – "
> "Don't," she said. "Don't."

She only, paradoxically, breaks down when she hears that Adrian will be back for a week or more.

She does so because of her sense of passing time. "The clock on the table beside her sounded deafening again, beginning to mark off the ten days at the end of which terror was the red light at the end of the tunnel." The story is full of motifs of the inevitable movement of time. The reader is aware of the four days that remain before Adrian's departure, for the story marks each day's passing. Adrian's parents' house is "full of it, ticking between simpering shepherdesses on the mantelpiece, grumbling out of the tall mahogany case in the hall, nervously stuttering against Adrian's wrist." Much talk is of the future – what Ruth will do after Adrian has gone, how long the war will last, how soon soldiers will be demobilized after it (in 1941, this is wishful thinking indeed!). On the night before the parting, Ruth notices their clock, which "went on sucking time, like an endless string of macaroni, into its bright, vacant face." In addition, "Every clock in London seemed to crash out the quarters outside their drawn curtains." Once her husband is gone, Ruth sets about filling up "the enormous empty room" of the time. She becomes calm and resilient in time clearly marked by the narrator, and it is the awful return of the days and hours that must be lived through again before her husband's second departure that makes her break down at the story's end.

The conclusion of "Goodbye, My Love" is surprising, but carries complete credibility. Panter-Downes may offer a limited perspective on the Second World War (could there be any other?), but it is a valid one. Her upper-middle-class protagonists are part of the time and conflict, as much as the evacuees and less well-off of whom the author also writes in "Battle of the Greeks" and "The Danger." In addition, she maintains a careful balance of sympathy and stricture toward her relatively well-heeled, well-educated, and articulate protagonists. In her exploration of the psychology of a character like Ruth, facing an awful experience (no matter how general it is), Panter-Downes is subtle and utterly convincing.

# Alun Lewis, "The Last Inspection" (1942)

Published in *The Last Inspection* (1942)

Alun Lewis's and Julian Maclaren-Ross's short stories look at the war from quite different points of view to those in Mollie Panter-Downes's work. Both offer a much more proletarian and demotic take on the conflict. All three writers, and Elizabeth Bowen, however, have this much in common that they see the war in terms of its effects on civilians or on soldiers out of combat. "The Last Inspection" is set somewhere in England on 31 December 1940, in what can be seen as one of the darkest moments of the Second World War for Britain. France has fallen; the British Army has been trounced in northern France; the *Luftwaffe* is bombing British cities; the U.S.A. has not yet entered the war. An unnamed elderly brigadier is making his last inspection of an extensive camp area. He is to make it by train, stopping to inspect troops at each barracks along the line. The train pulls a diner and a saloon car round the camp while the Brigadier and his entourage of officers and ladies dine lavishly and drink good wine and whisky. The story focuses largely on the civilian train driver, Fred Tube, and his fireman, Mogg Evans. They are cynical and insubordinate. The inspection is not completed because the Brigadier and his party cannot be bothered leaving their warm carriage. The war seems far away. At the end of the text, however, Fred Tube is told that there is a telegram waiting for him. He fears for his family in the (working-class) East End of London.

Narration is complex in "The Last Inspection." On one hand, the narrator is a third-person observer, but on the other, he constantly shifts his language to present different points of view, the Brigadier's and what can only be described as a disenchanted other ranks' perspective. The narrator's language

*The British and Irish Short Story Handbook*, First Edition. David Malcolm.
© 2012 David Malcolm. Published 2012 by Blackwell Publishing Ltd.

is, in any case, fundamentally informal. "Everything was O.K. In the loco sheds... everything was O.K.," the story begins. The locomotive is referred to as "Old Baden-Powell" and "old B.P." When the narrator introduces Tube and Evans, he does so in contemporary demotic clichés.

> Fred Tube was driving old B.P. He was driver on the London to Brighton line in civvy street, cool as a cucumber at seventy an hour.
> Morgan Evans was firing her. He had a boil on his neck and was browned off. He chucked his cotton waste away and sat on a packing case and yawned.

Here, the omission of an article before "driver," "civvy street," "cool as a cucumber," "browned off" (annoyed, vexed), and "chucked," all give a populist, *homme du peuple* aura to the narrator's language and perspective. This is reinforced when he refers to "us" and "the rest of us" at various points of the text. The subtle shifts in language and point of view are illustrated by the following passage. Note how observation becomes observation from a particular demotic and lower ranks' point of view and how the language becomes clearly that of "the boys," the ordinary soldiers at the paragraph's end.

> They were all waiting, the colonels and captains turned out like new pins by their batmen, the women in sables and astrakhan with little veils on their hats and silk stockings showing right up to their knees. And in the middle of them a mountain of flesh and khaki in a brass hat with a lovely red band round it, the Brigadier. Beside him, his daughter, a blonde whom the boys called Unity, and beside her, at a decent interval, her fiancee [sic], a dark thick moustache and a cap pulled down over his nose. He was only a second lieutenant and he wouldn't have been allowed to come if he hadn't got engaged to Miss Unity, so he got engaged. He was due for a couple more pips now, no doubt. Leave it to Unity, as the boys said; it was a kind of slogan in the camp – when the latrines wanted cleaning and that.
> And off they all went.

The jaunty, proletarian disrespect of this passage is achieved by the absence of finite verbs in the two central sentences about the Brigadier and his son-in-law, by the informal lexis such as "a brass hat with a lovely red band round it," "a couple more pips," and "wanted cleaning," and by the clearly satirical intent behind the narrator's observations of the Brigadier ("mountain of flesh and khaki") and his future son-in-law, who is a moustache and a cap, and no more.

However, at times, the narrator adopts the Brigadier's language and point of view, although it becomes rapidly clear that this is done to debunk the old windbag and fraud. The reader is meant to hear the Brigadier puffing, apoplectic and rubicund, in the following.

It's only natural when you're retiring, you want to see for yourself whether any work has been done during your tenure of office, how things have been getting along, sort of thing; because when you're at the helm you haven't any time to go dashing into the stokehold to supervise the trimmers, have you?

The phrase "sort of thing" and the final part of the above ("because when...") give the old soldier's voice. The narrator shifts to it at other points in the text. The Brigadier has wanted to extend and complete the railway line. "There was no real urgency in peace time. Now things were different. National emergency, supreme effort." But later, his real priorities become apparent, and through his own idiom. "It was *his* line, his monument. But first lunch."

But it was cold and morbid out, and – damn it – it all began to drizzle a bit; the windows of the diner were wet with drizzle outside and with condensing heat inside; and lunch took longer than they expected. You can't knock such good red wine and old scotch back in a hurry, it's a crime, and when a fellow is retiring like that, well, it's a shame to gabble the speeches off and hurry off and get wet and catch a cold as like as not. So they canceled the inspection of the new line. With regret.

The brigadier's own language is used to expose his fraudulence.

"The Last Inspection" is, generally, a deeply insubordinate and disrespectful text. Why are there so many sergeants in the locomotive shed? "Nobody knew what half of them were doing." "Yes, Miss," replies Evans to the self-important and bullying Regimental Sergeant Major. "Leave it to Unity," the soldiers say when they have to clean the latrines. The narrator points out that the Brigadier has spent a lot of time in London, lobbying for his pet project, "before the Blitz." Presumably he has been less frequently in London since the Germans have begun their bombing campaign. The work on the new rail line has its drawbacks for the those working on it – "in winter it was rough on them because they couldn't keep warm without working, but in summer it was O.K." When Evans has listened to the brigadier and his entourage in the dining car, he returns to Tube. "The war's nearly over, Fred," he declares. "We've dug for Victory and saved for Victory. And now they're drinking for it."

Indeed, for most of the story the war seems very distant. The sergeants in the locomotive shed talk of dogs. Tube and Mogg discuss long underwear. The Brigadier's circuit of the camp serves no military purpose, the loop in the line has never been completed, and the inspection never takes place anyway. Much effort is expended so that the brigadier and his entourage can have a fine lunch (while Tube and Mogg eat bully-beef sandwiches). In the dining car, the party is in full swing: "There were four speeches, three by colonels about the Brigadier and one by the Brigadier about the three colonels." The question in the story is implicit: how will this help to win the war? But at the story's end, the war becomes real. There is a telegram waiting for Tube.

> "O Christ," said Fred turning grey at the thought of his wife and kids in Shoreditch. "Oh Christ. Oh Christ."

At this moment of war's actuality, it is Tube's civilian companion who offers aid. "Mogg took his arm gently."

"The Last Inspection" is a satirical indictment of the system and hierarchy that has brought Britain to where it is on the last day of 1940. The Brigadier stands for an order that, one way or another, has had its day. He dines in jollity with his women and officers, while London burns. But perhaps in the insubordination that runs throughout the story, there is some hope. Perhaps, too, there is hope in Evans's gesture toward Tube. Perhaps, further, there is hope because this is, after all, the last inspection.

# Mary Lavin, "At Sallygap" (1943)

Published in *Tales from Bective Bridge* (1943)

"At Sallygap" is the fifth, and central, story in Lavin's *Tales from Bective Bridge*, bringing together the volume's principal motifs of entrapment and escape, and of love and the bitter despair of soured relationships. The text divides into three sections, distinguished principally by physical setting. In the first, the main figure Manny Ryan travels by bus on a summer afternoon outside Dublin in order to find a supplier of eggs for the shop he runs with his wife Annie. As he travels to the Sallygap on the edge of the city, he recounts to a stranger his abortive attempt, made many years previously, to leave Dublin for Paris. The second part relates Manny's afternoon and evening in the comparatively rural setting of Sallygap. On a whim he does not take the bus home, but walks in the countryside, arriving late in the city. The third section presents his fearful approach to his home. He is certain his wife will be angry with him, and, indeed, she is. Annie Ryan is deeply dissatisfied with the even tenor of their marriage, with Manny's passivity, and she sits brooding over her life. A detailed evocation of the shabby squalor of the Ryans' home and the hopeless durance – for both partners – of a loveless marriage ends the story. The Joycean interpretation of Ireland as paralysis is echoed in Lavin's text. Her created world is reflected in the poisonous subfusc of MacGahern's Ireland.

The narrator is a third-person omniscient one, but a narrator that moves very close to the two central figures, Manny and Annie, allowing their thoughts and feelings to come to the reader directly. Usually, the narrator's language is that of the subjects, relatively informal, but occasionally the narrator does raise the linguistic level in order to convey feelings that Manny, for example, cannot put into words himself. As he walks home from Sallygap, the "night's potent beauty" begins to work on him.

*The British and Irish Short Story Handbook*, First Edition. David Malcolm.
© 2012 David Malcolm. Published 2012 by Blackwell Publishing Ltd.

> The dark hills and the pale silk-shining sky, and the city pricking out its shape upon the sea with starry lights, filled him with strange feelings of sadness and joy mingled together. And when the sky flowered into a thousand stars of forget-me-not blue he was strangled with the need to know what had come over him.

Not only does the narrator's language closely shadow the characters', but through free indirect speech/thought the central characters speak almost directly to the reader. Immediately after the above passage, Manny reflects on what he is doing.

> Yesterday, if anyone came to him and suggested that he'd do such a thing, he would have split his sides laughing. And tomorrow, if he were to persuade Annie to take a walk out in the country, she'd look at him as if he were daft. The Dublin people couldn't tell you the difference between a bush and a tree. Manny stood to recover his breath. That was a fact. All the Dublin people were good for was talking. They'd talk you out of your mind.

The narrator does the same with Annie. Here, she thinks of her husband.

> He wasn't a bad sort, the poor fellow, always wanting to take her to the Gaiety when the opera was on. He wasn't to blame for being so weak. His hands always went dead when he was cold. His face got a terrible blue color in frosty weather. She thought about the peculiar habit he had of sleeping with his feet outside the bedclothes. And she began to feel uneasy about the past as well as about the future. She walked up and down the dark room.

Here there is a seamless movement between narrator ("She walked up and down the dark room") and subject ("His face got a terrible blue colour in frosty weather").

In addition to the above movement from narrator to character, the narrator allows characters to speak directly for themselves. Substantial parts of the text consist of dialogue, between Manny and the young stranger on the bus, and, to a lesser degree, between Manny and Annie. Almost a third of the text is made up of Manny's own account of his failed attempt to leave for Paris. "At Sallygap" opens up the lives and experiences of its central characters, in their own words, and in something like their own thoughts and feelings.

Besides her characters' psychologies, and, indeed, through her characters' lives, Lavin clearly aims at a specific depiction of Ireland. The image of Dublin, and by extension Ireland, in the story is dispiriting. From the start, the city is seen as small ("Dublin was all exposed") and the motif of the mail-boat pushing through the grey sea toward England suggests the centrality of the theme of escape. Manny's tells a tale of how he and some of his friends, musicians all, become disgusted with Dublin and the vulgarity of Dubliners. They plan to try their luck in "gay Paree." At the last minute, he, however, turns back from the ferry to England, leaving his fiddle on board; and his instrument, his passport to something more, to the brilliant charms of Paris, is shattered in being thrown down to him. He kicks its pieces into the harbor water, where it floats "along with the potato peels and cabbage stalks." Although the sordid Dublin of the story's end contrasts with the rural world of Sallygap, the countryside is scarcely vibrant in its hues. There are flowers, but Manny cannot name them, and what he does see, a grimy thatched cottage, a puddle of cabbage water in the road, a duck's inspecting the puddle, is tawdry. But it is the city itself, both its public and domestic sites, that fill Manny, and, indeed, Annie with horror.

> ... he thought of the old men standing at the pub ends of the streets, ringing themselves round with spits. He thought of the old women leaning against the jambs of the doorways, with white crockery milk jugs hanging out of their hands, forgotten in the squalor of their gossip. He thought of the children sitting among the trodden and rancid cabbage butts on the edge of the paths, whispering over again the gossip they had heard when they crouched, unheeded, under some counter.

Manny's and Annie's kitchen, with its "nauseous" smell of gas, its undignified squalor, the desiccated four-hour-old meal, the square of brown paper from the rubbish for a tablecloth, the filthy teacup with a layer of old sugar at the bottom, matches the exterior milieu. Both stand as observations of a reality, and as metaphors for the state of Ireland and Manny's and Annie's marriage.

Against this is set the glamour of the Paris that Manny never reached: bright lights, music, life, passion, and beautiful women. Manny talks of the city thus on the bus, and recurs to it at the story's end, contrasting it with the slow hatred and death he sees in Annie's eyes. Annie herself is a complex figure, at once an embodiment of repression and circumscription, and yet also a woman who rebels against the mild emptiness of Manny and her life with him. Within the limits of her imagination, she, too, longs for an escape from her circumstances, in violent, lurid passion. One has a strong sense of the utter hopelessness of characters' lives. Manny has fluffed his one chance to escape. His brief moment of freedom from the city and his sordid life will only happen once. He knows he will never go to Sallygap again.

Not all is dark in the story. "There are gentle souls," the narrator notes, "who take nothing from their coarse rearing, and less from their chance schooling, but who yet retain their natural gentleness, and sometimes it flowers, as Manny's did, in the hills." Even the city itself can be "so fair and so serene, so green and blue and gilt," that Annie turns from it to nurse her despair and anger. But the story ends with Manny's recalling his smashed fiddle on the harbor water, and motifs of self-loathing and shabbiness. Ireland and Dublin and its citizens seem hopelessly mired in inertia. Beckett's homeless paralytics are not too distant.

# Elizabeth Bowen, "Mysterious Kôr" (1944)

Published in *The Penguin New Writing* (1944) and in book form in
*The Demon Lover, and Other Stories* (1945)

"Mysterious Kôr" is a story about three people and London in war-time.
The time setting is sometime after 1941, but (it appears) before 1944 and
the Allies' invasion of France. It was hard enough to find a place to stay, one
character reflects, even "before the Americans came"; now it is impossible.
Two lovers, Pepita and Arthur, walk through the streets of London, eerily
illuminated by a full moon. They quote a poem to each other that they both
know, Andrew Lang's "She" (1888), a text that reworks motifs in H. Rider
Haggard's novel *She* (1887). They talk of an imaginary city, Kôr, that
London resembles, but which for Pepita is also a refuge from the actuality of
war-time. They have arranged for Andrew to spend the night in the flat
Pepita shares with another young woman, Callie. He is to sleep on the divan
where Pepita normally sleeps; Pepita is to share a bed with Callie. Neither is
happy at the prospect. The lovers reach the flat where Callie is waiting for
them, partly in excitement, partly in apprehension. There are awkward
moments, for Pepita really wishes to spend the night alone with Arthur. The
girls go to bed. Pepita falls asleep. Hearing Arthur moving about, Callie gets
up. Callie and Arthur talk in the darkness, about the city, the war, and
Pepita. Callie goes back to bed. Pepita dreams of Kôr.

Traditional story material is attenuated in "Mysterious Kôr," which thus
becomes a study of place and psychology in war-time. London, itself, or
rather a London transformed by war and moonlight, is central to the text.
"London looked like the moon's capital – shallow, cratered, extinct."
The light "drenched the city and searched it; there was not a niche left to

stand in." The streets are brightly, almost unbearably brightly, illuminated. People stay indoors, threatened by "something more immaterial," and ill-defined, than German bombers. Everything is illuminated. Callie feels when she switches off the light in her bedroom that something is happening outside – "outdoors, in the street, the whole of London, the world. An advance, an extraordinary movement was silently taking place." It is the moon's light that transforms the street, from the houses to some small glittering object, and the objects in her room. The story does not describe war damage, but rather the utter transfiguration of the city in the moonlight.

The oddness of the city at night, lit up as if it were day, is matched by other motifs of strangeness and disruption in the text. The blackout is absurd. Every tile on every roof is visible. Day has been turned into night. The traffic lights continue to change even though there are no cars on the road. The gates of the park have no gates, and the sky is "glassy." Arthur feels at times that he might be anywhere; he looses track of where he is. The girls' flat is a flimsily partitioned Victorian drawing room; the conservatory half a floor down is now a bathroom. Callie's cretonne housecoat becomes silver brocade in the moonlight. Her hand as it lies in the strange illumination becomes someone else's.

In this oddly transfigured world, three characters meet and talk, and the reader sees the war through their eyes. Before that, the third-person omni-scient narrator offers a panoramic view of this eerie London – the houses, the streets, the park, a few figures moving through the city. The two lovers talk to each other. The lunar cityscape makes Pepita think of Lang's poem about a ruined city, the "Mysterious Kôr" of the title. Pepita sees the war as having changed everything. Her views are a mixture of optimism and pessimism. She may hate "civilization," but "This war shows we've by no means come to an end. If you can blow whole places out of existence, you can blow whole places into it." However, the place she imagines that will survive is the imaginary Kôr, a ruined, but perfect and untouchable place, independent of anyone but the two lovers.

After a transition passage, in which the narrator provides details of Pepita's and Callie's lives and the sleeping arrangements that await the lovers, the text moves to Callie, tall, blonde and virginal, while Pepita is small, dark, and has a lover. Callie follows rules, goes to bed early, switches off the lights at the right time, worries about using too much gas, and is concerned that Arthur's walking in his boots will disturb the neighbors. She does not fully understand that she should leave the lovers alone in the flat. For her, Arthur is a kind of ideal figure, a soldier, a man. Pepita, on the other hand, is aware of the complexities and realities of personal relationships. She would, in some ways, prefer Arthur to sleep somewhere else.

The intricacies of close-quarters in the tiny flat (who uses the bathroom when, the thinness of the walls, having to share a bed with your flatmate when your lover is a few inches away) produce tensions in the three characters. Pepita, however, after some bitter words with Callie, is able to fall into an intense sleep. In the dark of the living room (and it is important that the two characters, in any case strangers, can scarcely see each other), Arthur talks to Callie about his relationship with Pepita, how his absences must unsettle her. He talks of war as something that takes time from people: "They forget war's not just only war; it's years out of people's lives that they've never had and won't have again." He talks of the escape to Kôr, and how, alarmingly he thinks, Kôr is real for Pepita. In this war-time world, it is all they have. Cannot we want the human, Callie asks. "To be human's to be at a dead loss," says Arthur yawning. Callie, the good girl, the hopeful, has no answer to this. She sees that the moon's eerie light is passing and goes to bed.

Finally, the narrator shifts to the sleeping Pepita, as she pursues her dream of Kôr. Arthur is "the source," but not "the end" of her dream. It is to Kôr that she goes – "down the wide, void, pure streets, between statues, pillars and shadows, through archways and colonnades." It is a depopulated world of "stairs down which nothing but the moon came," and "the ermine dust of endless halls." It has "wide, void, pure streets." It is London transfigured by moonlight, and yet also far from the war that has become normality, a dislocated normality, but still the seemingly inescapable here and now.

"Mysterious Kôr" is in some ways a difficult story. Its view of the war is at once direct and yet tangential. It deals not with battles, or even with the danger of bombing, but rather with three people's minds on a night of bright moon in 1942 or 1943 (perhaps). It is a dislocated, uneasy, eerie world that they inhabit. Their conversations are rarely directly about the war, but rather about its consequences for them: having nowhere to go to be together and make love, the loss of time, the need to escape somewhere, anywhere, from the here and now. They respond to the war differently: Callie with good-humor and bemused offense, Arthur with a shrug, Pepita with frustration and a radical flight to an imaginary world. The story absorbs one with its image of lunar London, terrifyingly exposed, and its believable and moving depiction of its three central characters. It goes beyond the individual, however. Kôr is ruined capital of a collapsed empire and a vanished civilization. London's days, too, must be numbered.

# Julian Maclaren-Ross, "The Tape" (1944)

Published in *The Stuff to Give the Troops* (1944)

The narrator of "The Tape" is a private in the British Army during the Second World War. His name is Ford; he is a big man; he is poorly educated; he speaks in non-standard English throughout the story. The tale he tells is of his relationship with another private called Phil, an educated young man, and a "socialist" (Phil calls himself), who does not believe in distinctions of rank, nor in one man's being put in authority over another. Ford and Phil are close. They sleep side by side, they do picket duty together, and they spend free time with each other. However, as Ford relates, the pressures of people and system force them apart. Phil is persuaded by his sergeant, and by his girlfriend, to become a lance-corporal, the lowest rank of N.C.O. (non-commissioned offer), but the first step on the path to becoming an officer. The "tape" of the story's title is sown on his sleeve, which delights Phil's girlfriend. The "tape" drives a wedge between Phil and Ford. By army regulations, privates and N.C.Os are not allowed to spend time together. Phil and Ford cannot do picket duty together; they cannot spend time together in the same canteen; they cannot be seen drinking together in a local pub. Ford eventually comes into conflict with authority, and quarrels with Phil when the latter supports the army hierarchy in this matter. Now that he is without his friend, Ford gets drunk, strikes a corporal who has always been his enemy, and serves a six-month jail sentence. He meets Phil once more, but his former friend is ill at ease. He is on his way to O.C.T.U. (Officer Cadet Training Unit – officer school), and Ford has a prison haircut. They say goodbye and never meet again.

*The British and Irish Short Story Handbook*, First Edition. David Malcolm.
© 2012 David Malcolm. Published 2012 by Blackwell Publishing Ltd.

The story is a poignant personal account (but told without any expectation of sympathy) of the complexities of the British class system, even in a war-time army, even in the midst of a people's war. Everything works to separate Ford and his friend, even they themselves. Ford urges Phil to take the "tape," and his arguments are not foolish. If people like you are not officers, he points out, who will we get? But once the decision has been made, the relationship between the two soldiers cannot survive. Sergeants, other N.C.Os, officers, Phil's girlfriend, and Phil's own sense of responsibility destroy it.

Ford speaks directly to the reader in his own voice. His language is non-standard and has the markers of spoken narrative (particularly long sentences held together by polysyndeton or parataxis – coordination by "and" rather than subordination). For example, the following is representative of his voice.

> I said we could still meet downtown in the Y.M. so long's we walked down different ways, and for a time we did that and it was O.K. But old Phil weren't the same, this bust-up he'd had with his girl had worked on him proper, and one day he come up to me and he said, "Fordy, it's no good, I've got to put in for this blasted commission" he said, "I can't help myself," and I said That's the stuff Phil, I'd do the same in your place, I told him.

Here the informality of Ford's voice is achieved through the use of "and" in both sentences, and by the repetitions of "he said" and "I said" in the second one. It is also marked by lexical items such as "so long's," "weren't" (for "wasn't"), "bust-up," "worked on him proper" (instead of "properly"), and "come" (for "comes" or "came"). Examples of Ford's highly informal and lower-class English could be multiplied. They give Ford's voice a verisimilar and pungently demotic quality.

As in many of Maclaren-Ross's army stories, the reader is also confronted with the abbreviations, the acronyms, and the informal lexis of the 1940s British Army: "Sarnt," "O.C.T.U.," "Corp," "L/C," "Old Man" (the commanding officer), "mucked off," "2 teas and a couple of wads" (sandwiches), "char" (tea), "Naffy" (N.A.A.F.I., that is, Navy Army and Airforce Institutes, that is the service canteen), "glasshouse" (military prison), "a fizzer" (a charge), and, of course, the sinister "Tape." The world of the 1940s army is brought vividly to life through the language, and also through Private Ford's accounts of training ("but the next two periods was [sic] Bren and that wasnt [sic] so bad"), drill ("He kept that up about 10 minutes without a break cause we'd not done it smart enough the 1st time"), "Gym" (physical exercise), most seemingly done in thoroughly unpleasant and freezing weather ("I tell you it was that cold you couldn't hardly feel your feet inside your boots" and "road was that slippery with ice you couldn't run even with slippers on"). Ford also recounts repeated conflicts with petty authority, the difficulties of getting back to barracks on time, and, eventually, a catastrophic drinking session with Scottish soldiers ("a lot of Jocks") from another part of town. The private British soldier, the much put-upon other ranks of the 1939–1945 conflict, the "poor bloody swaddies" of Hamish Henderson's great and equally demotic lament, "The 51st (Highland) Division's Farewell to Sicily" (1948), the men who eventually did help (along with lots of other men and women like them and unlike them, Americans, Russians, Poles, Free French, and all the rest) to see off the Germans and liberate Europe, is allowed to speak for himself in "The Tape." (The comparison with Kipling in his British India and First World War stories is instructive and worth commentary.) It is striking that Maclaren-Ross's Ford does not ask for sympathy. That is the way things are, regrettable, but inevitable. But by not asking for sympathy, he gets it. Maclaren-Ross's "The Stripe" is a moving vignette of the Second World War, and, like many of his war-time stories, tells the reader more about what life must have been like in the British Army for men like Ford than anything short of a long period reading in the archives of the Imperial War Museum in London.

# Denton Welch, "Narcissus Bay" (1948)

Published in *Brave and Cruel, and Other Stories* (1948)

In his brief life, Denton Welch wrote only a few short stories; however, they are very good and deserve to be much better known than they are. One of his most enigmatic and powerful stories is "Narcissus Bay." The narrator is an unnamed young European (presumably British, although it is not stated) boy who recounts a series of events that take place on a summer afternoon at Wei-hai-wei in China. While on his own in a "glade" in a wood, he sees four men and a woman coming down through the woods from the mountain. Two men are prisoners; the other two men are their captors. The woman follows them. She has clearly been badly beaten. The boy imagines a story of assault that can explain this procession. He then runs to the nearby beach. He tells his story to two girls. (Chinese? European? One does not know, although they speak French at one point.) They rush off to town to see something of the incident. The narrator then visits the home of a boy of his acquaintance, Adam Grant, a fat boy whom he finds, seemingly unwell, on a wicker chair. The narrator tells his story again. The boys take tea with Adam's mother and another younger boy and his nurse. Later, Adam torments the smaller Derek with, *inter alia*, tales of swordfish, jelly fish, and shark attacks. Adam and the narrator walk along the beach. The narrator, knowing that Adam is not allowed to swim, praises the water and bathes fully clothed in a rock pool. The narrator then returns home and thinks of the men and woman again, and of a shrine in the mountain he has seen with his mother.

The story material is seen from the child's perspective. The language may be at times more sophisticated than one would assume to be available to a young boy, but there is no overt attempt on the narrator's part to interpret the events

*The British and Irish Short Story Handbook*, First Edition. David Malcolm.
© 2012 David Malcolm. Published 2012 by Blackwell Publishing Ltd.

from an adult perspective. Indeed, the story's ambiguity depends on the lack of adult recension offered in the text. However, the reader is invited to interpret what is related.

The bulk of the story is composed of three sequences, each one of which has common elements: cruelty, imagination, and story telling. In the first sequence, the narrator observes the five figures coming from the wood and the mountain. "It was the most barbarous sight I had yet seen," he says, "and I held it to me with all the violence of a new possession." The violence of what he sees is very marked.

> The woman as she passed me held out the broken stick in pantomime. She ran her cries together, making them into a sort of whining song. The two men holding the ropes jerked the necks of their victims, swore at them, spat on their yellow-brown backs.

Then, in his imagination, the narrator reconstructs what he is sure must have been the events leading up to what he sees. He makes up a story of the two prisoners' beating the woman, of her cries, and of the arrival of the village policemen. Whether any of this is true or not, one does not know. Indeed, the narrator goes beyond what he thinks led up to the march down the hill; he imagines the scene in the court house in the nearby town, which has not yet taken place.

The following sequence with the two girls on the beach involves the same elements. The girls are habitually cruel to their Belgian governess. The poor, plump woman, the butt of the girls' ridicule has retreated to knit behind rocks (again the narrator imagines this). The narrator tells his story, deliberately aiming to fascinate the girls. He attempts "to describe the horror to them and the unreal, magic atmosphere" of what he saw in the woods. He tells them "about the ropes, the wounds, the blood, and the broken stick." He notes that "I had stirred them," despite their outward disdain. They rush off to the town to see what they can see of the incident, leaving the rotund governess "jellying" after them.

The narrator then goes to the Grants' home. Again, he tells his story to the costive Adam, whom he rather despises. He tells his story with deliberate search for the "greatest effect," "without any colour," and "with maddening slowness and vagueness." His listener is excited by the story. It is worth noting that the narrator exercises his imagination with regard to Mrs. Grant, creating an image of her (as superstitious) for which he has not a shred of evidence. After tea, Adam, perhaps inspired by the narrator's tale, torments the credulous Derek with "horror stories" of sword-fish coming at him out of the toilet bowl, of jelly fish that will blind him, and of sharks that will tear off his limbs. Later, the narrator inflicts a milder form of torture on Adam. Knowing the boy is not allowed to swim, he splashes happily in a rock pool.

In the story's final sequence, the events of "the early afternoon came back to me with a sudden violence," and the narrator sees it all again, the prisoners, the abusive guards, the bloodied and weeping woman. He then imagines the shrine he has seen on the mountain from which the men and woman came. He conjures the shrine up, with its vermilion plaster, its black roof, and its statuettes of gods surrounded by plates of food and gold and silver votive offerings. He thinks of the gods "all painted bright and gilded, gazing down, unmoving, caught in a trance, just watching everything." They are not exactly cruel, but are quite indifferent to human life and to the suffering of the woman and the men.

The narrator is like the gods in the mountain shrine. He disdains those around him: the girls on the beach have "thick arms and legs" that are "covered in reddish fur." They are quite vile to their governess, who is, herself, a grotesque creature in the narrator's eyes, "jellying" as she runs after her charges. Adam Grant is slightly grotesque for the narrator too with a "flannel band" round his stomach to fight a chill there. He certainly behaves monstrously to the pathetic younger Derek. Toward the story's end, all the narrator wants is to be on his own. After all, this is Narcissus Bay. "I longed to go away and be alone," he tells the reader. And later, "I wanted to be alone to watch the orange sun sink down into the sea." He marks his oddness by bathing fully clothed, partly at least to vex Adam. He returns along the beach on his own with a lantern.

> The oiled cotton of the lantern was painted with large scarlet and black characters. I danced and jumped about, making the light bob up and down and throw shadows like ghosts. Showers of drops fell from my soaking clothes. Far out in the bay the phosphorous was beginning to fringe the wavelets.

This enigmatic story of childhood experiences becomes a study of the beginnings of a creative mind of a certain kind. The narrator's imagination and storytelling skills are foregrounded, as is the cruelty that interests him (and which both interests others and runs through their own conduct). At the end of the text, he is like one of the brightly colored gods in the shrine, looking at human life with a clear-eyed but chilly detachment. He is on his way to becoming the kind of writer who could write "Narcissus Bay."

# Frank O'Connor, "Eternal Triangle" (1954)

Published as "The Rising" in *Cornhill Magazine* (1951),
as "The Tram" in Atlantic Monthly (1954),
and in *More Stories* (1954)

O'Connor is one of the major short-story writers of post-independence southern Ireland, and in the mid-twentieth century was one of the country's best-known literary figures, widely published in the U.S.A., where he also regularly taught. His influence on the twentieth-century short story was marked, especially through his widely read and widely taught polemic *The Lonely Voice: A Study of the Short Story* (1962). (O'Connor's much quoted central idea in the volume is discussed in Part 2 of this handbook.) His stories have been extensively discussed, especially the canonical "Guests of the Nation" (1931), and stories such as "First Confession" (1939) and "My Oedipus Conflict" (1965). The last two stories show O'Connor mining a rich vein of Irish small-town and rural life, presenting it with charming humor. Such stories cater to a sentimental vision of Ireland found in émigré Irish communities, and in a wider U.S. public. They also, however, insist on the importance and artistic interest of relatively humble Irish life, and can be seen as part of a necessary post-independence literary nationalism. O'Connor, however, also dug into a darker vein of the narrowness and strangulating stagnation of life in mid-century Ireland, in stories like "The Shepherds" (1944), "A Story by Maupassant" (1969), and "The American Wife" (1969). After the first political stories of the *Guests of the Nation* volume (none of which, apart from the title story, is reprinted in O'Connor's *Collected Stories* [1982]), O'Connor stuck to the comedy and constrictions of Irish mores, but at various points he revisited the subject matter of *Guests of*

*The British and Irish Short Story Handbook*, First Edition. David Malcolm.
© 2012 David Malcolm. Published 2012 by Blackwell Publishing Ltd.

*the Nation*, examining the story of the nation critically, if with comedy. One such story is "Freedom" (1952); another is "Eternal Triangle" (1951), under its various titles.

"Eternal Triangle" offers a particular point of view on the events that start the Easter Rising in Dublin in 1916. The narrator, a respectable, responsible watchman is sent to guard a broken down tramcar. On his way, he encounters both Irish nationalist Volunteers and loyalist cadets. He finds his tram damaged, and waits, guarding it, till a breakdown gang should arrive. It never does. The narrator finds himself in the middle of a gun battle between nationalists in a nearby park and pro-British forces in the hotel opposite. In the course of the day, he is joined by a woman (of loose morals, the narrator claims) who has gone out for some sugar, only to be caught up, like him, in the fighting. A Volunteer soldier uses the tram for cover to fire at the hotel, and then leaves. The couple in the tram are joined by a drunk who staggering along the street barely escapes being killed, despite valiant efforts to surrender to either side. The three spend the night in the tram, as the city burns in the background. In the morning, the pro-British forces tell them to go. The watchman refuses; after all, it is his duty to stay till relieved; the British officer tells him he is relieved. He then goes home, spending a week in bed, disgusted with what he sees as the nonsensical waste of the rebellion.

The story's title is ambiguous. Does it refer to the three people, two men and a woman, trapped in the tram? Despite the woman's attempts to initiate sexual contact with the watchman, there is no real sexual tension in the text. Or does the title refer to another eternal triangle: the two opposing forces in a rebellion or revolution, and the humble unheroic citizen, unengaged on either side, concerned only to get on with his job?

For "Eternal Triangle" looks at the founding moment of the Irish Republic through the eyes of someone who wants nothing to do with it at all. The narrator, who is unnamed, and, thus, a universalized figure, bemoans the destruction of property, and wonders about who will pay the bill for all the destruction this "revolution" entails. The reader knows little about him, except his job, and his attitude toward the upheaval of historic events. He has no dislike of the British, and, in fact, thinks they have done Ireland some good. "I'd like to know where you and the likes of you would be only for the English," he tells his female companion. He wants the police to come and put a stop to the silliness of the uprising (a sentiment in which the woman concurs). He continually recurs to the destruction of property, which leaves him "disgusted." He is a person of no social standing, but a deep sense of responsibility. Of indifferent education, he speaks ungrammatically. "A man in my position," he says, "have to mind his job and not bother about what other people are doing." But he knows that he and his kind end up paying for the "damage" of history.

The story constantly presents the events of this corner of Dublin in April 1916 as nonsensical and even farcical. Both sides expend large amounts of ammunition without hurting anyone. They do pointless damage to public and private property. The violence begins and ends equally arbitrarily, and, indeed, the two sides in the conflict are correlated both in the narrator's mind, and in the organization of the action in the text. All three central figures (watchman, woman, and drunk) are caught up in events by chance. The drunk's attempts to surrender are comic and grotesque. At one point, lying on his back in the street, he surrenders by putting his legs in the air. The whole business of rebellion is sent in a thoroughly unheroic light. The defense of Ireland and Ireland's cause is placed in the mouths of a sentimental demi-prostitute and a drunk. The city seems to burn to no end.

The narrator himself is not without a negative aspect however. His remaining at his post, to defend the tram, in the midst of a gun battle is only marginally less absurd than the pointless exchanges of fire. He considers himself relieved of his duty only when a British officer tells him that he is. He refuses to look at the "droves" of prisoners being marched away by the British when he does emerge from his week in bed. But his is a fascinating and discordantly unheroic Irish voice on the matter of 1916. He is, despite (or perhaps because of) everything about him, strangely heroic, doing his duty in most adverse circumstances. As he himself says, people like him pay the bills for revolutions.

Like the much better-known "Guests of the Nation," but in a much more comic fashion, "Eternal Triangle" attempts to demythologize recent Irish history, and suggest another perspective on the anti-colonial struggle. It is a text that deserves much more recognition than it has hitherto received, successfully fusing the comic and the mundane with the grand and historical.

# J. G. Ballard, "The Terminal Beach" (1964)

Published in the magazine *New Worlds* (1964) and in book form in
*The Terminal Beach* (1964)

"The Terminal Beach" is one of Ballard's most complex and ambitious short stories, a text in which science fiction and the avant-garde meet to produce something rich and strange. The story material is as follows. Traven, probably a former U.S. airman once involved in bombing raids both against Japan and perhaps elsewhere, crosses the Pacific to Eniwetok atoll. In the documented world, this atoll, in the Marshall Islands, is the site of battles between Japanese and U.S. forces in 1944, and, subsequently, of U.S. nuclear weapon testing. In Ballard's short story, the atoll is now, after the Third World War, an abandoned nuclear testing ground, covered in debris and a multitude of military structures. Traven takes up residence on the narrow atoll, exploring it as best he can in his physically reduced state. He discovers various parts of the sinister and grotesque landscape: abandoned B-29 bombers, ruined bunkers, submarine pens with mutated life forms, testing pools, some of which are filled with plastic dummies, used to test the effects of nuclear explosions, and, above all, a very large area of concentric concrete blocks. Traven is searching for something or seeking to appease his own conscience. He sees the specters of his dead wife and son. He injures his foot. He becomes progressively weaker. A biologist and his pilot land on the atoll, help him, and talk to him. They leave and a naval search party comes to look for Traven. He hides from them among the plastic corpses. He discovers the body of a dead Japanese man, who appears to have recently committed suicide on the atoll. Traven and he converse. At the end of the story, Traven has mounted the Japanese man's corpse on a chair so that he appears to be an archangel looking

*The British and Irish Short Story Handbook*, First Edition. David Malcolm.
© 2012 David Malcolm. Published 2012 by Blackwell Publishing Ltd.

over the apocalyptic landscape while Traven's wife and child draw nearer to him and he dreams of burning bombers falling from the sky.

"The Terminal Beach" clearly breaches the protocols of realism. It is set in an undocumented time: there was no Third World War after the mid-1960s. The protagonist and a dead character speak. There are specters. However, the text is rooted in a documented reality: Eniwetok atoll is a real place; the text quotes from a book by the British psychologist Edward Glover; the atoll is littered with the recognizable debris of mid-twentieth-century civilization, B-29 bombers, a jukebox, a broken cola bottle, army food cans, old magazines. While the text's narrative is traditional in its largely logical, chronological ordering of events, the story's narration is altogether odder. Like the created world of the story, it moves between the traditional and something innovative. On one hand, it is given by a traditional third-person narrator, with a point of view often, although not always, restricted to Traven's. The narrator, however, is able to explain things that Traven cannot, and often adopts a perspective beyond that of the main character, for example, in explaining how weapons testing has fused the atoll's sand into layers or by addressing the reader directly to urge him or her to try to imagine what Traven may be seeing. In addition, the narrator at one point attempts to sum Traven up in an unusual and enigmatic way.

**Traven: In Parenthesis**
Elements in a quantal world:
   The terminal beach.
   The terminal bunker.
   The blocks.
The landscape is coded.
   Entry points into the future=Levels in a spinal landscape=zones of significant time.

The text is odd in other ways too. It quotes a text by Edward Glover about the psychological consequences of nuclear war and weaponry, without integrating that in the world of the text. The dialogue between the dead Japanese man and Traven is given as a mini-play, a dramatic dialog with stage directions. Further, throughout, the story is divided into twenty-one subsections, each marked by a heading that indicates the subject of the following section. The bizarre and disturbing qualities of the topography of the atoll and of Traven's experiences on it are reflected in the story's narrational strategy.

As I have noted above, time in the story is both documented and undocumented. It also moves through three different levels within the text: the historical, the local, and the apocalyptic. The historical time level of time has to do with the location of the story in relation to the Second World War and the bombing of Japan, and also in relation to a moratorium on atomic testing and a Third World War. Further, the atoll is set in relation to dead civilizations like Assyria and Babylon, and to past eras, such as that of the dinosaurs. The local passage of time is clearly marked in the text. The Japanese man has been on the island for perhaps five years. The magazines upon which Traven sleeps are four or five years old. It takes Traven six months to cross the Pacific. He lands on the atoll at midnight. He inspects bunkers for several hours; he sleeps a few nights in the open. He exhausts his supply of food after two months. The story is full of time markers: "Later," "Shortly after," "On the day before," "Near the end," "ten minutes later," and so on. In addition, there is an apocalyptic time level. At various points, Traven feels he has entered a "zone of no time," and there are frequent allusions to another time order: to Pentecost, to Armageddon, to the time of the raising of the dead, and to the Apocalypse itself. The sun stands in the sky over Eniwetok ("the thermonuclear noon") and the sea forms a backdrop to events, as the sun and sea do in Revelation (for example, 1: 16, 6: 12, and 8: 12 [sun], and 4: 6, 10: 5, and 15: 2 [sea]).

Indeed, the atoll's landscape is an apocalyptic one, a world destroyed and damaged, full of sinister human artifacts, an utterly man-made, concreted-over, and contaminated wasteland.

> The desolation and emptiness of the island, and the absence of any local fauna, were emphasized by the huge sculptural forms of the target basins set into its surface. Separated from each other by narrow isthmuses, the lakes stretched away along the curve of the atoll. On either side, sometimes shaded by the few palms that had gained a precarious purchase in the cracked cement, were roadways, camera towers and isolated blockhouses, together forming a continuous concrete cap upon the island, a functional megalithic architecture as grey and minatory... as any of Assyria and Babylon.

The lines of concrete blocks, of "vast number and oppressive size," a labyrinth in which Traven regularly becomes trapped, are a central feature of this ravaged world. They are a monument to human industrialized, technological, military madness, the legacy of a civilization that must be near its end.

Some of the motifs that run through "The Terminal Beach" should be quite apparent by now: debris and ruin, the vanished past, death (the plastic corpses, the specters of Traven's wife and son, the dead Japanese man, the whole rationale behind Eniwetok), and the end of all things. Other motifs, however, are also prominent and add to the meaning of these. There are constant reversals and inversions. The atoll, which is a product of the present, and now belongs to the past, also points to the future: it holds "the mass graves of the still undead." It is "the fossil of future time." Traven comes ashore on a "concrete beach." The girl in the photograph, Traven claims, has adopted him, not vice-versa. The jukebox's list of records is replaced by a list of descriptions of chromosome mutations. Traven remembers that his son at birth looked "millions of years old."

The landscape that Traven inhabits is also filled with enigmatic signs. The palms are like "the symbols of a cryptic alphabet." They are called "enigmatic." The slits in a bunker are "like runic ideograms," or "tutelary symbols of a futuristic myth," and the sunlight falls within the bunker like "five emblematic beacons." Traven's journey through the artifacts of the island is described as "symbolic," and the charts of mutated chromosomes are "abstract patterns [which] were meaningless." Traven puzzles over them and later appends the list of records from the selection panel of the jukebox: "Thus, embroidered, the charts took on many layers of associations." To Osborne, Traven insists that "For me the hydrogen bomb was a symbol of absolute *freedom*." A "crescent-shaped shadow" is a "cipher" that leads him to the Japanese man's corpse. The dead Dr. Yasuda describes the atoll is "an image of yourself free of the hazards of time and space." At the story's end, Traven constructs for himself an image of the apocalypse.

The atoll itself, it becomes clear in the course of the story, is a cipher, a symbol, an image – of Traven's mind and body, of that of *homo hydrogenensis*, the creature of the atomic age. His own past has been that of one of the agents of the kind of world he moves through, part of a bomber crew, responsible for the deaths of Dr. Yasuda's family, and those of others, in part responsible for the monstrosity of Eniwetok. Osborne, the visiting biologist, sees him as haunted by guilt for his past. "The island is a state of mind," writes Osborne. It is "an Auschwitz of the soul," the narrator remarks. The camera bunker in which Traven sleeps has five apertures, parallel to the human five senses. The atoll is also called "a spinal landscape," and its megaliths offer Traven some sense of "absolute calm and order," cutting off the rest of the island, as if he enters into the striated folds of his own brain.

The atoll is finally a multivalent metaphor/symbol. It embodies modern civilization's future, a concrete wasteland given over to death. It embodies Traven's mind, the desolate mental topography of *homo hydrogenensis*. "The Terminal Beach" is a text the oddness of which parallels the mutated fauna and flora of Eniwetok. In it, Ballard offers a disturbing evocation of a human-made apocalypse that carries force beyond its immediate time of composition. After all, the atoll is "a fossil of future time," holding "the graves of the still undead."

As a final note, one might point to the following. The echoes of a Beckettian fictional universe in "The Terminal Beach" are unmissable (see the discussion of "Lessness," in this part on page 282): the tattered and enfeebled Traven dragging his ulcerated body through a desolate and depopulated and debris-strewn landscape; the correlation of topography and body (the apertures in the bunker, the spinal atoll). Here, science fiction meets the avant-garde, and produces a work of richness and distinction.

# Samuel Beckett, "Lessness" (1970)

Published in French as "Sans" (1969),
translated by Beckett as "Lessness" and published in
The New Statesman (1970) and The Evergreen Review (1970),
and in John Calder's Signature Series (1970).

Beckett's work challenges boundaries and conventions: French or English? Irish or cosmopolitan avant-garde? Short story or prose poem? His texts are extreme cases. How far can one deviate from tradition and convention? How can one make it new and still be understood? How far can you go to make it new?

"Lessness" is not a literal translation of the title of the French original. "Sans" means "without." Beckett's translations are not translations in a traditional sense, but rather rewritings in another language of what was first written in French. However, the title "Lessness" points appropriately to absences that one finds in the text. As Sinéad Mooney notes, in Beckett's work one can observe "Successive experiments in 'weakening' of conventional narrative... syntax" (Mooney 2006: 1). With regard to short fiction, she writes of Beckett's "evisceration of the short story" (Mooney 2006: 87). Certainly, in "Lessness," as in all of Beckett's late (post-1940) short fiction, there is a clear abandonment, or severe attenuation, of conventional features of prose fiction: character, setting, and action itself. In "Lessness," Beckett goes even further than in some other pieces. Like other avant-garde artists in the twentieth century, he relinquishes a degree of control over his text by a partially aleatory method of composition. This method is more complex than the following description can suggest, but it captures the central aspect of it.

The twenty-four-paragraph story consists of sixty different sentences, each used twice, and there are twelve paragraphs in each half of the story. Paragraph length and sentence order within paragraphs are arranged randomly. All this

The British and Irish Short Story Handbook, First Edition. David Malcolm.
© 2012 David Malcolm. Published 2012 by Blackwell Publishing Ltd.

was accomplished by the creation of six groups of thematically related sentences, another list indicating the order of their selection, and a third list indicating the number of sentences in succeeding paragraphs.

(Cochran 1991: 58)

(Beckett's procedure is further discussed by Pountney (1987: 55–75) and Cohn (1973: 265).)

Such an aleatory organization of textual materials (provided the reader is aware of it) carries much meaning. It emphasizes the motif of human powerlessness, and indeed that of the arbitrariness of things, that runs throughout Beckett's work, including "Lessness." But, of course, the author does not relinquish complete control over the text. Individual words are chosen by Beckett and their combination within sentences is also a matter of choice. Indeed, the numbers involved in the creation of the text are meaning-bearing. As Cohn (1973: 263) points out, for example, the number of sentences is sixty (the number of minutes in an hour), and the number of paragraphs is twenty-four (the number of hours in a day). The theme of time is clearly foregrounded here. Time is not progressive, nor does it bring substantial change. The second half of the story is the same material repeated in a different order.

Absence and arbitrariness (within limits) mark the language of "Lessness." Let us consider the first sentence of the text: "Ruins true refuge long last towards which so many false time out of mind." There is no punctuation within the sentence (and throughout "Lessness" no sentence is punctuated except by a final full stop). In the absence of such guides to reading, the words can be put together in a variety of ways. Does "true" belong with "ruins" (this could be a poetic text that permits adjective-noun inversion), or with "refuge" Or with neither? Is it the ejaculation "True!"? Is "last" a verb (the predicate of "ruins"), or part of an adverbial phrase, "(at) long last"? Does "false" belong with "many" or "time"? Is "time" part of the fixed phrase "time out of mind," or is "out of mind" meant to stand on its own, indicating insanity or a breakdown in rational thought? Punctuation would not resolve all of these difficulties (to the impoverishment of the text, of course), but it would fix some of the semantic problems.

Further, words one might expect in such a sentence are also absent. There is an almost complete absence in "Lessness" of finite verbs. This is true in the first sentence. But other words too seem lacking. One could add several to narrow down the range of meanings. For example: "Ruins **are a** true refuge **at** long last toward which so many **go but they prove** false time out of mind." Or perhaps: "Ruins **it is** true **are a** refuge long **and they** last towards which so many false **persons go for a** time **when they are** out of **their** mind." None of that will improve Beckett, it must be said, and other readers will certainly see other possibilities, but the lack of linguistic cohesion in Beckett's text, and the semantic indeterminacy and malleability that it opens and encourages, should be evident.

On another level, however, the language is cohesive. In the first sentence (and this device is repeated throughout "Lessness"), the phonological orchestration of the text is evident. One can note a dense sequence of alliteration (/r/,/l/and/t/), a combination of alliteration and consonance (the /s/sounds of "Ruins," "last," "towards," "so," and "false"), and assonance (the/ʊ/sounds of "Ruins true refuge," and the/aɪ/of "time" and "mind"). Every sentence in "Lessness" (and the title too) could be analyzed thus. Such orchestration offers a sense of order in the arbitrary and gap-ridden language, and also produces what J. M Coetzee describes as the "haunting verbal beauty" of some of Beckett's later prose (Coetzee 2006: xi).

On yet another level, the text is strikingly coherent. Words and motifs are repeated throughout the text, and given that the second half of the text repeats everything that goes before, if in a different order, these repetitions are even more marked. On one hand, there are: "ruins," "endlessness," "no sound no stir," "grey," and "sand." On the other, perhaps more positively, there are: "refuge," "pale blue," "blue celeste," "only upright," "dream," and "step." A desolate, drab, post-cataclysmic world, an endless wasteland of isolation and inertia, contrasts with hints, however fleeting, of something better, brighter, more dynamic. But the lonely and afflicted wilderness dominates. "No sound no stir ash grey sky mirrored earth mirrored sky." In it the sole human being is a pitiable creature. He/she is "Little body grey face features crack and little holes two pale blue" and "Little body ash grey locked rigid heart beating face to endlessness." The paradox of all this presentation of apocalyptic drab emptiness, as critics have pointed out (Mooney 2006: 95), is that Beckett puts it down in severely beautiful and teasingly enigmatic language. "Lessness" is at the border of the short story and at the border of comprehensibility, but is unignorable in its searing vision of things and in the challenges it offers to readers.

# Gabriel Josipovici, "Mobius the Stripper: A Topological Exercise" (1974)

Published in *Mobius the Stripper: Stories and Short Plays* (1974)

The title and subtitle of Josipovici's short story indicate its intellectual ambitions. A mobius strip is a surface with only one side, well known in popular culture from the etchings of the Dutch artist M. C. Escher. It can be seen as a symbol of infinite return and regression, inasmuch as anyone traveling along a mobius strip returns to the point of origin. If you walk a mobius strip, in the end you get nowhere. "A Topological Exercise" also refers to mathematics. Topology is a "branch of mathematics that that deals with those properties of figures and surfaces that are independent of size and shape and are unchanged by any deformation that is continuous" (*The New Shorter Oxford English Dictionary* [1993]) – a fancy version of *plus ça change, plus c'est la meme chose*? If the average humanist's brain is reeling at this point, one can scarcely be surprised. The sophisticated references are important and mark out the story's ambition, but, at the same time, the allusion to the mobius strip indicates simply that human life is not a linear progression (in fact, not really a progression at all), and the reference to topology suggests no more than that we are all pretty much in the same boat.

"Mobius the Stripper" breaches narrative convention in one major way. It consists of two narratives printed together. The top half of each page consists of the story of Mobius, a male strip-tease artist; the lower half contains the story of an unnamed narrator who is facing writer's block, partly occasioned by a sense of oppression *vis-à-vis* the achievements of the great writers of the past. This typographical exercise reflects the two-sided/uni-sided nature of

*The British and Irish Short Story Handbook*, First Edition. David Malcolm.
© 2012 David Malcolm. Published 2012 by Blackwell Publishing Ltd.

the mobius strip. It also draws attention to the text as text and the two stories as stories, in a metafictional gesture much beloved of experimental writers. The two stories are not independent, however. The narrator in the narrative of the lower half of the page is aware of Mobius and his act, and in fact sees him in a park at one point, without knowing it is he ("A fat man with one of those Russian hats"). Both he and Mobius refer to similar important writers, especially Proust. At the end of the second narrative, the narrator/writer "began to write" what is, one assumes, the narrative of Mobius that has been at the top of the story's pages all along. Thus, the reader, like the ant on a mobius strip, returns to the beginning.

Typological oddity, however, should not disguise traditional aspects of the text. It remains firmly within conventions of literary realism, and metafictional musings are the stuff of James's "The Real Thing" and "The Lesson of the Master," Woolf's "The Mark on the Wall," and almost any piece of Beckett's short fiction. The narrative on the upper half of the page has the following story material, improbable perhaps, but not impossible. Mobius is an immigrant in London. Although a fat man of indeterminate age with odd English, Mobius works successfully as a stripper in a Notting Hill strip club. He talks as he takes his clothes off, explaining that he is stripping away the contingent and superficial layers of his personality, trying to get down to the central core of himself. "Take off the layers and get down to the basics," declares the narrator of this part of the story. "One day the flesh would go and then the really basic would come to light. Mobius waited patiently for that day." He strips obsessively and with dedication, living for his evenings in the strip club. He works seven days a week, and becomes annoyed when the proprietor takes a holiday and closes the club. He finally formulates his project as an attempt to distinguish for himself and for the audience the difference between "clockwork" and "necessity." Clockwork is linear and mechanical, the superficial and predictable. "But Necessity she a goddess. She turn your muscles to water and your bones to oil. One day you meet her and you will see Mobius is right." This formulation makes Mobius himself reflective. "If he was giving them [the audience] the truth where was his truth?" he asks himself. He prepares to kill himself. "So I come to myself at last," he says. "To the center of myself. . . . Is my necessity and my truth. And is example to all."

The second narrative, on the lower half of each page, is related by a writer who is trying to write. He is terrified by the blank paper before him. If you can write anything, he despairs, how can you write anything? He wants to be left in peace and quiet by the rest of the world, especially by a young Englishwoman with big feet called Jenny who keeps encouraging him to come out and see exciting and strange phenomena – an Indian fakir, a man who keeps seals in a bath, Mobius the Stripper. The narrator/writer feels oppressed by the great writers of the past, paralyzed, unable to produce anything that is his. He runs through various beginnings and linking phrases, pointing to their sad tiredness, their near cliché-like status. (These are echoed in the voices that Mobius hears in his head throughout the text.) He is able to write when he laughs, sees that life is nothing (he echoes T. S. Eliot's "The Hollow Men" [1925] here), writes his own name at the top of the page, and then starts a story. "Perhaps it was only one story, arbitrary, incomplete, but suddenly I knew that it would make its own necessity and in the process give me back my lost self." Presumably, it is the tale of Mobius, and his realization of nothingness as the core of life.

Like all good metafictional games, "Mobius the Stripper" has some serious points to make about life and literature. Stories are stories, it reminds the reader. They are made; they are not transparent, natural windows on the world. Personality and identity are a layer of narratives, wads of fictions, which others envelop us in, which we wrap ourselves in. "To strip," as Mobius puts it. "To take off what society has put on me. What my father and mother have put on me. What my friends have put on me. What I have put on me." How, if we are writers, do we escape the achievements of the past? How can we escape the clichés of tradition and convention? As ordinary human beings, how can we penetrate the inessential to what is really us? And if we get there, what will we find, if not an empty void and death?

"Is not seshual. Is metaphysical," Mobius insists of his act, arguing that it differs from his fellow showgirls' routines because he attempts to reach a metaphysical "TRUTH!" But although not "seshual," both narratives are grounded in a more mundane level of reality as well as that of literary and philosophical abstraction. First, "Mobius the Stripper" is a humorous story. The central conceit of the upper-page narrative, a fat foreign man taking off his clothes to existential reflections is comic. So, too, are Mobius's exchanges with showgirls, his manager, and the police. The narrator/writer's reflections on the agony of literary influence are similarly humorous. He imagines the writer's situation as that of a diminutive rugby player carrying a bundle of soiled diapers while being charged down by a team of gigantic opponents consisting of a stellar line-up of, *inter alios*, Dostoyevsky, Swift, Hugo, Homer, and Decartes, with above all "Joyce, small and fiery, his moustache in perfect trim," and a "languid and bemonocled" Proust, "always drifting nonchalantly behind them." This is comic writing of a high order, and it is worth stressing that one of the narrator/writer's important steps to writing is to laugh.

Second, Mobius is an immigrant to Britain. He speaks odd English. When challenged by the police, he asks if he needs to show his British passport. The narrator/writer, too, feels it important to stress Jenny's "fresh English face," and it is noticeable that his favorite and feared team of writers includes a predominance of non-English players. Only Chaucer, Lawrence, and Milton would unambiguously get a game for England, and even Lawrence and Milton, by social class and republican politics respectively, are at an angle to many traditional English identities. When Mobius realizes what the core of being and what Necessity is, it is worth stressing that he does so in terms of annihilation, of the rendering of the human body down to products. "She turn your muscles to water and your bones to oil." As an Anglo-Jewish writer, Josipovici surely does not choose this definition of death and necessity lightly. The Holocaust is implied by Mobius's words here. Josipovici's mobius strip, his topological experiment, does not exist entirely outside the contingencies of history. It may be a meditation on eternal recurrence and on writer's block, but it is also an examination of exile and the weight of history.

# Michael Moorcock, "Waiting for the End of Time..." (1976)

Published in as "Last Vigil" in the magazine *Vision of Tomorrow* (1970) and in book form in *Moorcock's Book of Martyrs* (1976)

Michael Moorcock, along with J. G. Ballard, is responsible for some of the finest science-fiction short stories in English, texts that can interest even those that are not *aficionados* of the genre. (In addition, as Part 3 of this study makes clear, Moorcock's heroic fantasy texts are no mean achievements.) "Waiting for the End of Time..." a late example of his work, demonstrates the power and possibilities of the genre. The story is set on a planet, Tanet, only a few hours from its end. Its galaxy is "condensing," collapsing inwards. "Megaquasars" at the center of the galaxy are combining into a single Mass. Suns are swallowing their planets, only in turn to be swallowed by larger suns, and then ultimately by the Mass. Suron, the protagonist, has tried to avert this process, of which humanity has been aware for a thousand years, by constructing a city-machine that can move the planet, one of its galaxy's outer bodies, out of its sun's range. His plan has not averted apocalypse. Suron and his partner Mis'rn watch things coming to an end and reflect on the process of destruction. Suron is resigned, Mis'rn more fearful. Suron has seen something moving on what he thought was now the deserted planet. He sets off to investigate and finds an "anthropoid quadruped," Mollei, the last survivor of a species Suron's kind exterminated "a long time ago." Mollei's species is rational and civilized, if quadruped and furred. Mollei himself has lived for ages, and does not know hate. Indeed, he has learned human speech from a less evolved human whom he calls his "friend." Suron and Mollei discuss the impending disaster. When Tanet's moon crashes on its surface, Mollei is wounded and asks to die alone, as he has lived. Suron leaves and, after

*The British and Irish Short Story Handbook*, First Edition. David Malcolm.
© 2012 David Malcolm. Published 2012 by Blackwell Publishing Ltd.

collapsing on his way back to his tower refuge, is found by his partner. They contemplate the end of things side by side. But the narrator indicates that this is not, in fact, the end of things. As Suron and others have suspected, the collapsing galaxy almost immediately begins a cycle of rebirth. Suns, planets, living beings will occur again. "For Time meant nothing," the narrator informs the reader, "and Death meant nothing and Identity meant only a little."

In terms of narration and narrative, "Waiting for the End of Time..." offers nothing that is not part of the conventions of realism. Its genre-specific elements are on the level of the text's created world and its denizens. In this created world, both time and space are undocumented and on an impressively grand scale. Tanet is an undocumented planet. The story is clearly set in an undocumented future time, far from the story's time of composition (or perhaps it is simply a different time, a past time unrecorded by twentieth-century humanity). The vast cosmic processes the text details have not yet hit humanity. It should be noted that the narrator posits a cyclical sequence of destruction and rebirth for the galaxy in the story. This is not the end of things as such. The scale of fictional events is enormous.

The technology of Tanet is impressive also: a city-machine that could in principle move a planet to another galaxy, dwellings that respond to delicate signs from their inhabitants, power packs that allow movement and control of one's immediate environment, furniture that manifests itself just when one wants it, vast immaterial bands that encircle a planet powering and protecting human habitations. Humans, too, in this world are a repertoire of speculative possibilities. Suron and Mis'rn are hermaphrodites, humanity having evolved from its "pre-hermaphroditic" stage. Their bodies are transparent. Sex is a "graceful ballet of emotion," the participants "scarcely touching each other." They also speak a rather formal and mellifluous English, but that seems appropriate to their spiritual calm and intelligence. Mollei, the "anthropoid quadruped," is similarly a creature of speculation, unknown in the documented twentieth-century world of the story's composition.

Moorcock's world, in short, is different from that of his readers, but it fascinates – as Wells's and Ballard's worlds do – by its positing of potentialities, by its opening up areas of possible experience that the realist short-story cannot. Further, the world of Tanet is not without relevance to the staid *empirique* of human society and history. Suron's humanity has a history of expansion, conquest, and genocide, as the reader's has. Human self-conquest – "what the ancients," as Suron has it, "called 'a state of grace'" – a calm, a benignity, a love of others and the Other, is not an undesirable aim in the make-up of twenty-first century humanity. The ironic "too late" of the story – humanity has got thus far, only to be wiped out by a cosmic process – is a salutary warning to human readers, just as the vast galactic collapse puts all our petty concerns in perspective. The story achieves a kind of biblical grandeur in its conclusion that readers might do well to heed. "For Time meant nothing and death meant nothing and Identity meant only a little."

# Sylvia Townsend Warner, "The King of Orkney's Leonardo" (1976)

Published in *The New Yorker* (1976) and in
*One Thing Leading to Another, and Other Stories* (1984)

Townsend Warner's work, both in longer and shorter fiction, is not nearly as well known as it deserves to be. Her short fiction is extensive, and the stories usually grouped together as the "Kingdoms of Elfin" stories are both *sui generis* and also part of a strong (and underrated) non-realist tradition in twentieth-century British short fiction.

"The King of Orkney's Leonardo" is typical of the *Kingdoms of Elfin* stories. The conceit is the following. Elfins and elfin statelets exist alongside the documented human world, interacting with it in various ways, but existing always at a tangent to the human world. The elfins, the fairies, are winged and can be invisible if they choose. Sir Huon and Lady Ulpha, aristocratic but impoverished fairies, have a son. Although they have difficulty settling on a name for him, he is eventually called Bonny. Extremely handsome, he attracts the attention of the Chancellor of the nearby Elfin court. There, the beautiful boy draws the love of the Princess Lief, "Queen Gruach's daughter from the Kingdom of Elfwick in Caithness." She takes him there and makes him her consort, despite her mother's hostility. Bonny, now renamed Gentil, tolerates but does not reciprocate Lief's love, despite her best efforts. He loses any enjoyment in life until one day in spring he falls in love with a young peasant. This infatuation leads, however, to his mutilation. While hovering near the young man, the peasant, who is hedging, chops off half of one of Gentil's ears.

*The British and Irish Short Story Handbook*, First Edition. David Malcolm.
© 2012 David Malcolm. Published 2012 by Blackwell Publishing Ltd.

The unfortunate fairy is now horribly mutilated by Elfin standards and withdraws from all society. He is brought back to liveliness by a picture of a young man, most like himself, a Leonardo recovered from a shipwreck. The beauty of the portrait moves him to appreciate Lief and her beauty. Although their relationship can never be one of passion, it becomes rewarding and endures. Gentil is finally completely healed by discovering turbans in a picture in the castle library. He dons a turban, embraces Islam, and he and Lief travel to Aberdeen and then on to Northern capitals, buying pictures as they go.

The narrator is omniscient, the narrative linear, but the reader feels that he/she is being taken on a narrative trip that is not entirely logical and consequential. Bonny encounters Lief and she seems to him to reject her. However, she has actually fallen in love with him and immediately carries him off to Elfwick. The Leonardo portrait redeems – in a sudden blinding epiphany – Gentil and his relationship with Lief. When Lief wishes to offer Gentil an escape from the castle, she finally thinks – of course – of the court library. A turban solves all problems. Instead of just wearing the headdress, Gentil converts to Islam, and, most bizarre of all, instead of going to Mecca opts for Aberdeen. Part of the story's humor – and it is a comic story – lies in such inconsequentialities.

Much of the rest of the humor in "The King of Orkney's Leonardo" can be found in the world of Elfin and its differences from and similarities to the human world, a world implied and at times presented in the text. The story has a dark and sometimes sinister humor, but humor nevertheless. Something of the differences between the Elfin and the human world is made clear when the narrator speaks of Elfwick. "Its savagery," she notes, "was practical, its violence law-abiding. Though it had grown comfort-loving, it had never become infected with that most un-Elfin weakness, pity." The Elfins are at an angle to traditional human morality. In Elfwick, they live from shipwrecks. Gentil himself observes with surprise and initial incomprehension how his new companions watch excitedly as a ship is swept toward the shore in a storm. They turn away gloomily when they see that it has escaped their clutches. Gentil hopes that at least they would save any sailor that reaches shore. "Knocked on the head like a seal," Lief says coldly. The Elfins have no time for witches – "mortals all, derided by rational elfins," observes the narrator. There is, indeed, a savage rationality about these immortals. They need to make sure of shipwrecks and are prepared to do anything to achieve them, even go to the vile mortal witches, bringing them money and a basket of live cats for their spells. When in a glorious storm, the ship that brings the Leonardo founders off their shore, they pitilessly kill the brave black sailor who protects the picture and show no remorse.

But, of course, the Elfins' cold good sense and lack of pity cannot but strike the reader as having human counterparts, and much about the Elfins is shared with mortals. Lady Ulpha's sense that childbirth is somehow "vulgar" is funny, but does not sound quite inhuman. Nor does the *Schadenfreude* of Bonny's parents as they observe their son making an impression of Princess Lief, an emotion that is shared by Lief's waiting-woman as she watches her "fawning on an upstart from Galloway." Gentil's becoming smitten with the handsome young peasant surely points to a universal human experience, and the wound inflicted on him may not be possible in a human world but, metaphorically speaking, must be recognizable to many readers. The same can be said of Gentil's ennui and world weariness, Lief's attempts to combat these, and Gentil's eventual redemption by an epiphanic encounter with great art. Circumstances may be comically at odds with traditional human experience, but Elfin is not wholly alien to the human reader.

"The King of Orkney's Leonardo" succeeds on several levels. It is a fine humorous short story; it creates a world that is tangential (alien and yet not quite alien) to the human one, but provokes thought about human standards of behavior. It is also a sober and yet moving story of love and its possibilities. Also, the story presents itself simply as a bravura piece of writing, a splendid self-advertising creation. An alien world is invented; the narrator brings the reader through a sequence of somewhat inconsequential and improbable events. The text unashamedly draws attention to is own fictiveness, provoking reflection on the making of stories (it is all so clearly invention) and on their power (this tale of fairies keeps our attention and provokes our laughter).

# William Trevor, "Another Christmas" (1978)

Published in *Lovers of Their Time, and Other Stories* (1978)

The range of William Trevor's short fiction is considerable, covering Ireland in the 1950s and England at various periods, moving from poor farmers on bleak Irish hills to old-age pensioners in London and tourists in Israel. He also writes memorably about the Irish in England, about individuals drawn from the millions of immigrants who have made their life on mainland Britain. "Another Christmas" is about some of the complexities of that immigrant existence. It is also centrally about Ireland (and Ireland-in-England) and the difficulty of escaping its complex and dismal history.

The story is narrated in the third person, but entirely from the point of view of Norah. She has come to London twenty-one years ago with her husband Dermot, from Wexford. They have lived and worked in London since then, she as a shop assistant in a department store, he as a meter reader for North Thames Gas. They belong, thus, to the peripheral and seemingly insignificant characters that are so typical of Trevor's work. They have had five children. They have lived for many years in the same house in Fulham, and have become friendly with their English landlord, Mr. Joyce. He has fallen into the custom of visiting them each Friday evening and every Christmas. The story's present is two days before Christmas Eve. Norah is hanging the Christmas decorations in their living room. Dermot is observing her. They engage in conversation about domestic matters, but finally Norah broaches the topic that has been troubling her for some time. She is certain that Mr. Joyce will not visit them this Christmas. In August of that year, one Friday evening, after watching a T.V. report about an I.R.A. bombing in England, something has happened. As the story is set in the mid-1970s, there have been many such

*The British and Irish Short Story Handbook*, First Edition. David Malcolm.
© 2012 David Malcolm. Published 2012 by Blackwell Publishing Ltd.

outrages and many such reports, and Mr. Joyce's comment of "Maniacs" is his standard one. However, on this occasion, instead of silently acquiescing, Dermot insisted (politely and calmly, but immovably) that the bombing is the consequence of decades of injustice towards Catholics in Northern Ireland. Mr. Joyce has ceased to visit them after that evening. Norah attempts to persuade Dermot to go to Mr. Joyce to apologize. He refuses and insists on the rightness of his conduct. His calm refusal to see what he has done wrong drives Norah to a kind of despair. She feels that her husband, and herself by acquiescing in his behavior, have committed an awful wrong against an elderly Englishman, against someone who has never treated them badly – when he might have – because they are Irish. Dermot's insistence on loyalty to an Irish Catholic view of things has resulted in "a cruelty." The "troubles" have brought out "the worst" in him, and perhaps her.

As befits a story about the weight of history, the text interweaves past and present in the organization of its narrative. It moves between the present in the mid-1970s and the past in the 1950s or during the years between Dermot's and Norah's arrival in the U.K. It focuses particularly on the events of the mid-1970s, the I.R.A.'s bombing campaign on mainland Britain, and Norah's and others' responses to those malign years. It also points to the future. "Another Christmas" does not only refer to a sequence of past Christmases, now shattered and discontinued, but also, in Norah's imagination, to a future Christmas, when perhaps the English will turn on the Irish in their midst.

Trevor is a miniaturist in most of his short fiction, using a small number of characters and restricted milieux to suggest substantial themes. "Another Christmas" is particularly economical and successful in this respect. A Fulham living room in a late afternoon before Christmas in 1975 (the story is precise in terms of time setting) becomes a site for the interplay of the tragic legacies of Irish history. Dermot's cold arguments about the consequences of decades of wickedness are, indeed, valid, but so is Norah's emotional distress, her shame both for her husband's words and for the violence of the Irish bombers. Mr. Joyce's ritual condemnation of Irish terrorism is justified, but it is based on an ignoring of history.

Further, the story is a powerful presentation of the complexities of Irish immigrant life (and *mutatis mutandis*, that of other immigrant groups). The story's central conflict over I.R.A. violence is integral to this life, but so, too, are the details that Trevor so carefully points to. These include the religious images on the living room walls, the scenes of Waterford that accompany them, and the green clock on the mantelpiece. Norah's and Dermot's children's names and their Catholic education, along with Norah's involvement in the local Catholic church also belong here. The couple have done well in Britain. Their grown children are successful. But Norah comes to feel that she and her husband have made "a trap" for themselves.

> Their children spoke with London accents. Patrick and Brendan worked for English firms and would make their homes in England. Patrick had married an English girl. They were Catholics and they had Irish names, yet home for them was not Waterford.

A central aspect of "Another Christmas" is its evocation of the mind and feelings of Norah, a typically (for Trevor's work) unglamorous but psychologically and morally substantial figure. The story is shaped round her reflections on her life in England and her conflict with her reasonable, civilized, and (she comes to think) monstrously wrong husband. It focuses, above all, on her outrage at the outrages that Irish history involves and that Irish people have perpetrated for Church and country. She even feels that the problems of Northern Ireland are not hers, and that she has, in any case, never cared greatly for either Catholic or Protestant Northern Irish. She desires to run out onto Fulham Broadway, her hair flying, violently condemning the bombers to passers-by. But all she can do is talk to her husband and, when that fails, fall into silent musings and shame. As a scrutiny (from one particular point of view) of the matter of Ireland and an evocation of Irish immigrant experience, "Another Christmas" is subtle, complex, and deeply moving.

# Angela Carter, "The Erl-King" (1979)

Published in *The Bloody Chamber, and Other Stories* (1979)

"The Erl-King" has a simple story material, indeed a substantially attenuated one. A young woman enters a forest in autumn. In "a darkening clearing," she meets a Pan-like figure, surrounded by woodland creatures. He takes her to his house where he lives from the produce of the forest. He lays her on his bed and strips off her clothes. They make love. She visits her lover frequently. At first enthralled by the strange Erl-King, the young woman fears that he will imprison her, as he has imprisoned wild birds in cages of his own weaving. The young woman strangles her lover with his own hair, and frees the birds, which change into the young girls they once were. She cuts off his hair to restring an old fiddle that belongs to the Erl-King. Of their own accord, the strings call "Mother, mother, you have murdered me!"

Like the other texts in *The Bloody Chamber*, "The Erl-King" is a reworking of traditional legends and folk-tales. In this story, the Erl-King is part forest recluse, part wild man of the woods, part Pan. He lives entirely from the forest, mushrooms, berries, his own cheeses, an occasional rabbit. Only his nanny goat is not native to the woods. He possesses supernatural or quasi-supernatural powers: drawing wild birds to him; shedding leaves when he combs his hair; transforming girls into birds. The wild fox will lay its muzzle on his leg. After his death, his fiddle plays by itself. The name "Erl-King" drives from Goethe's poem about the powerful and sinister "*Erlkönig*" (King of the Alders) who carries off a child as he and his father ride "*so spät durch Nacht und Wind*" (so late through night and wind). In fact, Carter's story is barely connected to Goethe's "*Erlkönig*" – story material and characters, both predator and victim, are very different – except in the dangerous and seductive glamour of the Erl-King.

*The British and Irish Short Story Handbook*, First Edition. David Malcolm.
© 2012 David Malcolm. Published 2012 by Blackwell Publishing Ltd.

The text's narration is suitably odd for a story of possession. The narrator moves through all three persons in the course of the text. It starts in the second person: "You step between the first trees and then you are no longer in the open air; the wood swallows you up." The second person turns to third: "A young girl would go into the wood as trustingly as Red Riding Hood to her granny's house... and, here, she will be trapped in her own illusion. ..." Then the first person emerges:

> the intimate perspectives of the wood changed endlessly around the interloper, the imaginary traveler walking towards an invented distance that perpetually receded before me. It is easy to lose yourself in these woods. The two notes of the song of a bird rose in the still air, as if my girlish and delicious loneliness had been made into a sound.

For most of the rest of the text, the narration remains a first-person one. However, the addressee changes. For much of the story it is an unnamed one, but toward the story's end, the narrator addresses the Erl-King directly. "What big eyes you have. ... Your green eye is a reducing chamber." She then switches back to referring to him in the third person. She herself changes as she murders her lover "I shall take two handfuls of his rustling hair. ... Then she will open all the cages and let the birds free."

Time reference in the story is equally disrupted. The text shifts from past tenses to present tenses throughout. For example, when she first meets the Erl-King, the narrator moves from past to present. "It was a garden where all the flowers were birds and beasts. ... The rusty fox, its muzzle sharpened to a point, laid its head upon his knee. ... he knew I had arrived. He smiles. He lays down his pipe, his elder bird-call." In a substantial part of the story, habitual actions are given in present tenses, particularly the present simple. There are very few references to past or future. Once the narrator decides not to succumb to the Erl-King's charms, these become more important. "Your green eye is a reducing chamber. ... I will be drawn down into that black whirlpool and be consumed by you. ... When I realized what the Erl-King meant to do to me, I was shaken with a terrible fear. ..." The text reverts to the present simple as the narrator prepares for the murder; the act itself, however, and its aftermath are given in future forms: "I shall strangle him with them. ... She will carve off his great mane with the knife he uses to skin the rabbits. ... Then it will play discordant music. ..."

Shits in narration and shifts in time reference have two functions. First, they disorient and disturb. The oddness of the story material is embodied in technique. Second, the shifts suggest the universality of the experiences and situations depicted. It is not just about "me," but about "you" and "she" too. It is not just about now, but about past and future also.

The story is about erotic fascination and resistance to that fascination. The narrator – for she often refers to herself as "I," as well as using other pronouns – clearly feels a deep attraction to the man of the woods. She waxes lyrical of his charms.

> He strips me to my last nakedness, that underskin of mauve pearlized satin, like a skinned rabbit; then dresses me again in an embrace so lucid and encompassing it might be made of water.

Later she talks more of their lovemaking.

> His touch both consoles and devastates me; I feel my heart pulse, then wither, naked as a stone on the roaring mattress while the lovely moony night slides through the window to dapple the flanks of this innocent who makes cages to keep the sweet birds in. Eat me, drink me; thirsty, cankered, goblin-ridden, I go back and back to him to have his fingers strip the tattered skin away and clothe me in his dress of water, this garment that drenches me, its slithering odor, its capacity for drowning.

The rapture of the erotic is embodied elsewhere in the narrator's language. She has a fondness for richly inventive lists: animals, mushrooms, berries, herbs. In the opening paragraph, she achieves a gongoristic height that captures the exotic, ecstatic, fabulous quality of her experience. She writes of the sky and "these vertical bars of a brass-coloured distillation of light coming down from sulphur-yellow interstices in a sky hunkered with grey clouds that bulge with more rain." The light strikes the wood "with nicotine-stained fingers." In the forest, "the rains of the equinox had so soaked the earth that the cold oozed up through the soles of the shoes, lancinating cold of the approach of winter." "Lancinating" sums up the linguistic verve of this text – an early seventeenth-century word for piercing that is not in common use today.

Unusual lexis and erotic transport come together in the following.

> And now – ach! I feel your sharp teeth in the subaqueous depths of your kisses. The equinoctial gales seize the bare elms and make them whizz and whirl like dervishes; you sink your teeth into my throat and make me scream.

But this is a sexual rapture that must be resisted, for it will lead to capture and imprisonment. The narrator rejects the fate of the many singing birds in their cages and, in a reversal of the male lover's action in Robert Browning's "Porphyria's Lover" (1842), she strangles her wild lover with his own hair. However, the man of the woods in Carter's story is an "innocent," neither a monstrous male tyrant nor a madman. The narrator sees him as an "innocent," and he seems to lead an almost blameless life close to nature and the beasts. He even keeps a clean kitchen. The end of the story invites a shift in readers' sympathies. The restrung violin calls out "Mother, mother, you have murdered me!" The narrator becomes a sinister man-slayer at this point, and the violin's song reflects the refrain of "Edward, Edward," the medieval ballad of a mother's cruelty.

The stories in *The Bloody Chamber* are about the intricacies of male-female relationships. Carter rewrites traditional tales in exciting and intriguing ways. The agenda is feminist, but, even for the unreconstructed, Carter earns her politics by an inventive brio and a linguistic virtuosity, as well as complexity about male oppression and control and female acquiescence and resistance.

# Clive Sinclair, "The Evolution of the Jews" (1979)

Published in *Hearts of Gold* (1979)

The narrator of this brief and poignant fable is Shlomo, a Yiddish-speaking Jewish giraffe. He never uses the word 'giraffe' of himself, but refers to him and his kind only as Jews. He insists, in fact, that giraffes are the lost tribe of Israel. "How do I know?" he asks. "My father told me. What proof can I give? For starters, there's the statue of Moses wearing horns. Just like mine." They have wandered far and evolved much. "If every other creature in the world wanted to do you in you'd also head for the lowlands and grow a long neck. And four legs are faster than two." Shlomo's story is sad and funny. He is pursued by anti-semites (that is lions). He is tempted to deviate from the dietary restrictions imposed by the rabbis. Although forbidden to eat fruit from the ground, Shlomo follows a trail of tantalizing fallen fruit, at the end of which he falls into a trap. He is captured by what he calls "The worst anti-semites of them all. Men!" These, however, turn out to be Israelis, and Shlomo is brought to a zoo in Jerusalem. Here he feels happy. He is among fellow Jews. The anti-semites are behind bars. But even here he cannot stop worrying. He sees his compatriots grow lion-like. They carry guns and talk of battles. He wishes to warn them, but he cannot speak. At the story's end, Shlomo suffers the fall he has dreaded all his life, even more than he has feared the anti-semites. He is again tempted to try to eat the fruit of a tree that has been forbidden him. He falls, breaks his legs, and cannot rise. He decides that though he is dumb, his fate is a "warning to Israel." "I am a prophet!" he declares.

*The British and Irish Short Story Handbook*, First Edition. David Malcolm.
© 2012 David Malcolm. Published 2012 by Blackwell Publishing Ltd.

"The Evolution of the Jews" is a funny, sad, and political beast fable, in a long and resilient tradition of the genre. Shlomo speaks in a racy short-sentenced English that sounds as if it is meant to represent an Anglicised Yiddish (for Shlomo declares that one of the reasons his Israeli captors do not understand him, is that they do not speak Yiddish). Shlomo is discussing his sexual encounter with a lady giraffe.

> Just my luck this afternoon I got a real athlete. A dozen times in four hours she made me perform. Then the lookouts spotted the lions. Two of the brutes. Moving in our direction. "Run!" they signaled. Fat chance!

Here, he is describing the outcome of the lion attack. He has floored one of the brutes, but now the other is clinging to his back while the intrepid Shlomo gallops down an escarpment.

> I am safe. So long as I do not stop. But then above the thunder of my hoofs I hear a deeper rumble in the heavens. And I feel rain upon my muzzle. What *mazel*! The lion springs off my back leaving long raking scars – the butcher – and runs around catching raindrops on his tongue. The drought is over. God be praised. The Jews will live a few more days.

Shlomo is a creature of tradition. He refers to figures from Jewish legend and history: Moses, Samson, and Haman (the evil embodiment of anti-semitism). His life, and that of his fellow giraffes, is governed by tradition: he must make love to a female giraffe in a certain way; he may only eat of some kinds of fruit (mimosa and acacia), and then only in trees. His life, too, is one of persecution, blame, humiliation, and fear.

> "Remember you are a Jew," my father said when I was old enough to stand on my own four feet. As if the anti-semites would let me forget! They have been killing Jews in the miombo ever since the drought began. Before that there were pogroms in the nyika to the east.

All animals are the enemies of the giraffes; they are blamed during the drought for stealing the clouds. Even when the drought breaks, there is only a temporary quasi-peace – "Except for the odd outbreak of anti-semitism we are left alone." One of Shlomo's uncles came to an untimely end, strangling himself on a tree. "When we discovered him lions were already feeding from his hind legs. Ugh!" Shlomo himself is pursued by the vile, anti-semitic lions.

However, once he is transported to the safety of Israel, he sees dangers in a Jewish land. Here, his evolution into a long-necked fearful creature is contrasted with another evolution around him.

> What is there to worry about? I'll tell you. The evolution of the Jews. Make no mistake, evolution happens every day. I tremble for the kids. I am frightened by the way the hair forms thick and mane-like upon their heads. By the way their teeth grow sharp, their nails claw-like. And each time I see a Jew carrying a gun I shiver.

A militarily powerful Israel, able to defend itself, scares Shlomo. He warns that such "evolution is the secret weapon of the anti-semites," that "evolution is not inevitable." "But in Israel I am dumb," he concludes sadly.

Life as a persecuted creature in the miombo is bad, but what he sees in Israel disturbs him. In the end, Shlomo's fate is brought about by reaching for what is forbidden – in his case an orange; in his view, in the case of his fellow Jews, perhaps power, domination, military might.

In this story, Sinclair, a distinguished if controversial Anglo–Jewish author, takes on a central topic in much Anglo–Jewish and American–Jewish writing: the legacy of European Jewry, persecuted for centuries, murdered in the Holocaust, and the relation of that Yiddish-speaking world and culture to those of modern Jewry and of Israel. The latter is especially one of Sinclair's recurrent themes. Shlomo has words of warning to the modern Jewish world, but he himself is an ungainly and ultimately comic figure, a bit of a *nebech*. Sinclair's fable provokes the reader to thought and provides no easy answers to the questions it poses.

# John McGahern, "The Conversion of William Kirkwood"(1985)

Published in *High Ground* (1985)

John McGahern, despite publishing a relatively small number of short stories (*The Collected Stories* of 1992 contains only thirty-four short stories), was, by the time of his death in 2006, regarded (rightly) as one of the pre-eminent short fiction writers of his generation in English. The subjects of his short fiction closely follow those of his novels: the constrictions of Irish rural life in the mid-twentieth century; the *anomie* of those adrift in the city; blighted hopes; wretched family relationships, especially between sons and fathers; the bitterness of those who feel independence has brought little; and fragile glimmers of hope offered for a moment in love. Many of his short stories, too, take on the phonological, lexical, and syntactic patterning of the novels. One group of short stories particularly stands out in his œuvre: that is, the trio of stories in *High Ground* that aim at a historical sweep and focus that is unusual in short fiction in general, and that take on the (little touched on) subject of the Protestant legacy of and in southern Irish history and its presence in the modern Irish Free State and Republic. These stories are "Oldfashioned" (which was to be the title story of the *High Ground* volume), "Eddie Mac," and "The Conversion of William Kirkwood."

The last of these is a continuation of the material in "Eddie Mac," a story of betrayal by the eponymous protagonist, both of his lover Annie May and his employers, the Protestant Kirkwoods. "The Conversion of William Kirkwood" begins some years after Eddie Mac's departure to England, leaving Annie May pregnant, and taking the best of the Kirkwoods' cattle with him to sell in order to fund his escape. The Kirkwoods have insisted on their servant's bringing up the child in their big house, now sadly run-down.

*The British and Irish Short Story Handbook*, First Edition. David Malcolm.
© 2012 David Malcolm. Published 2012 by Blackwell Publishing Ltd.

The child, Lucy, is made much of by the older Kirkwood, and, after his death, by his son, also called William Kirkwood. The three, Annie May, Lucy, and William, live out the late 1920s and 1930s in relative isolation from the rest of the world, from Catholics and, indeed, Protestants alike. The child grows up devoted to William Kirkwood, as is her mother. They are poor, and Kirkwood's Protestantism and class history sets him (and, by extension, the women) apart from their Catholic neighbors. Paradoxically, it is the Second World War ("The Emergency" in neutral southern Ireland) that brings Kirkwood into the community. A scion of the officer class of the British Army becomes, without hesitation, an officer in the Irish reserve. Despite initial resentment, his fairness and efficiency bring him respect. His neighbors start to help him with his land, and he in return helps them. The new establishment of the new state, the teacher and the police sergeant, suggest he convert to Catholicism and later get married. Kirkwood has himself considered both steps, and by the story's end has both joined the Catholic Church and is about to marry the daughter of a prospering local Catholic landowner. The price of integration, however, will be steep. Lucy is alienated from her one-time father figure, and Mary Kennedy makes it clear that Annie May must be dismissed from the house before the marriage with Kirkwood. The story's conclusion is, to some extent, open-ended, and, predominantly, dark: Kirkwood is alone in his house's kitchen (where he has spent so much of his life with Annie May and Lucy), considering how to avoid driving out the people who have meant most to him in his life so far. Once again, as in "Eddie Mac," Annie May is to be betrayed.

This story, at once joyous and sad, is narrated by an omniscient third-person narrator, who is able to see into the hearts and minds of many characters, and, indeed, at times employs free indirect speech to give the responses of the community to Kirkwood and his actions. It is striking, however, where the narrator remains silent. He is very economical in giving Annie May's thoughts about Kirkwood's marriage; he tells the reader nothing about Lucy's response to the story's later events. The reader learns of her actions, but has no insight into her feelings. Similarly, Kirkwood's mind is given mostly through his utterances. It is the community (the teacher and Garda sergeant, the priest, and Mary Kennedy) whose thoughts and feelings are most frequently set out. This is appropriate in a story about the power of the communal.

The narrator is also selective in his conduct of the narrative. Mostly told in a linear fashion – with a considerable analepsis in the early section of the text, recounting the years after Eddie Mac's departure – the story substantially consists of representative moments, selected from many over several years from the late 1920s through the 1940s: Kirkwood's helping Lucy with her homework; the enfeebled Kirkwood senior's inability to lift the roofs off his beehives; the neighbors' coming to help Kirkwood stack his hay; the drinks after military exercises in which Kirkwood is encouraged to convert and marry; Kirkwood's visit to the McLoughlins' home; the Sunday on which Mary Kennedy visits Kirkwood's home, and he visits hers; and the final scene of the story in which Kirkwood sits alone in his kitchen pondering the future.

The narrator is selective, too, in his details of time and place. Both are, as is common in McGahern's work, both specific and vague (and, thus, generalized). There are place names, to be sure, and the reader knows from "Eddie Mac" that the story is set somewhere near the Shannon river, but its action takes place in deliberately universalized, generic rural southern Ireland. Similarly, there are time markers aplenty: Lucy's age, the end of the wealth and authority of the Anglo–Irish Protestant landowning class, and "The "Emergency." However, there is a deliberate avoidance of particular years (the story contains not a single date). Once again, there is an attempt to generalize and even universalize the action.

The steps by which Kirkwood moves toward integration into the community are set out with credibility and clarity. They are embedded in a selective, but lucidly illuminating choice of detail: the peculiarities of Kirkwood's Protestant phonology, which Lucy inherits in part; his dilapidated house, with its unoccupied rooms, its unworked land, its overgrown orchard; the *realia* of haymaking in uncertain weather; a provincial clothing store with its brass money cups clanging on wires; and Kirkwood's visit to the school teacher McLoughlin's home, where, surrounded by the bric-à-brac of a lower middle-class Catholic home, "[n]ot in all the years of his Protestantism had he ever felt his difference so keenly." The story's approach to Kirkwood's integration is like the algebra lesson that Kirkwood gives Lucy at the story's start. She professes not to understand abstractions, but follows Kirkwood's procedures well when he uses concrete objects to illustrate equations.

There is a near inevitability in Kirkwood's progression. He becomes interested in Catholicism through his helping Lucy with her homework. From generations of British Army officers on his mother's side, he performs his role in the Irish reserve with efficiency and aplomb. The next steps to the Church and to marriage have a logic to them. The community wants it, and Kirkwood, for all his oddness and difference, likes his neighbors enough. He enjoys being part of the large Kennedy family celebration. But McGahern also makes readers aware of complex motives underlying actions. Kirkwood gets a taste for being part of things and for being recognized and appreciated. For the community, he is a prize: his conversion is a communal celebration. Mary Kennedy knows exactly what she will get from a marriage with

Kirkwood, and also knows that Annie May, and the past, must go before she moves into the big house. The marriage will also bring benefits for Kirkwood. His farm will become viable again through the connection with the prosperous Kennedys.

McGahern's "The Conversion of William Kirkwood" is an ambitious and successful attempt to extend the range of his short fiction, both in terms of temporal scope and in terms of subject matter. It does not present Ireland as a site of dulling constraint (although there is enough of that in McGahern's other short fiction), but with extreme economy and shrewdness offers a picture of the integrational forces of community and history. This process, while moving, humorous, and positive, is seen with clarity and its costs and consequences are never dodged. It is part of a complex *œuvre*, but stands on its own as a fascinating (and very original) work by a great short-story writer.

# James Kelman,
# "Forgetting to Mention Allende"
# (1987)

Published in *Greyhound for Breakfast* (1987)

In an interview published in 1989, Kelman remarked that

> I think the most ordinary person's life is fairly dramatic; all you've got to do is follow some people around and look at their existence for 24 hours, and it will be horror. It will be just horror. You don't need any beginning, middle, and end at all. All you have to do is show this one day in maybe this one person's life and it'll be horror.
>
> (qtd. in Macdonald 2006: 133)

While the "horror" in "Forgetting to Mention Allende" is not as extreme as in some of Kelman's short stories, it is bad enough. The protagonist Tommy McGoldrick is unemployed. His wife works long hours as a supermarket cashier. He looks after their three children and decorates the flat they have just moved into. The story follows McGoldrick through part of his day from just before noon until mid-afternoon. He gives food to his young daughter, makes her take a nap, and brings her to her nursery school. He talks to an older man who has brought his grandchildren to the school. McGoldrick buys himself a pie on his way home and eats it. His elder son returns, and he attempts to have a conversation with the laconic youth. He gets ready to paint some of the apartment. Two Mormon missionaries call, but McGoldrick avoids having a conversation with them. McGoldrick realizes that he has not mentioned the Chilean president Salvador Allende to them. He lights a cigarette, makes a cup of coffee, and uses the bathroom.

The narrator of the text is both distant from and integrated with McGoldrick. The narrator refers to the principal character in the third person, but

*The British and Irish Short Story Handbook*, First Edition. David Malcolm.
© 2012 David Malcolm. Published 2012 by Blackwell Publishing Ltd.

the story slides seamlessly in and out of free indirect and free direct speech. The movement into Tommy's consciousness is often marked by the narrator's shift into southern Scottish, more specifically Glaswegian Scots. Thus, McGoldrick sits down after giving his little daughter two biscuits.

> When he sat down on the armchair he stared at the ceiling, half expecting to see it bouncing up and down. For the past couple of hours somebody had been playing records at full blast. It was nearly time for the wean to have her morning kip as well. The same yesterday. He had tried; he had put her down and sat with her, read part of a story: it was hopeless but, the fucking music, blasting out.

"Wean," "kip," the use of "but" as a phrase terminator, and "fucking" all mark a narrational shift to McGoldrick's language, to an informal demotic, and to Scots. The protagonist, to a degree, takes over, as does his language. This narrational strategy carries political significance. McGoldrick, his life, and his language are worthy of literary, moral, and political attention, the story insists.

"Forgetting to Mention Allende" gives a substantial part of McGoldrick's day, the domestic tasks he performs, the unexciting acts he accomplishes, the spaces of empty time he lives through. He lives on a "scheme," in public housing; he and his family are not well-off; he is unemployed. He does admirable things: he looks after his young daughter with affection, he talks politely to an older man, he tries to talk to his son, he starts to decorate his apartment, and he prepares to cook the evening meal. But the narrative elisions scream out in the text. What is the backstory to the events the story records? Why is Tommy without work? What does he feel about the reversal of traditional roles in his family? His wife is exhausted when she comes home. How is their relationship surviving his unemployment? How does Tommy feel when he talks to the older man and the latter starts to jibe at the unemployed? How will Tommy's relationship with his elder son develop (for it does not look promising at present)?

Above all, why is the story entitled "Forgetting to Mention Allende," and why does Tommy feel vexed that he has forgotten to mention the (one presumes) dead Chilean president (overthrown by a U.S. backed *coup d'état* in 1973)? The narrator and the story eschew answers to these questions, but the very ellipses demand that the reader reflect on Tommy's and his family's situation. Why might Allende be important to Tommy? Why might he want to mention Allende to the "bastards," the door-to-door missionaries he assumes are Mormons, and therefore to his mind associated with the U.S.A?

It is usual, in line with Kelman's own observation about his fiction quoted above, to emphasize the "horror," the negative aspects, of the worlds depicted in the author's fiction. But one can also see his work as a celebration of the powers of survival of people in very difficult situations. As I have noted, McGoldrick is an admirable figure, doing what he can to make things work better. The fact that he takes a long time to get started with his painting is one of the understated points in the text. Kelman is both inviting a middle-class criticism, and yet inviting, too, the intelligent reader to ask himself/herself what he/she would do in such circumstances. Further, although McGoldrick appears trapped in a hopeless situation, he has a consciousness of who he is and what he believes, a firmness alongside a basic decency and politeness. He knows, the work implies, that his position is part of a global process of exploitation and capitalist indifference. The fact that he survives and keeps on going, and does not lose sight of a broader world, offers hope in the context of drab "horror."

The Scottish author's celebration of the strength and dignity of working-class language echoes some of D. H. Lawrence's short fiction. Further, although working within the conventions of realism, Kelman's short fiction echoes more self-referential and less realist-bound work. His fascination with the drab repetitions of unglamorous lives, and the inertia of much life on the peripheries of respectable society, reflects motifs in Beckett's fiction and drama. In his insistence of the possibility and the importance of lower-class strategies of survival (for those involved and for humanity in general), he is in tune with the short fiction of John Berger, in, for example, his stories in *Pig Earth* (1979).

# Mary Dorcey,
# "A Noise from the Woodshed"
# (1989)

Published in *A Noise from the Woodshed: Short Stories* (1989)

Much praised and much criticized, Mary Dorcey's work in the short story revisits some traditional topics of Irish short fiction with an innovative sexual frankness. She also in "A Noise from the Woodshed" combines a political and social agenda with a technique that draws on the legacy of Beckett's experimental fiction.

"A Noise from the Woodshed" differs radically from the conventions of realism that dominate in the twentieth-century Irish short story. The narration does not employ a first- or third-person narrator, in any of their variants. It is an example, relatively unusual, of a second-person narration. As in most such narrations, the "you" is really an "I" addressing itself. However, it is a second-person narration, and this carries consequences, both in terms of breaching norms, and also because it suggests an attempt to generalize the speaker's experience. She is not just "I," but is "you" too. The voice speaks in its choice of pronoun for all women, and this universality is emphasized by an explicitly general perspective on female life throughout the story.

"A Noise from the Woodshed" is further norm-breaching in its presentation of its story material. In a sense, the text is traditional (although its lesbian subject matter is provocative). The story material is as follows. A woman is saved from a flooded path by another woman. They fall in love. They make love. The "you" of the text returns home with her female savior ("she"). They get to know each other, and the first woman (she who has been saved) learns of her lover's previous companion who has left. They live a life of Edenic relaxation, making love, drinking fine wine, pottering around the house. After hearing unusual noises in the woodshed, they investigate and find two

American women sleeping naked there. They have been invited to do so by the owner of the house. They plan to work to improve the house. "You" and "she" go for a picnic by a river in the woods.

This traditional (albeit lesbian) love story is, however, presented in a manner unusual in short fiction. It is both given through and overlaid by lyric effusions and feminist polemics. Being much closer in its evident patterning to the language of poetry, the language of "A Noise from the Woodshed" is self-referential in a way that is a manifest breach of realist convention, as the lesbian romance it details breaches the social norms suggested in the story (and those of the time and place of its publication). Language is foregrounded throughout the text. Sentences are persistently long, full of parentheses, participial phrases, and subordinate and coordinate clauses. Almost any passage taken at random can illustrate Dorcey's language in this text. In the following, note how a shorter sentence (and more the sort of sentence one might find in a dozen short stories) leads into a much longer one.

> So that day, when she came along, it was almost too late for you. When she swept you up in the nick of time, and carried you over the waters, and laid you down in the long grasses, and committed love with you, and staggered home drunken and laughing, shouting for joy and just for the sake of it, and did not stagger out again for days, being so busy, preoccupied with bodily surfaces and passages, and all that talking to be gone through – that day was no commonplace day – rest assured.

The second sentence in the above quotation is marked by syntactic parallelism ("When... and... and... and... "), achieved through polysyndeton. It has minor examples of homoeoteleuton ("laughing, shouting"), a device much more marked in other passages. There is alliteration – "shouting for joy and just for. . . ." There is paronomasia, the punning on the cliché "rest assured." The remainder of the text is equally self-referential. Prominent among Dorsey's devices in it is the list. The above quotation is continued thus:

> If it were, even you out there in the wilderness would have heard by now. That day was one of the special days, of triumph and discovery, of breaking through, opening the door from the given into the dreamed of: the possible world in the making, and you made it in the making, the making of anger and questions and loving, and laughter up there loftily in the loft, swaying in arms and trees, babes in arms, love a bye baby, the cradle will fall, and down will come tyranny, silence and all.

Lists ("of triumph and discovery, of breaking through, opening"), alliteration ("babes in arms, love a bye baby"), homoeoteleuton ("breaking... opening...

making… making… making… loving… swaying), puns ("loftily in the loft"), playing with fixed and well-known phrases ("the cradle will fall" instead of "the cradle will rock") – all combine to produce a richly exuberant verbal romp.

But this linguistic extravaganza has its polemic edge, celebrating the female and setting its responsibility, its openness, its joyousness, and possibility against a male world of selfishness, instrumentality, and violence. "There are soldiers and surgeons and scientists waiting to cure to death, waiting to kill for peace," the narrator warns. The female is Edenic, as the biblical lexis in the first quotation above – "and carried you over the waters, and laid you down in the long grasses" – suggests. It comprises a world of joy, peace, freedom, and carefree intercourse (in all senses) with others. The female/feminine world is not, however, wholly positive. It is chaotic and temporary; around the protagonists many things remain frustratingly (for the protagonists) undone. In addition, the narrator is occasionally self-mocking; the woman-written symphony she talks of never does get composed. Nonetheless, there is powerful feminist-lesbian appropriation of traditional (often biblical) symbol and motif – the river that is to be crossed, the savior that comes for one, and the flowers among which the lovers make love. To add a further dimension to the story's language, the syntactic and lexical elevation of the text is frequently, in comic and self-deprecating fashion, juxtaposed with a domesticity, references to the mundane (looking after a home, caring for children) that is, in this world, far from unimportant.

In one of the passages quoted above, the narrator talks "of triumph and discovery, of breaking through, opening the door from the given into the dreamed of: the possible world in the making, and you made it in the making." The language of the text, its organization of its story material, and its unusual narration all go to enact the newness, the millennial aspirations of the speaker. All will be made afresh beyond the river in the love and plans of two women, and those others in the woodshed. The text enacts this newness again and again.

Dorcey's short story sits four-square in an Irish tradition of critique of the restrictions of traditional life. "What's that?" asks the narrator. "There, where the chimneys rise smoking and the television aerials wave and the walls stretch long and concrete and she said oh, that; that's one of the power stations for the nuclear family. . . ." Her explicit feminist-lesbian agenda adds a radical dimension to that critique. Her language makes material the innovation to which her protagonists aspire. Beckett's avant-garde story-telling is turned to political and moral purpose.

# James Lasdun, "Ate/Menos or The Miracle" (1992)

Published in *Three Evenings, and Other Stories* (1992)

"Ate/Menos or The Miracle" is a sinister and disturbing story, even by James Lasdun's standards. It is also a morally complex examination of the force of religion and the force of deception. The narrator, who at one point calls himself Oliver, is a young man at a loose end on a Sunday in London. He takes a walk and decides on impulse to enter an Anglican Church, St. Simeon's, where he takes communion, although he declares "I am not a believer, let alone a Christian." He describes his act as driven by the Homeric states of either *ate* or *menos*. "*Ate*," he informs the reader, "drives a man to commit demonic acts of rashness for which he is duly punished. *Menos*... is moral spunk; a sudden access of energy, confidence, strength." He is not sure which applies in his case. After the service, the narrator feels "fueled" by his act of sacrilege, and when he is mistaken by a woman in the street for the theater director Matthew Delacorta, he decides to deceive her by pretending to be a person he is not. The woman, Madeleine, some ten years older than the narrator, is an actress and she desperately wishes to take advantage of this chance meeting. The two return to her grandly decaying home. There, the narrator encounters Madeleine's autistic daughter Kiku (or Suky), who has to live in a padded room and play with toys that have no sharp or hard surfaces. All the time, the narrator continues to foster the illusion that he is Matthew Delacorta. Madeleine and he get drunk; they have sex. Madeleine's husband turns up and declares the narrator not to be Delacorta. In a climactic conclusion, the narrator mentally torments the autistic Kiku, and makes his escape. As he flees, he hears a female voice in an anguished wail of "No, no, no... o... o... o... ." It is far from clear what happens in the end: Kiku is

*The British and Irish Short Story Handbook*, First Edition. David Malcolm.
© 2012 David Malcolm. Published 2012 by Blackwell Publishing Ltd.

distressed; a kettle boils violently filling the kitchen with steam; the reader's attention has twice been drawn to a line of kitchen knives on the wall.

The story is set on a Sunday in autumn. The day of Christian observance appears to mean little to the narrator, or to anyone but the few, mostly elderly, people attending the service in St. Simeon's. The place is London, according to the narrator, a materially solid place of "bricks and paving stones and plate-glass windows." St. Simeon's, where the narrator commits his sacrilege, possesses "ugly portals" and smells of "cold stone and candlewax." Madeleine's flat is a strangely church-like arrangement of old moth-eaten fabrics, worn furniture, and tarnished artifacts. Its Gothic qualities are reinforced by the revelation of Kiku's pretty but bizarre padded room with its swathed furniture and floppy toys. Madeleine's bedroom is "dismal," strewn with the debris of an unhappy life. Her kitchen, as I have suggested above, becomes nightmarish at the story's end: gratuitous cruelty, a menacing boiling kettle, a woman's wail. Places are disturbingly unattractive in "Ate/Menos or The Miracle," oppressively material, ugly, decaying, disordered, and frightening.

The places of this created world are seen by the narrator, and he himself is an ambiguous and sinister figure. His voice is a very educated, literate, and grandiloquently eloquent one. The following is a sample of his language. Note the sophisticated lexis *passim* and the complex syntax of the third sentence.

> The ramifications of my connection with Madeleine – was she succumbing to my charm, to Delacorta's, to my version of his charm – went on like an infinite mathematical series. We had entered a realm where we were subject more to the laws physics than those of human nature. And just as, under random stimulus, a quark is said to leave its own equivalent of a spoor along all the paths that it might have taken, but did not, as well as along the one it did, so I felt myself refracted into a mirror-hall of multiplicit possible selves, each one of them pressing a ghostly claim to being the sole channel through which these events were flowing. It was a vertiginous feeling.

The narrator is not just a skilled user of language, but an ambiguous figure. He once (to Kiku) gives his name as Oliver; the rest of the time he masquerades as Matthew Delacorta, just as he masquerades as a believer in St. Simeon's. He starts the day off listless, without the energy even to turn off a religious service on the radio. "How weak I felt, how powerless," he says in the fact of the solid materiality of London. He then attains force from his act of sacrilege, and exercises power over Madeleine, a power he is always conscious of. But he is a liar, a seducer, and a trickster. He performs tricks for an unimpressed Kiku, his "life's accomplishments," he declares. He tells Madeleine the truth, and gives her an accurate account of his day, knowing that she will accept it as fiction. Even he feels himself in need of cleansing after he has drunk Madeleine's "foul" cocktails and had sex with her under quite false pretenses. His whole performance reeks of wickedness. "What are you?" Madeleine's husband asks him, not "Who?" He may be in doubt as to whether *ate* or *menos* drives him. Most readers surely are not. His actions are "demonic acts of rashness," indeed. One wonders only whether there is any punishment in store for him.

Throughout the text, there are motifs of illusion and deception. The narrator wishes to maintain the "flattering" delusion that he is a person of consequence. He lies continually to Madeleine, even when he tells the truth. He calls his presence in Madeleine's house a "deception," and their inter-actions "a bogus intimacy." So advanced is his sense of deceit that he even feels Kiku is pretending to be what she is. As the day proceeds, the narrator thinks that he sees "not so much a sacrifice of truth, as a diminishing of it to an entirely valueless quality." At one point, "I had a glimpse of the scale of my deception. It was so colossal I could hardly credit it." Madeleine's face powder, too, covers a rather older face than the narrator at first thought. She both hides the physical effects of her aging and also boldly and tempo-rarily shows them. But her honesty only highlights the narrator's mendacity.

Underlying the sordid story material of "Ate/Menos or The Miracle" is a religious and spiritual lexis. This is obvious in the pagan and Judaeo-Christian vocabulary of the title. Some of this religious lexis has been noted above. The story starts with the narrator listening to a "religious programme" on the radio. As he walks the streets of London, he thinks of "the ordinariness, the celestial ordinariness, that Sunday morning confers on London streets." The narrator acknowledges that he commits an act of "sacrilege," by taking communion, the wafer like an "honesty pod," at St. Simeon's among the "old souls" of the congregation. When asked to tell Madeleine a story, the narrator reflects on his inability to create either a fictional or real "Human being *ex nihilo*." He sees Madeleine's bedroom as the "inner sanctum," and wonders as he copulates with Madeleine without a condom, "Was I with Satan or with the Angels?"

The religious lexis is not just Christian, and the title combines the pagan with the Judaeo-Christian. The narrator feels he has "stolen fire from Olympus," by taking communion. Afterward, "I wasn't sure whether I felt demonically mischievous, or consumately benevolent." "I was riding high on my *Ate*, my *Menos* – whichever it was," he notes later. After having sex with Madeleine, he thinks it "had abandoned me." However, the lexical substrate of the story is firmly Christian. This is emphasized by names: Madeleine is derived from Magdalene; Felix, the lighting man's name, carries religious connotations; Dominic is Madeleine's estranged husband; and Matthew is the name of one of the evangelists. Like the line drawing of a cube, to which the narrator refers, which shows "two mutually exclusive boxes," depending on how one looks at it, the story material of "Ate/Menos, or The Miracle," embodies a secular and a spiritual level. These are, however, not "mutually exclusive," but rather imbricated with each other. The sordid secular tale illustrates a set of metaphysical interactions, and vice-versa.

"Ate/Menos, or The Miracle" is a difficult story to sum up. It is similar to the Gothic excess of Madeleine's home, suggesting almost too many interpretative possibilities, in the end ambiguous. Clearly, the text suggests that underneath the material surfaces of our cities and our lives, metaphysical realities lurk. The narrator can be seen as manifesting some metaphysical principle of inspiration that induces rashness or madness. He can certainly be seen as a demonic visitant to Madeleine's and Kiku's world. Does he bring about anything positive? Will he make Madeleine see the emptiness of her life? Will he push Kiku from autism into the world? Would that be good or bad? What has happened at the end of the story?

Or is the narrator a self-serving trickster, putting his own shameful behavior in a context of ecstasy and divine *afflatus*? Lasdun's story is rich and sophisticated, a provocative exposition of a corrupt and corrupted world. Or perhaps it is something else. The text challenges the reader on several levels.

# Bernard MacLaverty, "A Silent Retreat" (1994)

Published in *Walking the Dog and Other Stories* (1994)

As Michael Parker points out in the illuminating introduction to his anthology *The Hurt World: Short Stories of the Troubles* (1995), the violence, injustices, complexities, and divided loyalties of the armed conflict in Northern Ireland after 1968, and, indeed, earlier acts in the "Troubles" attendant on the partition of Ireland in the 1920s, have provoked a range of substantial short fictions by writers such as Michael McLaverty, Mary Beckett, David Park, and Anne Devlin. One of the most important Northern Irish short-story writers of the last forty years is Bernard MacLaverty. (MacLaverty now lives in Scotland and writes novels, but his work in short fiction, a large part of which has a Northern Irish subject matter, is a major part of his output.) His short story "A Silent Retreat" is a subtle and disturbing engagement with the tensions of the deeply divided community of Northern Ireland.

The story tells of an encounter on two late wintry afternoons between a sixteen-year-old Catholic grammar-school boy, Declan MacEntaggart, and an only slightly older Protestant part-time policeman, Irvine Todd. Declan attends a Catholic boarding school run by priests. Irvine is a B-Special, a part-time armed policeman. (B-Specials were an exclusively Protestant semi-military, semi-police formation and were used in support of regular police and British Army units from the 1920s through to their disestablishment in 1970. Protestants saw them as defenders of a free Ulster; Catholics saw them as agents of Protestant state oppression.) They smoke. They banter. Irvine asks Declan questions about Catholicism. He is curious for Declan is, in fact, only the second Catholic he has ever talked to. Irvine also – unsolicited – tells Declan something of his life as a milkman and a B-Special. On the second

*The British and Irish Short Story Handbook*, First Edition. David Malcolm.
© 2012 David Malcolm. Published 2012 by Blackwell Publishing Ltd.

afternoon, the tensions underlying their conversations become acute. The working-class Irvine feels that he is being patronized by Declan, mocked for his lack of formal education. He emphasizes his physical dominance and official authority by menacing Declan (in a comic fashion that is not comic at all) with his machine gun. Declan walks away. Irvine's final words are the shouted and prophetic "Fuck the future."

The text is narrated in the third person, but employs Declan's point of view exclusively. Indeed, free indirect speech is employed at points to give a closeness to Declan's mind and feelings. The reader sees Irvine mostly through Declan's eyes. Much of the story, however, is delivered through dialogue, and, thus, Irvine is partly allowed to speak for himself. The language of the dialogue is often informal. MacLaverty aims to capture especially Irvine's voice through phonetic spellings and capitalization. Irvine uses "fuck" extensively. Declan, notably, does not use obscenities and speaks a more standard English. The narrative is very limited, covering only a few minutes on two late afternoons. However, in the small space offered by the encounter, MacLaverty creates a subtle and dark vision of human (and Irish) division.

The opposition between Declan and Irvine is marked. Declan's name, MacEntaggart, could scarcely be more Catholic, as Irvine (whose surname is the resolutely Protestant Todd) laughingly points out. Declan comes from the countryside, from a Nationalist/Republican stronghold; Irvine comes from the outskirts of Belfast. Irvine has left school at fourteen, and is a milkman; Declan is a grammar school boy thinking of becoming a priest. Irvine has the authority of uniform and machine gun; Declan has none of those, only education and the sense of superiority that comes with it. Their beliefs are radically different. Declan talks of God; Irvine has no such belief. However, despite his crudities of expression, Irvine is far from stupid or thoughtless. He listens to Declan, who at times parrots (and helplessly knows he parrots) what he has been taught in school. Irvine's materialism has a savage power to it that Declan's platitudes do not. He slaps the walls of the gaol. These are realities no words can will away. In addition, Irvine is, despite his intense Protestant loyalty, in the B-Specials mainly for a little extra money. If it paid well enough, he would be satisfied being a milkman. He also, one should note, knows the history of Ulster (at least *his* history of Ulster) better than Declan does. (There were A-Specials, he points out, despite Declan's mocking.)

But in spite of their radical, and finally unbridgeable differences, the two young men are strikingly similar. Both are linked to restrictive institutions, in Irvine's case the B-Specials and the gaol, in Declan's case the boarding school. If Declan is to become a priest, he will wear a black soutane like the B-Special uniform. Both young men hide from Declan's Dean and Latin teacher. Both are in breach of rules, smoking and smoking together. "You and me – talking.

It's against the rules, fuck them. Okay?" as Irvine puts it. The sadness, and – in the light of the later history of Ulster that the story implies – the tragedy of the situation is that no lasting positive relationship can be formed between them. The title is multi-layered. There is no silence that will let God's voice come through. There is no escape from the walls and stones and uniforms of this world. Declan literally retreats in silence from Irvine's half-joking, half-frightening brandished machine gun.

The time setting of "A Silent Retreat" is not clear. There are Republican prisoners in the gaol that the B-Specials are guarding. But neither Declan nor Irvine allude to the Civil Rights campaign of the late 1960s. The Gallager's Blues cigarettes that the young men smoke at one point did not disappear from the market until the 1970s, but Irvine carries a Sten gun, a rather old-fashioned weapon for any period after the 1950s. In a sense, the precise time setting does not matter. If it is the 1950s or 1960s, the future is in any case dismal. The story's two afternoons are dark and cold. One can scarcely see others for the obscurity.

# Hanif Kureishi, "We're Not Jews" (1995)

Published in *London Review of Books* (1995) and in book form in
*Love in a Blue Time* (1997)

"We're Not Jews" is centered on the experiences of Azhar, a young boy
growing up in early 1960s Britain. His mother is a white Englishwoman; his
father is an Urdu-speaking immigrant to Britain, who identifies himself as a
Pakistani, although he has actually never lived in Pakistan. The main action of
the story concerns a few hours in which Azhar and his mother are returning
from an interview with Azhar's headmistress. There are, however, sections of
the short story in which some details are given of the circumstances of Azhar's
life (the number of his father's relatives who live with them, for example) and
of his father's life and ambitions. Azhar's mother has gone to his school to
complain about Azhar's being bullied because of his ethnicity. On their way
home, they are harassed by one of the worst bullies and by the bully's father,
Little Billy and Big Billy, who are working-class and white. The harassment is
very distressing to Azhar's mother. In the course of it, browbeaten and hurt,
she produces the phrase of the title. Accused of being immigrants, she insists,
"We're not Jews." On the way home, she makes a detour to a public lavatory
where she tries to calm herself. She does not have to instruct Azhar to say
nothing of the encounter; he understands all too well that he should not. The
story ends with Azhar watching his father, his grandfather, and one of his
uncles listening to a cricket match on the radio, exclaiming in a mixture of
Urdu, Punjabi, and English. The ending is open. How will Azhar's life
develop? Who will he become? How will he deal with his complicated,
mixed origins? How will he fight the racists?

The story is set in a large British city. It feels like London or its suburbs, but
could be anywhere in the south-east of England. The settings are not

*The British and Irish Short Story Handbook*, First Edition. David Malcolm.
© 2012 David Malcolm. Published 2012 by Blackwell Publishing Ltd.

attractive. This is post-war urban Britain. Especially toward the story's end, places become ugly: the bomb site that Azhar and his mother cross, and the municipal public toilet in which the mother tries to calm herself. The time is the mid-1960s: there are still conductors on buses; Azhar's mother wears gloves; there is a bomb site; there is a reference to the Vietnam War; and Big Billy rides his motorbike on bank holidays down to the coast. The time setting is important. Race relations are not good, but they will get worse. Azhar's future will not be an easy one.

The story is related in the third person, but entirely from Azhar's point of view. Even analepses provide information that is known to Azhar. Important characters are the two racist bullies, whose shared name indicates that their racism will be passed down through generations. Working-class white males, they contrast with the benign retired middle-class school teacher who helps Azhar's father with his writing. Azhar's mother is not presented in detail, although she is a central figure. A white woman who has married an immigrant from the Indian subcontinent, she is clearly devoted to her son, and like him displaced in England. She has no connection with Pakistan and the Indian sub-continent, and hates spicy foods and too much sun. She comes from the neighborhood in which the family now lives. Big Billy knows her very well. She does not know how to defend herself against the racists, only able in her distress to insist that her family is different. They are not immigrants; they are not Jews (whom she with her 1930s background would identify with foreignness and immigration).

Azhar's father is particularly complex. A doctor's son, he is a manual worker in England. His great ambition is to be a writer, and, to that end, he follows correspondence courses and sends articles to newspapers and magazines, all of which reject his work. English is "his, but not entirely, being 'Bombay variety, mish and mash'." He is clearly very frustrated in England, unable to break out of the world of immigrant manual labor, on the peripheries of British culture and society. He talks of Pakistan as "home," although he has never been there, and, in fact, his family has lived for generations in China and India. Azhar is as displaced as his mother and father, and realizes this in the course of the story. He learns about racism, both in the behavior of Little Billy and his classmates, and in a conversation with a friend about South Africa. He also starts to work out how to deal with racists. When his mother and he leave the bus, Azhar thinks what to do.

> As he went past he wasn't going to stare at the Billys, but he did give them the eye straight on, stare to stare, so he could see them and not be so afraid. They could hate him but he would know them. But if he couldn't fight them, what could he do with his anger?

At the end of the text, Azhar is surrounded by the Bombay world of his father, grandfather, and uncle. They speak languages he does not know, but he is used to that and laughs when they laugh, mouthing words he does not understand. He is at home nowhere, at least nowhere yet.

Words and languages are a dominant motif in the story. Azhar's mother makes sure that he reads, taking him every evening to the public library near his school. Azhar's father "loved books and wanted to write them." His typewriter stands on the table beside the beer and the radio (covered with the names of distant cities, exotic words only, for the radio can never pick up those stations). Words are weapons by which the Billys torment Azhar and his mother. At first, Azhar's mother teaches Azhar to respond to racist taunts by calling Little Billy "common" – the language of class disdain being used to fight that of racial contempt. The two families (Azhar's and the Billys) can be contrasted in terms of language and language use. Azhar's father is presumably bi- or tri-lingual (English, Urdu, Punjabi); Big Billy is inarticulate even in one. Azhar's father is linguistically resourceful and educated enough to make a Nietzschean pun about his neighbor's motorbike. As I have noted above, the reader sees Azhar at the story's end, "whirling, all the while, in incomprehension," surrounded by streams of Indian sub-continent tongues.

"We're Not Jews" is a memorable story about a child's opening experiences in what will be a long personal history of conflict, incomprehension, and displacement. (Many of the other stories in *Love in a Blue Time* vividly illustrate such histories, for example, the complex "With Your Tongue down My Throat.") The story firmly generalizes Azhar's experience, while nowhere eliding its particularity. South African apartheid, the dislocations of centuries of the history of peoples from the Indian sub-continent, these add resonances to Azhar's experience on the lower deck of a bus in England sometime in the 1960s. The story's title as well as Azhar's father's own warnings relate Indian/Pakistani experience in England to Jewish immigrants' experiences and to the Holocaust. When Azhar's mother is pushed by the racists beyond endurance, she cries for help to the indifferent or unnoticing passengers on the bus. "The noise she made came from hell or eternity," the narrator notes. Confined in the cubicle in the grim public toilet with his despairing and defecating mother, Azhar feels all the terrors of one in a long line of the displaced and the persecuted. "His teeth were clicking; ghosts whispered in his ears; outside there were footsteps; dead fingers seemed to be clutching at him."

# Patricia Duncker, "Stalker" (2003)

Published in an earlier version in *New Writing* 8 (1999)
and in book form in
*Seven Tales of Sex and Death* (2003)

"Stalker," like many of Duncker's stories, is a remarkable mixture of genres and kinds of text: myth and legend, detective story, social-psychological text, and pornography. The textual mixture is appropriate to the mingling of past and present, mythological and contemporary, fear and desire that permeates the whole story. The mixture is compounded by the presence of a police report, emails, and a lecture in the text. The narrator is Semele, the beautiful, nearly forty-year-old wife of an eminent Oxford archaeologist. In the story's present time, from which the narrative starts, Semele is accompanying her husband, Macmillan, who is excavating a complicated and multilayered site in the eastern Mediterranean, at a spot called Hierokitia. Macmillan's overriding desire is to discover the site of a famous temple of Zeus. In the course of the story, he and his team come upon a beautiful Roman mosaic pavement and eventually the site of the sanctum of the temple. Interwoven with the account of archaeological discoveries are Semele's accounts of her adolescence and the brutal murder in later life of her friend Lindsay de la Tour. The savage sexually motivated murder of the beautiful and celebrated TV journalist is followed by the equally vicious killings of her lesbian partner Helena Swann, and the lover that Lindsay was about to leave her for, Diana Harrison. All three murdered women are glamorous and successful. At the beginning of the story, Semele feels that she, too, is being stalked by some powerful, indeed bestial, male figure, whom she both fears and desires. At the story's end, in a thunder storm she sees the approaching headlight of a mysterious, Hermes-like messenger on a motorbike who has told her that the "boss" wants to see her.

*The British and Irish Short Story Handbook*, First Edition. David Malcolm.
© 2012 David Malcolm. Published 2012 by Blackwell Publishing Ltd.

The story has marked supernatural elements. The women's attacker seems no ordinary human, but a creature of massive size and strength, who further is able to evade the security cameras that surround Lindsay's home. Semele even considers that he is a "shape-shifter." The murderer of Helena even seems to have come from the pond in her garden. The cases are unsolved. Semele imagines her stalker to have "hands... covered in dark animal fur, like a werewolf." The supernatural motifs are coupled with classical allusions. Some of the characters are living out mythological/legendary stories. Helena, Diana, and Semele are all classical figures. Helen of Troy is the offspring of the rape of her mother Leda by Zeus in the form of a swan. Diana is also a daughter of Zeus, from a less violent, but still irregular liaison. Semele is a lover of Zeus, destroyed when she is tricked into asking to see Zeus in his full divinity. She is the mother of Dionysus, the god of frenzy and wild excess.

These mythological allusions are reinforced throughout "Stalker." Semele's husband uses myths in his work, and argues that they have connections with actual history. The curtains in Semele's room in Greece show a nymph pursued by a satyr. The pavement uncovered at Hierokitia (the name itself uses the Greek word "*hiero*" that signifies holiness or sacredness) shows a woman and a disguised god, later revealed as Zeus in the guise of a swan beginning his rape of Leda. Helena Swann is found murdered in her hospital bed, and the room is "filled with clouds of feathers" from her shredded duvet. She has also been killed "by some kind of blunt mechanical instrument, shaped like a clamp," perhaps a bird's beak. The messenger that comes on a motorbike for Semele is a reincarnation of Hermes or Dionysos himself. "His hair is an unusual reddish blonde. He stands, arrogant and uncaring, in the leaden luminous air, grotesquely overdressed in black leather."

The supernatural story, embroidered with classical motifs, is, however, rendered in some measure verisimilar. This is achieved by the presence of other genres, the detective story (the murders are investigated by the police) and by the social-psychological observations in the text (for example, the presentation of the disappointed wives of Oxford academics, and the tourists that descend on Greek islands in summer), by references to Semele's husband's scholarly publications, and by the incorporation in the text of a lecture on the archaeological site at Hierokitia. There is also the skeleton of a time scheme in the story. Lindsay's murder took place seven years before the story starts, and various other events are located along a time line.

The central focus of the story is female desire and fear. Semele is both frightened by and fascinated by her imagined stalker.

> And then, suddenly, he is there. I feel the ferocity of his glare upon my naked
> shoulder blades and the frail nape of my neck. I dare not look round. His stare

moves across my back, down to the neat curves of my arse, tucked into the light wicker frame of my chair. I am sitting naked, undressed by his consuming gaze. . ... All the men around the table sense my excitement.

Semele claims that she has played sado-masochistic sexual games with Lindsay when they were younger. The nymph on the Greek curtain is "egging... on" the satyr. Lindsay let her attacker in to her home. Semele insists that "our desires, so often unuttered, are fluid, protean, inconstant." She goes toward the messenger of her stalker at the end of the text.

Yet Semele is well aware of the violence committed against women against their wills. She sees the attacks on Lindsay, Helena, and Diana as part of a male hostility toward successful, independent women.

Most women submit to sexual outrages far short of rape, and yet they rightly feel that they have been violated. . . have you ever been forced to lift your skirt before a gaggle of sneering boys? Have you ever had your knickers ripped with a penknife so that they could get a better look? Have you ever had the neck of a Coke bottle rammed up your arse while the man who has his knees on your back curses your stinking pussy? Well, it wasn't rape, your Honour. We were only having a bit of fun.

Semele is also aware of the lives of disappointment of so many women she knows, help meets to successful men, themselves deeply unhappy at how their lives have turned out. Semele loathes their half lives, their "long women's whine of doom," and will not be part of it. Better, she suggests, the ecstasy of the wild and bestial. Like Carter's "Erl-King" (see above), "Stalker" is a complex reflection on the intricacies of female desires and fears in a male-dominated world.

Disturbing in its configuration of female sexuality and disorienting in its mixture of genres, "Stalker" is a rich and powerful text, illustrating the vigor of the non-realist genres in the British short story.

# China Miéville, "Foundation" (2003)

Published in the *Independent on Sunday* (2003) and
in book form in *Looking for Jake, and Other Stories* (2005)

"Foundation" is a supernatural story with a marked political agenda. In the Acknowledgements to *Looking for Jake, and Other Stories*, Miéville writes that sections of the text are based on a documented atrocity committed by U.S. troops during the First Gulf War (1990–1991). The protagonist is an unnamed American ex-soldier in the Gulf War. During the conflict, on February 25, 1991, he has taken part in burying dead and living Iraqi soldiers in what remains of their trenches. He has also witnessed apocalyptic scenes of burning oil wells and disorientated, dying soldiers. On his return to his home town, he starts to build an extra room onto his house, but stops when he sees a vile dark liquid (blood? oil?) rising in the foundation he has started to build. No one else can see this. He also starts to hear the voices of the dead speaking to him from the foundations, and a year after his involvement in the atrocity, he realizes that "The city around him was built on that buried wall of dead. Bone-filled trenches stretched under the sea and linked his home to the desert." He begins to work as what others call a "house-whisperer." For ten years, he has followed a successful career as one. The dead that lie under the foundations of all buildings tell him whether the construction of any building is sound and what will happen to it. On one occasion he lies, declaring that a building sound that is not. He hopes that when it collapses, the dead will be satisfied by their victims. But they are not.

> The foundation wants nothing from him. His offering means nothing to the dead in their trenches, crisscrossing the world. They are not there to taunt or punish or teach him, or to exact revenge or blood-price, they are not enraged or restless.

The story material is not given in chronological order. It follows a typical supernatural story pattern – a situation is presented and then explained. The narrator, who is limited to the protagonist's point of view, presents the "house-whisperer's" unusual ability, and then gives the source of it, by recounting his dreams and finally the details of the military action in which he participated. Motifs of the supernatural story, in its horror subset, are apparent from early on in the story. The protagonist himself, despite his smile, is clearly disturbed by his own ability. His dreams of apocalypse, which are also dreams of his past, torment him. A "dark, thick and staining liquid" rises from the hole he digs by his house, "clinging to his spade, cloying, unseen by any but him." In the foundation of any building, he sees a mass of dead men.

> A stock of dead men. An underpinning, a structure of entangled bodies and their parts, pushed tight, packed together and become architecture, their bones broken to make them fit, wedged in contorted repose, burnt skins and the tatters of their clothes pressed as if against the glass at the limits of their cut....

They speak together and say: "we cannot breathe," "we cannot breathe and we shore you up and we eat only sand," and "we do not end, we are hungry and hot and alone." The protagonist imagines that these are ghosts who can be appeased by a blood "offering." In the end, they continue their eerie whispering.

War – the source of the supernatural disturbance – is presented as horrifying: an apocalyptic landscape of toxic clouds and red light, in which decaying, howling, lost figures wander. The actual atrocity, the burying of Iraqi soldiers alive and dead, is recounted in a more sober, documentary fashion (here one sees an echo of M. R. James's deployment of verisimilitude devices), although, throughout, the Iraqi soldiers in their dugout are treated metaphorically as material, as "cement," "the contents, the mulch and ragged soup," and "the untidy detritus," to be "patted down," "packed," "hosed down," "shoved down," and "finished off" by the equipment of their opponents.

"They are the foundation of everything around him," the protagonist realizes at the end of the story. The dead have followed him across the oceans, and they underlie all the buildings of his world. "Every home is built on them." "The city around him was built on that buried wall of dead. Bone-filled trenches stretched under the sea and linked his home to the desert." He can never be rid of them and he will hear their whispering forever.

Miéville is a writer of strong political convictions. Many of his stories, like "Foundation," address important topical issues from an anti-establishment, anti-war position. Whatever the reader's own politics are, "Foundation" can be seen as a powerful and sinister piece of work, one that turns the super-natural and ghost story to original and fresh ends. The metaphor of the dead of foreign wars lying beneath the buildings of the super-power carries a striking resonance. At the very least, "Foundation" provokes reflection and discussion, and admiration for its author's imaginative powers.

# Key Collections

Many of the short stories discussed in this volume are accessible in widely available collections. Several, however, are not. This lack of availability is evidence of the short story's uncertain canonical status. The following bibliography contains suggestions of useful and obtainable collections in which key texts and the works of key authors can be found. Where possible, I have chosen the most recent good edition of a volume.

**Richard Aldington**
*Roads to Glory*. London: Chatto and Windus, 1930.

**J. G. Ballard**
*The Complete Short Stories*. London: Flamingo, 2001.

**Samuel Beckett**
*The Complete Short Prose, 1929–1989*. Ed. S. E. Gontarski. New York: Grove Press, 1995.

**Frances Bellerby**
*Selected Stories*. Ed. Jeremy Hooker. London: Enitharmon Press, 1986.

**John Berger**
*Into Their Labours* (*Pig Earth*, *Once in Europa*, and *Lilac and Flag*). London: Granta/Penguin, 1992.

**Elizabeth Bowen**
*The Collected Stories of Elizabeth Bowen*. Intr. Angus Wilson. London: Vintage, 1999.

**Angela Carter**
*The Bloody Chamber, and Other Stories*. London: Vintage, 2006.

### Arthur Conan Doyle

There are so many editions of the Sherlock Holmes stories that it makes no sense to recommend any one in particular. Penguin editions are readily available.

### Joseph Conrad

*The Cambridge Edition of the Works of Joseph Conrad* provides definitive editions of Conrad's fiction. In the meantime (and, indeed, thereafter, for volumes in this series are not cheap), readers will have to use popular editions, such as those issued by Penguin.

### A. E. Coppard

A good collection of Coppard's inter-war stories is: *Selected Tales*. London: Jonathan Cape, 1946. Another useful collection is: *Selected Stories*. Ed. Doris Lessing. London: Jonathan Cape, 1972. *Dusky Ruth, and Other Stories* was published by Penguin in 1974.

### Hubert Crackanthorpe

The best edition of Crackanthorpe's fiction is: *Collected Stories* (1893–1897). Facsimile Reproductions (with an introduction by William Peden). Gainesville, Florida: Scholars' Facsimiles and Reprints, 1969.

### Ella D'Arcy

Original copies of D'Arcy's *Modern Instances* are difficult to obtain. There is a facsimile edition: *Modern Instances*. London and New York: Garland Publishing, 1984 (but this edition is hard to obtain too).

### Mary Dorcey

*A Noise from the Woodshed*. London: Onlywoman Press, 1989.

### Patricia Duncker

*Seven Tales of Sex and Death*. London: Picador, 2003.

### Walter de la Mare

*Short Stories, 1885–1926*. Ed. Giles de la Mare. London: Giles de la Mare Publishing, 1996.
*Short Stories, 1927–1956*. Ed. Giles de la Mare. London: Giles de la Mare Publishing, 2001.

### Hugh Fleetwood

*The Beast*. London: Hamish Hamilton, 1978.

*Fictional Lives*. London: Hamish Hamilton, 1980.
*The Man Who Went Down with His Ship, and Other Stories*. London: Hamish Hamilton, 1988.

**Graham Greene**
*Complete Short Stories*. Ed. Pico Iyer. London: Penguin, 2005.

**Thomas Hardy**
*The Withered Arm, and Other Stories*. Ed. Kristin Brady. London: Penguin, 2006.
*Wessex Tales*. Ed. Kathryn R. King. Oxford: Oxford University Press, 2009.

**Henry James**
The Library of America has three volumes of James's short fiction. However, there are many cheaper editions available published by Penguin, Oxford University Press, and Wordsworth Editions.

**M. R. James**
*Count Magnus, and Other Ghost Stories*. Ed. S. T. Joshi. London: Penguin, 2005.
*The Haunted Doll's House, and Other Ghost Stories*. Ed. S. T. Joshi. London: Penguin, 2006.

**Gabriel Josipovici**
*Mobius the Stripper: Stories and Short Plays*. London: Victor Gollancz, 1974.

**James Joyce**
*Dubliners*. Ed. Terence Brown. London: Penguin, 2000.

**James Kelman**
*Greyhound for Breakfast*. Edinburgh: Polygon, 2008.

**Rudyard Kipling**
The definitive *The Sussex Edition of the Complete Works of Rudyard Kipling* was published in 35 volumes between 1937 and 1939. But there are many cheaper editions of the short stories. Those published by Penguin and Oxford University Press are good.

**Hanif Kureishi**
*Collected Stories*. London: Faber and Faber, 2010.

**James Lasdun**
*Three Evenings, and Other Stories*. London: Secker and Warburg, 1992.
*It's Beginning to Hurt, and Other Stories*. London: Jonathan Cape, 2009.

**Mary Lavin**
*Tales from Bective Bridge*. London: Michael Joseph, 1945.
*In a Café: Selected Stories*. London: Penguin, 1999.

**D. H. Lawrence**
*The Cambridge Edition of the Letters and Works of D. H. Lawrence* offers definitive editions of the short stories. Cheaper editions are widely available from Penguin. See: *Selected Stories*. Ed. Louise Welsh. London: Penguin, 2007; *The Prussian Officer, and Other Stories*. Ed. John Worthen. London: Penguin, 1995. "Tickets, Please" is published in *The Penguin Book of First World War Stories*. Ed. Barbara Korte. London: Penguin, 2007.

**J. Sheridan Le Fanu**
*In a Glass Darkly*. Ware: Wordsworth Editions, 1995.

**Doris Lessing**
*Stories*. London: Everyman, 2008.
*To Room Nineteen: Collected Stories – Volume One*. London: Flamingo, 2002.

**Alun Lewis**
*The Last Inspection*. London: George Allen and Unwin, 1942.

**George Mackay Brown**
*Hawkfall*. Edinburgh: Polygon, 2004.
*A Time to Keep, and Other Stories*. Edinburgh: Polygon, 2006.
*A Calendar of Love*. Edinburgh: Polygon, 2011.

**Julian Maclaren-Ross**
Maclaren-Ross's short fiction, and much else by him, is available in: *Bitten by the Tarantula, and Other Writing*. Ed. Paul Willets. London: Black Spring Press, 2005. A good collection of short stories is: *Selected Stories*. Ed. Paul Willets. Stockport: Dewi Lewis, 2004.

**Bernard MacLaverty**
*A Time to Dance, and Other Stories*. London: Penguin, 1982.
*Walking the Dog, and Other Stories*. London: Penguin, 1995.

**Katherine Mansfield**
*The Collected Stories of Katherine Mansfield*. Ed. Stephen Arkin. Ware: Wordsworth Editions, 2006.

**E. A. Markham**
*Something Unusual*. London: Ambit, 1986.
*Ten Stories*. Sheffield: Sheffield Hallam University/PAVIC Publications, 1994.

**W. Somerset Maugham**
There are many editions of collections of Maugham's short stories. The following are two recent ones.
*Far Eastern Tales*. London: Vintage, 2009.
*Short Stories*. London: Vintage, 2010.

**Ian McEwan**
These are two recent editions of McEwan's short fiction.
*First Love, Last Rites*. London: Vintage, 2006.
*In Between the Sheets*. London: Vintage, 2006.

**John McGahern**
*The Collected Stories*. London: Faber and Faber, 1992.
*Creatures of the Earth: New and Selected Stories*. London: Faber and Faber, 2007. (This posthumous collection has new material and also omits some of the stories in the 1992 volume.)

**China Miéville**
*Looking for Jake, and Other Stories*. Basingstoke and Oxford: Macmillan, 2005.

**Michael Moorcock**
Moorcock's bibliography is vast. The following is a representative collection of his short fiction.
*Earl Aubec, and Other Stories*. London: Millennium/Orion Books, 1993.

**George Moore**
*The Untilled Field*. Ed. Richard Allen Cave. Gerrards Cross, Buckinghamshire: Colin Smythe, 2000.

**H. H. Munro ("Saki")**
*The Complete Short Stories*. London: Penguin, 2000.

**Frank O'Connor**
*Collected Stories*. Ed. Richard Ellmann. New York: Vintage, 1981.

**Seán O'Faoláin**
*The Collected Stories of Sean O'Faolain*. Boston and Toronto: Little, Brown and Company, 1983.

**Mollie Panter-Downes**
*Good Evening, Mrs. Craven: The Wartime Stories of Mollie Panter-Downes*. Ed. Gregory Lestage. London: Persephone Books, 1999.

**T. F. Powys**
*God's Eye A-Twinkle: An Anthology of the Stories of T. F. Powys*. London: Chatto and Windus, 1947.
*Fables*. London: Faber and Faber, 2011.

**V. S. Pritchett**
*The Complete Short Stories*. London: Chatto and Windus, 1990.

**Jean Rhys**
*The Collected Short Stories*. Ed. Diana Athill. New York and London: Norton, 1990.

**Alan Sillitoe**
"The Loneliness of the Long Distance Runner" is published in: *New and Collected Stories*. London: Robson Books, 2003.

**Clive Sinclair**
*Hearts of Gold*. London: Allison and Busby, 1979.

**Muriel Spark**
*The Collected Stories*. London: Penguin, 1994.

**Robert Louis Stevenson**
There are many editions of Stevenson's short stories. These are good, recent ones.
*Markheim, Jekyll and The Merry Men*. Edinburgh: Canongate Classics, 2008.
*Tales of Adventure*. Edinburgh: Canongate Classics, 2008.

**Sylvia Townsend Warner**
*One Thing Leading to Another, and Other Stories.* Ed. Susanna Pinney. New York: Viking, 1984.
*The Music at Long Verney: Twenty Stories.* Ed. Michael Steinman. Washington, D.C.: Counterpoint, 2001.

**William Trevor**
*The Collected Stories.* London: Penguin, 1993.

**H. G. Wells**
*The Complete Short Stories of H. G. Wells.* Ed. John Hammond. London: Dent, 1998.

**Denton Welch**
*Brave and Cruel.* London: Hamish Hamilton, 1948.
*The Stories of Denton Welch.* Ed. Robert Phillips. New York: E. P. Dutton, 1985.

**Oscar Wilde**
*The Complete Short Stories.* Ed. John Sloan. Oxford: Oxford University Press, 2010.

**Virginia Woolf**
*Selected Short Stories.* Ed. Sandra Kemp. London: Penguin, 2000.
*A Haunted House, and Other Stories.* San Diego, New York, and London: Harcourt, 2002.

# References and Further Reading

*55 Stories from The New Yorker.* London: Victor Gollancz, 1952.

Adams, Don. "Doris Lessing: *African Stories.*" In: Cheryl Alexander Malcolm and David Malcolm, eds., *A Companion to the British and Irish Short Story.* Oxford: Wiley-Blackwell, 2008: 440–447.

Aiken, Conrad. "Stories Reduced to Essentials," 1927. In: Cheryl Alexander Malcolm and David Malcolm. *Jean Rhys: A Study of the Short Fiction.* New York: Twayne, 1996: 118–119.

Allen, Walter. *The Short Story in English.* Oxford: Clarendon Press, 1981.

Archer, Stanley. *W. Somerset Maugham: A Study of the Short Fiction.* New York: Twayne, 1993.

Baldwin, Dean. "The English Short Story in the Fifties." In: Denis Vannatta, ed., *The English Short Story, 1945–1980: A Critical History.* Boston: Twayne, 1985: 34–74.

Baldwin, Dean. "The Tardy Evolution of the British Short Story," *Studies in Short Fiction* 30.1 (winter 1993): 23–33.

Beachroft, T. O. *The Modest Art: A Survey of the Short Story in English.* London, New York, and Toronto: Oxford University Press, 1968.

Bergonzi, Bernard. *Wartime and Aftermath: English Literature and Its Background, 1939–1960.* Oxford and New York: Oxford University Press, 1993.

Boccardi, Mariadele. "The Story of Colonial Adventure." In: Cheryl Alexander Malcolm and David Malcolm, eds. *A Companion to the British and Irish Short Story.* Oxford: Wiley-Blackwell, 2008: 19–34.

Bloom, Jonathan. *The Art of Revision in the Short Stories of V.S. Pritchett and William Trevor.* New York and Basingstoke: Palgrave Macmillan, 2006.

Böker, Uwe. "Zu Produktionsbedingungen, Verbreitungsformen und Leserschaft der Kurzgeschichte im 19. und 20. Jahrhundert." In: Arno Löffler and Eberhard Späth. *Geschichte der englischen Kurzgeschichte.* Tübingen and Basel: A. Francke Verlag, 2005: 23–43.

Bowen, Elizabeth. "Introduction: The Short Story," *The Faber Book of Modern Stories.* Ed. Elizabeth Bowen. London: Faber, 1937: 7–19.

Bowen, Elizabeth. *Collected Stories.* London: Vintage, 1999.

Brosch, Renate. *Short Story: Textsorte und Leseerfahrung.* Trier: Wissenschaftlicher Verlag, 2007.

Carter, Angela, ed. *Wayward Girls and Wicked Women.* London: Virago, 1986.

Cave, Richard Allen. "Introduction." In: George Moore. *The Untilled Field*. 1903. Ed. Richard Allen Cave. Gerrards Cross, Buckinghamshire: Colin Smythe, 2000: vii–xxvii.

Cochran, Robert. *Samuel Beckett: A Study of the Short Fiction*. New York: Twayne, 1991.

Coelsch-Foisner, Sabine. "Finding a Voice: Women Writing the Short Story (to 1945)." In: Malcolm, Cheryl Alexander and David Malcolm, eds. *A Companion to the British and Irish Short Story*. Oxford: Wiley-Blackwell, 2008: 96–113.

Coelsch-Foisner, Sabine. "H. G. Wells's Short Stories: 'The Country of the Blind' and 'The Door in the Wall'. " In: Cheryl Alexander Malcolm and David Malcolm, eds. *A Companion to the British and Irish Short Story*. Oxford: Wiley-Blackwell, 2008: 174–182.

Coetzee, J. M. "Introduction," *Samuel Beckett: The Grove Centenary Edition, Vol. 4 Poems, Short Fiction, Criticism*. Ed. Paul Auster. New York: Grove Press, 2006: ix–xiv.

Cohn, Ruby. *Back to Beckett*. Princeton: Princeton University Press, 1973.

Coppard, A. E. *Selected Stories*. London: Jonathan Cape, 1972.

Crackanthorpe, Hubert. *Last Studies*. London: Heinemann, 1897.

Craps, Stef. "Virginia Woolf: 'Kew Gardens' and 'The Legacy'." In: Cheryl Alexander Malcolm and David Malcolm, eds. *A Companion to the British and Irish Short Story*. Oxford: Wiley-Blackwell, 2008: 193–201.

Dunleavy, Janet Eagleson. "Mary Lavin, Elizabeth Bowen, and a New Generation: The Irish Short Story at Midcentury." In: James F. Kilroy, ed. *The Irish Short Story: A Critical History*. Boston: Twayne, 1984: 145–168.

Eagleton, Mary. "Gender and Genre." In: Hanson (1989) 55–68.

Fallon, Erin, Feddersen, R. C., Kurtzleben, James, Lee, Maurice A. and Rochette-Crawley, Susan. *A Reader's Companion to the Short Story in English*. Westport, Connecticut, and London: Greenwood Press, 2001.

Feddersen, R. C. "Introduction: A Glance at the History of the Short Story in English." In: Erin Fallon, R. C. Feddersen, James Kurtzleben, Maurice A. Lee and Susan. Rochette-Crawley. *A Reader's Companion to the Short Story in English*. Westport, Connecticut, and London: Greenwood Press, 2001: xv–xxxiv.

Flora, Joseph M., ed. *The English Short Story, 1880–1945: A Critical History*. Boston: Twayne, 1985.

Fowler, Alastair. *A History of English Literature: Forms and Kinds from the Middle Ages to the Present*. Oxford: Basil Blackwell, 1987.

Gąsiorek, Andrzej. "The Short Fiction of V. S. Pritchett." In: Cheryl Alexander Malcolm and David Malcolm, eds. *A Companion to the British and Irish Short Story*. Oxford: Wiley-Blackwell, 2008: 423–430.

Gray, John. "On T. F. Powys," *New Statesman* 3 December 2001: 54–55.

Greaves, Richard. "Paralysis Re-considered: James Joyce's *Dubliners*." In: Cheryl Alexander Malcolm and David Malcolm, eds. *A Companion to the British and Irish Short Story*. Oxford: Wiley-Blackwell, 2008: 165–173.

Green, Roger Lancelyn, ed. *Kipling: The Critical Heritage*. London: Routledge and Kegan Paul, 1971.

Greene, Graham. "On the Short Story," *Journal of the Short Story in English* 4 (spring/printemps 1985): 11–24.

Grubisic, Brett Josef. "British Gay and Lesbian Short Stories." In: Cheryl Alexander Malcolm and David Malcolm, eds. *A Companion to the British and Irish Short Story*. Oxford: Wiley-Blackwell, 2008: 356–371.

Gullason, Thomas H. "The Short Story: An Underrated Art," *Studies in Short Fiction* 2 (fall 1964): 13–31.

Gullason, Thomas H. "The Short Story: Revision and Renewal." 19 (summer 1982): 221–230.

Hanson, Clare. "Introduction." In: Clare Hanson, *Short Stories and Short Fictions, 1880–1980*. London and Basingstoke: Macmillan, 1985: 1–9.

Hanson, Clare. "'Things Out of Words': Towards a Poetics of Short Fiction." In: Hanson (1989) 22–33.

Hanson, Clare. *Short Stories and Short Fictions, 1880–1980*. London and Basingstoke: Macmillan, 1985.

Hanson, Clare, ed. *Re-Reading the Short Story*. Basingstoke and London: Macmillan, 1989.

Harmon, Maurice. "First Impressions: 1968–78." In: Rafroidi and Brown (1979): 63–77.

Harris, Wendell V. *British Short Fiction in the Nineteenth Century: A Literary and Bibliographic Guide*. Detroit: Wayne State University Press, 1979.

Head, Dominic. *The Modernist Short Story: A Study in Theory and Practice*. Cambridge: Cambridge University Press, 1992.

Henderson, Eric and Geoff Hancock, eds. *Short Fiction and Critical Contexts: A Compact Reader*. Ontario: Oxford University Press, 2010.

Hosmer, Robert Ellis, Jr. "The Short Stories of Muriel Spark." In Cheryl Alexander Malcolm, and David Malcolm, eds. *A Companion to the British and Irish Short Story*. Oxford: Wiley-Blackwell, 2008: 456–463.

Hunter, Adrian. *The Cambridge Introduction to the Short Story in English*. Cambridge: Cambridge University Press, 2007.

Ingarden, Roman. *The Literary Work of Art: An Investigation on the Borderlines of Ontology, Logic, and Theory of Literature*. 1930. Trans. George G. Grabowicz. Evanston, Illinois: Northwestern University Press, 1973.

James, Henry. "An Appreciation." In: Hubert Crackanthorpe. *Last Studies*. London: Heinemann, 1897: xi–xi.

Jarfe, Günther. "Gabriel Jospovici." In: Cheryl Alexander Malcolm and David Malcolm, eds. *British and Irish Short Fiction Writers, 1945–2000. Dictionary of Literary Biography*, vol. 319. Farmington Hills, MI: Thomson Gale, 2006: 121–127.

Jarfe, Günther. *Die moderne britische Short Story: Eine Einführung*. Berlin: Erich Schmidt Verlag, 2010.

Kilroy, James F. "Introduction." In: Kilroy, James F., ed. *The Irish Short Story: A Critical History*. Boston: Twayne, 1984: 1–19.

Kilroy, James F., ed. *The Irish Short Story: A Critical History*. Boston: Twayne, 1984.

Kiberd, Declan. "Story-Telling: The Gaelic Tradition." In: Rafroidi, Patrick and Terence Brown, eds. *The Irish Short Story*. Gerrards Cross, Buckinghamshire: Colin Smith/Atlantic Highlands, N.J.: Humanities Press, 1979: 13–25.

Korte, Barbara. *The Short Story in Britain: A Historical Sketch and Anthology*. Tübingen and Basel: A. Francke Verlag, 2003.

Lasdun, James. "A Genius for Misery: William Trevor and the Art of the Short Story." *Times Literary Supplement*, 23 September 1996: 23.

Lee, Hermione, ed. *The Secret Self: Short Stories by Women*. London and Melbourne: Dent, 1985.

Lessing, Doris. "Introduction." In: A. E. Coppard. *Selected Stories*. London: Jonathan Cape, 1972: vii–xii.

Lestage, Gregory. "Afterword: Mollie Panter-Downes and *The New Yorker*," *Good Evening, Mrs. Craven: The Wartime Stories of Mollie Panter-Downes*. London: Persephone Books, 1999: 191–203.

Lewis, Mitchell. "Michael Moorcock." In: Cheryl Alexander Malcolm and David Malcolm, eds. *British and Irish Short Fiction Writers, 1945–2000. Dictionary of Literary Biography*, vol. 319. Farmington Hills, MI: Thomson Gale, 2006: 245–256.

Lewis, Mitchell R. "Science Fiction and Fantasy after 1945: Beyond Pulp Fiction." In: Malcolm, Cheryl Alexander and David Malcolm, eds. *A Companion to the British and Irish Short Story*. Oxford: Wiley-Blackwell, 2008: 372–383.

Linklater, Alexander. "Reclaiming the Story." *Prospect* (September 2005): 24.

Löffler, Arno and Eberhard Späth. *Geschichte der englischen Kurzgeschichte*. Tübingen and Basel: A. Francke Verlag, 2005.

Lonergan, Patrick. "Irish Short Fiction: 1880–1945." In: Cheryl Alexander Malcolm and David Malcolm, eds. *A Companion to the British and Irish Short Story*. Oxford: Wiley-Blackwell, 2008: 51–64.

Macdonald, Graeme. "James Kelman." In: Cheryl Alexander Malcolm and David Malcolm, eds. *British and Irish Short Fiction Writers, 1945–2000. Dictionary of Literary Biography*, vol. 319. Farmington Hills, MI: Thomson Gale, 2006: 128–136.

Mackay Brown, George. "Introduction." In: George Mackay Brown. *Witch, and Other Stories*. London: Longman, 1977: vi–xi.

Mackay Brown, George. *Witch, and Other Stories*. London: Longman, 1977.

Maher, Eamon. *John McGahern: From the Local to the Universal*. Dublin: The Liffey Press, 2003.

Malcolm, Cheryl Alexander and David Malcolm. *Jean Rhys: A Study of the Short Fiction*. New York: Twayne, 1996.

Malcolm, Cheryl Alexander and David Malcolm, eds. *British and Irish Short Fiction Writers, 1945–2000. Dictionary of Literary Biography*, vol. 319. Farmington Hills, MI: Thomson Gale, 2006.

Malcolm, Cheryl Alexander and David Malcolm, eds. *A Companion to the British and Irish Short Story*. Oxford: Wiley-Blackwell, 2008.

Malcolm, David. *Understanding Ian McEwan*. Columbia, S. C.: University of South Carolina Press, 2002.

Malcolm, David. "W. Somerset Maugham's Ashenden Stories." In: Cheryl Alexander Malcolm and David Malcolm, eds. *A Companion to the British and Irish Short Story*. Oxford: Wiley-Blackwell, 2008: 227–235.

Matthews, Brander. "Kipling's Deeper Note." 1926. In: Green (1971) 337–341.

Maunder, Andrew, ed. *The Facts on File Companion to the British Short Story*. New York: Facts on File, 2007.

Maxwell, William. "Foreword." In: Sylvia Townsend Warner. *The Music at Long Verney: Twenty Stories*. Ed. Michael Steinman. Washington D. C.: Counterpoint, 2001: vii–xv.

May, Charles E. "The Unique Effect of the Short Story: A Reconsideration and an Example," *Studies in Short Fiction* 13 (1976) 289–297.

May, Charles E. "The Nature of Knowledge in Short Fiction," *Studies in Short Fiction* 21.4 (1984) 327–338.

May, Charles E. "Prolegomenon to a Generic Study of the Short Story," *Studies in the Short Story* 33 (1996) 461–473.

May, Charles E., ed. *The New Short Story Theories*. Athens, Ohio: Ohio University Press, 1994.

May, Charles E. *The Short Story: The Reality of Artifice*. New York: Twayne, 1995.

Menikoff, Barry. "Class and Culture in the English Short Story," *Journal of the Short Story in English* 8 (spring 1987): 125–139.

Miller, Gavin. "George Mackay Brown: 'Witch,' 'Master Halcrow, Priest,' 'A Time to Keep,' and 'The Tarn and the Rosary'." In: Cheryl Alexander Malcolm and David Malcolm, eds. *A Companion to the British and Irish Short Story*. Oxford: Wiley-Blackwell, 2008: 472–479.

Millhauser, Stephen. "The Ambition of the Short Story," *The New York Times Book Review*, 5 October 2008: 31.

Mooney, Sinéad. *Samuel Beckett*. Tavistock, Devon: Northcote House and The British Council, 2006.

Moore, George. *The Untilled Field*. 1903. Ed. Richard Allen Cave. Gerrards Cross, Buckinghamshire: Colin Smythe, 2000.

Moosmüller, Birgit. *Die experimentelle englische Kurzgeschichte der Gegenwart*. Munich: Wilhelm Fink Verlag, 1993.

Nyman, Jopi. "The Detective and Crime Story: 1880–1945." In Cheryl Alexander Malcolm and David Malcolm, eds. *A Companion to the British and Irish Short Story*. Oxford: Wiley-Blackwell, 2008: 65–80.

O'Connor, Frank. *The Lonely Voice: A Study of the Short Story*. 1962/1963. Cleveland and New York: Meridian Books, 1965.

Orel, Harold. *The Victorian Short Story: Development and Triumph of a Literary Genre*. Cambridge: Cambridge University Press, 1986.

Orlet, John David. "T. F. Powys. " In: John H. Rogers. "Introduction. " British Short-Fiction Writers, 1915–1945. Ed. John H. Rogers. *Dictionary of Literary Biography*, vol. 162. Detroit, Washington D.C., and London: Bruccoli Clark Layman/Gale Research, 1996: 307–313.

Parker, Michael. "Introduction." In: Michael Parker, ed. *The Hurt World: Short Stories of the Troubles*. Belfast: The Blackstaff Press, 1995: 1–10.

Parker, Michael, ed. *The Hurt World: Short Stories of the Troubles*. Belfast: The Blackstaff Press, 1995.

Pasco, Allan H. "On Defining Short Stories." In: Charles E. May, ed. *The New Short Story Theories*. Athens, Ohio: Ohio University Press, 1994: 114–126.

Perényi, Eleanor. "The Good Witch of the West." *New York Review of Books* 32 (18 July 1985): 27–30.

Poe, Edgar Allan. "Review of *Twice-Told Tales*." 1842. In: Henderson, Eric and Geoff Hancock, eds. *Short Fiction and Critical Contexts: A Compact Reader*. Ontario: Oxford University Press, 2010: 395–396.

Pountney, Rosemary. "The Structuring of *Lessness*." *Review of Contemporary Fiction* 7 (1987): 55–75.

Pickering, Jean. "The English Short Story in the Sixties." In: Vannatta, Denis (ed.). *The English Short Story, 1945–1980: A Critical History*. Boston: Twayne, 1985: 75–119.

Powys, T. F. *God's Eyes A-Twinkle*. London: Chatto and Windus, 1947.

Pritchett, V. S. "An Interview," *Studies in Short Fiction* 13 (1976): 423–427.

Pratt, Mary Louise. "The Long and the Short of It." In: May, Charles E., ed. *The New Short Story Theories*. Athens, Ohio: Ohio University Press, 1994: 91–113.

Prentice, Charles. "Preface." In: Powys, T. F. *God's Eyes A-Twinkle*. London: Chatto and Windus, 1947: ix–xv.

Pritchett, V. S. "An Interview," *Journal of the Short Story in English* 6 (spring 1986): 11–38.

Rafroidi, Patrick and Terence Brown, eds. *The Irish Short Story*. Gerrards Cross, Buckinghamshire: Colin Smith/Atlantic Highlands, N.J.: Humanities Press, 1979.

Reid, Ivan. *The Short Story*. London: Methuen/New York: Barnes and Noble, 1977.

Rogers, John H. "Introduction." *British Short-Fiction Writers, 1915–1945*. Ed. John H. Rogers. *Dictionary of Literary Biography*, vol. 162. Detroit, Washington D.C., and London: Bruccoli Clark Layman/Gale Research, 1996: ix–xv.

Rosenberg, Tracey. "Science Fiction." In: Andrew Maunder, ed. *The Facts on File Companion to the British Short Story*. New York: Facts on File, 2007: 372–373.

Russell, Paul March, "The Gardener." In: Andrew Maunder, ed. *The Facts on File Companion to the British Short Story*. New York: Facts on File, 2007: 164–166.

Scofield, Martin. *The Cambridge Introduction to the American Short Story*. Cambridge: Cambridge University Press, 2006.

Séjourné, Philippe. "La nouvelle à la recherche d'un troisième souffle." *Journal of the Short Story in English* 1 (1983): 7–16.

Shaw, Valerie. *The Short Story: A Critical Introduction*. London and New York: Longman, 1983.

Stanford, Derek. "Introduction." In: Stanford, Derek, ed. *Short Stories of the 'Nineties: A Biographical Anthology*. London: John Baker, 1968: 13–47.

Stanford, Derek, ed. *Short Stories of the 'Nineties: A Biographical Anthology*. London: John Baker, 1968.

Taylor, Debbie. "Endangered Species." *Mslexia* 16 (January-March 2003): 9–13.

Townsend Warner, Sylvia. *The Music at Long Verney: Twenty Stories*. Ed. Michael Steinman. Washington D. C.: Counterpoint, 2001.

Treglown, Jeremy. *V. S. Pritchett: A Working Life*. London: Pimlico, 2005.

Vannatta, Denis (ed.). *The English Short Story, 1945–1980: A Critical History*. Boston: Twayne, 1985.

Winston, Greg a. "Mary Lavin." In: Cheryl Alexander Malcolm and David Malcolm, eds. *British and Irish Short Fiction Writers, 1945–2000. Dictionary of Literary Biography*, vol. 319. Farmington Hills, MI: Thomson Gale, 2006: 151–164.

Winston, Greg b. "E. A. Markham. " In: Cheryl Alexander Malcolm and David Malcolm, eds. *British and Irish Short Fiction Writers, 1945–2000. Dictionary of Literary Biography*, vol. 319. Farmington Hills, MI: Thomson Gale, 2006: 197–205.

Wilson, Angus. "Introduction." In: Bowen, Elizabeth. *Collected Stories*. London: Vintage, 1999: Bowen, Elizabeth. *Collected Stories*. London: Vintage, 1999: 7–11.

# Index

*The British and Irish Short Story Handbook*, First Edition. David Malcolm.
© 2012 David Malcolm. Published 2012 by Blackwell Publishing Ltd.